D1083948

# MANEUVER WARFARE

# MANEUVER WARFARE

## An Anthology

Editor: Richard D. Hooker, Jr.

Foreword by Gen. John R. Galvin, USA (Ret.)

PRESIDIO

*To Old Soldiers with Young Minds*

Published by Presidio Press
505 B San Marin Dr., Suite 300
Novato, CA 94945-1340

Library of Congress Cataloging-in-Publication Data


Maneuver warfare : an anthology / editor, Richard D. Hooker Jr., foreword by
    John P. Galvin.
        p.    cm.
    Includes bibliographical references and index.
    ISBN 0-89141-499-1. — ISBN 0-89141-518-1 (pbk.)
    1. Maneuver warfare. 2. United States—Military policy.
  I. Hooker, Richard D.
  U250.M36 1993
  355.4'2—dc20                                              93-8900
                                                            CIP

Typography by ProImage
Printed in the United States of America

# CONTENTS

# Foreword

This is a timely book. First, the long years of East-West confrontation are now Cold War history; gone is the era in which we spent too much time on the size of forces and not enough on the possible uses of them, and when our concept of forward defense of Western Europe did not encourage a maneuver outlook. Second, we now enter a time in which American military forces—and indeed those of most of the world—will undergo great change in every aspect of their being, and especially in their size. As we draw down the military structures, prescient nations will try to safeguard the quality, the effectiveness of their residual forces. In the military institution quality has many aspects, and one of the most important is the state of mind of the leaders at all levels.

Can we keep and nurture a vibrant, inspired core of officers and enlisted leaders, open-minded, forward-looking, innovative, absorbed with the questions inherent in the combinations of time, space, and combat? The example that is set by this seminal work of authors, not all of them military, not all Americans, many quite young, some with full careers behind them, says yes, indeed we can. It's refreshing to see with what energy those writers have taken up the venerable controversies over maneuver vs. firepower, *Auftragstaktik* vs. *Befehlstaktik*, fluid vs. linear battle, war of movement vs. "industrial warfare," and the style of fighting that seeks to pit strength against enemy weakness and break the enemy's will vs. the commitment to attrition as the main decider of battle. They hold maneuver warfare up to the light and study it from all angles, judging it as a concept, comparing it to other options, measuring the way it affects and is affected by military institutions and organizations and psyches. They also place maneuver warfare in the tapestry of history and seek there the lessons it can give.

Rommel is here with his *Infanterie grieft an,* those fascinating personal tales of small unit maneuver that taught the generation of German officers who fought WWII. Later, as the Desert Fox, riding in his halftrack with the single word *"Greif"* emblazoned in red letters across its sides, he would elevate his earlier creed into broad sweeps of armored battle in which he always tried to roll his tanks not against those of the enemy but against vulnerable targets in his opponent's rear areas.

The French are here with Bob Doughty's story of their remarkable change from maneuver to linear battle in WWI and then their fateful decision to stay "linear" at the outbreak of WWII. Wavell is here, in his early North Africa whirlwind desert fighting, as are Falkenhorst and Dietl, masterminds of the campaign of maneuver that snatched Norway from the teeth of the Royal Navy in April of 1940.

The concept of maneuver warfare needs this kind of debate. It is an idea that has always been open to critique, to interpretation, and especially to misinterpretation. The Soviets, trying to learn from the master, Marshal Tukhachevsky, searched for a combination of maneuver and firepower that resulted in the creation of the echeloned attack, an unwieldy formation that could be easily disrupted. When we responded with the concept of follow-on forces attack, aimed at upsetting the timetables of this lumbering style of combat, the Soviets saw their mistake and built the operational maneuver groups. Those self-sustained and fast-moving corps gave them much greater potential for maneuver, but Soviet doctrine remained fixed on achieving flexibility at the operational level by calling for strict predictability at the tactical level. Changes toward emphasis on maneuver were too few and too late for the Soviets in the confrontations of the Cold War, but there is much to be learned from their experience.

Saddam Hussein purchased enough high technology fighting systems to make his armed forces into a veritable powerhouse, but one that had no sense of maneuver and no ability for such work. It takes a lot to maneuver at the operational level; that is, to command and control armies on the move in combat. A single example: the ability to maneuver on the three-dimensional battlefield of today and tomorrow is contingent on air defense. Local air superiority and defense against ballistic missiles, along with protected communications, are major contributors to maneuver. Saddam's mindset, however, was attrition, not maneuver, and he made the mistake of thinking ours was, too.

A healthy and absorbing combination of different approaches keeps this book as a whole from being doctrinaire. The writers are bold; they take a catholic and eclectic approach to maneuver warfare, relating it, for example, to the psychology of combat, to the mechanics of innovation, to the uses of deception, and to the aims of low-intensity conflict. The reader "listens in" on a running conversation in which there is much give-and-take. Dan Bolger regales us with an entertaining and powerful assault against the proponents of maneuver warfare, advising them to "strike their tents and retire to write their memoirs," whereas Rich Hooker is a stout and articulate supporter of maneuver. Jim McDonough, on the other hand, astutely points out that no concept like maneuver warfare stands alone, that there can be successful shifting from linear to fluid battle or, more likely, the two can be going on at the same time. At both tactical and operational levels, maneuver of a part of the force is often dependent on linear operations by supporting forces. At the same time, maneuver has to be understood and accepted in all of its ramifications or it simply will not work. Several authors correctly note that in the U.S. armed forces there is a reluctance to "go too far in one direction," meaning to push too much the concept of maneuver warfare. As we come out of a period in which NATO doctrine dominated our thinking and linear defense was the political and military order of the day, we must look closely at ourselves, and, if we do, we will see (and John Foss, former commander of U.S. Army Training and Doctrine Command, has warned of this) that maneuver has had too little emphasis in our conceptualizing of training. This obviously applies to joint and combined training as well, if we consider that future warfare will be three-dimensional and will be fought by coalitions.

Maneuver warfare, as a concept, is a habit of thinking about the purpose of engagements, battles, campaigns, one that asks the question, How can I seize and hold the initiative, stay ahead of my enemy's ability to think and act, dismantle this enemy, cause his collapse, take him apart? The answer leads then to a spacial question, which is, Where should I be with reference to him? "Straight up the middle" is usually the wrong answer.

We needed this book. I hope it will be volume one of a series to come, as others join the fray and help to point out the way ahead.

Gen. John R. Galvin, USA (Ret.)

# Introduction

As this is written, the American military finds itself facing an organizational dilemma of the first order. After a brief period of public praise following its outstanding performance in the Gulf War, the military services, and particularly the Army and Marine Corps, will draw down to lower levels than they have known for some five decades. Understandably, they are absorbed with solving the problems of downsizing the force, revising the National Military Strategy, and minimizing the impact of the turbulence and turmoil that attend such massive systemic change.

The implications of a dramatically reduced force structure (the active Army, for example, will lose between one-third and one-half its combat divisions) suggest, however, that increasing the combat power of those units that survive the cuts must be a top priority for uniformed and civilian leaders and force planners. To remain a viable instrument of statecraft, to effectively deter potential opponents or defeat them in battle if deterrence fails, a smaller military should explore ways to improve its combat performance that do not require more expensive technology.

Is it reasonable to suppose that a smaller military might actually be better? This is a vexing question that divides even the contributors to this volume. Seasoned professionals know that at some point, size and mass always matter. A better way to frame the debate is to challenge the military to make its surviving units better than they were before—to offset the loss of mass with other forms of combat power.

Maneuver warfare is one promising approach to this dilemma. Informed by ancient practitioners of the military art such as Sun Tzu and Epaminondas, its modern roots lie in the Prussian and German armies.

Prostrate after the destruction of its field army at Jena-Auerstädt, Prussia revived under the enlightened leadership of Scharnhorst, Gneisenau and a score of lesser reform-minded military intellectuals. By 1866 the outlines of a distinctly different approach to war were visible, an approach that emphasized decentralization, rapidity of thought and action, and the search for decisive results through maneuver.

Searching for ways to break the riddle of the trenches in 1916, German commanders built upon these strengths and their earlier *Jäger,* or light infantry, traditions, which emphasized open-order tactics and high-quality, independent junior leaders and soldiers, to create a highly flexible defensive doctrine. When applied to the offense shortly thereafter, these ideas led to spectacular tactical and operational successes in the Baltic and on the Western Front in 1917 and 1918.

Strategically compressed between the mighty bulk of Russia in the east and France and Britain in the west, the German empire in 1914, and again in 1940, was compelled to look for solutions to the dual threats of inferior mass and a two-front war. The result was maneuver warfare, an intellectual approach to war which relied, not upon superior firepower and industrial strength, but upon a strikingly different dialectic: the use of strength against weakness to deliver a rapid knockout blow.

Called "blitzkrieg" (a superficial and imprecise term coined by journalists), the German style of war did not owe its success wholly to technology in the form of the tank, the airplane and the wireless. Nor did it emerge fully formed in the invasion of Poland in 1939. This distinctly German form of warfare evolved slowly over two centuries, always in competition with other forms and theories of warfare (even within the Prussian and German militaries).

Influenced by foreign military thinkers such as Liddell Hart, Fuller, and Tukhachevsky, and incorporating new technology in the form of armored tank and infantry units, self-propelled artillery and close support aviation, the Germans achieved similar successes from 1939 to 1941.

Superior doctrine and tactics could not, however, compensate for the strategic deficiencies of the German High Command. While retaining its tactical superiority to the end of both world wars, the German army succumbed to the numerical and industrial superiority of its opponents and the strategic failures of its senior commanders in 1918 and again in 1945.

The Israeli Defense Forces, in one of the more striking paradoxes of history, adopted this approach to war as a way out of Israel's own strategic dilemma. Like Germany, Israel found itself surrounded by numerically superior enemies it could not match, in Fuller's phrase, "in weight of metal." Although Israeli social and military culture is as different from Prussian militarism as it is possible to be, the similarities between the German and Israeli styles of war are more than coincidental.

Lacking the physical resources of its adversaries, Israel turned to leadership and doctrine for answers to its strategic conundrum. In four conventional conflicts, the IDF, employing speed, a rapid operating tempo, decentralized command and control, and outstanding junior leadership, defeated its stronger Arab opponents in a matter of weeks. To outward appearances an undisciplined, even amateurish force, the Israeli military remains today the preeminent military force in the Middle East and perhaps the most battle-worthy army in the world. Like the Germans, the Israelis have learned in the hard crucible of war an enduring prescription for success.

While cultural and organizational factors unquestionably intrude, the fact that two such different societies and military cultures could employ a similar approach to warfighting suggests that the American military is not necessarily constrained by its history and traditions from embracing a new and different paradigm. Indeed, the times may demand it. This question—how the American military should approach its fundamental missions of deterrence and defense, given severe resource constraints—lies at the heart of the maneuver debate.

This volume was conceived with several objectives in mind. First, it attempts to explore this model of maneuver-based war and assess its potential for solving the pressing organizational challenges alluded to above. Second, it represents an effort to reenergize and build upon the creative debates of a decade ago and carry forward the intellectual momentum of what was, at its best, a fascinating and important exchange of ideas and commentary on the military art. Lastly, it introduces a rising generation of military thinkers and analysts whose work will play an important role in shaping the post–Cold War military establishment.

The essays presented herein are loosely organized into three sections. The first offers a critical and theoretical discussion of maneuver warfare as a concept and system of ideas. The second addresses the institutional and organizational implications of maneuver warfare.

The final section of the book consists of a series of historical essays which portray successful applications of maneuver concepts or contrast them with other styles of war.

No attempt has been made to confine the contributing authors to prescribed format or subject. The anthology should be read as a collection of essays, perhaps only tangentially linked, each making its own independent contribution to an evolving body of thought. If the reader is moved, either in affirmation or contradiction, to contribute in some way to the synthesis of ideas that attend this topic, the efforts of the contributing authors will be well rewarded.

# PART 1
## THE THEORY OF MANEUVER WARFARE

In this century, and particularly in the last fifteen years, maneuver warfare as a bounded system of ideas has been raised from the level of casual observation to that of true theory. Where previously historians attempted to isolate and identify the unifying themes or ideas that animated successful military commanders, today it is possible to advance a distinctly different theory of warfare which, while not approaching the mathematical precision of the "hard" sciences, nevertheless meets the standards of contemporary social and political science.

In this sense, theory can be understood as a system of ideas that seeks to explain reality and serve as a guide to action. As an attempt to identify recurring phenomena and the relationships that define their interaction, theory thus defined is both descriptive and prescriptive. This is not to suggest that maneuver warfare can be reduced to lists of imperatives and rules leading to battlefield success. Rather, it can be seen as a more efficient and effective thought process and a framework for analysis to guide the military decision maker toward the solution of complex battlefield problems.

Here we present affirmative and critical views of the maneuver argument, together with original essays on strategic settings, operational art, low-intensity conflict, the origins of the German system of mission tactics, and the psychological basis of maneuver warfare defeat mechanisms. Taken together, these discussions delimit the spectrum of the maneuver debate and suggest new directions for study and analysis.

# The Theory and Practice of Maneuver Warfare
## William S. Lind

For fifteen years, a major debate over maneuver warfare has raged around and within the American armed forces.[1] In 1989, the U.S. Marine Corps issued a new basic doctrinal manual, FMFM 1, *Warfighting*, which explicitly adopted maneuver warfare as doctrine. The U.S. Army had adopted many of the basic concepts of maneuver warfare as doctrine earlier, in the 1982 edition of FM 100-5, *Operations*. Recently, the Army has begun using the term "maneuver warfare" as well.[2]

What is maneuver warfare? To begin answering that question, it is helpful first to ask another: what is maneuver? That question has three basic answers, in that there are three ways the word "maneuver" is commonly used.

The first is simply as a synonym for movement. This is encountered in such phrases as "tactics of fire and maneuver," where the movement of the rushing element is described as "maneuver." Or a company commander may say, "I maneuvered my company to the assembly point." He means nothing more than he marched his company to that point. This is in effect a colloquial use of the term "maneuver," and has little to do with maneuver warfare.

The second meaning of maneuver is movement relative to an enemy's position. This definition is reflected in the Army's FM 100-5 field manual: "Maneuver is the movement of forces in relation to the enemy to secure or retain positional advantage." This is historically the most common use of the term "maneuver," and such maneuver has been an important element of warfare since the dawn of recorded history. Usually, it means moving around the enemy's front to hit his flanks or rear. From the Battle of Marathon in 490 B.C. through Cannae to Napoleon's *manoeuvre sur les derrières* and von Moltke's *Kesselschlacht*, maneuvering to hit the enemy's flanks or to encircle him has often been the commander's objective, and when achieved it has often been decisive.

3

Maneuver warfare incorporates this second sense of the word maneuver. But it also moves beyond it. In the term "maneuver warfare," maneuver refers to an entire style of warfare, one characterized not only by moving in relation to the enemy to gain positional advantage, but also—and even more—to moving faster than the enemy, to defeating him through superior tempo. The theoretical understanding of war as a competition in time even more than in position is a recent development, largely of the last fifteen years.[3] In practice—which preceded the theory—a style of warfare based on tempo is, in the 20th century, largely a product of the German Army.[4] It is this development to which we refer in the term "maneuver warfare," and it is best seen in a historical context.

If we look at modern warfare—warfare roughly since the Peace of Westphalia in 1648—we can see three distinct approaches, or styles, which, as they succeeded one another, may be thought of as "generations." First-generation warfare was dominated by the tactics of line and column. Its period was from about the middle of the 17th century to about the middle of the 19th, and it reached its apotheosis in the wars of the French Revolution. The most important weapon in first-generation warfare was the smoothbore musket, and the tactics, especially those of the line, flowed in large part from the characteristics of that weapon.

First-generation warfare remains of more than historical interest, because elements of it are still very much with us. Linear tactics still turn up in modern engagements, even though the result is usually disaster.[5] Military drill derives from and reflects the tactics of the first generation. Most important, the culture of first-generation warfare remains dominant in most military services. As the first-generation battlefield was a battlefield of order—the Prussian Army of Frederick the Great was lauded as a "perfectly oiled machine"—so the military culture is a culture of order. Uniforms, ranks, saluting, and drill are all largely products of the first military generation. So is the general obsession with order, control, centralization and standardization which characterizes militaries—characteristics which, as we shall see, are not necessarily helpful on modern battlefields.

Second-generation warfare emerged in the middle of the 19th century, reaching its high point in the French "methodical battle" tactics of the latter stages of World War I. Adopted wholesale by the U.S.

Army and Marine Corps in World War I, the "methodical battle" remained the basis for American ground force doctrine until the 1980s. Because thousands of officers trained in methodical battle doctrine remain on active duty, actual practice in many units remains well within the realm of the second generation.[6]

The second generation arose largely in response to the replacement of the smoothbore musket with the rifle. In the face of rifled muskets—and later, breechloaders, repeaters, machine guns, and quick-firing artillery—first-generation tactics of line and column proved suicidal, as Grant discovered at Cold Harbor. Second-generation tactics, however, remained linear; in the defense, the objective remained "holding the line" and preventing any penetration, and the attack aimed at moving a line of friendly troops forward. The techniques changed—e.g., the advance was by alternate rushes and the defense dug in—and the line was thinned out laterally, but the basic concept of what the attack and the defense were trying to do remained the same.

World War I brought another change in weaponry that in turn brought the second generation to its fulfillment: indirect artillery fire. Previously restricted largely to sieges, indirect artillery fire came to dominate World War I on the western front. With that domination, infantry tactics of the second generation underwent a fundamental change, in that the actual destruction of the enemy was left largely to the artillery. The French Army expressed this in the motto, "The artillery conquers, the infantry occupies."

While the first-generation culture of order reflected a battlefield of order,[7] the second generation attempted to impose order on an increasingly disorderly battlefield. The French doctrine of the inter-war period showed this clearly. That doctrine prized obedience over initiative, centralized decision making (for more efficient control of the artillery), and discouraged any departure from "the plan."

If World War I saw the full flowering of second-generation warfare, it also witnessed the birth of the third generation, maneuver warfare. More than that, it saw maneuver warfare's full conceptual development.[8] This birth and growth occurred in the German army, the *Kaisersheer*.

While the Allies sought the answer to the "riddle of the trenches" in ever-more-powerful artillery bombardments and, later, the tank, the Germans sought a tactical answer.[9] After a number of false starts, including von Falkenhayn's disastrous flirtation with attrition warfare, the Germans settled on an approach that took advantage of some of their traditional virtues: their fondness for decision in battle, the initiative of their junior leaders and their "every problem demands a unique solution" attitude toward tactics. Combined with improved artillery techniques and weapons—such as a light machine gun, portable trench mortars, hand grenades, and flamethrowers that gave unprecedented power to small units—the Germans of 1917 and 1918 won impressive tactical victories.

That the Germans were unable to do more than win battles was largely a function of operational considerations. While Allied tactics were, as a general rule, cruder than German tactics, the Allied rail net gave them the ability to shift reserves from one point of the front to another quickly. The Germans, on the other hand, had to move their muscle-powered armies across miles of shell-torn wilderness. At a time when horses and men were both underfed and in short supply, winning the race against Allied locomotives was out of the question. When, however, the Germans between the wars replaced muscle power with the internal combustion engine, the tactics they had developed in the First World War became one of the cornerstones of blitzkrieg.

What were these new German tactics?[10] Conceptually, the purpose of battle shifted: the goal was no longer simply to kill enemy soldiers or destroy enemy equipment, nor just to hold or advance the line. Rather, it was to take enemy units as a whole out of play.[11]

On the defense, the enemy was expected and allowed to penetrate. At first, he encountered only light resistance from outposts. As he went deeper, resistance stiffened. Built around machine-gun nests designed for 360-degree defense, this resistance was intended to break up the momentum and cohesion of the attack. Frequently, the main belt of machine-gun positions would be on reverse slopes; when the Allies encountered them, their own artillery could not observe to support them, while German artillery that had remained concealed suddenly opened up. Then came the coup de grace in the form of a powerful German counterattack that drove to the previous German front line and encircled the attacker.

The new German defensive tactics were the first nonlinear tactics. The same was true of their offensive "infiltration" tactics. Under the cover of fire from artillery and other supporting arms, small units organized for independent action—the famous storm troops—used favorable terrain, particularly culverts, ravines, and similar features, to bypass enemy strong points and penetrate into the depth of the enemy's positions. Once into the Allied defenses, they drove on forward as fast as they could, disregarding the progress, or lack of it, of units on their flanks. A successful penetration was immediately reinforced. The objective was not the enemy infantry—that was cut off, pocketed, and left for follow-on forces to deal with—but the enemy's rear, especially his artillery. The goal was to collapse whole enemy units and sectors—and it worked.

In a famous passage, Sir Basil Liddell Hart likened this type of attack to flowing waters:

> If we watch a torrent bearing down on each successive bank or earthen dam in its path, we see that it first beats against the obstacle, feeling and testing it at all points. Eventually, it finds a small crack at some point. Through this crack pour the first driblets of water and rush straight through. The pent-up water on each side is drawn towards the breach. It swirls through and around the flanks of the breach, wearing away the earth on each side and so widening the gap. Simultaneously the water behind pours straight through the breach between the side eddies which are wearing away the flanks. Directly it has passed through it expands to widen once more the onrush of the torrent. Thus as the water pours through in ever-increasing volume the onrush of the torrent swells to its original proportions, leaving in turn each crumbling obstacle behind it. Thus Nature's forces carry out the ideal attack, automatically maintaining the speed, the breadth, and the continuity of the attack.[12]

These World War I German tactics, offensive and defensive, remain the basis of modern maneuver warfare tactics: a defense in depth that combines positions on reverse slopes, ambushes, and small units operating independently to harass, confuse, and pin, with a powerful counterattack intended to cut off and encircle; and an attack that penetrates in multiple thrusts aimed at weak points, reinforces successes and exploits without too much concern for flanks, uses speed as its preeminent weapon, and again seeks the enemy's rear and encirclement.

So is that all there is to maneuver warfare? If so, the challenge to the American Army and Marine Corps to move from second- to third-generation tactics would seem relatively easy. But in fact there is a great deal more to it. Behind these tactics lies a series of concepts, all of which are central to the tactics—the one cannot be done without the other—and all of which represent fundamental change, cultural change. They move the military culture from being a culture of order, attempting to impose order on the inherent disorder of war, to a culture that can adapt to, use, and generate disorder, that is in harmony with it.

The transformation is a difficult one. It begins with understanding just what these concepts of maneuver warfare are. The first is an understanding of war itself. Maneuver warfare theory accepts that war is by its nature disorderly. It is dominated by uncertainty, rapid and unexpected changes, and friction. Maneuverists view Clausewitz's concept of friction—that in war everything is simple, but even the simplest thing is extremely difficult—as his most important contribution to military theory. This view of the nature of war underlies all other maneuver warfare concepts, because it demands that they all be consistent with it. Concepts that contradict it—such as "synchronization," one of the four main concepts of the Army's AirLand Battle—must fall out, because the nature of war simply will not admit them. Something that is dominated by surprise, rapid change, and friction cannot be synchronized; it is not a railway timetable. War demands "thriving on chaos."

How does one thrive in this chaotic mess called combat? Principally, by driving change instead of being driven by it; in other words, by being faster than the enemy. The principal weapon in maneuver warfare is speed; not just speed in movement, though that is important, but speed in everything, which is sometimes called tempo. In maneuver theory, war is above all a competition in tempo, which is to say in time. It is no accident that the most successful commanders in maneuver warfare have been men like Gen. "Schneller Heinz" Guderian and Gen. Hermann Balck, whose motto for his staff was, "Don't work hard—work fast!"

While great captains have instinctively understood the importance of time and speed, the anchoring of maneuver theory in time competitiveness was accomplished only recently, in the work of Col. John Boyd, USAF. Synthesizing from both air and ground combat, Boyd determined that conflict can best be understood as time-competitive cycles of observing, orienting, deciding, and acting. Each side begins by observing, through military intelligence, reconnaissance, the commander's own eyes and ears, etc. On the basis of the observation, each orients; that is to say, each makes up a mental picture of his situation relative to his opponent. On the basis of the orientation, each makes a decision to do something; then he acts. Assuming the action has changed something, each must then observe again, and the cycle begins anew.

Whoever can go through this "Boyd Cycle" or "OODA Loop" consistently faster gains a tremendous advantage, primarily because by the time his opponent acts, his own action has already changed the situation so as to make the opponent's action irrelevant. With each cycle, the time margin by which the enemy is irrelevant grows. Striving ever for convergence, the opponent finds himself obtaining wider and wider divergence. His situation is not only bad, but it is steadily getting worse; and it is getting worse at an ever-accelerating pace. Eventually, he tends to realize what is happening to him, to understand that nothing he can do will work. At that point, he often panics and runs or simply gives up. If he does keep fighting, he is ineffective, because his cohesion is shattered; the trinity of "order-counterorder-disorder" has pulled him apart. He can no longer fight as an organized whole.

The question, "How does one fight effectively in the chaos of combat?" is thus answered, "By consistently being faster than the enemy." But that raises another question: "How can one consistently be faster?"

The first answer is, "Through practice of the operational art."[13] Operational art is the linkage between tactics and strategy. It is the art of using tactical events—battles and, equally, refusals to give battle— to strike directly at an enemy strategic center of gravity, a "hinge" in the enemy's system which, if shattered, will bring it down. How does operational art increase speed? Largely by permitting its practitioner to avoid unnecessary fighting. Fighting—battles and engagements— slows things down. By fighting only where and when necessary in order to get at an enemy's strategic center of gravity, battle is minimized and speed is increased.

The concept of avoiding fighting carries over to the tactical level as well. In maneuver warfare tactics, the goal is not "close with and destroy" but "bypass and collapse." Attacks are not on the enemy, but through him. The German storm troops of 1918 engaged the enemy only to the degree necessary to get past him and into his rear. The situation is the same in the counterattack. The more static elements in the defense of course do seek to engage the enemy, but the primary object of that engagement is to absorb the enemy's attention, pin him, and set him up for the counterattack.

The attack or counterattack in turn is done through what the Germans call "the tactics of surfaces and gaps." A reconnaissance screen, running as the advance element of an attack, looks for where the enemy is—surfaces or "hard spots"—and gaps or "soft spots," where he isn't. The reconnaissance screen "pulls" the units behind it around the surfaces and through the gaps, minimizing contact and keeping up the speed of the attack. Any successful penetration is immediately reinforced, widened and deepened.

Does this promise bloodless war? The answer is, "It depends on the situation." Faced with a high-speed attack that comes where they aren't, penetrates deeply, and encircles, some forces collapse with little fighting; the war with Iraq provides a good example. Other opponents will continue to fight, and while their effectiveness will be reduced, some bloody combat may nonetheless ensue. In general, maneuver warfare offers no promise of bloodless war, but it does offer less bloody war than a head-on bash directly into the enemy's strength.

The tactics of surfaces and gaps have at least one remarkable feature about them: since the precise direction of the attack follows a continuing reconnaissance pull, it is being set not by colonels in headquarters, but by corporals, sergeants, lieutenants, and captains—by people at the bottom of the chain of command. In effect, the decisions flow upward, not downward, and those above act to support what has been decided and done by those below.

This suggests maneuver warfare involves radical decentralization of authority, and that is in fact the case. If we again consider speed, the reason is obvious. If decisions can only be made after information is collected and transmitted up the chain of command, and the decisions must then flow back down that chain before action results, the decision cycle will be slow indeed. Speed requires that decisions be made at the lowest possible level.

How can this be done without creating chaos as every junior leader "does his own thing"? Through another of maneuver warfare's central concepts: *Auftragstaktik*, or "mission tactics." This has been (under a variety of terms) the guiding tactical principle of the German army at least since 1870. Simply put, it involves telling a subordinate what result he is to obtain, usually defined in terms of effect on enemy,[14] then leaving him to determine how best to get it. Orders specify output, not input. This is true at every level, right down through the fire team and the individual soldier. In turn, everyone is expected to know what result is wanted at least two levels up.

This sounds simple, and once people are accustomed to it, it is. But in terms of the traditional military culture of order, it is revolutionary. That culture is accustomed to subordinates who do exactly what they are told, when they are told, and don't mess things up by taking initiative. It pushes the noses of junior leaders down into the muck of detail and minutiae, and woe be unto him who dares to look up at the "bigger picture." He will quickly and forcefully be told, "That's above your pay grade!"

Mission tactics breaks dramatically with this. It wants, indeed demands, subordinates who think, make independent decisions, assume responsibility, and show initiative. By specifying the result the superior wants, and that more than one level up, it gives the subordinate the "big picture" he can use to ensure that his actions, while independent, work in harmony with the actions of others because they are all trying to achieve the same goal, the same result.

In practice, the subordinate is usually given two reference points. The first is his superior's intent: the overall result he wants to achieve at the end of the action (e.g., "I want to stop his advance to the north, cut him off from the south, and encircle him against the river to the east"). The second is the subordinate's specific mission, which is his "slice" of the intent, also expressed in terms of results ("Smitty, I want your battalion to stop his advance north"). If events bring the two into conflict, the intent—what the Germans sometimes call "the ticket to the end of the line"—is overriding. For example, if in this situation the enemy halted his own advance and dug in, Lieutenant Colonel Smith might choose to add his battalion to the battle group that is moving to cut the enemy off from the south. He would do that on his own initiative, especially if time were pressing, which it usually is, or if communications were bad, which they often are.

Mission tactics may be thought of as a series of contracts between superior and subordinates.[15] The superior, in his contract, pledges to make the result he desires crystal clear to his subordinates (no more casting bones and reading chicken entrails to determine "what the Old Man really wants"), to leave the subordinate maximum latitude in determining how to get the result (no more inch-thick battalion operations orders), and—perhaps the greatest change—to back him up when he makes mistakes. Mission tactics allows honest mistakes; maneuver warfare and "zero defects" are incompatible. Maneuverists recognize what Germans call "the inherent right of the lieutenant to make rash, brash mistakes."[16]

On his part, the subordinate contracts to discipline himself to ensure that his actions serve to accomplish the mission and achieve the commander's intent. This is another of the cultural shifts maneuver warfare requires: whereas first- and second-generation tactics relied on imposed discipline, maneuver warfare demands self-discipline.

The subordinate also pledges to be highly active in pursuit of the result his commander wants. This is the other side of the coin of tolerating mistakes; the subordinate has to be willing to risk making them. While the German army tolerated mistakes that came from too much boldness, it was intolerant of those that proceeded from overcaution or unwillingness to make a decision. Again, this calls for a shift in institutional culture; second-generation tactics often speaks well of initiative, but traditional military culture in fact frowns on it. The junior officer or NCO quickly learns that if he does nothing except what he is told, he will not get in trouble, whereas if he does something without being told, he may. A third-generation military acts precisely the opposite way; it rewards initiative, even when in terms of solving the problem, it doesn't work.

Finally, in their mutual contracts, both superior and subordinate pledge to focus *outward* on the situation, the enemy, and what must be accomplished to defeat him, rather than *inward* on process, procedure, format, and hierarchy. If a captain, by virtue of being in the right spot at the right time, knows what a reinforcing battalion should do better than does the battalion's commander, then the battalion commander allows the captain to direct it. If the situation requires someone to depart from what he was ordered to do, he acts according to the situation. If the press of time does not allow the normal staff planning process to operate without slowing down the action, the process is jettisoned. The situation is sacred, not the colonel's dignity, nor the five-paragraph order format, nor the chain of command.

At this point, it should be clear that there is much more to *Auftragstaktik* than sticking a paragraph labelled "commander's intent" in the usual overly detailed, overly structured five-paragraph order (maneuverists do not worry about the form of an order, but rather about its content). Mission tactics means a whole different way of thinking and behaving—a change in culture—from what prevails in second-generation warfare. If it does not bring that kind of change, if it is simply a new "buzzword" attached to business as usual, then it is nothing.

The relationship of mission tactics and its accompanying decentralization to speed is obvious. But is speed the only principle of war in maneuver warfare? No. There is one other: focus. It lies at the heart of a central maneuver warfare concept, *Schwerpunkt*, or focus of effort.[17]

While a specific unit—division, battalion, or company—is designated the focus of effort, the "focus" is much more than that unit. At root, it is the commander's bid to attain a decision. In second-generation warfare, the goal is usually an incremental gain. In maneuver warfare, the goal in each situation is to attain a decisive result. When a commander designates a unit as his focus of effort, he is saying, "this is the unit I will use to achieve a decision."

Conceptually, the opposite to focus is fairness. When a commander is being "fair," he parcels out missions, supporting arms, logistics and forces equally to everyone. When he is building a *Schwerpunkt*, he determines what action he thinks will be decisive, then ruthlessly focuses combat power to be stronger than the enemy in that action (a principal reason why smaller forces practicing maneuver warfare often defeat larger ones that aren't). He often takes major risks elsewhere in order to focus. Units not part of the *Schwerpunkt* are left largely to fend for themselves with their own resources.

Designation of the *Schwerpunkt* is one of the commander's main responsibilities. If his character is weak, he will have trouble doing it; he will tend to try to "cover all the bases." If his military judgment is weak, he may simply be unable to choose a *Schwerpunkt*, because he will be unable to think through how he intends to fight the battle.

Along with the intent and the mission, the focus of effort expresses the commander's conceptualization of the battle; how he intends to fight and win it. Together, they tell his subordinates what is in his mind. (If they are devoid of content, they may tell them that there is nothing in his mind at all.)

What happens if the commander designates a *Schwerpunkt*, but the situation changes in such a way as to make it inappropriate, for example, while aimed at a gap it unexpectedly hits a surface? The answer is, he changes it. If a neighboring unit finds itself moving forward easily while the *Schwerpunkt* is blocked, he redesignates the neighboring unit as the *Schwerpunkt*. With the redesignation come the supporting arms, reinforcements, and so on. Thus, the *Schwerpunkt* may and often does shift, but there always is one.

A common error in understanding the *Schwerpunkt* is to think it translates, especially in the attack, into a single, powerful thrust. In fact, maneuver warfare depends heavily on multiple thrusts. Multiple thrusts generate massive confusion for the enemy and serve to disguise the *Schwerpunkt*. They also generate opportunities for shifting it.

These are the defining concepts of maneuver warfare.[18] They do not add up to a new formula, recipe, or method. Methodical battle—the focus inward on process rather than outward on the situation—is the opposite of maneuver warfare. Methodical battle was the French doctrine in 1940, just as maneuver warfare was the German doctrine; the result when the two clashed was decisive, largely because the Germans drove events at a tempo faster than the French method could accommodate.

Understanding of maneuver warfare has been spreading in the U.S. Army and the U.S. Marine Corps since the debate over it began in the 1970s. But an academic understanding alone is not sufficient for a soldier or an army. Understanding maneuver warfare is one thing; being able to do it in combat is very much more. Only an institution-alized ability to do it brings victory.

What changes must the American military make to institutionalize maneuver warfare? The most important are in the personnel system. Maneuver warfare demands highly cohesive units, which means the personnel system must promote personnel stability instead of constant rotation. People must be assigned to specific billets as individuals, with regard to their individual talents and character, not simply on a "warm body" basis. The officer ranks, especially field grade and above, must be lean, not bloated with thousands more officers than there are real jobs. An officer surplus inevitably leads to centralization, overcontrol of subordinates, and large headquarters that make decisions by committee, all of which work against speed.

Military education must focus on development of judgment, not transmission of knowledge.[19] That is accomplished largely through study of history and through putting people in military situations, forcing them to make decisions, then critiquing those decisions. The bulk of the time in military schools and colleges should be devoted to map exercises, sand tables, tactical exercises without troops (TEWTs), war games, staff rides, etc. Most training should be force-on-force and free play. Scripted, "scenario" exercises are useful only for training opera companies. Only free-play training brings in the central element of war, the free, creative will of an opponent.

All training exercises must be followed by rigorous, thorough, honest critiques, where no commander is spared, however exalted his rank. Much of the value of training is lost when critiques are exercises in Hapsburg court etiquette, where everyone's dignity is carefully protected and the object is to make everyone look good and feel good. At the same time, no one's career should suffer because of a mistake in an exercise.

As this essay has endeavored to make clear, the most important changes needed to make maneuver warfare a reality are in institutional culture. The culture of a maneuver warfare military is very different from the culture of order that grew out of first-generation warfare and carried on through the second generation. It is parallel in some ways to what we think of as the Japanese corporate culture: decentralized, participatory, and focused outward on the product and its success in the marketplace. It goes too far to call it a culture of disorder, but through decentralization and shared objectives, it is a culture that is comfortable with a disorderly world and can function effectively in that world.

In Desert Storm, the American ground forces, Army and Marine Corps, on the whole practiced maneuver warfare. There were certainly exceptions: for example, we had in effect the 1st German Marine Division and the 2d French Marine Division, in terms of the styles each employed. But the overall picture suggests the ship has come onto the new course, even if it has a long journey ahead of it before it is safe in the maneuver warfare harbour.

What is critical now is that the journey continue. Desert Storm does not demonstrate that all is now well and the military can return to a pleasant slumber. The test was an easy one, because for the most part the enemy did not fight. It is probably desirable that the first test be an easy one. But if it leads to complacency, to a belief that the American armed forces have suddenly become the Wehrmacht in terms of their ability to do maneuver warfare, it will have been an operational victory but a strategic defeat. If, on the other hand, Desert Storm stimulates the American forces to fulfill the promise they showed in that campaign, then it will mark a historical turning point. Which it will be, only the people in our armed services can determine.

# Notes

1. The debate began in 1976, sparked by a paper finally published in March 1977. See William S. Lind, "Some Doctrinal Questions for the United States Army," *Military Review* (March 1977), p. 54.

2. See Gen. John Foss, "Advent of the Nonlinear Battlefield: AirLand Battle-Future," *Army* (February 1991), p. 24.

3. Thanks to the work of Col. John Boyd, USAF, ret.

4. This is not to say previous history saw no instances of tempo-based warfare; the Mongols are an obvious example.

5. David H. Hackworth and Julie Sherman, *About Face: The Odyssey of an American Warrior* (New York: Simon and Schuster, 1989), p. 503.

6. For a definitive description of methodical battle, see Robert A. Doughty, *The Seeds of Disaster: The Development of French Army Doctrine, 1919–1939* (Hamden, Conn.: The Shoe String Press, 1985).

7. Toward the end of the first generation, the disorder of the battlefield was increasing, driven in part by a revival of light, as opposed to line, infantry. However, the culture of order remained dominant. See J. F. C. Fuller, *British Light Infantry in the Eighteenth Century* (London: Hutchinson and Co., 1925).

8. From a dinner conversation with General Hermann Balck. When asked if the bulk of German thinking on maneuver warfare had been developed 1914–1918 or 1918–1939, he replied that it had all been developed 1914–1918.

9. The two best works on the new German tactics are Bruce I. Gudmundsson, *Stormtroop Tactics: Innovation in the German Army, 1914–1918* (New York: Praeger Publishers, 1989) and Timothy J. Lupfer, "The Dynamics of Doctrine: The Changes in German Tactical Doctrine During the First World War," *Leavenworth Papers,* No. 4 (Ft. Leavenworth, Kans.: U.S. Army Command and General Staff College, 1981).

10. While new as a complete "package," these tactics had a heritage that dated back decades. For example, the practice of assigning a subordinate a mission and leaving him wide latitude in accomplishing it can be seen in the Prussian army by 1813. See Charles Edward White, *The Enlightened Soldier: Scharnhorst and the Militaerische Gesellschaft in Berlin, 1801–1805* (New York: Praeger Publishers, 1981).

11. Balck said that in 1914, the German goal had been to kill enemy soldiers and destroy enemy equipment. As the war went on, the goal changed to taking entire units out of play, with the size of the enemy unit that was the objective steadily growing. From a conversation with General Hermann Balck, cited above.

12. Captain B. H. Liddell Hart, "The 'Man-in-the-Dark' Theory of Infantry Tactics and the 'Expanding Torrent' System of Attack," *Journal of the R.U.S.I.* (February 1921), p. 13.

13. A very good short treatise on operational art is the United States Marine Corps' FMFM1-1, *Campaigning*.

14. Sometimes the objective may be defined in terms of terrain, e.g., in the seizure of key terrain features. But this is a fairly rare exception, and when it is used, the subordinate should still understand why the terrain is key, i.e., how it relates to the enemy.

15. Thinking of mission orders as a series of contracts between superior and subordinate was first suggested by Col. John Boyd.

16. OTL i.G. Dieter Farwick and OTL i.G. Gerhard Hubatschek, *Die Strategische Erpressung* (Munich: Verlag for Wehrwissenschaften, 1981), p. 168.

17. The question frequently arises of the relationship between maneuver warfare and the "principles of war." Maneuverists generally eschew any such list of principles, on the grounds that war cannot be fought by following lists. However, Col. Michael D. Wyly, USMC, Ret., the Marine Corps' premier maneuver warfare theorist, argues that if someone wants principles of war for maneuver warfare, there are only two: speed and focus.

18. A number of concepts could be added, such as the central importance of the reserve, the use of combined arms, flexibility and innovation in techniques, etc. However, the author would argue that while important, they are not defining.

19. A French officer, writing immediately after France's defeat in 1940, lamented that in French military schools, "The teaching was more concerned with developing knowledge than exercising judgement." Daniel Vilfroy, *War in the West: The Battle of France, May-June, 1940* (Harrisburg, Penn.: Military Service Publishing Co., 1942), p. 89.

# Maneuver Warfare Reconsidered

## Daniel P. Bolger

"There is less here than meets the eye."
Tallulah Bankhead

We all remember the images: the stark black-and-white photos of the Korean bug-out, the *Pueblo* crew in captivity, the blasted wreckage of Fire Base Mary Ann, overloaded Huey choppers on the roof of the Saigon embassy, burnt-out helicopter carcasses rusting in the Iranian desert, and a devastated Marine barracks in Beirut. To believe the press pundits, the U.S. military that won World War II became the gang that couldn't shoot straight.

If so, a phoenix has arisen. How did the United States of America field armed forces that performed so superbly, and won so completely, in the recent Gulf War? Here is one story that is making the rounds . . .

Once upon a time, in the bad old days after the fall of Saigon, a good many soldiers, Marines, retired military men, and concerned civilians began asking themselves what had gone wrong with the American war effort in Southeast Asia. Given the scale of the debacle, finding problems proved pretty easy.

Some claimed that the military had been just about to win when they were stabbed in the back by a cowardly coterie of unscrupulous journalists, pinko college students, weak-kneed liberal politicians, and other sundry mouth-breathing malcontents. Others stated that the armed services and their civilian handlers botched the strategy by choosing either a conventional or unconventional fight when the opposite would have worked. A discouraged few argued that America's war in Vietnam had always been doomed, and that the real tragedy involved the military's inability or unwillingness to confront this unpalatable situation.[1]

19

All of these analysts started from the premise that the crux of the matter involved the unique nature of the Southeast Asian War. A far bolder, and more persuasive, group of critics took the opposite approach. They argued that the real trouble arose inside America's military structure. In their view, Vietnam amounted to a major symptom of a far more serious disease: America's defense establishment preferred the wrong way of war.

These vocal defense reformers, in and out of uniform, based their beliefs on excursions through the deep reservoirs of military history. Based upon their studies, they demanded that America give up what they called a historical tendency to embrace "a firepower/attrition style of warfare" for what they perceived as a more promising approach.[2] They called their concept "maneuver warfare," and spoke of lightning victories at small cost.

Like the prescient intellectuals they were, these diligent maneuverists endured years of alienation at the mercy of suspicious bureaucrats. They liked to think of themselves as unappreciated visionaries, hovering out on the far fringes of military oblivion, out in that netherworld populated by myopic wargame enthusiasts, fussy academics, pretentious congressional staff defense "experts," and perennially disgruntled junior officers. In their romantic view, these persecuted prophets struggled for years in obscurity, ignored and unappreciated by the mossbacked traditionalists entrenched in the upper echelons of the U.S. defense establishment. Still, they trusted that the weight of history and the need for fundamental change in a discredited system would eventually bring their ideas to the fore.

After a decade or so of dogged persistence in the inherent correctness of their so obviously valid views, the maneuver enthusiasts at last gained recognition for their purity of thought. Scales fell from the eyes of senior officers and civil policymakers, who apologized for being so blind to the brilliance and cogency of the maneuverists' arguments. The services, particularly the Army and Marines, enshrined "maneuver warfare" as their fighting doctrine by the mid-1980s.[3]

For finally coming around to proper military thinking, America received a reward beyond its wildest dreams. Racing tanks and screaming jets led U.S. forces to a smashing, nearly bloodless triumph in the desert, culminating in an awesome 100-hour blitzkrieg against Iraq. It all worked, just like the maneuver warfare proponents always predicted.

Truly, the entire country can and should be thankful to those hardy maneuver warfare pioneers who, as *US News and World Report* recently explained, led "The Fight to Change How America Fights."[4] Being the modest, duty-bound types that they are, the vindicated maneuverists will settle for choice promotions, key government appointments, hefty consulting fees, healthy military retirement benefits, university sinecures, honorary degrees, and occasional adulation as demigods. After all, it's only fair for men who made a wrong thing so right.

Does that story seem ridiculous to you? It ought to.

Maneuver warfare is bunk. No competent soldier, let alone the entire U.S. military establishment, should embrace it. Subjected to serious scrutiny, maneuver warfare's theoretical assumptions turn out to be laughably flimsy. Not surprisingly, so are the battlefield prescriptions that flow from such flawed premises.

## MANEUVER WARFARE AS WE KNOW IT

What do proponents define as maneuver warfare? Sometimes, it seems like the answer is "anything that works," as these people refuse to be pinned down on paper or on the battlefield. Still, like Supreme Court justices in search of pornography, they know it when they see it.

Defense consultant Edward N. Luttwak writes that in maneuver warfare, "instead of seeking to destroy the enemy's physical substance, the goal is to incapacitate by *systematic* [emphasis in original] disruption."[5] A maneuver-oriented general intends to knock out the foe by "presenting him with surprising and dangerous situations faster than he can react to them, until he comes apart."[6] Maneuverists aim to shatter the enemy's army, not simply cut him to death through slow attrition.

As one summary of the theory states, "maneuver warfare means different things to different people, but it does embrace a set of common assumptions and prescriptions."[7] One has to dig a bit through the available literature, but these assumptions and prescriptions can be identified.

Maneuver warfare derives from four assumptions. A maneuverist believes that the human activity known as war can be understood through the medium of social science. Second, he believes that war is war, whether conducted at low or high intensity, at the tactical or strategic level, on land, sea, or air. With this view of conflict, the maneuverist posits a critical variable for victory, the need to emphasize the dislocating effects of maneuver over the killing effects of firepower.[8] Finally, he turns to military history to prove his thesis, and discovers that the most effective armies have employed what he would call maneuver warfare.[9]

Prescriptions flow from these assumptions. First, maneuverists urge commanders to avoid enemy strength and fiercely attack weaknesses. Second, they encourage subordinate initiative to seize fleeting battlefield opportunities. Third, they prompt commanders to win wars at the operational level, free from the intrusion of politics from above or friction from below.[10]

It all sounds great, especially when the payoff appears to be a quick, resounding victory. Too bad that it has very little to do with the messy realities of war.

### FAULTY ASSUMPTION #1: WEIRD SCIENCE

Why do maneuver proponents think the way they do? What made them isolate maneuver as the vital determinant of victory? Maneuverists say that they derived their thoughts from history, but the lack of any such body of thought in the human record prior to the stylings of mid-1970s America indicates that the thesis probably preceded the search for evidence. That's a common enough approach in physics or chemistry, but war is not a hard, or "exact," science. Maneuver warfare thinkers arrived at their conclusions by trying to understand war through the tools of social science, sometimes called "soft" or, more appropriately, "weird" science.

The very term "social science" is an oxymoron, an annoying point that most true believers prefer to avoid. Hard science deals with things: rocks, stars, atoms, moons, and meatballs. Things usually do the same things when you mess with them in the same way. Glass does not cut diamonds. Diamonds always cut glass. These materials have very predictable ranges of response. Ninety-nine times out of a hundred, and usually much more reliably, real scientists can predict those responses—from things.

Add "social" to science, though, and you've added people, and the neat curves and mathematical certainties go haywire. In scientific terms, the human mind and spirit create an exceedingly large set of variables. The permutations and combinations seem endless. Unlike things, humans respond to stimuli in many different ways. Do a certain something to a person and his reaction can vary widely from time to time.

This is so even in fairly simple matters. If I slap you, you may do nothing, you may cry, you may hit back, or do all of those in an unpredictable sequence. I can never really be sure what you will do.

Do something to a group of people and the potential responses multiply exponentially. Sure, there is a range of possibilities, but after a while, the range grows so large that it and infinity might as well be the same. It appears more than a little presumptuous to try to predict the behavior of hundreds of thousands of independent human beings, each with free wills, unique thoughts, and irrational emotions. Yet economists, sociologists, criminologists, psychologists, and a hundred other pseudoscientists allege otherwise and strive mightily to make people toe the line, whether it be the Laffer Curve, the Law of Diminishing Returns, or the Devil's Theory of Baseball Parks. Damned if people don't keep screwing up the experimental data. No wonder social scientists prefer to postulate a "rational actor" (Mr. Spock, call your office) or just give up and play with rats.

When it works, social science tells you what you already know: "a person maximizes happiness and minimizes pain," "most children love their mothers," or "people tend to enjoy the company of others." All very nice—but so what?

When social science fails, as it often does, it predicts things that don't happen: "recession coming," "political realignment," or (a particular howler these days) "the inexorable triumph of socialism." Usually, this is all harmless claptrap that at least allows a few soft scientists to put food on their children's plates. But sometimes the failures can prove to be colossal. Witness some of social science's greatest hits: Thomas Malthus's population projections, Lyndon Johnson's Great Society, the Cabrini-Green Housing Project in Chicago, and the Union of Soviet Socialist Republics.[11]

Given this sort of track record, why would anyone try to use these blunt instruments to study humans in war? Perhaps maneuverists don't know any better.

## FAULTY ASSUMPTION #2: WARS IS WARS

Having started from a social science perspective, a maneuverist next has to make his thinking fit the straitjacket imposed by his discipline.

His theory must be simple, powerful, and account for most of the situational variables. Otherwise, fellow social scientists will dismiss the theory as simply another "ad hoc" argument. The idea that most of life is ad hoc rarely occurs to social scientists, just as the vexing likelihood that most of war is ad hoc seldom troubles committed maneuverists.

Maneuver adherents refuse to be content with explaining a few pieces of the issue. Like all good social scientists, they seek to swallow the whole enchilada. One maneuver warfare manifesto explains it thusly: "Maneuver warfare addresses the spectrum of conflict from low to high intensity, and applies from the tactical through the operational to the strategic level of war. It is not bounded by the physical dimensions of land, sea, air, or space, but views warfare as multi-dimensional."[12] In short, these people think that a war is a war is a war.

There is some truth to that, but only at the very lowest levels, where the violence is so concrete that nuances disappear. U.S. military planners may refer to "operations short of war," but there is no such thing as "killed short of dead." For the rifleman about to squeeze off a round, for the pilot boring in against an enemy radar site, and for the sailor plying mine-infested waters, war is war, and there can be nothing low-intensity about it. Even in this aspect, few would disagree that the infantryman, the aviator, and the seaman live very different lives and experience very different kinds of wars, whatever the declared intensity.

Aside from the evident variances in land, sea, and air combat, wars also differ in scale. From a U.S. perspective, low-intensity conflicts, such as Panama (1989–90) or Grenada (1983), feature limited aims and severely limited means, which is to say no mobilization. Mid-intensity wars, like Korea (1950–53), Vietnam (1965–73), or Iraq (1990–91), call for limited aims and limited means, with some sort of partial mobilization. High-intensity wars would require unlimited means (full mobilization) to achieve unlimited ends, as with America 1941–45.[13] Nuclear weapons make an American war on the highest end of this spectrum exceedingly unlikely. All of these types of wars are not the same, as General of the Army Douglas A. MacArthur and Gen. William C. Westmoreland both discovered to their chagrin.

Aside from environment and scale, war differs markedly at the strategic, operational, and tactical levels. Statesmen select ends and provide means (strategy), generals apply the means where they work best to achieve strategic aims (operations), and the poor bastards at the bottom end fight it out (tactics). Things that work well at the operational level, such as deep turning movements and exploitations, really don't apply in grubby squad-to-squad gunfights.

Carl von Clausewitz and Sun Tzu might have worried about such distinctions, but today's maneuverists say that those differences really do not matter. This is principally because, despite their constant statements otherwise, maneuver enthusiasts show very little interest in anything but a rerun of World War II in Europe. Almost everything they write refers to mid-intensity, European-style mechanized ground warfare. The relevance of this fixation is questionable, as it currently accounts for about four days out of the last 4½ decades of post–World War II American military experience.

Maneuverists really do not have much to offer beyond their restricted area of interest, other than exhortations to apply a "maneuver mindset" to all phases and kinds of war. How does one avoid enemy strength when forced to storm a bristling embassy complex full of hostages? How much initiative can be granted to submarine commanders armed with nuclear weapons? Does knowledge of the operational level of war comfort a flier forced to hit a certain heavily defended Scud missile launcher to appease an American ally? Maneuver warfare thinkers' very few attempts to go beyond their preferred narrow band of 1939–45 blitzkriegs have been predictably silly, much like trying to apply techniques of mid–19th century Yankee whaling to servicing a modern home aquarium.

## FAULTY ASSUMPTION #3: MANEUVER UBER ALLES

Social science applied to war claims to simplify things down to their essence, and perhaps the meat of war rests in a few European campaigns of the mid-20th century. To use social science jargon, the critical variable is the relation of fire to maneuver. The latter must predominate to achieve success. So goes the line.

William S. Lind, a leading maneuver theorist, explains it this way: "The object in maneuver warfare is not to kill enemy soldiers, but to shatter the ability of whole enemy units—divisions, corps, even whole armies—to fight in an organized, effective way, and to panic and paralyze enemy commanders. The main means is not firepower, but maneuver."[14]

Fair enough; most generals would applaud that intention, although only a few would limit their options to maneuver.

Maneuverists do, since for them, the alternative is almost too horrible to contemplate. In some kind of bizarre tribute to Hegel, maneuver warfare is purported to have an evil twin, the "fundamentally antithetical" idea that the maneuverists call "attrition warfare." They define this as war in which "the object is simply to pour firepower on the enemy," "the massive application of firepower and technology as a substitute for skill, proficiency, leadership, and training."[15] Suggestions that perhaps a Hegelian synthesis could occur are dismissed with the same assurance that led Karl Marx to rule out any synthesis of the bourgeoisie and proletariat. Like Marx, maneuver advocates display the sure knowledge that a preconceived, normatively preferred outcome is more important than consistent internal logic in their argument.

The maneuver/attrition dichotomy must be resolved in favor of maneuver, as it is usually posed in Manichean terms. Would you prefer quick, decisive victory in the German drive on France in 1940 or in the recent Gulf War, or would you rather accommodate a bloody, ugly muddling about at Verdun or in Vietnam? It's that simple: Hannibal or Haig.

This maneuver/attrition split is a bogus one, invented with an eye toward avoiding Vietnam-era body counts. It cannot be found in any of the great works on war. Indeed, Carl von Clausewitz, Hans Delbrück, and Russell F. Weigley emphasize ends, not means, when they refer to "attrition." They distinguish between wars of annihilation and wars of attrition/exhaustion.[16] These estimable scholars did not dare try to separate maneuver from firepower, recognizing that they are too closely linked for that. The U.S. Army, which supposedly "adopted maneuver warfare as doctrine"[17] in the 1980s, summarizes a synthesis that Hegel could approve: "maneuver will rarely be possible without firepower and protection."[18] The maneuver warfare community backs and fills on this point, but always comes down on the side of maneuver. It's their reason to be.

## FAULTY ASSUMPTION #4: PERVERTED HISTORY

Like most social scientists, maneuver warfare advocates reach into the grab bag of history for examples to prove their case. Historians shy away from trying to derive "the lessons of history," preferring to gain fresh views of the human condition as revealed by studying the past. Historical researchers try to avoid explaining "everything," as events are, of course, unique to their time and place.

People motivated by social science do not feel so constrained. They have settled on maneuver as the answer to the challenge of battle, and so look for those historical episodes that seem to accord with that predisposition. Most of their examples are out of context. Others are just plain wrong.

Maneuver warfare theorists claim that their ideas motivated victorious generals of old. Thus, William Lind informs us that "maneuver warfare is not new. The first clear example of it is the battle of Leuctra in 371 B.C., between Sparta and Thebes."[19] While Epaminondas did execute an unconventional movement that unhinged the Spartans' flank, he has left no record that this was anything more than a battlefield trick. Firepower wasn't an issue.[20] Undaunted by the facts, Lind makes similar maneuverist claims for Hannibal at Cannae, and then blithely remarks that "this is what happened in many of history's most decisive battles and wars."[21] So there.

Those pre–20th century examples are placed in the literature mainly to let you know that maneuverists have some facility with the great captains and their battles. They could probably tell you who won and they can always tell you why—maneuver. The precise details don't much matter, unless you're actually trying to understand what happened. But these guys are social scientists, not archeologists or historians.

Maneuver warfare Valhalla is to be found in the 20th century, specifically in the gray ranks of the German army of World War II. "In modern times," says Lind, "the Germans have been the greatest practitioners of maneuver warfare. Their best maneuver warfare campaign was that against France in 1940."[22] Never mind that trouble in Russia the following summer.

Maneuverists have a bad case of what may be called, to borrow from a sister social science, "Wehrmacht penis envy."[23] These people love the Panzers, the Stukas, and the *Sturm und Drang* with the enthusiasm of any twelve-year-old boy who has yet to learn about Kursk, Omaha Beach, or Operation Cobra, let alone Bergen-Belsen. German words predominate in maneuver warfare parlance. Among the cognoscenti, it's always *Schwerpunkt*, never the pedestrian American "main effort." "Mission tactics" typically receive the appellation *Auftragstaktik*. Saying it in German somehow renders it all the more authoritative and more warlike.

To hear these people talk, you might never know that most of the great German triumphs turned out to be hollow performances, impressive compulsory figures that meant little in the final outcome.[24] They looked good losing, though, didn't they?

Even more to the point, whatever the Germans did to their unlucky neighbors, it was not maneuver warfare, a concept unrecognizable in German doctrine. Despite Lind's assurance that "the Germans had a new idea: blitzkrieg,"[25] ample evidence indicates that the Germans had, instead, a good army, good leadership, and some weak opponents. The term *blitzkrieg* came from a journalist's imagination.[26]

Perhaps to prove that they really are not closet Nazis, maneuver warfare folks also shower praise on the Israelis, pointing to the great victories of 1956 and 1967 in particular. The bloody noses at the outset of the 1973 War, not to mention the blitzkrieg into the Lebanese quagmire in 1982, merit less attention.[27]

Aside from the obvious differences between the United States and two militant land powers surrounded by conventionally armed hostile states, this knee-jerk praising of the Germans and Israelis is incomprehensible. These armies did not espouse or train "maneuver warfare," although some of their leaders have figured out how to mouth the right platitudes to ensure speaker fees and book contracts.

Indeed, studying the German and Israeli blitzkriegs clearly leads one to think that the critical determinant is not doctrine, but the low caliber of opponents. France, Holland, Denmark, and Belgium in 1940 or Syria, Egypt, and Jordan in 1967—in either case, given the rot in those armies, who could be surprised by the result? America learned this against the vaunted Iraqis. In commenting on the Gulf War, military writer Col. Trevor N. Dupuy noted that "there are no great victories when evenly matched armies and commanders face each other. The 1864 campaign between Grant and Lee is only one example."[28] The Germans found far tougher opposition in Russia and in Normandy, and the Israelis discovered that the Arabs of 1973 had learned much in six years.

Few would be so close-minded as to argue that Americans could not gain some useful insights from the German and Israeli military heritage. One might legitimately ask if it would not make more sense to look to our own military tradition. A global power confronted with many small challenges on land, sea, and air could uncover some useful perspectives from the frontier regulars, the Pacific campaigners of 1941–45, and the advisors and expeditionary warriors who have won a lot of small ones since 1945. Whatever the next war will look like, it probably will not resemble World War II in northwest Europe.

## PRESCRIPTION #1: AVOIDING STRENGTH AND ATTACKING WEAKNESS

Having defined their problem (How do you win a war quickly and decisively?) and provided the solution (relational maneuver), the maneuverists prescribe certain methods to create the sort of decisive actions they promise. Most of them come down to "hitting 'em where they ain't."

Maneuver warfare describes a nonlinear battlefield of "surfaces and gaps." The idea is to use your reconnaissance to pull you through the gaps, avoiding the defended surfaces. Once you find the gap, you designate your *Schwerpunkt* (no doubt genuflecting toward the shades of Heinz Guderian, Erwin Rommel, and Erich von Manstein in the process). Then you plunge through and tear the bad guys a new one.[29]

It's all great stuff, and who could argue that fighting like this would work well—in some wars, against some enemies, in some places, for some armies, and at certain times. But it is not a be-all and end-all. Avoiding strength and hitting weakness is hardly original or revolutionary. Worse, it may not accord in the least with the tactical situation at hand.

Advocates of maneuver act as if they have discovered the secret of transmuting lead to gold and can hardly convince anyone to believe them. "There's a real reluctance," says advocate Maj. David Grossman, "to drive around the enemy and have a bloodless victory. It seems contrary to the warrior mentality."[30] To be more accurate, sometimes it's contrary to military common sense.

The surfaces and gaps concept might be a revelation to dilettantes and armchair commandos, but that idea amounts to yesterday's news to experienced soldiers. To be precise, these sorts of tactics originated from German attempts to break the trench deadlock in the last two years of World War I. By 1939, the Germans were doing the same thing with tanks and dive bombers, and the world called it blitzkrieg. Today, the descendants of these infiltration tactics characterize most modern infantry, armor, and combined arms doctrine.[31] This is what we call conventional warfare.

Fighting the way everybody else does is rarely a road to glowing success, unless you can line up a scrap with the Iraqis, the Argentinians, or the Danes. But fighting by tried and true World War II means is pretty much what maneuver enthusiasts tell their disciples to do. It is not hard to conceive of battlefield situations in which avoiding strength and attacking weakness would be at best counterproductive and at worst disastrous.

Certain missions require troops to attack enemy strength. Examples include seizure of a key chokepoint (Vicksburg, 1863), a coup de main (Fort Eben Emael, 1940), assault of a critical airhead (Grenada, 1983), relief of an encircled force (Bastogne, 1944), reduction of a hostage situation (Entebbe, 1976), or a supporting attack intended to pin the enemy down (the Marines in Kuwait City, 1991). Sometimes a tough fight at the tactical level opens up opportunities for other units or at the operational level. But somebody has to open the penetration, take the key bridge, or charge in and free the captives. Invariably, they will take their lumps. By assuming that "wars is wars," maneuverists do not account for these important distinctions between what squads must do and what divisions could do.

Enemies vary widely in quality, and some do not panic when confronted by a blitzkrieg. Stolid Sam Grant did not flinch in the face of "Marse Robert" Lee's bold maneuvers in Virginia in 1864. Those maneuver warfare darlings, the Germans of World War II, discovered that Russians, Americans, and British elected not to fold up as readily as the French and Dutch. One antidote to maneuver warfare is brutally simple—stand fast and, as soon as you can, smash 'em right back.

The other solution is simply not to play. Enemies such as Mao Zedong's Chinese guerrillas, the Viet Minh, the Algerians, the Afghan mujahedin, Palestinian guerrillas, and America's Vietnamese opponents in Southeast Asia chose not to fight conventional armies conventionally. America helicoptered, tanked, and walked all over Vietnam and eastern Cambodia in campaigns that reflected many of the fondest desires of maneuverists. How many recall that the 1970 Cambodian operation aimed to locate and destroy the enemy Central Office for South Vietnam and thereby cripple Communist command and control? Not many maneuver enthusiasts have much to say about their model Israel's hapless efforts in the Lebanese mess or against the frustrations of the intifada. Maneuver warfare offers few answers to the challenges of protracted warfare.

Terrain plays a major part in any attempt to avoid strength and strike weakness. Sometimes, there is no choice about where to fight. The 1st Marine Division had only one way out of the Chosin Reservoir in 1950, and the Chinese knew it. American divisions staging for the Cobra breakthrough in 1944 needed to hold the high ground and road net around St. Lô. At Gettysburg in 1863, Joshua Chamberlain and the 20th Maine understood that Little Round Top would have to be defended to the death.

How armies deploy on available terrain, the force-to-space ratio, also makes a big difference in what can be done. It is easy to talk about a nonlinear battlefield and flanking maneuvers, but what happens when the front is continuous and the forces are arrayed in depth? In that case, gaps must be created by blood and explosives. The Luftwaffe's aerial firepower blew open the gap at Sedan in the 1940 campaign in France, whatever can be said about the daring German panzer push through the Ardennes. American bombers did similar work in the 1944 Normandy breakout. Of course, the 1991 campaign against Iraq offers a clear example of gap creation. Allied warplanes subjected Saddam Hussein's soldiers to a tremendous pummeling, battering the snot out of dozens of divisions for five weeks—only then did the Abrams tanks spring forward.

It is equally important to remember that, at the lowest levels, there really are no flank attacks. Some men pin the enemy with bullets and the rest move while the bad guys have their heads down or, better yet, blown off. Squads, platoons, and companies confronted with an unexpected assault turn to meet it, usually followed by the mobile reserves that armies keep to deal with surprises. The virtue of flanking comes from the fact that it forces the enemy to turn out of his prepared positions. Against a disorganized, ill-trained foe deployed ineptly across terrain favorable to the attack, plunging through gaps works.

Against a determined enemy, what looks like a gap can often turn out to be a fire sack.

The quality and quantity of friendly troops also affect an army's ability to avoid strength and hit weakness. Poor-caliber troops may well panic if they drive too deep against an enemy who refuses to collapse when bypassed—witness Eighth Army's precipitate rout in late 1950 at the hands of the relentless Chinese peasant infantrymen. Sometimes there are simply not enough mobile troops to pull off a blitzkrieg, as the Germans found out in Russia in 1941. Of course, how many panzers are enough? Nobody expected to need to solve that conundrum a few dozen miles short of Moscow, and all the nifty doctrine in the world could not make up for a few hundred too few tanks.

Time is the final determinant that can force an army to attack strength rather than weakness. Lt. Col. "H" Jones probably did not intend to lead his men into a tough frontal attack on Goose Green during the 1982 Falklands campaign, but domestic political pressures demanded that the British "do something" immediately. In a similar case, American Rangers jumped directly into a hail of gunfire at Point Salines airfield in Grenada in 1983, driven by rumors of an imminent hostage situation.

To meet these objections, the maneuverists maneuver. They say that weakness isn't always a spot in space and time, although that delineation was good enough for Clausewitz.[32] Edward Luttwak looks for weaknesses of all types, including the "command structure of the enemy forces, their mode of warfare and combat array, or even an actual technical system." The fault may be "physical or psychological, technical or organizational."[33] In short, it could be anything, and if you assail that flaw successfully, then you have accomplished another feat of maneuver warfare.

By this logic, the attack on Goose Green was not really a frontal attack, even though it looked like one, because the real Argentine weakness turned out to be a fear of close combat with British infantrymen. Operation Cobra, although it blew open the front with a mass bombardment, constituted maneuver warfare because it exploited the Germans' inability to concentrate mobile reserves rapidly. Pickett's Charge, of course, went awry since it attacked the strength at the center of the Union line at Gettysburg—had it worked, maneuver enthusiasts might say that it took advantage of the Yankees' fear of Southern bayonets.

Given this sort of sloppy categorization, anything that works can be characterized as maneuver warfare because it has found some kind of weakness. Failures are, of course, attacking strength and, hence, attrition warfare. This is called a tautology, a circular argument that cannot be proven wrong. Would that real combat worked out so neatly!

## PRESCRIPTION #2: ENCOURAGING INITIATIVE

Maneuver warfare doesn't just happen. It must be written down, then it must be practiced. To read the public record, one might believe that it had been written down. Peter Cary of *US News and World Report*, like William Lind, thinks that the American "Army's internal fight ended with a knockout blow for the 'maneuverists.'"[34]

The U.S. Army's own historian of the issue, John L. Romjue, indicates otherwise. He refers to reformers' views on U.S. tactics as "exaggerated" and "oversimplified." The Army intended to publish a complete fighting doctrine, based upon maneuver, firepower, protection, and leadership. The soldiers who wrote the new doctrine wanted "not maneuver for maneuver's sake, but its proper balance with firepower."[35] The maneuverists assumed that since they were consulted and some maneuver terminology made it into the doctrine, they had won.[36] None of the gleeful proponents considered the chance that their shrewd insights might amount to military common sense.

Not that it matters all that much what the manuals say. Written doctrine only goes so far. In the U.S. Army, where doctrinal books typically serve to hold doors open and justify extra shelving, hardly anybody really reads the doctrine. No surprise there—most of the doctrinal literature is stultifying and grossly redundant, forever being redrafted and reorganized. It tells you in grave terms what you already know, then furnishes handy laundry lists best summarized by Rogers' Rangers as "Don't forget nothing."[37] Even the service schools recognize that and rely on short summaries known as "advance sheets."

The U.S. Army depends instead on leadership experience gained through realistic training, not "how to" books. Tough, demanding new training centers at Fort Irwin in California, Fort Chaffee in Arkansas, and Hohenfels in Germany force modern soldiers to meet and defeat skilled opposing forces that outnumber them and play to win. Reliable simulation technology ensures that player units know "who shot John."

This training has paid off in combat, with Grenada, Panama, and the Gulf War offering good examples of trained troops fighting well.

The doctrine underwent the usual constant rewrites throughout the 1980s, but the training standards never wavered. At Irwin or Chaffee, victory became the bottom line, with doctrine a guide but not a requirement. American fighting men do battle the way they're trained by their own flesh and blood commanders, not in response to the dull verbiage in lifeless books. Of course, it's a rare American commander who doesn't have his own style of sizing up the situation and fighting his fight. Our tradition encourages that sort of personal approach.

Maneuverists act as if they were unaware of the American military heritage, particularly in the area of leader initiative. "Currently," notes Lind, "most military orders tell the subordinate exactly what to do, and he is kept closely under the control of his superior. That is not true in maneuver warfare, which can only be fought with mission-type orders. A mission-type order tells the subordinate what result his commander wants but leaves him a great deal of latitude in determining how to achieve it."[38] Of course, the maneuverists prefer to use the German term *Auftragstaktik*, and act like they have found another piece of the True (Iron) Cross.

In fact, mission tactics have typified the American military since 1775. Those exceptions, usually in sensitive political situations, make sense. Until recently, nobody thought it was important to write it down. It probably still isn't. Put a lieutenant in the jungle with a radio and he'll ask forgiveness, not permission. Try to micromanage him and he'll find the off switch. Contemporary armies are just too damned big and spread out to control like Frederickian Prussian automatons, regardless of what the computer guys promise.

The American tradition is best summarized by Gen. George S. Patton's dictum: "Never tell people *how* to do things. Tell them *what* to do and they will surprise you with their *ingenuity*." Patton led the Third Army across Europe with a series of half-page operation orders and, in the process, taught the *Auftragstaktik* crowd a thing or two about their trade.[39] From the Revolution to the Gulf, that has been the American method. Vietnam seemed like an aberration, with its flying command posts, but even there, the man on the scene usually made the call.

The troubles in Vietnam may have sprung from attempts to use new technologies and techniques developed to maintain positive control of nuclear weapons. When playing with Armageddon, it's not unreasonable to encourage a "zero defects" approach.[40] Why gamble with the future of humanity?

Low-intensity conflicts, where political interests are acute and military forces very limited, often feature very restrictive rules of engagement. Each casualty inflicted or suffered can affect policy and public support.

These restraints are not surprising. Nuclear submarine captains on patrol in the Barents Sea or rifle platoon lieutenants on patrol in the Korean Demilitarized Zone cannot and should not have the same latitude as their World War II counterparts. They aren't in World War II, after all.

Curbs on initiative always relate to risk, the military term for taking a chance on losing a lot of men and maybe the battle/campaign/war. Here maneuverists come afoul of their unwillingness to draw lines between small wars and world conflagrations. Risking the loss of a rifle platoon at Omaha Beach barely deserves notice. Risking a Marine platoon from the single battalion landing team in 1983 Beirut is an entirely different matter. This type of consideration certainly tied American hands in 1951–53 in Korea and throughout the Vietnam War.

Maneuverists chafe at such strictures. Their approach to warfare promises high payoffs, but it also runs risks of great losses, even in triumphs. Remember, somebody has to make gaps out of surfaces. Fellows like William Lind do not seem to mind. "Germany conquered France, Belgium, and Holland in only forty-three days," he notes approvingly, "with the loss of just 27,000 killed—small casualties by World War I standards."[41] Is it too much to ask that someone weigh the risk a bit before issuing blanket mission orders in small wars? El Salvador or Grenada may not be worth 27,000 U.S. dead.

## PRESCRIPTION #3: IN PRAISE OF
## THE OPERATIONAL ART

Maneuverists agree with the mainstream of military thought that "strategy is the art of winning wars" and "tactics is the art of winning battles."[42] Most doctrine writers inject an interim level, "the art of winning campaigns," formerly called "operations" by the U.S. Army and now known as "operational art."[43] As you would expect, the ever-efficient (though, by their won-loss record, not ever-effective) Germans achieved "spectacular operational successes in World War II"[44] and are said to offer a good model for planning campaigns.

In truth, the operational level of war can be a dangerous thing. Clausewitz said that war is a continuation of politics by other means. By sticking the operational art between strategy (setting ends and allocating means) and tactics (applying the means at the grunt-to-grunt end), soldiers may have created a bastard form of strategy, in which "military" considerations filter out those messy political issues.[45] The younger Helmuth von Moltke managed to help start World War I by such purely military calculations.

This accords nicely for maneuverists, whose world does not give much credence to political factors that may cause "stupid" things like an extra assault at Petersburg in 1864 or a march on Goose Green in 1982. Their German heroes botched this part pretty badly, winning a series of impressive victories in Europe from 1939 to 1942 that led nowhere but the grave.[46] The Israelis, too, showed great prowess in the operational art in 1956, 1973, and 1982, but to what end? The Soviets' brilliant series of strikes that opened the Afghan War could not affect the eventual blood-soaked stalemate. Meanwhile, the muddling Americans mix politics into all three levels of war and somehow contrive to run the world.

Operational art may have made it into the field manuals, but it will not be practiced in high-intensity nuclear axe fights nor in politically touchy low-intensity conflicts. Even mid-intensity fights will always have a strong political flavor. To echo Georges Clemenceau in the Great War, few wars are so unimportant that they can be left to the generals. Gen. H. Norman Schwarzkopf learned that lesson in 1991 even as he longed to take the big left toward Baghdad.

Like much of maneuver warfare, the operational art is a creature of mid–20th century mechanical warfare. It is a way to factor the politics out of war, which is like trying to take the wetness out of water.

## LEARNING FROM MANEUVER WARFARE

Maneuver warfare amounts to a bag of military Doritos—tasty and great fun to munch, but not very nutritious. Like most social science theories that attempt to explain complex human activities, it fails to explain very much beyond what sensible people, in this case students of warfare, already know. Faulty assumptions naturally breed poor prescriptions, and only a massive dose of hubris could make these diligent maneuverists so sure that they have derived the military equivalent of the Unified Field Theory in physics. Fortunately, nobody important seems to be paying all that much attention, and perhaps a few doctrinal buzzword bones tossed in their direction will appease these people.

Is there anything good about the concept of maneuver warfare? Absolutely! None of the good stuff is especially original, but that doesn't mean it's unimportant.

Maneuver warfare stresses that wars are won by men, not machines. Its proponents prefer history (albeit versions distorted by social science smash-and-grab techniques) to technology and, consequently, people to things. Their emphasis upon leadership is right on target and, in an age of computerized "command and control," maneuverists stand tall for the central importance of leader initiative.

Most important of all, the maneuverists have consistently challenged the American defense establishment to look at itself. The results might not be maneuver warfare, but they are unquestionably an improvement over the dejected wreck of a military that emerged from Southeast Asia. Maneuver advocates helped to move the Pentagon dinosaur in the right direction, no small task whatever the means.

That said, I would advise the maneuver warfare proponents to declare victory, strike their tents, and retire to write their memoirs. Remember, if you promote your version often enough, it may become the lie generally accepted as truth. The maneuver thinkers have hit a few juicy gaps with the doctrine writers and the planners. Still, if they really want to reshape the U.S. military into the World War II Germans or modern Israelis, I'd warn them to give it up. It's all surfaces from here, boys.

# Notes

1. Here are just a few examples that epitomize some of the key schools of thought on the American war in Vietnam. The stab-in-the-back theory is best presented in Gen. William C. Westmoreland, USA (ret.), *A Soldier Reports* (New York: Doubleday and Co., 1976). The idea that Vietnam should have been fought conventionally is ably stated in Col. Harry G. Summers, USA, *On Strategy* (Carlisle Barracks, Penn.: U.S. Army War College, 1981). The opinion that Vietnam should have been fought unconventionally is advanced convincingly in Maj. Andrew J. Krepinevich, USA, *The Army and Vietnam* (Baltimore, Md.: The Johns Hopkins University Press, 1986). Finally, one of the oldest and still most insightful versions of the hopeless war thesis can be found in David Halberstam, *The Best and the Brightest* (New York: Fawcett Crest, 1972).

2. This idea is developed in John Ellis, *Brute Force* (New York: Viking Press, 1990). A version of it, albeit much qualified and more balanced, appears in Russell F. Weigley, *The American Way of War* (Bloomington, Ind.: Indiana University Press, 1977).

3. Sen. Gary Hart and William S. Lind, *America Can Win* (Bethesda, Md.: Adler and Adler Publishing, 1986), pp. 34, 35.

4. Peter Cary, "The Fight to Change How America Fights," *US News and World Report* (6 May 1991), pp. 30–31.

5. Edward N. Luttwak, *Strategy: the Logic of War and Peace* (Cambridge, Mass.: Belknap Press, 1987), p. 93.

6. Hart and Lind, pp. 30, 31.

7. Maj. David A. Grossman, USA, and Captain Richard D. Hooker, Jr., USA, "What is Maneuver Warfare?" *The Maneuver Warfare Symposium Quarterly Newsletter* (17 January 1991), p. 2. This is one of the best short summaries of maneuver warfare fundamentals.

8. Ibid.

9. Hart and Lind, pp. 30–32.

10. Ibid., pp. 33, 34; Grossman and Hooker, p. 3.

11. An exciting new field of mathematics, chaos theory, is beginning to offer some insights into why it is so difficult to predict outcomes in an extremely complex model with multiple interrelated variables. Chaos theory attempts to describe such confusing phenomena as weather patterns. Some-

day, it may finally give the social scientists a tool that can help them. For now, it merely offers a few more voices noting that crude, general theories of human behavior don't explain or predict all that much.

12. Grossman and Hooker, p. 2.

13. U.S. Army, FM 100-5, *Operations* (Washington, D.C.: U.S. Government Printing Office, 1986), pp. 2–5.

14. Hart and Lind, pp. 30, 31.

15. Ibid., p. 30. For similar explanations, see also Luttwak, pp. 92, 93 and Grossman and Hooker, p. 2.

16. Weigley, pp. xxi–xxiii offers a good summary of Clausewitz and Delbrück, as well as Weigley's own views.

17. Hart and Lind, pp. 34, 35.

18. Department of the Army, FM 100-5, p. 12.

19. Hart and Lind, p. 31.

20. About the only thing authors agree on when discussing Leuctra are the date, place, opponents, and that the Thebans did something surprisingly effective to the Spartan flank. After that, every analyst has his own ideas. For example, Richard A. Preston and Sydney F. Wise, *Men in Arms* (New York: Holt, Rinehart, and Winston, 1979), pp. 26–27, call Leuctra a good example of the employment of combined arms and offensive tactics. Maj. Gen. J.F.C. Fuller, British Army, *A Military History of the Western World*, volume 1, *From the Earliest Times to the Battle of Leanto* (New York: Funk and Wagnalls, 1954), p. 83, refers to an attempt to "meet shock with supershock," hardly a description of maneuver warfare as explained by its adherents.

21. Hart and Lind, p. 7. At Cannae, the Romans rushed into a gap that turned out to be a surface.

22. Ibid., p. 31. See also Jeffrey Record, *Revising U.S. Military Strategy* (McLean, VA: Pergamon-Brasseys International Defense Publishers, 1984), p. 82.

23. The term "Wehrmacht penis envy" was coined by Prof. John J. Mearsheimer, currently the chairman of the Department of Political Science at the University of Chicago (and an accomplished historian as well as political scientist). Maj. Keith E. Bonn, USA, has elaborated on the use of the term in his recent doctoral dissertation in history entitled "When the Odds Were Even: The U.S. Seventh Army in the Vosges Campaign, 1944–1945," (Chicago: University of Chicago Press, 1991).

24. This idea of sterile military successes unwedded to political realities is masterfully developed in Michael Geyer, "German Strategy in the Age of Machine Warfare" in Peter Paret, ed., *Makers of Modern Strategy* (Princeton, N.J.: Princeton University Press, 1986). See in particular pp. 578, 579.

25. Hart and Lind, p. 31.

26. Matthew Cooper, *The German Army 1939–1945: Anatomy of Failure* (New York: Stein and Day, 1989), p. 116. He refers to blitzkrieg as a "myth" and notes the term's first appearance as "a piece of journalese" in *Time* magazine on September 28, 1939. See also Geyer, pp. 584–86.

27. Hart and Lind, pp. 31, 32; Record, p. 82.

28. Col. Trevor N. Dupuy, USA (ret.), "How the War Was Won," *National Review* (April 1, 1991), p. 31.

29. The idea of surfaces and gaps is thoroughly addressed, complete with examples, in William S. Lind and Col. Michael Wyly, USMC, *Maneuver Warfare Handbook* (Boulder, CO: Westview Press, 1985). For an abbreviated treatment, see Grossman and Hooker, pp. 3, 4.

30. Major Grossman is quoted in Cary, p. 30.

31. Captain Jonathan M. House, USA, *Toward Combined Arms Warfare* (Fort Leavenworth, KS: Combat Studies Institute, August 1991), pp. 34, 42, 182; Lieutenant Colonel John A. English, Canadian Army, *On Infantry* (New York: Praeger Publishers, 1984), pp. 1–28.

32. Carl von Clausewitz, *On War*, trans. Col. F. N. Maude, British Army (New York: Penguin Books, 1968), p. 267.

33. Luttwak, pp. 93-94.

34. Cary, p. 31. Although the U.S. Army did not accept maneuver warfare, one service did. The United States Marine Corps, in its 1989 *Fleet Marine Force Manual 1: Warfighting* (*FMFM-1*), explicitly embraced maneuver warfare as Corps doctrine. How this will actually be implemented remains to be seen. The Marines seem ill-suited to emulate the Germans or Israelis. Their forces typically deploy by battalions, have very limited armored support, and usually fight at the low-intensity end of the spectrum. In the Gulf War, some Marines sat offshore, frustrated by sea mines, but at least providing some threat to Iraqi coast defense divisions. The majority of the Marines launched a supporting attack with two divisions abreast along with several Arab contingents sandwiched in between. This attack (dare we call it a frontal attack?—it was, until it penetrated) pinned the bulk of the Iraqis in the Kuwait City area and thereby facilitated an envelopment by the U.S. Army XVIII Airborne Corps and VII Corps.

35. John L. Romjue, *From Active Defense to AirLand Battle* (Fort Monroe, Va.: U.S. Army Training and Doctrine Command, 1984), pp. 57–58. William S. Lind and fellow maneuverist Edward N. Luttwak were allowed to read and comment on early drafts of what emerged as the 1982 edition of FM 100-5.

36. Ibid., p. 58.

37. U.S. Army, *SH 21-76: Ranger Handbook* (Fort Benning, Ga.: U.S. Army Infantry School, 1987), p. i.

38. Hart and Lind, p. 33.

39. General George S. Patton, Jr., USA, *War As I Knew It* (New York: Pyramid Books, 1970), pp. 307, 308.

40. Paul Bracken, *The Command and Control of Nuclear Forces* (New Haven, Conn.: Yale University Press, 1982), pp. 212–20.

41. Hart and Lind, p. 31.

42. Ibid., p. 34.

43. Department of the Army, *FM 100-5*, pp. 9-11.

44. Record, p. 82.

45. Clausewitz, pp. 404, 405.

46. Geyer, p. 581.

# Maneuver Warfare and the United States Army

## Robert R. Leonhard

In the wake of the Gulf War, the term "maneuver warfare" has become fashionable. With memories of the curving, colored arrows that painted the maps of our news magazines during the 100-hour operation, we like to think of ourselves as having a maneuver-oriented army. But besides having some vague impressions of what maneuver theory is all about, our army has had difficulty merging its firepower mentality and traditional attrition strategy with the potentials of maneuver. Our way of fighting—or by extension, our whole perspective on war and strategy—simply does not match classic examples of maneuver warfare from the past. In my book *Art of Maneuver,* I tried to zero in on some definitions of maneuver theory in order to show the disconnects. One of the most difficult aspects of maneuver theory that continues to confound both theorist and practitioner alike is the matter of command and control. In this essay, we shall compare the two primary philosophies of command and control, see how each relates to maneuver theory, and then suggest what American-style maneuver warfare might look like in the future.

For many of my colleagues—some of whom have contributed to this book—maneuver warfare is inseparable from the German concept of *Auftragstaktik*. The word is translated literally as "mission tactics," and that has been the term embraced by the U.S. Army. Mission tactics is a misnomer of sorts, because it is in reality a philosophy of command and control, not a tactic.

I prefer the British use of "directive control" as being more descriptive, and it has the added benefit of not confusing the issue with the word *tactics*. The commander using directive control assigns his subordinates missions, but then allows them the freedom to figure out how to execute. He provides only enough guidance to focus the otherwise independent efforts of the subordinates and to synchronize fires and combat support elements with ground maneuver. The chief advantage of this method is that the subordinates, who have a better, more immediate grasp of the situation, have the freedom to make decisions faster than the commander could do.

## DEVELOPMENT OF DIRECTIVE CONTROL

Why has directive control become an issue within modern armies? Where did the idea come from? Certainly the antecedents of modern-day directive control were found in Napoleon's *corps d'armée* system. Although Napoleon carefully crafted and supervised his campaign plans, his organization presupposed the need for corps and division commanders to fight independently on occasion—at least until the rest of the army could concentrate. The vast expansion of the army and the logistical systems that supported it forced organizational changes that had immediate tactical ramifications, one of which was the delegation of authority.

But the most obvious place to look for the birth of modern directive control is in the German army of World War I. The battlefields of the Great War gave birth to a series of tactical innovations that challenged the rigidly centralized control of small units in battle. The machine gun and rapid-fire artillery forced units to disperse or die en masse. And with dispersion came a serious command problem: the colonels and generals could no longer assess the situation well enough and communicate at long enough ranges to effectively command their formations. Hence, with the wise tolerance of Ludendorff, the Germans developed a new philosophy of small unit command: they passed the control of the actual fighting to the captains, lieutenants, and sergeants on the spot.

This tactical novelty produced some startling successes (mostly defensive), and added to the development of infiltration tactics. According to many historians, these conceptual advances led to the more audacious and effective blitzkrieg tactics of World War II. But the point that we must carry away from all this is that directive control came into practice in order to redress the balance between decision making and the flow of intelligence and communications.

I have previously stated my concern with the prescriptive way in which the U.S. Army preaches the use of directive control. The student is left with the impression that directive control is the only right way to do business, and that if he uses it, his efforts on the battlefield will be successful. But the other approach to command and control, called *Befehlstaktik*, literally "orders tactics" or detailed control, has some distinct advantages as well. The commander using this form issues precise orders describing not only what to do but how to do it. The principal advantage is that the efforts of the subordinates are unified from the start. The commander can bring all his supporting assets to bear with precise and effective timing, because he does not have to guess what his subordinates might do at any given time. Of course, the disadvantage to detailed control is that success depends upon the commander assessing the situation correctly and formulating a good plan.

Rather than dogmatically espousing either concept of command and control as the only right answer, I believe that maneuver theory allows for either or both approaches. Consider an analogy using modern antitank munitions. Many of our tank-killing munitions are "dumb" rounds—that is, they are fired by the gunner and fly directly to the aim point without guidance. Others are guided missiles that find their way to the target by the gunner tracking it. Still newer technology allows the missiles to hit the target by seeking out the enemy vehicle themselves. But not even the most vociferous proponent of any of these technologies would suggest that the future force should select only one type of system. There is a tacit understanding that each type of weapon has its own strengths and weaknesses. For example, fire-and-forget munitions are typically cheaper, easier to train, and faster than guided missiles. But those that are guided—particularly self-guided—usually feature greater range, more effective attack profiles, and better hit probabilities against moving targets. The application of this logic to command and control is obvious. Detailed control has the advantages of unity of command, opportunity for rehearsal, and simplicity in training. Directive control gives greater flexibility in a changing situation, and it is best for finding and exploiting gaps. As I have shown in *Art of Maneuver*, detailed control is related to momentum in operations, while directive control is related to acceleration.

## DISADVANTAGES TO DIRECTIVE CONTROL

But what about mission tactics, or directive control? Are there any disadvantages related to this form? The answer is an unqualified yes, although doctrinaires invariably ignore them. First, it must be remembered that neither form of command and control will guarantee success. Directive control is a means to the end, not the end itself. Leaving the primary decision making to subordinates does not necessarily mean that they will choose correctly. In fact, it is a virtual certainty that the subordinate leaders have less training and experience than their commander. Directive control puts a greater burden upon these leaders, requiring them to navigate, formulate plans, synchronize combat and combat support assets, and communicate laterally to a greater degree than under detailed control. And subordinates can make mistakes as well as their commander. Further, they are one step farther away from the "big picture," so to speak. In the heat of battle, it is difficult to see beyond the exigencies of the moment.

This relates to the other principal disadvantage of directive control. Inherent in the use of directive control is the violation of the principle of unity of command. It is an age-old axiom of war that on the battlefield, one man must be in charge. As Napoleon said, "Better one bad general than two good ones." By giving subordinates the latitude to make their own plans, unity of command suffers.

Proponents of directive control would strongly protest this point. In response they would jump to their feet and shout yet another German word, "*Schwerpunkt!*" The concept of "the heavy point," or main effort, is the byword of those who employ directive control. The idea is that the commander, along with assigning a mission to his subordinates, describes his intent and designates a main effort as well. In the intent, the commander communicates his vision of the end of a successful operation—how the enemy force is to be defeated, how the friendly force will be disposed, and how their success will relate to other operations. The main effort, typically expressed in terms of a particular friendly unit, will have priority for fires, combat support, and service support throughout the operation. It is quite possible—indeed, even expected in many cases—that the main effort will shift during the operation in order to take advantage of sudden opportunities. The combination of the intent and the designation of the main effort ensures unity of command.

But it is important for us to understand that these measures are *compensating* ideas, designed to overcome the drawbacks of directive control. Directive control and the tactics related to it inherently result in diffuse operations. The main effort must be designated and the intent clearly explained in order to focus efforts that will otherwise tend to radiate and disperse. The commander employing detailed control, on the other hand, does not have to emphasize these unifying concepts as much, because they are implicit in his orders.

It is instructive to note why a given army may opt to use directive control or not. One of the most obvious examples of detailed, centralized control is the Soviet army. In the Soviet army, small unit initiative is simply unheard of: it is neither desired nor permitted. Yet to conclude that the Soviets do not fight according to maneuver theory would be ludicrous. Some of the best examples of maneuver warfare come from the Soviet offensives against the Germans in World War II. But why do the Soviets not use directive control? In *Art of Maneuver*, I suggested that their need for extremely deep penetrations caused them to emphasize momentum as a characteristic of their operations. Momentum (mass times velocity) is a vector quantity both in physics and in warfare; that is, it is directional. The army seeking momentum aims at a specific point or objective and relentlessly speeds toward it, seeking to overturn any opposition rapidly along the way. Such methods of operational maneuver do not emphasize sudden opportunities or rapid shifts in direction; rather, they rely upon preemption. The most effective method of controlling such an operation is with the use of detailed control by a centralized decision-making node. Hence, the Soviets favor this particular method.

But others have pointed more to the Soviets' collective cultural heritage, and to their military experience in particular. The centralized, autocratic, and totalitarian nature of both the tsarist and communist governments have had their effect on military command as well. Further, the birth of the Red Army during the Russian civil war saw an urgent need for rigid control of subordinates. Fighting along interior lines and against many fronts simultaneously, the Red Army took its orders from one central body, so that logistics and maneuver could be properly synchronized. And the nature of the army called for detailed control as well. The army was composed of many different nationalities, speaking different languages and carrying different loyalties. To allow control of operations to fall into the hands of any subordinate leader would have been to risk a revolt. Hence, we can conclude that detailed control was and is used in the Soviet army partly to overcome cultural heterogeneity. Likewise, we shall see that the U.S. Army has special characteristics that suggest the use of detailed control.

## DIRECTIVE CONTROL AND THE U.S. ARMY

We would be suspicious of a man who parades about insisting publicly that he does not beat his wife. We may suspect that the truth is exactly the opposite. Likewise, the U.S. Army is one of the most vociferous proponents of directive control (the term used is "mission tactics"). Our doctrine clearly expresses our intent to employ such methods, but there is strong evidence to suggest that in practice, we use detailed control at every level of command. From my personal observations during the Gulf War (I served in an infantry battalion in the 3d Armored Division), I saw no freedom for small unit commanders to make any decisions regarding battlefield maneuver. Brigade, battalion, and company commanders were told where to go, when to move, when to shoot, and when to cease fire. Above all, they were warned to keep their flanks tied in with friendly units.

A similar dynamic is evident in our tactical training centers, especially at the National Training Center at Fort Irwin, California. The keys to success in the training scenarios are unity of command, flawless gunnery, and good navigation. Battle is inevitable and cannot be avoided through clever maneuvering. Therefore, there is little opportunity or payoff for a small unit commander to find a gap in enemy defenses. This phenomenon is less obvious in mixed or close terrain. When terrain or vegetation reduces the small unit commander's ability to see, there is a natural tendency to rely on subordinates more. Nevertheless, the pace of operations at the training centers often precludes company commanders or platoon leaders from developing the enemy situation and finding routes around enemy resistance. There are exceptions to the rule, but they are few.

But whether we use directive control now is a question that is open to debate, and it is largely influenced by the personal styles of commanders. Of greater bearing on the question of directive control in the U.S. Army is the course of materiel developments that will be fielded around the turn of the century. It is my belief that, our doctrine notwithstanding, future technology in the fields of intelligence and communications will drive the U.S. Army toward detailed control more than ever before.

As noted above, the purpose behind directive control is to find the right balance between intelligence and decision making on the battlefield. Control of the battle is passed to lower echelons, because they have the relevant information and have it in a timely manner. But technological and doctrinal changes in the army strike right to the heart of that relationship. Army, corps, and division commanders of the future will have unprecedented amounts of intelligence. The exploitation of space, advanced airborne radar, and myriad other battlefield sensors will offer a revolutionary capability for senior commanders to see the enemy and terrain. With this new capability will come a series of new challenges and also some changes—perhaps implicit—in our command and control philosophy.

It is popular, particularly among combat arms officers, to voice doubts about our current and future intelligence capabilities. There are numerous examples from history, including some illuminating events during Operation Desert Storm, that point up the limitations of battlefield intelligence. It is an established pattern that the gathering of information is the easy part of the intelligence function. Rather, it is the interpretation, processing, and dissemination of intelligence that continues to challenge our systems and staffs. It is not the purpose of this essay to delve into the business of intelligence, however; and to some degree, the question of whether future technologies will be effective and timely or not is irrelevant. It will be the *existence* of those systems, not their effectiveness, that will drive doctrine.

But one aspect of intelligence processing is germane to the issue of command and control. It is a characteristic of all the future intelligence systems that they must be supervised and managed by large staffs of technically proficient soldiers. Hence, control of the intelligence process (and, by extrapolation, the command and control process) necessarily falls to the higher echelons of command, because they are the only ones with large enough staffs and enough resources (power, time, communications, etc.) to process the intelligence.

Information flow and decision making are perforce linked in military organizations; that is, a commander can be counted on to act on the information he receives. He will make decisions and issue orders based on his perceptions of the enemy and friendly situations. In the past, commanders came to realize (through the very good school of military defeat) that they consistently lacked information upon which to base tactical decisions in small units. Hence, as described above, decision making passed to lower echelons. However, if future technologies allow the senior commanders (and only the senior commanders) to have the important information, and to have it on a timely basis with a considerable degree of resolution and accuracy, then the control of the battle is inevitably going to return to them also. It is human nature for any commander to act on information. Indeed, if he does not, then the information is superfluous. Of course, the theory that the army is working under today states that the higher commanders will receive, process, and disseminate the intelligence, and then pursue mission tactics (directive control), allowing their subordinates to choose their own courses of action. This concept is—I can find no better term—pure hogwash. If the commander has the information, he will pass it to lower echelons as needed, but with that information will come orders. He who controls the intelligence controls the decision making.

The other major trend in technological advances comes in the realm of communications. In the sense of evolutionary improvements, one could safely say that headquarters of the future will be able to talk further, more securely, and more reliably than before. In addition, they will be able to send burst transmissions of data and even graphics. But the revolutionary aspect of communications development can be found in position location and reporting systems.

The first of these capabilities, position location, was employed with great effect during the Gulf War. Ground unit leaders can simply (and cheaply) receive a set of signals from navigation satellites and get a digital readout telling them their position in map grid coordinates. Even better, they can input a destination point and/or a movement route, and the position location device will direct them along their way. What a godsend for leaders! (If you've ever had the privilege of being hopelessly lost with a huge convoy of armored fighting vehicles behind you, you will appreciate the point!) There is no doubt that position location technology has come to stay. Future vehicles will be built with such devices embedded in the system.

But the next step beyond position location is position reporting, and it is this technology that (along with intelligence considerations) will most significantly contribute to the centralization of command and control. Although we don't dwell on it much (and never talk about it publicly), small unit commanders spend a great deal of effort and time looking for their subordinates and checking on their progress (or lack of it).

Position reporting in the future will be automatic and will eventually take the form of a commander being able to look on an electronic map and see his subordinates as little moving symbols. Even more significantly, there are indications that the same commander may be able to push a button and see not only his subordinate leaders, but *their* subordinates also. In other words, he would be able to see the positioning of friendly units two levels down the chain of command. Again, we stubbornly refuse to consider the implications, but it is a fact that the commander will act on the information he has, and when he can see locations two levels down, it is inevitable that he will issue orders concerning those units or individuals.

Hence, the picture we are left with is one in which higher headquarters (brigade, division, corps, and echelons above corps) have relevant information about both the enemy and friendly situation, and they have it either faster than or as fast as the lower echelon commanders. It is a matter of course that directive control will fade in significance in such a context, and centralized, detailed control will be the style of the future.

Other trends suggest this scenario as well. It is already an accomplished fact that control of fire support has passed upward in the chain to brigades, and that battalions (not to mention companies and platoons) have little or no influence over artillery. This relationship was accomplished due to the recurring belief in some minds that massed fires are more important than responsive fires. It is not my purpose here to reiterate my concern over the course of artillery doctrine in the U.S. Army (I have done so elsewhere). I mention it only because the practice results in a limited capability for small units to synchronize battlefield capabilities at their own level. Combined arms integration effectively occurs at ever-higher levels.

As fire support, communications, and intelligence technology (not to mention air defense, engineer, and other combat support technologies) become more complex, the ability of a small unit commander and his staff to comprehend, train, integrate, and synchronize the combined arms fight recedes. To command effectively in war, the commander must be able to simplify—to understand and make others understand the capabilities and limitations of his own systems (as well as those of the enemy). He must be able to concentrate his energies on *integrating* his various assets effectively, not on trying to comprehend the particulars of any one system. Unfortunately, the development of future weapon, sensor, and communications systems occurs at the hands of branch proponents and materiel developers who are expert in their own narrow field of expertise. There are few or no generalists in the process, and the synchronization of the multiple, complex capabilities thus developed happens or fails to happen due to the efforts of field commanders. In many cases, there is a lack of requisite expertise, and the control process must by default pass to higher echelons with bigger, more specialized staffs.

Added to these issues that impact mostly upon the tactical level of war are the strategic and operational trends within the US Army. The recent publication of TRADOC Pamphlet 525-5, *AirLand Operations*, describes an altogether new approach to warfighting for the future. The emphasis will be upon a limited forward presence in overseas regions, reinforced rapidly from assets within the continental United States. Most often, these operations will require joint (i.e., other services') and combined (i.e., other allies') participation and may even feature interagency cooperation. Again, the integration of other services, agencies, and allied forces connotes ever greater centralization of command.

For all these reasons, I believe the army's claim that it uses and will continue to use directive control is a false one. Rather, the command process will continue to centralize, and the tactical process in particular will be controlled at echelons no lower than brigade, and most often at division or corps.

Given that my conclusions are correct, does this mean that the U.S. Army will not be capable of prosecuting maneuver warfare in future conflicts? Because most of my associates consider directive control to be synonymous with, or at least a vital part of, maneuver warfare, the answer might be yes. But I have persistently stated that the means of control is not directly related to the means of defeat. And it is the means of defeat that defines maneuver warfare.

Maneuver warfare, if we allow ourselves an abstract approach, is based on the premise that the enemy's strength can be effective only within certain dimensional limits. That is, the enemy can concentrate his power only along a finite frontage (or width), length (or depth), height, and for a limited period of time. Maneuver warfare seeks to dislocate (i.e., avoid and therefore render irrelevant) that strength by focusing combat power in the dimensional extremes. In terms of classic ground warfare, we may easily envision the traditional outflanking movement. But maneuver theory likewise contemplates *temporal* dislocation, that is, dislocating enemy strength by attacking him either before he is ready (called preemption), or after his strength has culminated.

Likewise, maneuver theory attempts to collapse or disrupt the enemy (rather than destroying his physical components) in order to bring about his defeat. This does not mean that an army employing maneuver warfare must leave the enemy army intact. Destruction of the enemy is always an option, but maneuver theory would seek destruction only *after* defeat has occurred. Attrition theory, on the other hand, considers the destruction of the enemy's forces as a component of defeat, rather than as a result of it.

Disruption is brought about by successfully discerning and attacking the enemy's center of gravity. In *Art of Maneuver,* I showed that maneuver theory defines the center of gravity as the enemy's critical vulnerability—that aspect of the enemy whose neutralization causes paralysis within the enemy force. After disruption occurs, the enemy is typically unwilling or unable to fight.

The purpose of this short discourse on the means of defeat is to show that although the U.S. Army does not use directive control and is not likely to in the future, it can apply maneuver theory effectively. What would American-style maneuver theory look like? To begin, we must consider how maneuver theory relates to our national strategy of deterrence.

One of my favorite television shows when I was growing up was the martial arts/western action adventure *Kung Fu.* It was, however, something of a paradox each week to watch the ultimate man of peace beat the tar out of his fellow man at least twice each show. Why then did our half-American, half-Chinese priest, Mr. Caine, continually get into fights, despite his peaceful disposition? Obviously, the need for high television ratings bore on the problem. Taoist philosophy is fine, but I wanted to see someone get the hell kicked out of him. But if we were to suspend disbelief for a moment, why would such a character—if he had really lived—have gotten into so many fights? The problem was that Caine could not deter a fight. Deterrence theory suggests that to prevent an aggressive enemy from attacking, we must convince him that we are both willing and able to fight. Caine's fighting methods depended less on muscle than on technique. He was a highly trained martial arts expert, but that did not suffice to deter aggression. The problem was that Caine looked like a wimp.

Likewise, maneuver warfare theory—while unquestionably the superior method of fighting—makes a dubious deterrent. When an enemy contemplates war, he necessarily judges empirically, weighing tangibles and calculating probabilities. While being overwhelmed numerically is a common fear, no army ever imagines itself dislocated, disrupted or paralyzed. The tacit assumption in military planning is that everything will work, and that working, every component of the armed forces will be relevant somehow. Hence, if the U.S. Army were to embrace maneuver warfare theory, one of its primary challenges would be to target the mind of potential enemy governments and convince them of our fighting worth.

Strategic preemption, a bona fide form of maneuver warfare, is not generally an option for the U.S. for a number of reasons. First, a sudden attack on an unprepared enemy finds no place in our national strategy of deterrence. America does not go to war suddenly. Secondly, since our strategy almost invariably assumes allied participation, preemption recedes as an option simply because the addition of each ally (hence, another sovereign government) precludes rapid strategic decision making. Finally, the use of strategic preemption would challenge the already-sensitive constitutional balance between executive and congressional privilege in war making.

There is, however, ample opportunity for preemption at the operational and tactical levels of war. Concerning the former, however, the hastily written *AirLand Operations* concept paper, published in draft form in 1992, has articulated a theater concept of operations that commences with a "detection/preparation" stage. This is essentially a reiteration of our traditionally cautious approach to operations. The goal is to develop a comprehensive and accurate picture of the enemy, while at the same time building up forces in theater. (The Desert Shield/Storm experience is the scenario that the concept writers had in mind.) The flaw with such thinking is that it does not seriously consider the possibility of preemption by either side. The enemy is assumed to possess the unequaled stupidity of Saddam Hussein, and they will offer no sudden attempt to close off ports of entry before the buildup is complete. Likewise, the concept rules out a bold preemptive stroke by our forces, because it assumes that both mass and perfect intelligence are prerequisites for victory.

Maneuver aimed at dislocating the enemy will no doubt be a continuing feature of American-style maneuver warfare. I suspect, however, that it will manifest itself more at the operational level than at the tactical level, as it did in Operation Desert Storm. For all the reasons stated above, the initiative and control of operations will likely be in the hands of our commanders at corps level and above, with very little latitude granted to divisions, brigades, or small units. Even in low-intensity conflict (LIC), this pattern will likely pertain. It is a characteristic of LIC that political considerations reach down through the chain of command and influence even the lowest tactical echelons.

Armed with an unprecedented ability to see the enemy, future corps and army commanders will possess powerful means for outmaneuvering enemy forces on a grand scale. Of course, these capabilities will depend upon air superiority and uninterrupted communications. Given these conditions, the potential for theaterwide dislocation of the enemy is tremendous. Whether our doctrine and military leadership will take advantage of the possibilities is an open question. Future leaders trained to think in terms of caution, the avoidance of risk, and the simple mathematics of destruction by massed fires will be locked into attrition theory regardless of the instruments at their disposal.

As modern forces continue to grow in complexity, there is ever greater opportunity for disruption of those forces. A modern army dispersed over a large area can be totally paralyzed by the jamming of their communications. And none but light guerrilla forces could survive without open lines of supply. Hence, our operations against enemy forces will be most effective if we train our leaders to think of the enemy in holistic terms, not simply as a certain number of tanks, troops, and guns. An army is, in essence, a living organism characterized by selected strengths, weaknesses, and critical vulnerabilities. Maneuver warfare theory is all about collapsing the vulnerabilities in order to disrupt the rest of the force.

As an aside, I am curious why some commentators (within and without the army) declaim against maneuver warfare. Some indeed hold that when it comes right down to it, warfare is all about guns, guts, and blood, and any attempt to delay the basic confrontation is simply artful nonsense. According to this view, battle is the dominating feature of modern war: decision in battle is the bottom line, and our doctrine, organizations, leader development, training, and materiel developments should be focused there. Nothing could be farther from the truth. As potential enemy armies continue to modernize, as battlefields become dominated more and more by electronic communications, computers, and advanced weaponry, and as armies' need for logistical support grows, logic demands that we aim at disrupting and defeating, rather than destroying. The opportunities are there . . . but will we exploit them?

Consider a biological analogy. The maladies that might harm a single-celled organism are comparatively few. These lowest forms of life have so few systems that not much can go wrong beyond the physical destruction of the organism itself. But man—a much more complex form of life—can be attacked by unnumbered diseases and injuries that leave him incapacitated, regardless of his physical or mental strength. Complexity breeds vulnerability, and this truth is nowhere more obvious than in armies today. As Clausewitz noted, even the simple friction of moving or supplying an army can undo an organization, quite apart from enemy intentions.

For this reason, American-style maneuver warfare should aim at employing functional dislocation and disruption against future enemies. Our efforts should be characterized by large-scale employment of electronic warfare; air interdiction aimed at reducing the flow of supplies and reinforcements; and rapid, bold maneuver aimed not at enemy entrenchments, but at enemy supply bases, transportation centers, seats of government, and other critical vulnerabilities.

In the realm of tactics, the U.S. Army is in need of a renaissance in combined arms theory. In *Art of Maneuver*, I described the fixation within the army's combat arms (infantry, armor, and artillery) upon fighting their enemy counterparts: infantry killing infantry, tanks shooting tanks, and artillery bombarding artillery. While there is no doubt that a certain degree of such "like-system" fighting must occur in war, it is vital that the army train its leaders to think in other terms. Like-system fighting is a violation of combined arms theory, and it misses the natural economy of effort that can occur when systems are used to attack *unlike* enemy systems. Our tactical system should be built around creating favorable asymmetries: infantry killing tanks in close terrain, tanks overrunning surprised artillery groups, and artillery killing

# Thoughts About Maneuver Warfare

## John F. Antal

War is a matter of vital importance to the State;
the province of life or death; the road to survival or ruin.
It is mandatory that it be thoroughly studied.

Sun Tzu, The Art of War

A debate over the usefulness of maneuver warfare has raged in professional military circles for the past few years. Opponents of maneuver theory argue that maneuver theory is all "smoke and mirrors," that maneuver warfare is a concept that can only be portrayed in a historical context and is used by victors to explain how they defeated their dull-witted opponents. Fans of maneuver warfare theory argue that the Germans had the right idea in their concept of *Auftragstaktik*. Maneuverists call opponents of maneuver theory "attritionists." A maneuver-oriented military analyst may argue that maneuver versus attrition is the primary argument in styles of warfare, that maneuver warfare offers cheap victories, and that Operation Desert Storm vindicated maneuver theory concepts. Others, who seldom call themselves attritionists, argue that each military situation is unique; that Operation Desert Storm vindicated the decisive, attrition role of firepower. In any case, didn't the Germans lose World War II?

The debate over maneuver warfare is an important exercise. The debate involves the way we analyze military problems. In an era when the United States military will be asked to shoulder great responsibilities with fewer resources and less force structure, the debate takes on added importance. The answer to this debate will set the foundation for the United States Army of the 21st century.

Maneuver warfare is a thought process, not a particular set of tactics or techniques. It is based on a firm belief that the enemy should be trapped rather than merely pushed away. This belief influences the prosecution of combat throughout the entire structure of war. This essay proposes that maneuver warfare is an alternative to costly attrition. Furthermore, this essay proposes that maneuver warfare, and the command and control environment that must exist for maneuver warfare leadership to flourish, should be the preferred method for waging war for a leaner United States Army.

## THE STRUCTURE OF WAR

The first step in our analysis of maneuver warfare begins with an explanation of the levels of war. FM 100-5, *Operations* is the U.S. Army's capstone warfighting manual. This manual outlines the structure of modern warfare into three distinct levels: strategy, operational art, and tactics. Strategy is the "art and science of employing the armed forces of a nation or alliance to secure policy objectives by the application or threat of force."[1] Our methodology, therefore, will build on this structure by adding "policy" as a distinct level of conflict. A maneuver or attrition approach is decided upon at each of these different, yet interrelated levels of military and political action. This decision influences the style of conflict at each level (see Figure 1).

### Policy
War is a political act. A nation pursues the goals of policy with its elements of national power. There are five basic elements of national power: military, economic, political, geographic, and the national will. Each of these elements has an impact on how a nation executes a particular policy goal in a time of conflict. In the United States, policy is the realm of elected officials and is subject to the checks and balances of our democratic system. In autocratic nations the elements of national power are more centrally controlled and are often more ruthlessly employed.

All, or any combination, of the five basic elements of national power can be used to achieve a political end—a policy. Direct means can involve the use of the armed forces or the execution of economic measures such as an embargo, boycott, trade restriction, or trade tariff (to name only a few). Indirect means can involve the use of political action, the posturing offered by certain geographic advantages (deny, or threaten to deny, free access through a strait, or deny air traffic over one's territory), and the mobilization (or disregard) of one's national will.

All five elements impact to some degree on the outcome of a conflict. In a limited conflict a nation may rely upon one or two elements, such as military and economic power. In such cases, the application of the elements of national power are decisive only when they overpower or outmaneuver the opponent.

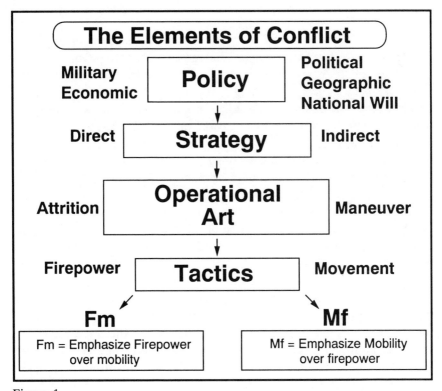

Figure 1

## Strategy

Policy sets the objectives for strategy. As stated above, military strategy is the art and science of employing the armed forces of a nation or alliance to secure policy objectives by the application or threat of force. Military strategy establishes the goals in theaters of war and theaters of operations. It involves the allocation of forces, the conditions on the use of force, and the specification of a desired end state. The famous British military philosopher Sir Basil Liddell Hart defined strategy as "the art of distributing military means to fulfill the ends of policy. For strategy," he continued, "is concerned not merely with the movement of armies—as its role is often defined—but with the effect.[2] An effective military strategy is designed to achieve specific political objectives.

Although there are many possible military strategies for any situation, there are only two general categories—the direct or the indirect. A direct strategy usually involves maneuvering the mass of one's forces against a critical enemy center of gravity.[3] A direct strategy usually involves the use of one of the elements of national power, military power, against the similar power of the enemy. At the strategic level, a direct strategy can involve the destruction of the enemy's army or his means to resist. A direct strategy usually requires overwhelming the enemy with massive numbers or massive firepower. America has employed a direct strategy in most of its wars in the 20th century.[4]

An indirect strategy, on the other hand, involves the destruction of the enemy's center of gravity in an oblique fashion. An indirect strategy involves avoiding enemy strengths and seeking to destroy his weaknesses in order to gain fast but cheap victory. An example of an indirect strategy could involve the destruction of a "key economic resource or locality, the strategic transport capability by which a nation maintains its armies in the field, or a vital part of the homeland itself."[5] Sir Liddell Hart proposed this concept as the strategy of the "indirect approach." The indirect approach attacks the enemy along the "line of least expectation and least resistance, resulting in the psychological dislocation of the enemy."[6] This "psychological dislocation often results in the enemy's defeat on a scale out of proportion to the effort employed. This strategy becomes very desirable for nations that possess small, but well-trained, competent military forces. Other options for an indirect approach involve the use of one of the elements of national power against a different element of the enemy's power.

The Vietnam War illustrates the difference between a direct and indirect strategy. France, and later the United States, aimed at a direct strategy of defeating the Vietnamese Communist regular and irregular forces. The center of gravity was determined to be the enemy's army and his military capacity. The Vietnamese Communists, on the other hand, fought an indirect strategy that involved a protracted war. The Communist strategy aimed to destroy the enemy's morale and his national will to continue the war. The Vietnamese Communists achieved this goal against the French after the French disaster at Dien Bien Phu. They achieved nearly the same result against the Americans with the 1968 Tet offensive. The Vietnamese Communists determined that their enemy's center of gravity was the enemy's national will to continue support for the war. Even though France and the United States won most of the military battles, America lost the war. The Vietnamese Communists outmaneuvered their adversaries at the strategic level of war.

## Operational Art

The operational level of war seeks to attain the goals set by strategy. It is the linking level between strategy and tactics. FM 100-5, *Operations* defines operational art as "the employment of military forces to attain strategic goals in a theater of war or theater of operations through the design, organization, and conduct of campaigns and major operations."[7] Operational art involves the decision to accept or decline battle, and where and when to fight. The essence of the operational art is to determine the enemy's center of gravity and develop a campaign plan to achieve decisive success.

There are two distinct styles of operational warfighting: attrition and maneuver. The attrition style emphasizes firepower. The maneuver style emphasizes movement. Attrition attacks strength; maneuver attacks weakness. The predominance of one operational style over the other has important implications on an army's doctrine, organization, and command and control philosophy.

The attrition style of warfare focuses on the destruction of the enemy's forces. Attrition deals with destruction of personnel and equipment over time. Attrition warfare reduces the enemy through the application of superior firepower or superior numbers. "Attrition warfare emphasizes the material aspects of war. It dehumanizes war to a mathematical equation. An attritionist sees the enemy as targets to be engaged and destroyed systematically."[8]

The American army has emphasized attrition warfare in most of its wars. Both world wars were won by the overpowering superiority of Allied firepower, numbers, and technology. The stalemate in Korea was "guaranteed" by this same kind of superiority. During the Vietnam War, the strategy of attrition reached its zenith as the American way of war. Combined with the zealous belief in the killing power of new technology, American commanders employed overwhelming firepower against the North Vietnamese army and Viet Cong. "It was a strategy that was based on the attrition of the enemy through a prolonged defense and made no allowance for decisive offensive action."[9] The war continued in spite of the awesome firepower. After twelve long years of fighting, America lost the will to carry on a war of attrition.

To win by attrition, a force must kill or incapacitate the enemy until the enemy can no longer resist. In essence, one side outlasts the other. In the past this operational technique has been the safest means for a numerically superior force to beat a smaller force. The "addict of attrition advances cautiously and tidily on a broad front to seize another piece of ground which directly threatens some vital interest of the erstwhile aggressor. This process is repeated until one side has gained overwhelming strength (Second World War) or becomes exhausted (First World War)."[10] This philosophy at its worst is typified by a British casualty list of about 420,000 men during the 16-day Battle of the Somme in 1916. In Vietnam it was represented by the indecisive commitment of an army dedicated to the policy of "body count." The bloody eight-year war between Iran and Iraq is a frightening example of high-tech, modern attrition warfare.

The attrition approach attempts to translate war into a science. The focus is on efficiency in the best use of mass numbers. Scientific management in the form of detailed planning, management of resources, and active centralized control guides the application of the force. Large armies and mass firepower require detailed planning to synchronize the force for maximum effect in time, space, and purpose. This tends to make attrition approaches to war slow-moving and predictable set pieces.

The attritionist must deploy a large army to ensure success. This approach is particularly attractive to countries that plan to raise large armies on short notice. Overwhelming numbers require less military skill to accomplish tactical and operational objectives. Large, mass-conscripted armies replace military skill with numbers. Firepower replaces maneuver. In turn, a lower level of military proficiency drives the requirement for centralized control and centralized planning. For almost two centuries the United States relied on a moderately trained, massed army to execute an attrition approach to war.

The unsuccessful attrition strategy of the Vietnam War forced the army to reevaluate its thinking about war. One famous American military author put it this way:

> Attrition is not a strategy. It is, in fact, irrefutable proof of the absence of any strategy. A commander who resorts to attrition admits his failure to conceive of an alternative. He rejects warfare as an art and accepts it on the most non-professional terms imaginable. He uses blood in lieu of brains. To be sure, political considerations left military commanders no choice other than attrition warfare, but that does not alter the hard truth that the United States was strategically bankrupt in Vietnam in 1966.[11]

Maneuver warfare, on the other hand, is based on a "desire to circumvent a problem and attack it from a position of advantage rather than straight on."[12] Maneuver warfare emphasizes the intangible human factors—leadership, organization, cohesion, and morale. The maneuver approach relies more on speed and surprise as multipliers of combat power than on sheer weight of numbers. *It seeks to trap the enemy, rather than merely pushing him back.* The maneuverist sees war as a matter of surfaces and gaps. To trap the enemy the maneuverist seeks to exploit the enemy's weak spots (gaps) and avoids his heavily defended areas (surfaces).

Germany's quick and decisive defeat of France in 1940 is the quintessential example of the potential of maneuver warfare. The fall of France was dramatic and stunning. Overall, the French outmatched the Germans in almost every category. The French had better tanks, and an army of 3 million men to a German force of only 2.5 million. In addition, the French had constructed a formidable series of defenses, the Maginot line, to reinforce themselves against German attack. The Germans attacked on 10 May 1940. The French surrendered over forty days later on 22 June.

The Germans attacked French weakness, aiming their panzer divisions at the enemy's weak spot (a gap), rather than attack the formidable defenses of the well-prepared Maginot line (a surface). In the "impassable" Ardennes, General von Rundstedt's Army Group A, consisting of three panzer corps with a total of seven hand-picked tank divisions, was opposed by weak regiments of the Belgian *Chasseurs Ardennais* and a few French motorized units. The density of forces at the critical time and place, the *Schwerpunkt*, greatly favored the Germans. The German spearheads quickly punctured this light screen and headed for the Meuse River. Once the fortified Meuse River was breached, the tank columns continued to roll to the English Channel. The attack by these panzer divisions, which comprised less than 5 percent of the total force structure of the Wehrmacht, led to the collapse of the French command system, the loss of their will to fight, and the eventual defeat of France. The German attack concentrated on destroying the enemy's command and control and cutting off the Allied combat forces from their lines of communication. The Germans did not try to systematically destroy every French combat unit. Instead, the Germans bypassed combat units (surfaces) and raced deep into enemy lines to destroy undefended supply dumps, staging areas, and command and control centers (gaps). Had they stopped to fight every Allied combat unit, the blitzkrieg might never have occurred and the outcome would have resembled the trench warfare of World War I. The "German thrust through the Ardennes in Belgium to the Channel coast of France in May 1940 was accomplished by a concentrated armored and motorized army. . . . It was a battle of movement . . ."[13]

Maneuver warfare is a thinking activity, an art, based on scientific foundations. "Maneuver theory draws its power mainly from opportunism—the calculated risk, and the exploitation both of chance circumstances and (to borrow a tennis term) of 'forced and unforced errors' by the opposition; still more on winning the battle of wills by surprise or, failing this, by speed and aptness of response."[14]

In the offense, maneuver warfare bases movement on active reconnaissance. During what are often called "reconnaissance-pull" operations, the maneuver-oriented commander supports success by driving his forces into areas that his reconnaissance has proven are weakly defended. General MacArthur's invasion at Inchon is a classic example of operational maneuver to "hit the enemy where they ain't" and cause their strategic dislocation. Like Napoleon at Ulm, the practitioner of maneuver makes every attempt to trap his enemy with his offensive maneuvers.

In the defense, maneuver warfare bases the response on the enemy. At the operational level the maneuverist seeks to defeat, rather than just destroy, the enemy by attacking the enemy's plan. Active measures are used to preempt the enemy attack and disrupt the enemy's operational timetable. Again, every attempt is made to trap the enemy rather than merely push him back. The Battle of Austerlitz is an example of this concept. Davout's corps defended against superior enemy forces for most of the morning while Napoleon waited for the right moment to launch his trapping envelopment through the center of the allied line. Thus, Davout's defense set the conditions for Napoleon's greatest triumph.

## Tactics

The style of operational art, either attrition or maneuver, has a great influence on the tactics of an army. On the battlefield, at the tactical level of war, the elements of attrition and maneuver often exist simultaneously. Obviously, attrition, the killing of the enemy, must occur in maneuver warfare just as maneuver often occurs in the deadliest war of attrition. Like the oriental concept of yin and yang, at the tactical level attrition and maneuver are complementary, yet opposite. "Maneuver and firepower are inseparable and complementary elements of combat. Although one might dominate a phase of the battle, the coordinated use of both characterizes all operations."[15] At the cutting edge of combat, war is a combination of fire and movement, of killing and moving.

The tactical level is where the fighting and dying takes place. The tactical level of war is where the operational plan, either attrition- or maneuver-oriented, is translated into action. Tactics is the "art by which corps and smaller unit commanders translate potential combat power into victorious battles and engagements."[16] Engagements are small conflicts between opposing forces, while battles are a series of related engagements. Engagements are normally measured in hours, while battles are normally measured in days. At the tactical level, the goal of an engagement is the destruction of the enemy force as an effective fighting unit. The enemy either is killed, surrenders, or runs away. An enemy is destroyed when he no longer has the physical means to resist as a coherent fighting force. An enemy is defeated when he no longer has the will to resist as a coherent fighting force.

The degree to which an army emphasizes firepower over movement is directly related to its style of operational warfighting. Every army chooses between the operational style of attrition or maneuver based on its past traditions, doctrine, capabilities, and training. An army that adopts a maneuver style of operational warfighting emphasizes movement over firepower. An army that adopts an attrition style of operational warfighting emphasizes firepower over movement. The tactical commander is concerned with finding, fixing, fighting, and finishing the enemy. To do this the tactical commander moves his firepower to gain an advantage over the enemy and destroys him with a combination of fire and movement. At the tactical level of war, therefore, there is only fire and movement.

Movement, however, does not imply movement without killing. Movement at the tactical level involves the emphasis of mobility over firepower. The mobility of the unit becomes its main weapon, and enables the firepower of the unit to have a greater effect with proportionally less mass. This situation is represented in the model by the symbol $Mf$ (representing "big MOBILITY and little firepower"). Movement aims at the defeat of the enemy.

Firepower, on the other hand, does not imply killing without movement. The destruction of the enemy force as an effective fighting unit remains the goal, but overwhelming mass is used as the means. Firepower at the tactical level involves the emphasis of firepower over mobility. The firepower of the unit becomes the main weapon, and the mass of its killing effect is moved to gain advantage over the enemy. This situation is represented by the symbol $Fm$ (representing "big FIREPOWER and little mobility"). Firepower aims at the destruction of the enemy.

The idea of "density of forces" is important to understand how fire and movement apply on the battlefield. The density of forces is the amount of force within a given space on a battlefield. The density of forces is a key factor in the ability of a military force to apply $Mf$

versus Fm. Density of forces can be overcome by either F (firepower; destroy the enemy) or M (mobility; move to make his density useless). A low density of enemy to friendly forces facilitates Mf, while a high density of forces often forces an Fm solution.

An excellent example of an indirect strategy inspired by a maneuver-oriented operational concept, emphasizing an Mf tactical technique, is the Arab-Israeli Six-Day War. The Israelis knew they could not win a war of attrition against their Arab enemies. Employing an indirect strategy that sought to bring about the defeat of their enemies in the minimum amount of time, the Israelis selected an operational strategy of maneuver. They attacked while their enemies were staging. The Israelis emphasized tactical movement over firepower, or Mf, employing their few elite tank units in their main effort. Rather than focus their effort on killing Arab soldiers, the Israelis used the momentum of their drive to disrupt the enemy's command and control. This resulted in the complete paralysis of the enemy's command system and the defeat of the Arab armies.

## ATTRITION VERSUS MANEUVER IN COMMAND AND CONTROL

Two competing command and control philosophies have emerged from the attrition and maneuver styles of the operational art. These concepts are the "detailed orders tactics" approach (centralized control), and the system of "mission tactics" (decentralized control).

Because of the relative lack of expertise of hastily assembled mass armies, control becomes the predominant command principle in attrition warfare. Control is achieved by centralized planning and centralized, active control over each piece of the combat equation. Centralized planning moves the mass in the assigned direction. Centralized, active control assists the efficient employment of massive firepower. Victory is declared when the enemy is annihilated. The end can be mathematically determined by an ever-increasing count of destroyed enemy personnel, vehicles, and equipment.

Detailed orders tactics is an orders-intensive approach to facilitate the continuous active control of subordinate units during combat. Active control requires technology and rigid organization. The orders-intensive system aims to continuously update the decision maker to assist him in making battlefield decisions. These decisions are based upon a detailed plan that covers the most likely course of action and enemy reactions. Adherents of this theory often propose a technological solution to command and control, with heavy emphasis on the ability to control elements during the battle. The subordinate's understanding is explicit, leaving nothing implied. With new technology such as computers and position-locating devices, the logical extension of this control philosophy is a "command through instruments" approach. It would be theoretically possible, using this approach, to direct the exact movements and actions of all units and subunits from one or more centralized control headquarters.

The other system, mission tactics, involves indirect control and implicit understanding. Mission tactics (*Auftragstaktik*) concedes that the tactical battlefield is too confusing to control centrally and that the commander must direct his operations through guidance rather than active control. The emphasis is on command. Commanders trust subordinates to execute their missions according to the plan and the commander's intent. If the plan is no longer valid due to the situation on the battlefield, the subordinate is expected to act rather than wait for orders that may never come. Subordinates are trained to think and execute as the commander would intend for them to act if the commander could see the situation and issue the orders himself. Since the commander cannot possibly foresee every eventuality, the subordinate's understanding of the commander's intent must be implicit rather than explicit.

In mission tactics, subordinates are not freewheeling agents, running around the battlefield without guidance. They are expected to execute the commander's scheme of maneuver and his branch plans on order. If the situation changes, and the plan no longer applies due to unforeseen circumstances, then the subordinate is expected to continue in the correct direction to secure the commander's intent. The subordinate's responsibility to execute the commander's will is ironclad; only the "how" in these emergency situations is missing. Thus, a force can continue to act even after positive control is lost, such as during radio jamming or when the command group is destroyed or knocked out of action.

Mission tactics is the preferred method of waging maneuver warfare. This is accomplished largely by verbal, mission-type orders issued by the senior commander overlooking the terrain where the battle will be fought. Subordinates are expected to make decisions within the guidelines established by the commander's intent. When decisions are made at the point of execution, advantage can be taken of battle opportunities as they occur, without loss of time. "Time is always critical and mission-type orders save time. The command style and staff functioning that contribute most to maneuver warfare is characterized by the application of mission orders."[17]

Mission tactics demand a high degree of military skill and discipline. Mission tactics are just as the name implies: the tactic of assigning a subordinate a mission without specifying how the mission must be accomplished. The manner of accomplishing the mission is left to the subordinate, thereby allowing him freedom—and establishing the duty—to take whatever steps he deems necessary based on the situation. Mission tactics are not new to the American army. They are rediscovered whenever the army has to learn the hard lessons of combat. The *CGSC Quarterly*, vol. XV, 1935, had the following information concerning mission tactics:

> In the past we have often used what may be called mission tactics and mission orders. Under this system, instructions and orders are not prescribed in minute detail; the reason being that the commander on the ground is the only person who can correctly judge existing conditions and take the proper action when a change occurs in the situation. In addition to the tactical reason, there is a strong psychological reason for such tactics and orders. The commander who is given a mission and made responsible for results will normally accomplish more because he can act in accordance with his own individuality.[18]

Carl von Clausewitz, the great 19th-century German war theorist, described action in war as "movement through a resistant element. . . . An understanding of friction is a large part of that much-admired sense of warfare which a good general is supposed to possess."[19] Clausewitz labeled this resistance as "friction," giving his term a similar definition to that used by the study of physics: He visualized battle as a process of move and countermove. Plans often go astray, and Clausewitz recognized that countless forces acted against the plan. Many of these forces could be anticipated before battle, but even a genius could not reduce friction to zero. The physical result of friction—a cold driving rain, the fear of death or injury, or the lack of sleep—can often leave a commander deprived of his better judgment and committed to take actions, in the heat of battle, that are not correct.

Clausewitz went on to explain that military operations will deteriorate quickly if the friction is not reduced by the "oil" of good planning, trained leadership, and ruthless execution. "Countless minor incidents—the kind you can never really foresee—combine to lower the general level of performance, so that one always falls short of his intended goal."[20] To combat friction, a commander must possess a determined and faithful commitment to accomplish his commander's intent.

This is where maneuver warfare can make a dramatic impact on the course of combat operations. For an army to adopt the maneuver approach and employ Mf tactics, it must embrace a leadership philosophy of mission tactics. Well-trained leaders guided by a clear understanding of the commander's intent can be an important lubricant to reduce friction. With the increased tempo of modern combat, success in battle usually falls to the side that can quickly and consistently take advantage of the enemy's mistakes.

To take advantage of the enemy's mistakes, you must be able to act faster than he can—what is termed "getting inside the enemy's decision/reaction cycle." The speed needed to do this does not necessarily come from faster-moving units or vehicles—although these things are very important—it comes from faster, more focused thinking. This thinking must isolate the critical criteria that set the conditions for success in battle, focus intelligence assets on those criteria, and anticipate enemy actions. AirLand Battle calls this agility. By successfully outthinking your opponent, by possessing greater agility, you present him with a series of situations to which he cannot react in time. If this continues, his actions will appear futile and his command and control system will cease to function effectively.

Developing a faster tactical decision cycle than your opponent means you must (1) lower the level at which decisions are made and allow trained, subordinate leaders maximum freedom of action guided by the commander's intent, (2) train cohesive units capable of independent action, (3) develop a streamlined information gathering and processing system that reports information internally, laterally, and to higher headquarters, and (4) instill the understanding that decisions will be made without the availability of perfect information.

Sun Tzu aptly portrays this situation in the following passage from *The Art of War*:

> Now in war there may be one hundred changes in each step. When one sees he can, he advances; when he sees that things are different, he retires. To say that a general must await commands of the sovereign in such circumstances is like informing a superior that you wish to put out a fire. Before the order to do so arrives, the ashes are cold. And it is said one must consult the Army Supervisor in these matters! This is as if in building a house beside the road one took advice from those who pass by. Of course the work would never be completed![21]

Uncertainty and confusion are inherent in battle. Certainty is a product of time and information. Faced with friction and the need to get inside the enemy's decision/reaction cycle, even the most confident military planner is often humbled. Centralized detailed orders tactics work against this trend. Communications frequently break down under combat conditions. Speed of decision making and speed in execution can be critical to reducing friction. Military decision makers benefit by reducing the communication time needed for both internal transmission of orders and for reporting to higher headquarters. A maneuver-oriented, mission tactics approach can help work around this friction.

Erich von Manstein, the famous German general who conceived the 1940 campaign plan against France, explained the difference between the two approaches this way:

> It had always been the particular forte of German leadership to grant wide scope to the self-dependence of subordinate commanders—to allot them tasks which leave the method of execution to the discretion of the individual. From time immemorial—certainly since the elder Moltke's day—this principle has distinguished Germany's military leadership from that of other armies. The latter, far from giving the same latitude to subordinate commanders on the tactical plane, have always tended to prescribe, by means of long and detailed directives, the way orders should actually be carried out or to make tactical action conform to a specific pattern. On the German side this system was considered a bad one.

It would, admittedly, appear to reduce the risk of failure in the case of a mediocre commander. Yet it only too easily leads to the executant's having to act against the exigencies of the local situation. Worst of all, in its preoccupation with security it waives the opportunity that may occur through the independent action of a subordinate commander in boldly exploiting some favorable situation at a decisive moment.[22]

## CONCLUSION

Two opposing styles of operational warfare dominate the tactical level of combat: attrition warfare and maneuver warefare. Attrition emphasizes firepower and an orientation on terrain. Maneuver emphasizes mobility and an orientation on the enemy. In the final argument the difference between attrition and maneuver styles boils down to a desire to *push* or *trap*. Maneuver warfare seeks to trap, bringing about decisive action, rather than pushing the enemy back and continuing the fighting. This philosophy extends to the entire structure of war. At the strategic level, the indirect approach offers the best chance to trap your opponent. At the strategic level, you accomplish this by what Sun Tzu once said was of supreme importance in war: "to attack the enemy's plan."[23] At the operational level, you trap the enemy by maneuvering against his weak spots rather than by pushing against his strength. At the tactical level, you execute fire and movement, in varying degrees of Mf or Fm, to trap the enemy and decisively destroy him.

The greatest confusion of the maneuver versus attrition debate occurs at the tactical level of war. At the tactical level, the style of war is directly related to, and greatly influenced by, the operational style of warfare that a military force adopts. A military force that adopts a maneuver warfare style emphasizes movement over firepower at the tactical level of war. A military force that adopts an attrition warfare style emphasizes firepower over movement at the tactical level of war. Each style of war, in turn, supports a corresponding command and control style.

The command and control style that best supports the attrition style of war is the system of detailed orders tactics. The leadership technique that best supports maneuver warfare is mission tactics. In detailed orders tactics, the plan is designed to cover each eventuality. The battle is managed through centralized control. Leaders are expected to force the plan to work at all costs. In mission tactics, the plan is a basis for changes. Successful mission tactics depends upon the initiative of competent subordinate commanders, trained to take advantage of fleeting opportunities and enemy mistakes. "Maneuver theory draws its power mainly from opportunism—the calculated risk, and the exploitation both of chance circumstances and (to borrow a tennis term) of 'forced and unforced errors' by the opposition; still more on winning the battle of wills by surprise or, failing this, by speed and aptness of response."[24] Mission tactics can only be executed by a highly skilled army that possesses talented tactical leadership. In this regard, the United States Army is better off than at any other time in its history.

The maneuver theory debate is an important one for the United States Army. The choice of a particular style of warfighting will set the style of command and control and establish the basis for the army's warfighting ability. The army has broken with its attrition-oriented past and set a solid maneuver-oriented foundation with the concept of AirLand Battle. FM 100-5 describes maneuver as "the dynamic element of combat . . . which enables smaller forces to defeat larger ones."[25] It is time to build upon this foundation, institutionalize the concepts of mission tactics and maneuver warfare, and groom the army's intellectual development to employ the smaller, but more capable army that we will need to win on the battlefields of the next century.

# Notes

1. U.S. Army, FM 100-5, *Operations* (Washington, D.C.: U.S. Government Printing Office, 1986), p. 14 (hereafter listed as FM 100-5).

2. Sir B. H. Liddell Hart, *Strategy* (New York: Praeger Publishers, 1967), p. 348.

3. FM 100-5, p. 179, defines a center of gravity as: "The center of gravity of an armed force refers to those sources of strength or balance. It is a characteristic, capability, or locality from which the force derives its freedom of action, physical strength, or will to fight. Clausewitz defined it as 'the hub of all power and movement, on which everything depends.' Its attack is—or should be—the focus of all operations."

4. Russell F. Weigley, *History of the United States Army* (New York: Macmillan, 1967), p. 472.

5. FM 100-5, p. 79.

6. Liddell Hart, p. 348.

7. FM 100-5, p. 10.

8. U.S. Navy, FMFM 1, *Warfighting* (Washington, D.C.: Headquarters, U.S. Marine Corps, 1989), p. 28 (hereafter listed as FMFM 1).

9. Col. Hoang Ngoc Lung, *Strategy and Tactics* (Washington, D.C.: U.S. Army Center of Military History, 1980), p. 71.

10. Richard E. Simpkin, *Race to the Swift: Thoughts on 21st Century Warfare* (London: Brassey's Defense Publishers, 1985), pp. 20-22.

11. Col. Dave R. Palmer, *Summons of the Trumpet* (New York: Ballantine Books, 1984), p. 148.

12. FMFM 1, p. 29.

13. Len Deighton, *Blitzkrieg, From the Rise of Hitler to the Fall of Dunkirk* (London: Fakenham Press Ltd., 1979), pp. 203–206.

14. Simpkin, p. 22.

15. FM 100-5, p. 41.

16. Ibid., p. 10.

17. Gen. Bruce C. Clarke, *Guidelines for the Leader and the Commander* (Harrisburg: Stackpole Books, 1963), p. 95.

18. Maj. Fred During, ed., and Capt. G.B. Guenther, assoc. ed. *Review of Military Literature, The CGSC Quarterly,* vol. XV (Ft. Leavenworth, Kans.: Command and General Staff College, 1935), pp. 142, 143.

19. Carl von Clausewitz, *On War*, ed. and trans. Michael Howard and Peter Paret (Princeton: Princeton University Press, 1976), p. 120.

20. Ibid., p. 119.

21. Sun Tzu, *The Art of War,* trans. by Samuel B. Griffith (New York: Oxford University Press, 1963), p. 63.

22. Field Marshal Erich von Manstein, *Lost Victories,* ed. and trans. Anthony G. Powell (Novato: Presidio Press, 1982 edition), p. 383.

23. Sun Tzu, p. 77.

24. Simpkin, p. 22.

25. FM 100-5, p. 12.

# Ten Myths About Maneuver Warfare

## Richard D. Hooker, Jr.

Now as never before since the end of the Second World War, external events are stimulating our armed forces to think creatively about the future. Although the services are focusing primarily on how to cope with force reductions, the prospect of dramatically smaller forces should also prompt the military to think about ways to improve and increase capability to help offset loss of mass and combat power. Maneuver warfare is one way to increase combat effectiveness without increasing size or budget outlays. However, many sincere and knowledgeable professionals view maneuver warfare with skepticism.

This essay seeks to clarify and refine the maneuver warfare debate. In so doing, the author acknowledges both the stature and high motives of many prominent figures, both in and out of uniform, who have expressed reservations about maneuver warfare in the course of this debate. Their criticisms are real and deserve a substantive response. If the times do indeed demand fundamental change, the price of failure requires the most searching examination before we move to replace current methods and theories of war with new ones.

Much of the criticism of maneuver warfare is not based on a careful reading and analysis of maneuver warfare as a body of thought or set of concepts. In the past decade, a number of conclusions were drawn which are now commonly accepted as fact. To judge maneuver warfare fairly on its merits, it is first necessary to address some of the more common misconceptions or "myths" that surround it.

### ASSUMPTIONS

Before addressing these common misconceptions, it may be useful to inquire into the basic assumptions that inform the maneuver warfare argument.

For many military professionals, the label "maneuver warfare" it-self evokes a certain measure of hostility that is a product of the con-tentious debates of a decade ago, as the so-called military reform movement took on the military establishment and asked it to reexam-ine what was widely perceived to be a uniquely American style of war.[1] In the views of its critics and many historians, this American approach to war focused on a few simple themes: mass, fires, an overwhelm-ing logistics effort, and a centralized and relatively methodical approach to battle.[2]

Some call this American style of war *attrition* warfare. American forces have not always sought victory through massed fires and over-whelming force. We have had our share of Waynes, Forrests, Mackenzies, and Pattons. But these outstanding American military figures were remarkable, perhaps, precisely *because* they departed from the mili-tary norms of the day. If one looks closely, it is possible to see in them and in others the outlines of a different way to fight, another way to look at war.

A second basic assumption is that, AirLand Battle doctrine notwith-standing, the emphasis on massed fires and the linear battlefield still retains a powerful hold on the institutional consciousness of the American military. The historical record supports this view, and so does an aggregated review of our performance at the National Training Cen-ter. A first look at the written material coming out of the Gulf sug-gests that "victory through superior firepower" remains central to the American way of war.[3] At least empirically, there is much to suggest that the physical destruction of the enemy by massed fire systems remains central to our view of war.[4]

A third assumption is that, contrary to the widely held views of many prominent figures both in and out of uniform, the American military is capable of evolutionary and even revolutionary change in its ap-proach to war. We are not necessarily wedded to techniques, doctrines, and routines that descend from our defining experiences in Northwest Europe in 1944 or the amphibious campaigns in the Pacific or the stra-tegic bombing campaigns over Germany and Japan.[5] All militar-ies change over time. In the coming decade we may have no choice but to change, to reach out for new concepts that offer hope of maxi-mizing the capabilities of what all agree will be a much smaller mili-tary establishment.

Such change is necessary and normal and natural. But what kind of change will it be? We have already begun to look at this question and attempt to formulate some answers. Prior to his retirement, Gen. John Foss at TRADOC published a series of papers describing a different kind of battlefield. He foresaw a future battlefield characterized by smaller forces, greater lethality, more mobility and increasing complexity, and he called it the nonlinear, or fluid, battlefield.[6]

Against credible opponents, an ordered or methodical view of the battlefield probably will not reflect reality—if it ever did. As Clausewitz argued so eloquently a century and a half ago, the battlefield is a place of friction, of chaos and uncertainty, of error and bad weather and missed opportunities. Those who believe otherwise, and there are many these days who see perfect transparency and perfect target acquisition just over the horizon, are engaging in an old, familiar game. They see, in the next technological advance, or perhaps the next doctrine, a way to bring about what all combat leaders desperately want: an ordered, understandable tactical and operational universe. They want a linear battlefield.

There may be times when the battlefield assumes a linear character. But in an age of rapid technological change, we can be confident that the human dimension of battle will retain its traditional importance. This is not to suggest that technology is not supremely important in war. But an emphasis on technology that neglects the role of human factors is fundamentally misplaced.

If the world is fated to remain a dangerous place (and all militaries are founded on the supposition that it is) and if the battlefields of the future will continue to be dominated by friction and a relative absence of order, how can a smaller, less robust force prevail? Maneuver warfare provides one promising answer. In its emphasis on the fluid nature of modern war, its recognition of friction, and its potential for rapid victory without the high casualties and enormous consumption of wealth that can attend modern war, maneuver warfare offers one answer to an increasingly compelling dilemma.

## MANEUVER MYTHS

With these assumptions and observations in mind, let us examine the more common criticisms of maneuver warfare, beginning with myth number 1: *Maneuver warfare is nothing more than another set of rules.*

All theories are based on a set of organizing concepts. For maneuver warfare, these include: emphasis on how to think, not what to do; targeting the opponent's will to resist, not just his physical resources; a preoccupation with decisive battle; and the application of strength against weakness.

However, it is difficult to find another school of thought that argues so strongly against the application of rules as a guide to battlefield behavior. This does not mean that the principles of war or AirLand Battle imperatives, for example, should be ignored or that they are not important. It does mean that rules, principles, concepts, or whatever we may choose to call them, are meaningless except in the context of the present operation.

> Combat situations cannot be solved by rules. The art of war has no traffic with rules, for the infinitely varied circumstances and conditions of combat never produce exactly the same situation twice. Mission, terrain, weather, dispositions, armament, morale, supply and comparative strength are variables whose mutations always combine to form a new tactical pattern. Thus, in battle, each situation is unique and must be solved on its own merits.[7]

Maneuver warfare eschews *absolute* rules absolutely. At Chancellorsville, Lee divided his force and divided it again, trusting to speed, deception and a certain moral ascendancy over Hooker to retrieve his exceedingly dangerous situation. At Tannenberg, the Germans left a single cavalry division to oppose the Russian First Army while redeploying three full corps southward to envelop and crush Samsonov. They took the principles of concentration on the one hand and economy of force on the other to new heights.

They did not think along methodical, tidy lines, as Montgomery or Hodges might have done, but instead gambled that the intangibles—speed, resolution, shock, and the enemy's lack of imagination—would fall their way. At Chancellorsville and Tannenberg the situation, not the rules of the game, was supreme.

Maneuver warfare preaches the futility of formulaic rules more strongly than any comparable theory of war. It is based on an intellectual tradition which stresses how to think, not what to do. The use of strength against weakness to break the enemy's will is the analytical framework that provides a guide to action. Experience, talent, intelligence, and will—and above all, character—are the ingredients that must exist to apply this thought process to local conditions. They are the essential characteristics that distinguish those who can adapt the principles of war to the local situation and win from those who will apply them by rote and lose—or win at great and unnecessary cost.

Myth number 2: *Maneuver warfare exalts maneuver and ignores firepower.* Understanding the relationship of fire to maneuver is central to understanding war. Fundamentally, this relationship is not a function of the quantity of the one versus the other. Despite direct quotes from the literature which state unequivocally that "the importance of firepower in maneuver warfare cannot be overemphasized,"[8] critics persist in the belief that maneuverists ignore or neglect the role of fires.

It is time to put this charge to rest. Armies fight with fires. Period. But some armies maneuver to mass fires with a view towards occupying terrain and physically destroying opposing forces. Other armies use fires to permit or facilitate decisive maneuver against weak points, in order to cause the collapse and disintegration of enemy forces. Some armies do both, whether by accident or not. But generally speaking, armies fight in the spirit of the one—as France did offensively in 1914 and defensively in 1940, and as we did in Korea and Vietnam— or the other—as reflected in the operating styles of the Wehrmacht, the Israeli Defense Forces, and the North Vietnamese army and the Viet Cong.

What is different in maneuver warfare is the *relationship* between fire and maneuver. In maneuver warfare, the object of maneuver is not to position fires for the ultimate destruction of the enemy. Ideally, fires are used to create conditions which support decisive maneuver—that is, movement of combat forces in relation to the enemy to destroy his will to resist. In the 1973 and 1982 wars, the Israeli Defense Forces used battalion-sized units as a base of fire to support maneuver by other forces moving to deliver a decisive blow. But overall, they possessed many fewer artillery systems and numbers of tanks than their opponents.[9]

Local conditions (for example, a holding operation) may dictate something different. But the "default setting" should be decisive maneuver supported by fires, and not the reverse. Armies that emphasize maneuver will not require huge quantities of fire support because the objective is not the physical annihilation of enemy forces and equipment.

Instead, concentration and timing are the keys to effective fire support. Fire systems must, of course, exist in reasonable numbers, but it should not be necessary to overwhelm the enemy with artillery. It is illuminating that large numbers of massed fire systems breeds a confidence that our maneuver capability does not.

Myth number 3: *Maneuver warfare is inconsistent with American military culture.* This is a favorite bromide with many critics who argue that America's predilection for "industrial" warfare is a cultural imperative. This critique can be summarized by saying that the American military won't change because it can't.[10]

Whether or not this critique is historically accurate, we cannot conclude that other armies have somehow cornered the market on such qualities as boldness, initiative, decisiveness, or strategic and operational vision, leaving none for the plodding Americans. We rapidly absorb new technologies. Racial and gender integration in the Army and impressive progress in interservice relations demonstrate our capability to move beyond entrenched organizational routines. Our own history yields abundant evidence of our propensity for innovation and initiative. These virtues remain an integral part of our organizational culture. They refute the charge that Americans are, at best, gifted amateurs who resist progress and change.

As an institution, we have shown ourselves capable of absorbing the lessons of the past and applying them to the present. There is no reason why a military as professional as ours, with the kind of intellectual resources we dispose and the caliber of soldiers and leaders we can boast, should conclude that we must remain wedded necessarily to the practices of the past. If we as a profession see a path to a better way, our reach need not exceed our grasp.

Myth number 4: *Maneuver warfare promises bloodless war.* In conventional conflicts decided by force of arms, the ideal outcome is the rapid collapse of the opponent without protracted combat. The United States and its coalition partners achieved such an outcome in the Gulf War, largely, it can be argued, through the application of maneuver warfare at the operational level of war. But in a contest between rival states, where the contending parties are roughly equivalent and armed with modern, lethal weaponry, maneuver warfare promises no free ride.

The 1866 Prussian-Austrian War, the 1940 invasion of France, and the 1967 Six-Day War each brought about the humiliation of powerful states by rivals of approximately equal strength. In each case victory was achieved quickly and decisively. But these victories were not bloodless. Some victorious units suffered terribly, and strategic success overshadowed many tactical defeats and reverses. No doctrine, no technology, no strategy can fairly promise overwhelming victory without cost.

Yet these three campaigns stand out in military history as brilliant examples of what can be accomplished through the dislocation in time and space of an opponent otherwise equal in numbers and weaponry. By avoiding known enemy strengths and striking at sensitive and vulnerable centers of gravity, the victors achieved the collapse and disintegration of their opponent's field forces in short order. They avoided a protracted series of wearing battles, with their inevitable casualties through disease, exhaustion and enemy fire. While no war is bloodless, maneuver warfare offers the possibility of reduced casualties through rapid operational and strategic success—by saving time, that most precious of military commodities.

Myth number 5: *There is no such thing as attrition warfare.* One sometimes hears that the existence of a maneuverist school "implies" the existence of an attrition school or theory, but that no such school exists; and that maneuver warfare throws its intellectual punch at empty air. Certainly there are very few advocates of attritional warfare. But there is a mass of historical data that supports a progressive emphasis on firepower and attrition at the expense of maneuver.

Only in the past decade has published doctrine explicitly addressed this imbalance, and we cannot yet know how well we have absorbed the philosophy of AirLand Battle. While its outlines seemed clearly visible in Operation Desert Storm at the operational level of war, at the tactical level combat very much resembled traditional "smash-mouth" warfare, with huge quantities of firepower being poured on enemy formations in lieu of maneuver.

This is not necessarily a bad thing, if our forces can quickly switch doctrinal gears in circumstances where attritional techniques do not apply. The historical record suggests that many American commanders, with notable exceptions, could not. A maneuver-focused force can adapt when faced with equal or superior firepower. A mass-focused force cannot.

It is perfectly true that there is no well-thought-out, perfectly articulated theory of attrition warfare. Yet the continuing outlines of an "industrial" approach to war, decade after decade and conflict after conflict, suggest that the mass vs. maneuver debate is both relevant and real.

Myth number 6: *Maneuver warfare is "just fighting smart."* There is nothing new or even particularly original about maneuver warfare. What is new is the attempt to organize successful concepts from the past around a unifying theme and then articulate that theme so it can be understood and applied more readily. Ardant Du Picq warned that technology changes, but human nature, and its influence in battle, does not. And while there is more than a grain of truth to myth number 6, it misses the mark by a wide margin.

Most leaders have been schooled to solve battlefield problems through the application of techniques and a standard suite of tactical solutions. These solutions presuppose near-perfect control. The desire for control is nothing more than a natural desire to impose order on disorder. When we lunge for a flank we are trying to do the same thing. We have been taught that flanks are vulnerable places and we should go for them.

The problem is that often they are not. The ability to discern strength from weakness is not a programmed response. It is an art form developed by years of practice, training and thinking about such things. It is, in fact, an intellectual discipline, practically derived.

In battle, very many leaders will do one of two things. They will bring heavy fires to bear and attack frontally, or they will suppress the enemy and maneuver to a flank. Both options are conditioned responses. They reflect patterned behavior. When and if they succeed, we call it "fighting smart."

Neither response, however, is based upon a thought process. Most leaders use the commander's estimate, the staff planning process and mission analysis to plan an operation. While these are useful and necessary mental checklists, they are at best a planning process—a way to organize one's time and ensure the completion of necessary planning tasks—but not a true thought process. They do not provide a mental framework for the analysis and solution of battlefield problems. They do not represent a theory or philosophy of warfighting, unless we consider the reduction of warfare to target lists, phase lines, and timetables a philosophy.

At a crude level, this thought process sounds something like: identify a decisive weakness, find or make a gap, ruthlessly exploit it, and continue to do so until the enemy collapses. The means used to do this—fires, maneuver, reconnaissance and intelligence, the will and vision of the commander, the courage and initiative of the subordinate—are means to this end. They are not ends in themselves. The labels are not important. The mechanical processes are not defining. What is important and defining is the thought process employed and the results achieved.

Myth number 7: *Maneuverists see maneuver as an end in itself.* This is a persistent claim whose origin is difficult to trace. Presumably it is a response to the label "maneuver warfare" and to criticism directed against the promiscuous use of firepower. A close reading of military history and of maneuver literature, however, quickly reveals the true end of maneuver operations.

Running throughout the memoirs of successful German generals of the First and Second World Wars is a preoccupation with decisive action. One cannot read von Mellenthin, von Manstein, Rommel, or Guderian without being struck by the constant emphasis on the decisive battle. Whereas attrition or "industrial" warfare "seeks battle under any or all conditions, pitting strength against strength to exact the greatest toll from the enemy,"[11] maneuver warfare seeks battle only under advantageous conditions *where a decisive result can be achieved.*

This obsession with forcing a decision is the defining characteristic of maneuver warfare. It undoubtedly descends from the experiences of the Prussian, German, and Israeli armies, who when faced with superior numbers and enemies on all sides developed a theory of war to compensate for numerical inferiority with intellectual and moral vigor. These armies could not afford to become locked in attritional exchanges where mass could dominate. Instead, they sought to create conditions where speed, tempo, focus, and initiative could be used to score a knockout.

These armies and others like them did not see maneuver as an end in itself. Maneuver warfare does not tout maneuver as an end in itself. To seek and gain the decision as rapidly and vigorously as possible is the true end of battles and campaigns. The Marine Corps' doctrinal discussion of *The Conduct of War* in its principal warfighting manual captures the essence of maneuver warfare simply and succinctly: "This is how I will achieve a decision; everything else is secondary."[12]

Myth number 8: *We're already doing maneuver warfare.* This claim derives from the publication of doctrinal materials, chiefly the U.S. Army's FM100-5, *Operations* and the Marine Corps' FMFM1, *Warfighting* and FMFM1-1, *Campaigning*, which incorporate a number of themes commonly associated with maneuver warfare. This doctrinal incorporation of maneuver concepts and thinking continues in the current revision of the operations manual, supported by other doctrinal publications and discussion in professional military journals.

Our recent experiences with armed conflict in Panama and Kuwait suggest that we may have grasped maneuver warfare at the operational level, but not at the tactical. Furthermore, there is much to suggest that technology, among other things, will make maneuver warfare at the tactical level even less likely to take hold in the American military.[13] And while maneuver warfare at the operational level of war represents a marked improvement in the effectiveness of the American military in the field, its absence at the tactical level forces us back to the familiar paradigm of mass and fires—whether or not this approach can work in a given theater, against a given opponent or at a given gradient on the spectrum of conflict.

What is the evidence that the U.S. practiced maneuver warfare operationally during Operations Just Cause and Desert Storm? The strongest indicator in both cases was an evident determination to strike swiftly at an identified center of gravity and avoid force-on-force engagements with large enemy units, except on favorable terms. A distinctive feature in both operations was the attempt to stun or paralyze the enemy's ability to command and control his forces—to shock the enemy's nervous system at the outset and prevent a coordinated response. In both campaigns, the operational plan sought to create conditions that would force a decision quickly, without the need for extended combat.[14]

At the tactical level, however, American forces seem to have performed in the traditional manner. U.S. soldiers were well trained and fought courageously. Their leaders proved themselves masters of the art of coordinating fire support, movement, and logistics. Allied officers serving in the Gulf were stunned at the ability of large U.S. heavy forces to organize for combat and mass overwhelming combat power. One British officer observed: "At the big unit level the Americans are simply not to be believed. Only a fool would get in their way."[15]

While U.S. forces may have carried traditional methods, techniques, and doctrine to new heights, they have not absorbed maneuver warfare at division level and below. Command and control remained rigidly centralized. Units moved in strict conformance to preplanned control measures. Fire control of artillery and close air support was consolidated at high levels; much was preplanned.[16] Units moved primarily to mass fire systems against enemy forces and expressed a clear preference for the use of fires over maneuver.

These methods worked well against a passive enemy. But they do not reflect the spirit of AirLand Battle doctrine at the tactical level, and they do not reflect a conceptual grasp of maneuver warfare.

Myth number 9: *Maneuverists have failed to define their terms*. This myth is sometimes colorfully packaged, as in the following: "Many discussants held that reformers had done their cause a great disservice by failing to identify and clarify the most significant empirical referents of the maneuver notion."[17] This kind of criticism is effective for at least two reasons. First, it deflects discussion from the real issues. Even though first-order questions ("Is there substance to the attrition critique?") and basic terms ("Maneuver is movement in relation to the enemy") are well defined, haggling over questions of precise definition, particularly when critics do not agree among themselves on the definitions of many common terms, trivializes the debate. Second, the charge of "lack of clarity and precision" often masks an unfamiliarity with the literature or grasp of the essentials of the maneuver warfare argument.

The study of war becomes more useful and relevant as its students strip away the peripheral to come to grips with the true nature of human conflict. Real progress becomes possible only to the extent that students and practitioners of the military art can focus on this essential question objectively. Both soldiers and scholars (as well as those who are both) have important roles to play in what is fundamentally a dynamic, Hegelian process. Neither has a monopoly on the truth.

By now, the important assumptions and the organizing concepts of maneuver warfare are well known and well articulated. There is a substantial body of literature on the subject, and no lack of advocates and critics on both sides of the issue. Experts may disagree on the validity or applicability of maneuver warfare as a theory of war. But the charge that it has never been adequately defined is thin indeed.

Myth number 10: *If you've never done it, you can't theorize about it.* Regrettably, much of the early debates about maneuver warfare focused on personalities. While civilians and academics charged senior military leaders with lacking a real understanding and historical grasp of their profession, military professionals responded with harsh criticism of the reformers' lack of combat experience and understanding of the realities of modern warfare. In the exchange, both sides sometimes failed to listen to the other; both missed opportunities to further the study of the profession.

No civilian theorist or historian has an answer to the charge that he lacks practical experience. No junior officer can rebut the criticism that he lacks combat experience or personal knowledge of the problems of command. Nevertheless, these are criticisms of individuals, *but not of their intellectual contributions to the debate.* These must stand or fall on their own merits, not on the résumés of their proponents.

Military history is replete with examples of oustanding military figures, such as Bedford Forrest, Wade Hampton, and Joshua Chamberlain, who possessed innate talent but lacked practical experience or professional training. Others, such as Alfred Thayer Mahan, Ardant du Picq, B. H. Liddell Hart, and Clausewitz himself, distinguished themselves as outstanding military theorists despite a lack of impressive credentials as wartime commanders. Their example suggests that a vigorous debate carried on in a collegial and constructive manner is essential to the furtherance of the military art.

## CONCLUSION

In this decade, budget realities and a rapidly changing strategic environment[18] place extreme pressures on the military services. A smaller, "poorer" military might not be able to squeeze much more performance out of the force without changing some of the rules. The time is right to take a hard look at ways to improve the capabilities of those forces that will survive the deep cuts that now appear inevitable.

It is natural to view the current organizational climate as a time of crisis. But it may also provide striking potential for positive change. Fundamentally, maneuver warfare is not about personalities or politics. It is about a better way to fight. It deserves mature consideration and reflection as we look at the defining challenges, and opportunities, that await us in the coming century.

# Notes

1. A partial list of well-known figures who comment on American preference for mass and firepower includes Weigley, Marshall, Hastings, Michaelis, Huntington, Fehrenbach, English, Hadley, Doughty, and Lind. J. F. C. Fuller was perhaps most outspoken in denouncing the American style of warfare as "ironmongery."

2. See Russell F. Weigley, *The American Way of War* (Bloomington, Ind.: Indiana University Press, 1977) and Robert A. Doughty, "The Evolution of U.S. Army Tactical Doctrine 1946–1976," *Leavenworth Papers No. 1* (Ft. Leavenworth, Kans.: U.S. Army Command and General Staff College, 1979).

3. *The Conduct of the Persian Gulf War* (Washington: Department of Defense, 1992) provides a good general overview of the Gulf War. The author also bases this conclusion on numerous interviews, personal conversations, and written correspondence with a large number of Army and Marine Corps officers from the grades of captain to lieutenant general. Analyses of tactical methods used in the Gulf War support the view that American emphasis on firepower and attrition is alive and well: "Maneuver commanders directed that when lead maneuver elements detected an Iraqi position, the artillery was to stop and plaster it with devastating fire. The object was to pound them to jelly . . ." Paul F. Pearson and Glenn K. Otis, "Desert Storm Fire Support," Association of the United States Army *Landpower Essay Series No. 91-2,* June 1991, p. 1.

4. "I saw the U.S. mass firepower better than any other nation in the world . . . maneuver merely got our firepower assets into position to annihilate the Iraqis, whether on the ground or during the preparatory air offensive—it's the American way—in spite of AirLand Battle Doctrine!" Letter from a field grade armor officer who participated in the Gulf War.

5. Carl Builder, *Masks of War* (Baltimore: Johns Hopkins University Press, 1989).

6. See John Foss, "Advent of the Nonlinear Battlefield: AirLand Battle-Future," Military Review (February 1991).

7. *Infantry in Battle* (Washington: The Infantry Journal Incorporated, 1939), p. 1.

8. William S. Lind and Col. Michael Wyly, *Maneuver Warfare Handbook* (Boulder, Colorado: Westview Press, 1985), p. 21.

9. Interview with Col. Giora Eiland, January 1986.

10. Samuel Huntington, "Playing to Win," *The National Interest* (Spring 1986).

11. FMFM 1, *Warfighting* (Washington, D.C.: Headquarters, U.S. Marine Corps, 1989), p. 28 (hereafter listed as FMFM 1).

12. FMFM 1, p. 73.

13. See Robert Leonhard's *Art of Maneuver* (Novato: Presidio Press, 1991), p. 120.

14. The Department of Defense official After Action Report for Desert Storm cites the following statement of Commander's Intent, published by Commander-in-Chief Central Command prior to the commencement of the offensive ground campaign: "Maximize friendly strength against Iraqi weakness and terminate offensive operations with the Republican Guard Forces destroyed and major U.S. forces controlling critical lines of communications in the Kuwaiti Theater of Operations." See *Conduct of the Persian Gulf War*, p. 317.

15. Interview with a British troop commander of the 17/21st Lancers detached for service with the British armored division in the Gulf War, 27 July 1991.

16. A number of field grade officers interviewed for this essay reported that in the Gulf their battalion commanders were unable to call for artillery fires, as fires were pre-planned or reserved for use at higher levels. See also Leonhard, p. 286: "From my own observations and my interviews with officers from the 3d Armored Division, 24th Mechanized Division, 1st Armored Division and 3d Armored Cavalry Regiment, battalions in battle had virtually no integrated fire support during the four-day operation."

17. The Military Reform Debate," *Final Proceedings: Senior Conference XX* (West Point: U.S. Military Academy, 1982), p. 37.

18. For a discussion of the shift in national security paradigms, see the author's "The Future of Conventional Deterrence," *Naval War College Review* (Summer 1992), with Ricky L. Waddell. See also *The National Security Strategy of the United States* (Washington, D.C.: U.S. Goverment Printing Office, 1991).

# The Strategic Setting

## Bruce B. G. Clarke

### INTRODUCTION

Washington's nervous breakdown may be the natural result of suddenly losing its sense of identity. After 45 years as freedom's champion in the cold war, it no longer seems to have much purpose in life. Europe, Japan and the rest of Asia are going their own way without us, and with disturbing success. Washington has been numbed by winning the cold war: powerless to rethink military policy, paralyzed by domestic problems.[1]

The author of this statement paints a grim future for the United States. He also highlights the critical strategic issue of today and this decade. What role does the United States wish to play in the years ahead? Does it wish to remain a global superpower with global responsibilities? This is the tough question that has Washington "numbed." Most pundits, in search for the elusive "peace dividend," are assuming superpower status will continue, in spite of the changes in the relative status of U.S. power. Colin S. Gray likened the current U.S. situation to the Byzantine Empire when he wrote:

When peace is not challenged, deterrence can seem to be easily achieved. Indeed, a society can come to believe that peace is its birthright. The 1990s are not the first period in history wherein the achievements of a generation of vigilance may be squandered. In 1025 . . . the Byzantine Empire was more secure than it had been for half a millennium. . . . Yet, forty six years later, the empire suffered a military defeat with such devastating consequences that it never truly recovered as a great power. What had happened?

Above all else, the politician-bureaucrats and intellectuals in Constantinople forgot that peace born of victory was both won very much by the sword, and could be protected only by the same.[2]

The purpose of this essay is to suggest a strategic enterprise and outline for the years ahead. This proposal is intended to have a synergistic effect with the essays in the rest of this book. A doctrine must support a strategy and the strategy must be reflected in the doctrine. This essay, then, is designed to set the strategic outlines that a doctrine of maneuver warfare should support. The subsequent sections of the book give more details on how to transition to a doctrine of maneuver warfare and provide examples of the concepts of maneuver warfare being applied.

In the process of highlighting the strategic enterprise that the United States must embark on, we will establish the *ends* that the United States should seek to achieve, discuss the *ways* that we should go about achieving these ends, and talk generally about *means* (resources).[3] The relationship of ends, ways, and means is, of course, the theoretical essence of strategy. (It must be remembered that both the relationship and the ends, ways, and means are the result of a political process.) Strategy has many levels of analysis. At the national level, national security strategy seeks to achieve U.S. goals (ends) through the synchronization and integration of foreign policy, defense policy, international economic policy, intelligence policy, and domestic policy. These policies are the ways, and the resources used are the means.

In the strategic debate following the Cold and Gulf wars, the focus has been on the military means. This debate began with President Bush's 1990 Aspen speech, where he said:

The decades-old division of Europe is ending—and the era of democracy building has begun. In Germany—the divided nation in the heart of a divided continent—unity is now assured, as a free and full member of the NATO alliance. The Soviet Union itself is in the midst of a political and economic transformation that has brought unprecedented openness—a process that is at once full of hope and full of uncertainty. . . . Our task today is to shape our defense capabilities to these changing strategic circumstances. In a world less driven by an immediate threat to Europe and the danger of global war—in a world where the size of our forces will be increasingly shaped by the needs of regional contingencies and peacetime presence—we know that our forces can be smaller.[4]

The only discussion of ways and ends in the Aspen speech was the following:

What we require now is a defense policy that adapts to the significant changes we are witnessing—without neglecting the enduring realities that will continue to shape our security strategy. A policy of peacetime engagement every bit as constant and committed to the defense of our interest and ideals in today's world as in the time of conflict and cold war.[5]

## THE PROJECTED INTERNATIONAL ENVIRONMENT

Many commentators today find it very difficult to even forecast the future, let alone develop a strategic vision.[6] The post–World War II paradigm, which was captured in NSC-68 (the 1950 document that encapsulated all of the elements of the containment strategy that the U.S. followed for 40 years), of a global struggle to contain communism and cause the Soviet Union to change has passed. Strategists and futurists alike are looking to the future through cloudy crystal balls. However, most will agree that forecasting the future based upon present trends suggests a world characterized by regional, secular, ethnic, and economic conflict that involves both states and groups with access to increasingly more sophisticated weapons.[7] Additionally, most agree that the future will be characterized by competition over resources, an erosion of sovereignty, and the creation of flexible coalitions. It is interesting to note that the United States' security partners are also its largest economic competitors and markets. This will be a subject of continuing debate as we seek to balance the economic and military aspects of our security strategy.

### Strategic Vision

In short, we have a forecasted future of regional, economic, social, and religious conflict and a vision defined by President Bush's October 1990 speech to the UN, where he said:

We have a vision of a new partnership of nations that transcends the Cold War; a partnership based on consultations, cooperation, and cooperative action, especially through international and regional organizations; a partnership united by principle and the rule of law supported by an equitable sharing of both cost and commitment. We should strike for greater effectiveness and efficiency of the United Nations. The United States is committed to playing its part in helping to maintain global security, promoting democracy and prosperity.

Relatedly, he said:

The civilized world is now in the process of fashioning the rules that will govern the new world order beginning to emerge in the aftermath of the Cold War.[8]

In his announcement of the commencement of hostilities in the Persian Gulf he said:

This is a historic moment. We have in the past year made great progress in ending the long era of conflict and cold war. We have before us the opportunity to forge for ourselves and for future generations a new world order, a world where the rule of law, not the law of the jungle, governs the conduct of nations.

When we are successful, and we will be, we have a real chance at this new world order, an order in which a credible United Nations can use its peacekeeping role to fulfill the promise and vision of the U.N.'s founders.[9]

Given previous-President George Bush's strategic vision of a new world order governed by the rule of law and policed by the United Nations, and minimal debate on it during the 1992 campaign, it is possible to outline a general strategy and to discuss some of the possible intermediate objectives that will need to be accomplished en route to the achievement of this strategic vision. There currently does not exist a domestic consensus on this vision, let alone an international consensus, in spite of the lack of discussion during the 1992 election campaign. However, the Clinton transition effort has not shown any significant variance with the ideas contained in the above quotes.

Henry Kissinger highlighted this point when he wrote:

> With few exceptions, all American leaders since Wilson have shared the propensity to disclaim national interest as their motivation. But is a disinterested foreign policy really a prerequisite for world leadership? Is there not a danger that other societies might perceive claims to disinterestedness as a subterfuge for unpredictability or as a blank check for capriciousness? We need not a disinterested foreign policy but a definition of national interest that commands consensus at home while accommodating the interests of other societies.[10]

However, the above vision of the future at least provides a start point for developing a strategy to achieve it, and thus to demonstrate how the tenets of maneuver warfare will have a synergistic effect with that strategy.

The basic strategy is one that seeks to develop and/or increase the power of the United Nations and related international organizations through legal, economic, political, and military means. To do this will require the achievement of numerous intermediate objectives. For analytical purposes these objectives fall into four general categories:

• organizational—those changes in international organizations to accommodate the increased frequency of conflict and the increased level of responsibility;
• political—those changes in how nations interact that allow the strengthened organizations to function;
• economic—those items, in addition to increased funding for international organizations, that will be necessary to accommodate and resolve the turmoil created by current international economic conditions; and,
• military—those actions necessary to ensure the availability of peace-enforcing and peacekeeping forces so as to enforce the rule of law that is envisioned.

Before beginning to describe some of the changes that one should anticipate or seek as we move toward this "new world order," a brief discussion of the importance of the outcome of the Persian Gulf conflict is in order. The fact that the allied forces in the Gulf conflict operated to fulfill a United Nations' mandate is of significant importance to the achievement of the new world order. Should the alliance have failed to enforce this mandate then the credibility of the U.N. would be very low. The alliance's success reinforces the United Nations' credibility that it will act with purpose. This success, it is felt, will deter others from similar types of behavior. Conversely, the inability to act decisively on Yugoslavia highlights the need for dynamic leadership during this period of transition between the Cold War and some future international system.

This highlights the dangerous nature of the next decade. The old world order is gone, and no stabilizing influence is fully engaged throughout the world. This suggests that the coming decade will be one characterized by uneven movement toward the following changes that seem to be the logical intermediate objectives as one moves from the present toward the ultimate strategic vision of a "new world order." It may require significant use of military power to achieve even these intermediate goals.

### Organizational Changes

A significant de facto increase in the power of the U.N. Security Council will mean an increase in the power of the five permanent members. Some derisively call the current arrangement "Pax Permanent Five."[11] With the growing power of other states, and the need to ensure representation of more of the geographic, economic, and religious sectors in this pluralist, multipolar world that we have envisioned, it seems natural that Germany, Argentina or Brazil, Japan, and possibly India should be added to the Security Council as permanent members. Given the difficulty in reaching unanimous consent of nine such diverse nations, there may need to be some method to prevent any one nation from preventing the U.N. from acting.

By necessity, the increased focus on the role of law implies an increase in the number and probably the type of cases to be handled by the World Court. This additional work load for the court implies an increase in the size of the court or the establishment of more than one court. One might even envision a system of regional adjudication bodies similar to the U.S. federal court system.

The involvement of the United Nations in an increased number of peace-enforcing and peacekeeping missions suggests that the U.N. Military

Staff Committee could take on added importance and responsibilities. This will become more evident in the section on military changes that will be necessary to achieve the above strategic vision.

The number and nature of the conflicts forecasted for the coming years could easily inundate the United Nations Security Council. In this light the establishment, reinvigoration or rechartering of such organizations as the Organization of American States (OAS), the Conference on Security and Cooperation in Europe (CSCE), or the Arab League become important. These organizations could work to resolve minor disputes between member states so as to reduce the number and type of conflicts that reach the U.N., or at least clearly define the problem so as to facilitate U.N. action.

## Economic Changes

The economic portion of the strategic vision is to increase global economic well-being by encouraging free trade—making the concept of comparative advantage work. To resolve international economic conflicts will require that the World Bank and other such organizations maintain their vitality. More importantly, however, the General Agreement on Tariffs and Trade (GATT), which is in its fourth year of unsuccessful negotiations, needs to be revitalized with the ultimate goal of eliminating protectionism. To lead in such an effort will require leverage that the U.S. economy alone may be unable to provide.[12]

## Political Changes

The most important political event that must occur is the surrendering of some sovereignty by the nations of the world. It is inconceivable that the above organizational changes can occur without nations making the tough political decisions necessary to surrender sovereignty to empower the World Court and the Security Council to act in lieu of the nations involved in a specific conflict. This is probably the largest impediment to achieving the above strategic vision.

The conclusion of regional and global arms control agreements is a critical part of the strategic vision. It is by means of such agreements that the intensity of future wars and the probability of surprise attacks will be reduced. The elimination of chemical weapons and limitations on nuclear weapons, and the delivery means of both, are examples of arms control agreements that will limit the intensity of future conflicts. To reduce the chances of surprise attacks, a regime of Confidence- and Security-Building Measures (CSBMs) that increases the transparency of activities within potential belligerents will be useful. The CSCE/CSBMs and the Conventional Forces Europe (CFE) agreement verification procedures may provide a start point and might be modified for other parts of the world.[13] Such agreements can be worked out either in the revitalized regional organizations or within the framework of the United Nations itself.

As mentioned, the size and operation of the United Nations Security Council will also have to be adjusted. This change, like most of the organizational changes stated above, will require political activity to bring about.

### Military Changes

There are obvious military implications to the arms control agreements mentioned above. However, for the foreseeable future it is impossible to imagine that nuclear deterrence will not continue to be an important part of the strategic mosaic—albeit one that we do not clearly understand. Deterrence of use of nuclear weapons by a splinter republic of the old USSR or a newly emerged nuclear state may not be the same as the nuclear deterrence that characterized the Cold War.

In the near term, it is hard to envisage nuclear weapons being allocated by any state to a U.N. peacekeeping or peace-enforcing force; however, as the number of renegade states that are not complying with the rule of law is reduced, it may become possible for all condoned nuclear weapons to be under the control of the United Nations. This would be a significant loss of independent action by a nation-state and should not be considered practical in the near term.

The most important military change will be the creation of what amounts to a U.N. military force for use in peacekeeping and peace-enforcing functions. Such a force would probably consist of forces earmarked by member states to participate on short notice in a U.N.– sponsored and supported military operation. Obviously, such a multilateral force would have numerous logistical, command and control, and doctrinal problems that would need to be worked out before the fact. (An international understanding of the tenets of maneuver warfare discussed in this book will be critical.) As mentioned, the U.N.

Military Staff Committee may need to be enlarged. Its main purpose would be to begin to work through all of the very complex tasks necessary to field and fight a true U.N. Corps. This concept may be key to U.S. acceptance of the entirety of the strategic vision. The American people will not support the United States providing 90 percent of every force sent abroad to enforce a United Nations' mandate. This also implies that nonparticipant states would incur some type of financial obligation.

As should be clear from the above discussion, there are numerous intermediate hurdles that need to be jumped en route to the strategic vision of a world where the rule of law predominates. This also means that there are numerous opportunities to go astray and trend toward a world of armed global pluralism where armed conflict is the norm.

All of the above discussion is an attempt to provide some structure to the end of "the new world order" and some ways that could be adopted to achieve the new world order. None of these ends or ways is uniformly accepted. This suggests a distinct disconnect between ends, ways, and means. We have some lofty goals, some fuzzy ways to achieve them, and we are reducing our military means before our economy is fully recovered or our political problems fully addressed.

## AN ALTERNATIVE APPROACH

While the United States decides what role it seeks to play and develops a strategy to replace the strategy of containment, it should take a conservative, go-slow approach to military force reductions. Failure to do so without a corresponding increase in political or economic power could place us in the position of the Byzantine Empire—we would have given up our one true claim to superpower status before we had an opportunity to develop an alternative source of power. We must maintain our options while we decide whether the above "new world order" and the intermediate objectives are truly desirable.

Whether the United Nations seeks to expand its peace-enforcing role in the future is, at this writing, academic. In the near term, while the U.S. seeks to develop a new strategic consensus and then move to achieve it, it is necessary not to give up the ability to fight as part of a coalition to protect U.S. interests and maintain global stability. This suggests that our near-term national security strategy should have the following components:

• Using extended conventional and nuclear deterrence to prevent armed aggression against the U.S., its allies, and friends. Should that deterrence fail, be able to fight as part of a coalition to at least restore the status quo, and more likely, to remove the source of the conflict.

• Using whatever leverage we might have, continue efforts to achieve the international economic and political goals and stability described above. These include:

  • A healthy and growing economy
  • A stable and maturing set of alliance relationships
  • A reduction in global terrorism
  • A reduction in the flow of drugs
  • A reduction in weapons proliferation

• Simultaneous with this "strategic delay,"[14] the U.S. would apply and focus its domestic energy on the causes of domestic inefficiency so that we can once again compete in the international arena.

## National Military Strategy

In furtherance of the above national security strategy we should posture ourselves in a manner that will allow economic recovery within the United States without eliminating our ability to influence events by the use of military force. Nuclear deterrence is critical to this effort. However, this may not mean deterrence by means of ICBMs and SLBMs. In a proliferated, regional, nuclear environment, other delivery means may be more credible. The dilemma of regional nuclear deterrence is that different delivery means may be more credible in different situations depending upon targets, locations, threat level, etc. Additionally, in an era of sophisticated conventional munitions, we may be able to substitute conventional weapons to accomplish nuclear missions.[15] This concept further demonstrates the dilemma of regional deterrence— we can destroy the requisite targets using conventional munitions, but conventional weapons do not have the requisite psychological impact to achieve a deterrent effect. In the realm of extended conventional deterrence, some have argued that the concept failed its first test— Iraq invaded Kuwait. One study argues that this was the result of a series of "barriers to signalling" that in essence suggests that Saddam Hussein did not believe that the U.S. could or would intervene.[16] Adoption of a maneuver warfare doctrine that has a decisive intent may be one way of signalling the seriousness of our conventional deterrent.

If extended deterrence fails, Secretary Weinberger's six points or tests[17] should continue to guide the employment of conventional military forces. In abiding by his points, we are driven to a doctrine of maneuver warfare that seeks to exploit an enemy's weaknesses by maneuvering to attack his decisive point/center of gravity. In this regard, we should develop "victory criteria" for any conflict we are going to be involved in.[18] In short, victory is achieved when one successfully defends his own center of gravity while simultaneously successfully attacking his opponent's, at least indirectly, with the result being that he changes the objectives that he initially sought in the conflict. The exact nature of both sides' centers of gravity is situation-dependent.

### Theater Military Strategy

It is at the theater level, as part of a coalition, that the precepts of maneuver warfare are the most applicable. In this regard, we should plan for four phases to such a conflict:

• The defense phase, in which primarily indigenous forces are defending against a potential aggressor, and the United States is using political and economic efforts while conducting a military show of force to dissuade or deter the aggressor from beginning offensive military operations.
• The defense and lodgment phase, in which a joint U.S. or host nation force is defending while the United States builds its forces and targets with the appropriate element of power the group that can change the opponent's objectives.
• The offense phase, in which attacks are conducted, not necessarily against the opposing force but against the opponent's strategy and its political center of gravity as it has been translated onto the battlefield.[19]
• The termination phase, in which hostilities may continue, but political actions are begun to terminate the conflict. At the end of this phase, civil-military activities to consolidate the victory and preclude future hostilities will be occurring.

In the near term we need to structure our military to be capable of conducting such coalitional maneuver warfare efforts. If we do this, we will have enhanced our ability to deter regional conflicts.

The concepts of maneuver warfare are critical to the third phase of any coalitional effort and are in perfect consonance with Secretary Weinberger's six tests. Most importantly, if these concepts are applied, as mentioned here, they will lead to decisive results and, as long as casualties are low and the hostilities short, the public will support the endeavor. These, of course, are the goals of maneuver warfare.

## CONCLUSION

The concepts of maneuver warfare discussed in the subsequent sections of this work are doctrinally critical if the U.S. is to be a responsible actor on the international scene, not only during this period of transition, but also in the coming pluralistic international system that may be the "new world order."

In the near term, as we conduct a "strategic delay"[20] to arrive at a strategic consensus on the U.S.'s role in the world, we must structure and train our military to be quickly decisive. We must also not take any precipitous actions that would preclude future strategic options. Once a strategic consensus is reached on the meaning of the new world order we can revise our strategies and doctrines to accommodate the desired future.

# Notes

1. Editorial, *The Patriot*, Harrisburg, Penn., 4 November 1991.
2. Colin S. Gray, *War, Peace and Victory* (New York: Simon and Schuster, 1990).
3. Col. Arthur F. Lykke (ret.), *Military Strategy: Theory and Application* (United States Army War College, 1989), p. 3.

We can express this concept as an equation: Strategy equals *Ends* (objectives towards which one strives) plus *Ways* (courses of action) plus *Means* (instruments by which some end can be achieved). This general concept can be used as a basis for the formulation of any type strategy—military, political, economic, etc., depending upon the element of national power employed.

We should not confuse military strategy with national (grand) strategy, which may be defined as:

> The art and science of developing and using the political, economic, and psychological powers of a nation, together with its armed forces, during peace and war, to secure national objectives.

Military strategy is one part of this all-encompassing national strategy. The military component of our national strategy is sometimes referred to as national military strategy—military strategy at its highest level, and differentiated from operational strategies used as the basis for military planning and operations. Military strategy must support national strategy and comply with national policy, which is defined as a broad course of action or statements of guidance adopted by the government at the national level in pursuit of national objectives. In turn, national policy is influenced by the capabilities and limitations of military strategy.

With our general concept of strategy as a guide—*Strategy* equals *Ends plus Ways plus Means*—we can develop an approach to military strategy.

"Ends" can be expressed as military objectives. "Ways" are concerned with the various methods of applying military force. In essence this becomes an examination of courses of action designed to achieve the military objective. These courses of action are termed military strategic concepts.

"Means" refers to the military resources (manpower, materiel, money, forces, logistics, etc.) required to accomplish the mission. This leads us to the conclusion that *Military Strategy equals Military Objectives plus Military Strategic Concepts plus Military Resources.* The conceptual approach is applicable to all three levels of war: strategic, operational, and tactical. It also reveals the fundamental similarities among national military strategy, operational art, and tactics. Strategists, planners, corps commanders and squad leaders are *all* concerned with *ways* to employ *means* to achieve *ends.*

The above is quoted with the permission of Colonel Lykke and the USAWC.

4. George Bush, "Transforming the U.S. Security Environment," *The Aspen Institute Quarterly* 2, no. 4 (Autumn 1990), p. 12.

5. *Ibid.,* p. 13.

6. Strategic vision is a much-used and barely understood concept. The reader will see the term used in this paper as the decision maker's view of what the state of affairs should be following hostilities or at some time in the distant future. Col. Dave Jablonsky's December 1991 *Parameters* piece "Strategic Vision in the Post Cold-War Era," pp. 2-3, draws on some of my work and argues that strategic vision can occur when we combine the outlook of the prophet with the authority of the politician, and the result is the statesman at the national level capable of providing strategic vision.

7. John Lewis Gaddis, "Toward the Post–Cold War World," *Foreign Affairs* (Spring 1991). Gaddis argues that the post–Cold War world will be characterized by competing processes—integration versus fragmentation. John J. Mearsheimer, "Why We Will Soon Miss the Cold War," *The Atlantic,* August 1990: pp. 35-37, 40-42, 44-47, 50. Mearsheimer argues that we may come to lament the loss of order that the Cold War gave to the anarchy of international relations. He argues that the prospects of major crises, even wars, in Europe is likely to increase dramatically now that the Cold War is receding into history.

8. George Bush, U.N. speech, October 1990.

9. George Bush, television address, 16 January 1991.

10. Henry Kissinger, "What Kind of New World Order?" *Washington Post,* 3 December 1991, p. A21.

11. Recent interviews with U.N. representatives of several nations noted varying views on this concept. Those who felt that their views were fairly represented by the current permanent five saw the situation as acceptable, while those not so represented were fearful of the consequences of the permanent five cooperating.

12. There are numerous references to the state of the U.S. economy. William Pfaff in his article "Redefining World Power" argues that a superpower is

strong militarily, politically and economically. The United States and the Soviet Union, with the end of the rivalry of the bipolar world, have lost superpower status. The Soviet Union is in economic and political decomposition and is more dangerous for it. The United States remains the world's most important military power, but is faltering economically and technologically. The need now is for the U.S. to look inward to the true national challenge. From *Foreign Affairs,* "America and the World," 1990/1991, pp. 34–48.

13. Catherine M. Kelleher, "Arms Control in a Revolutionary Future: Europe," *Daedalus* 120, no. 1 (Winter 1991), Cambridge, Mass. Professor Kelleher argues that the building of a new European security system will be the first test for a new, expanded concept of positive arms control.

14. The term "strategic delay" is meant to imply a time-buying strategy where we grudgingly give up power in the international arena in exchange for time—time to develop a new strategic consensus on the future U.S. role in the world.

15. James Blackwell et al., *The Gulf War: Military Lessons Learned* (Washington, D.C.: Center for Strategic and International Studies, 1991), Chapter VI.

16. *Ibid.,* p. 49.

17. Casper W. Weinberger, "The Uses of Military Power," *Defense '85,* January 1985, pp. 2–11.

18. Bruce B.G. Clarke, "Conflict Termination: A Rational Model," Strategic Studies Institute, May 1991, pp. 11-16. The thrust of this paper is that we need to determine how to induce either the leader or some chosen political group in the opponent's government to change that nation's objectives so that the source of the conflict is eliminated; then take actions that cause that faction to have both the desire and power to cause that change in objectives to occur. The above analysis suggests that victory will result from the successful defense of one's own political and military centers of gravity combined with action that, at least indirectly, attacks the opponent's center(s) of gravity with the result being that he changes his objectives.

19. I used the same phases in several critiques of AirLand Battle-Future. In letters to the editor of *Military Review,* October 1991, "Victory Criteria," and *Armor,* January 1992, I argued that emerging U.S. Army doctrine was totally flawed because:

• It did not reflect the coalitional nature of future conflicts that the U.S. might be involved in.

• It did not reflect a "victory criteria"—what it meant to win.

• It is parochial in nature.

• It is focused on the corps level.

20. See note 14.

# The Operational Art: Quo Vadis?

## James McDonough

What is the future of operational art? The answer lies in the directions that strategy will take. Where strategy goes, so go the operational concepts to serve it. Those operational concepts will most likely include more than combat or combat-related events. Operational art, after all, is more than just the tying together of wartime activities. Put another way, there is more to campaigning than the proper sequencing of a series of battles or tactical engagements. It includes all major actions, usually joint (meaning that more than a single military service or government agency is involved) and often combined (meaning several nations), that lead to the attainment of strategic objectives. Those actions may or may not take place under conditions of war. They are more likely these days to occur across the spectrum of peace, crisis, and war. Their commonality and their place in operational art is fixed by their focused pursuit of strategic objectives.

The first step, therefore, in divining the directions operational art should take is understanding the strategic environment. The second is understanding the strategic guidance received from appropriate higher authority. If the second step is missing, the first becomes more important. In a perfect world, one would expect that the strategic guidance would always be forthcoming and that it would precede the operational concepts; the latter, in turn, would precede the design of force structure. Ends, ways, and means could then be put together to attain national objectives. But this is not a perfect world. Seldom does it work that cleanly. The North Atlantic Treaty Organization, in light of the sudden dissolution of the Warsaw Pact and the withdrawal of Soviet forces from Europe, felt compelled in 1990 to revise its strategy. Forward defense and flexible response, which had sufficed to hold together the alliance for over twenty years while deterring an often-aggressive and always imposing Soviet military force, no longer seemed appropriate.

But prior to the completion of the strategy review process, political imperatives dictated that operational concepts and force structures be determined. The danger of the erosion of military commitment by alliance members was so great that structure had to be affixed even before consensus on purpose was reached. During the same time frame, the United States began to review its own strategic concepts. A "new world order," as articulated by the president, became its guiding principle.[1] But undefined and undeveloped, it led to uncertainty at every level as to how to structure to its end. Simultaneously, the Joint Chiefs of Staff offered a unified command plan that sought to bring order to the extensive reduction of military forces, a process momentarily interrupted by the Gulf War. In both NATO and Pentagon offices, operational concepts were preceding the solidification of strategy.

For the United States, the inability to predict with any precision the strategic background in which its military will operate is nothing new. General George Washington continually revised his strategy during the Revolutionary War to reflect the capabilities of his resources.[2] Eighty-five years later, President Lincoln was forced to wait until the right general emerged to affix a strategy and a follow-through to bring the Civil War to a successful conclusion. In the 1930s, we approached World War II with a series of plans—each of them color-coded so that together they became known as the "Rainbow Plans"—that projected one nation or another as enemy.[3] In the end, we had to pick the two plans that dealt with Germany and Japan and blend them into a national, and later a coalition, strategy. At other times, we have lacked the prescience to have even a generalized contingency plan. We were surprised by the suddenness of the Korean conflict and drifted into the complexity of Vietnam in the early and middle 1960s.

Nonetheless, operational art must begin with the definition of strategic objectives. The U.S. Army's central doctrine for warfighting, for example, states, "Operational planning begins with strategic guidance to the theater commander."[4] In the course of a single conflict, military men would like the objectives to be steadfast, but that may not always be the case. The strategic environment can change, as it did in Korea when the Chinese entered the war in November of 1950. Or the political support can change, as it did in Vietnam after the Tet offensive of 1968. One of the advantages to coalition forces in the Gulf War of 1990–1991 was the constancy of the stated strategic objectives. As the President of the United States originally put them, they were to:

1. get Iraqi forces out of Kuwait
2. restore Kuwait's legitimate government
3. achieve security and stability in the region
4. protect the lives of American citizens[5]

With such directness, planning could proceed along clear lines.

Whatever the nature of the strategic guidance, the operational level commander seeks to establish the military conditions within his theater of war or theater of operations that lead to the accomplishment of strategic objectives. Since those strategic objectives and theaters exist in a variety of patterns, concepts of operational art must be broad enough to apply to any one of them, yet specific enough to provide direction in their application.

Given that every campaign—whether it pertains to an environment of peace, crisis, or war, or any mixture thereof—is unique, the question arises as to whether an overarching operational concept can be of any use. The answer is yes, provided that the operational concept makes it clear above all else that the solution—usually referred to as the campaign plan, but applied as the operational art—must be thought through relative to the conditions in which it will apply.

Whether we label them principles, precepts, verities, or imperatives, no sets of guides can be blindly prescribed. Well-reasoned thoughts reduced to lists have the seductive appeal of simple truths, when in reality, no truths are simple. None exists in isolation from others; each contains the seeds of its own dialectic.

In 1983 Huba Wass de Czege wrote a chapter for the book, *The Defense Reform Debate*, that argued there could be no easy formulas for achieving victory in our nation's wars.[6] At that time, he was a lieutenant colonel in the U.S. Army tasked to write that service's central warfighting doctrine. The piece he produced (with the backing and wisdom of several senior military officers) was eventually to become known as the strangely spelled "AirLand Battle Doctrine." Eight years and one rewrite of FM 100-5 later, it would be applied in Panama and the Persian Gulf with dramatic success.

Yet the caution he sounded in 1983 still applies today. There are no simple formulas. Each war—indeed, each crisis—is unique unto itself. Certain principles apply, but the varying options for their implementation are limitless. Put together correctly, the chances for operational and strategic success rise; put together incorrectly, the chances for success plummet. There are no guarantees. Selection, analysis, and decision take place in an environment of uncertainty. Risk, ever defiant of precise measurement, lurks in every corner.

In the aftermath of what seemed an easy victory in the Gulf, some would forget Wass de Czege's note of caution. It all seemed so easy. In the blink of an eye, coalition forces—led by the United States, following its plan, and dominated by its strength—routed the world's fourth largest army, destroyed or neutralized a modern air force, and nullified a regional naval power. The cost in friendly casualties was mercifully low, much less than even the most optimistic estimates. It was war as any military would like to fight it: quick, overwhelming, decisive, and virtually (relatively speaking) painless for the victors.

There is danger in all of this, however. If we are not careful, we could succumb to the temptation to believe that we have arrived at a solution, that we do indeed have a formula for success. In a changing world such complacency could prove disastrous.

Doctrine, after all, is dynamic. It must be reflective of constantly changing strategic and tactical environments, and the operational art, whose job it is to connect the two, must be responsive to these changes.

Tactics, for example, are affected by pivotal changes in technology. During the American Civil War, the development of the rifled musket led to the prevalence of entrenchments and the dispersion of military formations. By the time of the Boer War, smokeless powder and the consequent invisibility of the defender made massed infantry assault and the cavalry charge virtually suicidal.[7] During World War I, the advent of barbed wire and the machine gun led to the dominance of defense, while the introduction of the tank in the latter part of that war, and the refinement of its capabilities in the years that followed, led to the resurgence of the offense—the latter not recognized by the French until 1940, much to their regret.[8]

So too in the Gulf War did technology have its effect on tactics. Iraqi air forces were severely disadvantaged by their air-to-air tactical doctrine, which mandated ground control and a necessity to come at the opponent from behind. Coalition air, on the other hand, completely negated any advantage Iraq may have gained from interior lines. On the ground, the greater ranges and mobility of Western armored and artillery forces, combined with superior tactical doctrine and training, turned battlefield engagements into a coalition-dominated exploitation.

Nor is it ever a simple case of technology driving tactics. Sometimes tactical—and operational—doctrine drives technology. Usually, it is a mixture of both, an endless chicken-and-egg relationship that leaves one wondering which came first. In the inter-war years, navies at first resisted the impact of technology on sea operations, then pursued new technologies avidly when it was perceived what advantages could be gained.[9] So too did air power advocates of the 1930s go after the technologies that allowed them to validate their theories during World War II.[10]

As Chris Bellamy put it in the conclusion to his *The Future of Land Warfare*, war is a series of complex interactions:

> We have seen the stretch of air-land operations, their greater intensity and cost, thus making war even more total, the intermingling of these operations with those at sea, in the upper air and in cosmic space and their absolute dependence on the latter, not least because of the need for over the horizon target acquisition. All this may well mean that in the Western theatre, major "air-land warfare" as a discrete phenomenon has, in at least two senses, spaced itself out of existence.[11]

Bellamy's view of air-land warfare as passé in the "Western theatre" (meaning, in this sense, the European area) may be premature. The partition of Yugoslavia and the breakup of the Soviet Union may yet lead to some application of force requiring air, land, and sea forces to resolve crises and settle disputes. But his admonition that warfare is complex deserves heeding. As we develop the operational art, we must avoid simplistic prescriptions that promise more than they can deliver. Above all, we will need balance.

For example, maneuver warfare, while an important component of the operational art, cannot exist devoid of its counterpart—firepower. We maneuver in order to bring fire on the enemy. We bring fire on the enemy so that we can maneuver. One should not happen—indeed *could* not happen—without the other. To assert there is a "maneuverist school" with superior theoretical views is to imply there is a "firepower school" (usually labeled a "firepower-based attrition warfare school") with inherently inferior ideas. As Wass de Czege said in his defense of AirLand Battle at West Point in August 1982 (two months before the publication of the 1982 FM 100-5), it is a false dichotomy.[12]

Over the years, the notion of maneuver warfare has moved to a dominant position in our operational concepts. In 1949, the U.S. Army *Field Service Regulation* (the forerunner of the later, less prescriptive, *Field Manual*) stated, "Maneuver in itself can produce no decisive results, but if properly employed it makes decisive results possible through the application of the principles of the offensive, mass, economy of force, and surprise." By the 1954 edition that had been changed to read, "Maneuver must be used to alter the relative combat power of military forces." Further strengthening appeared in 1962 and 1968 when the appropriate passage began, "Maneuver is an essential ingredient of combat power" and in 1982 with the statement "Maneuver is the dynamic element of combat . . . the effect created by maneuver is the first element of combat power." But by 1986, FM 100-5 attempted to temper the zeal with which maneuver was described while taking the concept a step further: "Maneuver occurs at both the operational and tactical levels . . . operational maneuver seeks a decisive impact on the conduct of a campaign . . . tactical maneuver seeks to set the terms of combat in a battle or engagement." At a later point in the manual, it went on to add, "At all levels, successful application of this principle requires not only fire and movement, but also flexibility of thought, plans, and operations, and the considered application of the principles of mass and economy of force."[13]

Despite this official attempt to balance the views on maneuver, attachment to the concept as if it were the Holy Grail of land warfare advanced unabated into the '90s, distinguished in some circles by its capitalization as "Maneuver Warfare,"[14] an almost mystical beknighting (via English grammar) of an otherwise perfectly common—and useful—concept. It is well to remember that while maneuver is a vital element of both tactical- and operational-level warfare—and therefore of the operational art—it is not the sole criterion of success. It is a part of the whole complex web of warfare that must be applied intelligently, or not applied as the case may be.

In his foreword to the Richard Simpkin book, *Race to the Swift*, Gen. Donn Starry asks the rhetorical question, "What does win?" His answer:

> By far the majority of winners in battle in which the beginning force ratios were generally within . . . "reasonable" limits . . . were those who somehow seized the initiative from the enemy, and held it to battle's end. Most often the initiative was successfully seized and held by maneuver. This seems to be true whether defending or attacking, outnumbered or outnumbering.[15]

The idea is that maneuver is important, but only insofar as it seizes the initiative. The latter is the essential ingredient of success in warfare. One is reminded that ends, ways, and means should never be confused.

If maneuver is not an end in itself, neither is nonlinearity. While nonlinear operations may open up opportunities in a theater of operations allowing for integrated and mutually supporting activities in space and time,[16] linear operations will still be needed. If large ground formations (e.g., divisions, corps, and above) must retain the flexibility to move to decisive points in theater and on the battlefield rapidly, other units must be capable of linear operations. Battalions and brigades, for example, will often be compelled to take up linear formations in both the attack and defense. Logistical units, when pressed to any degree by a determined enemy, may find it necessary to seek safety behind well-established lines. Although it is true that operational-level maneuver—whether it be U.S. Grant encircling Vicksburg or H. Norman Schwarzkopf left-hooking to the Euphrates—requires a boldness free of the shackles of fixed lines, we must be cognizant of the need for integrated operations and their sustainment. Field Marshal (Viscount) Slim, the reconquerer of Burma in 1944 and as fine a practitioner of operational art as any produced in World War II, found it imperative to pull the corps of his 14th Army back to the Imphal-Kohima plain in order to consolidate his lines, establish a continuous front, and draw the Japanese into a disadvantageous battle before retaking a bold, nonlinear offensive that eventually drove his enemy to precipitous defeat.[17] His genius for the operational art was reflected in his wise selection of a mixture of linear and nonlinear operations put together in such a manner as to gain and retain the initiative and eventually produce victory.

The history of militaries and their attendant doctrines shows an unfortunate tendency to tip too far in one direction or another when incorporating operational concepts. "Offense à la outrance" was the battle cry of the French army in 1914 as it charged forth to be swallowed whole (almost) by the juggernaut of the German Schlieffen Plan. The French military (and political) leaders of that era were still smarting from the humiliation they had received at the hands of the Prussians in their 1870–71 war. Never again, or so they said, would they remain on the defensive. Sedan and Metz had taught them the futility of such initiative-lacking operations. With a misguided zeal they preached the maxim of the offensive—to the brink of their ruin only one month into the Great War.

From his vantage point in Arabia, Lt. Col. T. E. Lawrence reflected on the military's infatuation with bold ideas to the point of excess. After the war, he wrote, "Napoleon had spoke in angry reaction against the excessive finesse of the eighteenth century, when men almost forget that war gave license to murder. We had been swinging out on his dictum for a hundred years, and it was time to come back again."[18]

His analogy is apt—"swinging out." The pendulum of military thought tends to pick up a momentum of its own and flies well beyond the balance point before it catches itself. In the past decade or so, American concepts of operational art have become infatuated with offense. The defense-dominated FM 100-5 of 1976 (labeled the "Active Defense") gave way in turn to the offensive-minded AirLand Battle of the 1982 and 1986 versions of FM 100-5. By spring of 1991, the U.S. Army was developing an operational concept that barely managed to mention the word "defense" once or twice in its entirety.[19]

But there can be no offense without a defense. Each contains within it elements of the other. "The defense is a shield of blows," said Clausewitz, who, by the way, believed that defense was the stronger form of war. And at different levels of war, various combinations of offense and defense might apply. Rommel in the North African desert sought every opportunity to take the operational offensive, but he always endeavored thereby to seize terrain that would force his enemies to attack him and from which he could defend tactically at some advantage. Von Manstein on the Russian front, viewed by many as the greatest German operational genius of World War II, was on the operational defensive from 1943 on, but he never failed to regain the initiative by launching lightning tactical attacks that threw his enemy off balance.

Warfare is like that, a mixture of ever reforming combinations: attack and defense, maneuver and firepower, linearity and nonlinearity, mass and economy of force, simplicity and surprise, command and initiative, centralization and decentralization. Though more art than science, the operational level of war demands a rigor of calculation. Correlation of forces, firepower densities, rates of supply, march tables, portages, lift tonnages, load cubes, weapons' probabilities of kill, unit personnel strengths, state of training, and maintenance readiness are all important considerations for the operational planner. But measurements by themselves are meaningless. It takes creative initiative to incorporate all of the details and data while seeing the larger possibilities beyond.

Beware the simple solutions. In the aftermath of the Gulf War, the Center for Strategic and International Studies put out a crisp analysis of the major lessons learned. The strategic and political insights reflected well-reasoned views of the study's panel of experts. In commenting on the changed nature of war, however, the conclusion was that linear warfare was a relic of the past, a World War II anachronism that could find no intelligent place in the modern world.[20]

We need to ask ourselves, "Is that so?" No doubt the world is changing—and with it the techniques of warfare. But there is always a balance point. Error—and the concomitant potential for disaster—lurks on either side of it. To change too much can be as dangerous as not to change at all.

And if warfare has always been that way, the future promises to make it even more complex and less predictable. There will be rapidly changing technologies, continually surprising us with their rate of advance. The strategy itself is changing.[21] While deterrence will remain a prime objective, it will be complemented by the notion of "compellance," which is a word not to be found in the dictionary but is taken to mean for any others to do your will. Forward defense will be replaced by power projection, a capability dependent on the ability to introduce our forces quickly anywhere in the world. This predisposes the need to operate in joint, interagency, and combined formations. Military forces will be asked to pursue national objectives in an environment of peace, crisis, and war. No single service will be sufficient to the task. It will take intelligent combinations to resource the operational art adequately, and it will take study, analysis, and creativity to develop the right operational campaigns.

Attainment of national strategic objectives will remain the fundamental task of operational art. As these objectives are set in environments other than strictly defined wars, the operational-level considerations must be expanded to deal with them. Considerations heretofore ignored, such as the resolution of crises and the reestablishment of peace, must enter into the campaign plan. An endgame design that goes beyond the cessation of hostilities seems to be at the moment a lost art. Both in Panama and Iraq, otherwise brilliant campaigns were marked by the need for improvisation once hostilities ceased. It was almost as if the American military expected that once the last shot was fired, its job was done. This proved not to be the case in either event.

Should the United States find itself involved in a long-term crisis—as could be the case in Yugoslavia—its military will have to think through the entire range of operational-level options. For one thing, there may be a significant difference between peacemaking and peacekeeping. The former implies at least some application of force, if only to separate the hostile parties. This may range from conventional armies and air forces to irregular forces. Simultaneously, one could envision a need for air-land-sea operations that developed a conventional military campaign, while a parallel campaign sought to bring a guerrilla, terrorist, or civil war—or aspects of all three—under control.

Cessation of hostilities in the one area may not bring peace in the other. Nor would complete termination of hostilities promise to be a permanent condition. Peacemaking could quickly transition to peacekeeping, an activity that might imply a long-term presence.

Are we prepared for that? The current wisdom appears to say no. At the moment, our national military strategy envisions short-term contingencies and judges the probability of protracted commitment to troubled spots of U.S. forces to be slight.[22] In times of shrinking military resources, this may be wishful thinking. At the turn of the last century, similar theories of short wars abounded.[23] Campaigns at Königgrätz in 1866 and at Sedan and Metz in 1871 brought hostilities quickly to an end. The costs of mobilized armies to industrialized nations were seen as prohibitive. The argument went that none of the advanced nations of the world—who so desperately needed their manpower to keep the factories producing—could afford the consequences of a long-term war. Even the anomaly of the Boer War was explained away as the exception that proved the rule. Few public spokesmen, such as the Polish banker Ivan Bloch,[24] were bold enough to make contrary predictions. The few, of course, were right, and the many were wrong. When war came in 1914, it seemed to recognize no limits of time, blood, or wealth.

As the premier world power of the age, the U.S. cannot afford operational concepts that are presumptuous. We in the military sometimes evince a degree of arrogance. Since we have enjoyed air superiority in all of our wars, we continue to expect we will be unimpeded in our control of the skies. Since our sea lines of communications have not been interrupted since World War II, we merely consider the bottoms needed, portages available, and distances involved in order to calculate logistics possibilities. We do not concern ourselves with the possibility of interdiction. And since our last three interventions have been short-lived, we expect more of the same in the future.

But, of course, all this optimism may be ill-placed. Our enemies may get smarter; they may show greater determination. Or the problems themselves just might be thornier. It would be wise for the military to remember that, in the end, the U.S. military does not pick its fights. It goes where it is sent. Nowhere in former Secretary of Defense Casper Weinberger's six principles does it read that the U.S. military must agree to its commitment.[25]

That brings us back to where we began. The operational art must be able to achieve the nation's strategic objective. That is its sole purpose. It must do that in conditions of peace, crisis, and war. And it will be able to do that not by the application of preordained formulas, but by a keen appreciation of the conditions at hand and the possibilities available in developing the right campaign design. This calls for a mastery of the fundamentals and the creative genius to put them together in innovative, successful patterns. Further, operational art must retain balance. Its practice will become increasingly complex, yet will not cause abandonment of well-established principles. Future warfare must be both offensive and defensive in nature, combining firepower with maneuver into both linear and nonlinear battle and major operations to retain initiative, reach decisive victory, and achieve strategic objectives. That is the future—and the past—of operational art.

# Notes

1. The U.S. military's attempt to refine a strategy built up steam during late 1990 and early 1991. The J-5 of the Joint Chiefs of Staff, then Lt. Gen. Lee Butler, gave a public airing of his views first to the National Press Club in September and finally, before moving on to his job as Commander in Chief, Strategic Air Command, to the Air Force Academy in early March. The Chairman, Gen. Colin Powell, explained his views before the Senate Armed Services Committee on 21 February 1991. Within ten days of his testimony, Operation Desert Storm had both begun and ended. In late July of 1991, a working paper entitled "United States National Military Strategy for the 1990s and Beyond" was forwarded for coordination, and in August the President published his "National Security Strategy of the United States."

2. David Palmer, *The Way of the Fox* (Westport, Conn.: Greenwood, 1975).

3. Louis Morton, "Germany First: The Basic Concept of Allied Strategy in World War II," *Command Decisions*, ed. Kent Roberts Greenfield (Washington, D.C.: Office of the Chief of Military History, United States Army, 1960), pp. 11-47.

4. U.S. Army, FM 100-5, *Operations* (Washington, D.C.: U.S. Government Printing Office, 1986), p. 28.

5. President George Bush, televised address, 8 August 1990. See *U.S. State Department Dispatches*, 3 September 1990, p. 52.

6. Huba Wass de Czege, "Army Doctrinal Reform," in Asa Clark et al., *The Defense Reform Debate* (Baltimore: The Johns Hopkins University Press, 1984), pp. 101–120.

7. James J. Schneider, "The Theory of the Empty Battlefield," *RUSI*, September 1987, pp. 37–44.

8. For an excellent discussion of the doctrinal and tactical failures of the French in the era see Robert A. Doughty's *The Seeds of Disaster* (Hamden, Conn.: Archon Books, 1985) and *Breaking Point* (Hamden, Conn.: Archon Books, 1990).

9. Trevor N. Dupuy, *The Evolution of Weapons and Warfare* (Fairfax, VA: Hero Books), pp. 202–212.

10. Ibid., pp. 240–252.

11. Chris Bellamy, *The Future of Land Warfare* (London: Routledge, 1990), pp. 299–300.

12. Wass de Czege, op. cit., Clark et al., *Defense Reform Debate*.

13. FM 100-5, pp. 12, 175.

14. Capt. Richard D. Hooker, Jr., "Redefining Maneuver Warfare," *Military Review,* February 1992.

15. Richard Simpkin, *Race to the Swift* (London: Brassey's Defense Publishers, 1985), p. x.

16. U.S. Army, TRADOC Pam 525-5, *AirLand Operations* (Washington D.C.: U.S. Government Printing Office, 1991), p. 15.

17. Viscount Field Marshal Slim, *Defeat Into Victory* (London: Macmillan Publishers Limited, 1987).

18. T. E. Lawrence, "The Evolution of a Revolt," *Army Quarterly and Defense Journal,* October 1920.

19. TRADOC Pam 525-5.

20. James Blackwell et al., *The Gulf War: Military Lessons Learned* (Washington, D.C.: Center for Strategic and International Studies, 1991), p. 11.

21. Lt. Gen. Lee Butler, USAF, J-5, Joint Chiefs of Staff, address to U.S. Air Force Academy, Colorado Springs, Colo., March 1991.

22. Steven J. Argersinger, "Peacekeeping, Peace Enforcement, and the United States," U.S. Army War College paper, May 1991.

23. Geoffrey Blainey, *The Causes of War* (New York: The Free Press, 1978), pp. 206–227.

24. Ivan Bloch, "The Future of War," *The Contemporary Review*, September 1901.

25. Casper Weinberger, speech to the National Press Club, Washington, D.C., November 28, 1984. Reprinted in *Defense*, January, 1985, pp. 2–11.

# Maneuver Warfare and Low-Intensity Conflict

## Ricky L. Waddell

Maneuver warfare is a contentious issue precisely because it defies easy definition and easy understanding. It is more misunderstood than understood. The same can be said for low-intensity conflict (LIC). If maneuver warfare is a thought process that applies across the spectrum of conflict, as some suggest, how does it apply to LIC?

This essay will focus on some of the definitional controversies concerning maneuver warfare and LIC with the object of identifying the salient points of each. Next, I will apply the key concepts of maneuver warfare to some aspects of LIC at the strategic, operational, and tactical levels. The concept that maneuver warfare is a thought process that seeks to pose our strengths against our adversaries' weaknesses will be the constant focus across all three levels. I will demonstrate that maneuver warfare concepts have the most utility at the tactical level of LIC, and diminishing relevancy as we ascend the levels of war. However, these concepts retain conceptual usefulness at all levels. Given the breadth of the two topics, the level of historical detail in the argument must give way to the need for broad conceptualizations.

## LOW-INTENSITY CONFLICT

Low-intensity conflict is variously defined. To some, LIC describes a kind of war, namely that of insurgency or revolution. To others, LIC defines the most likely military operations in an age of nuclear deterrence that precludes large-scale conventional operations. Geographical definitions are also in vogue; for some, LIC only occurs in the Third World (another concept that defies easy definition).

Indeed, some authors merely skip definitions altogether. In *Low-Intensity Warfare*, the editors, Michael T. Klare and Peter Kornbluh, refer to LIC variously as "The New Interventionism," "a doctrine for countering revolution," and "a war for all seasons."[1] In *Uncomfortable Wars: Toward a New Paradigm of Low Intensity Conflict*, the editor, Max G. Manwaring, refers alternatively to "uncomfortable wars," or "small wars," and in the essay where the editor presents the new paradigm, LIC becomes simply "Insurgency Wars."[2]

The doctrinal manuals used by the US Army at least give a verbal definition. In FM 100-5, *Operations*, LIC is described as a "form of warfare [that] falls below the level of high- and mid-intensity operations and will pit Army forces against irregular or unconventional forces, enemy special operations forces, and terrorists."[3] In FM 100-20, *Military Operations in Low Intensity Conflict*, the official definition is

> a political-military confrontation between contending states or groups below conventional war and above the routine, peaceful competition among states. It frequently involves protracted struggles of competing principles and ideologies. Low-intensity conflict ranges from subversion to the use of armed force. It is waged by a combination of means, employing political, economic, informational, and military instruments. Low-intensity conflicts are often localized, generally in the Third World, but contain regional and global security implications.[4]

The official definition is too broad to be truly useful.[5] This imprecision has led critics to charge

> so deliberately broad and ambiguous is the official description of low-intensity warfare that it embraces drug interdiction in Bolivia, the occupation of Beirut, the invasion of Grenada, and the 1986 air strikes on Libya. Also included are a wide range of covert political and psychological operations variously described as "special operations," "special activities," and "unconventional warfare."[6]

A criticism often heard from within the military is that "'LIC' may be many things, but what it is not is conflict that is low in intensity."[7] To the soldier in a firefight or in a minefield, war is war.

The types of operations covered in FM 100-20 give a more specific definition of what the U.S. military considers to be in the realm of LIC: insurgency, counterinsurgency, combatting terrorism, peace-keeping operations, and contingency operations.[8] The only topic missing is antinarcotics operations, which could be subsumed in several of the other categories. Hence, it is easier to define LIC negatively in reference to what it is not than in terms of what it is: it is not mid-intensity conflict of the sort waged in the recent Gulf War between large mechanized units. Neither is it high-intensity conflict of the sort we planned to wage with mechanized units and nuclear weapons against the Soviets in Central Europe. The best positive definition is, perhaps, the laundry list of events covered in the LIC manual; these are commonly understood by critics and practitioners alike to be LIC operations.[9]

Definitional controversies aside, LIC is acknowledged to be a persistent problem for the U.S. The 1980s were a growth period for writings on various LIC topics, both in professional military journals and in the academic press. One scholar, Martin Van Creveld, goes so far as to claim that low-intensity conflicts may, in fact, replace large-scale conventional wars as mankind slips into a kind of new Dark Age.[10]

## MANEUVER WARFARE

Maneuver warfare is grounded in an acceptance of the confusion and disorder of war, and how commanders at all levels can use that confusion and disorder to defeat the enemy.[11] To do this, advocates contend, a soldier has to adopt a new way of thinking that eschews formulaic prescriptions: "Instead of a checklist or a cookbook, maneuver warfare requires commanders who can sense more than they can see, who understand the opponent's strengths and weaknesses and their own."[12] Clausewitz, with his own unending emphasis on the uncertainties of war, also cautioned against relying too heavily on "learned monographs."[13]

Two works of which maneuver warfare is the intellectual descendant can be seen in the light of "learned monographs": Liddell Hart's *Strategy* and Colonel John Boyd's "Patterns of Conflict" briefing (on which one maneuver advocate, William Lind, relies heavily for the basis of his own thoughts).[14] A subtle similarity exists between these works. Both purport to tell us of a more effective, lower-cost way to victory. For Liddell Hart, his survey of over 280 campaigns and battles led him to conclude that the victor in the overwhelming majority of them utilized some form of the indirect approach—essentially some variation of turning movements, envelopments, infiltrations, ruses—anything that did not smack of the lackluster frontal assault, or as Lind might put it, "meeting him [the enemy] club-to-club."[15] For Boyd, it is the OODA (Observe, Orient, Decide, Act) loop. All one has to do to win is to get inside the adversary's decision cycle. Maneuver warfare links these two concepts: Orient-Observe-Decide-Act faster than the enemy, and hit him strenuously, but indirectly, with operations aimed at his decisive weaknesses.

Note that both the OODA loop and the indirect approach have important psychological dimensions. How we orient and what we observe has much to do with the filters and screens we bring to any decision-making task—how we mentally pick objects that we need to observe from the surrounding environment.[16] If maneuver warfare is a thought process, then the proper means of orienting and observing are skills that soldiers can learn. If LIC is somehow different from other conflicts, then the skills may also be different than those needed for fighting in Central Europe.

The psychological dimension of the indirect approach is grounded in the fear of suddenly finding an adversary on one's flank or in one's rear. It also comes from the fear of the advantage that an enemy gains from being able to operate unobserved as your forces face a different direction; from the fear that the enemy is capturing the supplies you need for sustainment and, more importantly, cutting off your line of retreat. Liddell Hart contended that the "indirect approach is closely related to all problems of the influence of mind upon mind."[17] Consistent with this, *Strategy* is filled with references to the influence of psychological factors, dislocation of the opponent's mind and forces, importance of distractions, and upsetting the opponent's balance.[18]

The indirect approach and the OODA loop complement each other in that a force that employs the former disrupts the planned decision cycle of its adversary. This disruption forces the enemy to adjust plans, locations, and dispositions of subordinate units. The initiative passes from the enemy to you. Lind talks about "Boyd cycling the enemy" until the enemy force panics and loses cohesion.[19] By attacking the psychological cohesion of the opponent, smaller forces can defeat larger ones, and larger ones can win at lower cost than if they adopted bludgeoning, force-on-force styles of warfare.

The OODA loop and the indirect approach, on which the concepts of maneuver warfare depend, sound too easy: just out-OODA your opponent on his flank, he disintegrates, and you win. Piece of cake. Lind, though, rightly points out that the thought process of opposing the enemy's weaknesses with our strengths in ways creative enough to cause the enemy to disintegrate is "seldom easy."[20]

At least in the abstract, the psychological effects of using strength against weakness have much utility at all levels of LIC. As LIC tends to occur in ambiguous political situations where the goals of our own efforts are often unclear and the methods suspicious, the psychological dimension is all the more important. However, some of the filters and glues that aid the mental process at the tactical level have less saliency for LIC as we ascend to the operational and strategic levels.

## STRATEGY

What is strategy? FM 100-5, *Operations* defines strategy as "the art and science of employing the armed forces of a nation or alliance to secure policy objectives by the application or the threat of force."[21] If maneuver warfare is a thought process that allows us to pick the essential elements of information from our environment so that we might apply our efforts in the most efficient manner, then it should apply to the strategic level as well as the tactical. The efficiency is obtained by adhering to the "first commandment" of maneuver warfare: "attack weakness, avoid strength,"[22] and also by maintaining a consistent focus of all strategic efforts. The U.S.-Soviet competition over the last 45 years can serve as an example of what these concepts mean. This is an especially apt example, since it is in the context of that competition that the concern for low-intensity conflicts arose in the late 1970s and early 1980s.

Low-intensity conflict came to the fore in strategic thought in the early 1980s precisely because members of the foreign policy and academic communities in the United States perceived that growing Soviet influence in the Third World posed dire threats to U.S. access to the markets and raw materials of those areas. Additionally, others feared that Soviet-Cuban support for insurgency in El Salvador and for the Nicaraguan Sandinista regime threatened to turn America's strategic southern flank.[23] In maneuver warfare terms, perhaps this represented

an acknowledgement of the difficulty the United States had in dealing with radical revolutionary situations; it was a principal strategic
weakness. For our adversaries in the Cold War, then, to exploit this
weakness was the essence of strategic wisdom. Fortunately, the U.S.
security community did recognize the strategic implications of low-
intensity conflicts, and a blizzard of studies, articles, training programs,
and force structure changes has been the result.

Along with the exploitation of your adversaries' critical weaknesses,
the maneuver warfare concept of "focus of effort" is also useful at
the strategic level. In maneuver warfare terms, what was the strategic
focus of effort of America's foreign policy since 1945? I submit that
it was the continued implementation of containment of Soviet power.
Containment was based on perceived economic and political weaknesses of the Soviet system which would provoke debilitating crisis
in that system in the long run. In the 1970s, though, following the
withdrawal of the United States from Vietnam, Soviet adventurism in
the Third World grew dramatically: Angola, Ethiopia, Grenada, Nicaragua,
and Afghanistan were the more spectacular examples. These actions
did not appear to be the actions of a power about to go into crisis.
Indeed, by their actions primarily in the Third World, actions that often
involved low-intensity conflicts of one type or another, the Soviets
appeared menacingly strong.

The foreign policy and security community, however, recognized
that the difficulties posed by revolutionary conflicts could cut both
ways in the superpower relationship. Hence, one significant change
in the 1980s over the experience of the 1960s counterinsurgency era
was the U.S. efforts at fostering insurgencies in Nicaragua, Afghanistan, and Angola. Once we perceived the situations in these areas were
still fluid, and that forces and populations existed that would fight against
inclusion in the Soviet orbit, we found a potential weak place (a "gap"
in maneuver warfare terms) in the Soviet strategic disposition, and we
moved, albeit in the fitful manner of pluralistic democracies, to exploit
that weakness. We did unto the Soviets as they had done unto us.

We should not be surprised that either of the maneuver warfare concepts
of a central focus of effort, or opposing the adversary's critical weaknesses with our strengths, is present in strategy. These are very old
principles, even though the processes involved in each are quite difficult.[24] More troublesome to strategy is the maneuver warfare concept of mission orders.

In maneuver warfare, mission orders tell subordinate commanders "what to do," but not "how." According to FM 100-5, though, national strategy "assigns forces, provides assets, and imposes conditions on the use of force."[25] Presumably, mission-type strategic orders are still useful for contingency and antiterrorist operations.

While these two operations are often styled "unconventional," the conduct of raids, punitive expeditions, or coups de main has a long history. These operations are understood well by the military profession. Consequently, it is entirely possible that the National Command Authority could give the order for an operation such as Urgent Fury or Just Cause to a unified or specified commander without dictating how the operation should proceed, except by designating broad parameters in terms of time, geographical limits, and extra assets available. This is so because these two categories of LIC operations are tactical in nature of execution, but generally strategic in importance. It should not surprise us that a concept, such as mission orders, designed to enable tactical commanders to react more quickly than their enemies should retain saliency at this level.

On the other hand, mission orders do not fit as well in situations involving insurgencies and peacekeeping, precisely because the "how" takes on crucial political significance. As FM 100-20 makes clear, "indirect, rather than direct, applications of U.S. military power are the most appropriate and cost-effective ways to achieve national goals in a LIC environment."[26] Further, "political objectives drive military decisions at every level from the strategic to the tactical."[27]

Hence, strategic guidance to the military in an insurgency, counterinsurgency, or peacekeeping situation may be quite restrictive in terms of availability of forces, acceptable levels of operational and tactical activities, rules of engagement, and treatment of and contact with the host nation population. The military "how" may not be entirely specified in such strategic missions, but the options available to military commanders may be so circumscribed as to leave them few choices.

Given a general strategic focus, the maneuver warfare thought process would then ask where is the adversary decisively weak, and can we focus our strengths on that weakness? In the case of the U.S.S.R., perhaps history will show that the Soviets were indeed quite weak economically and weak politically with respect to world opinion. Economic and political weaknesses were their strategic center of gravity.

Proinsurgency operations such as those the United States undertook in the LICs of Afghanistan, Angola, and Nicaragua could then be seen in the light of forcing the Soviets to pay a higher economic price for the extension of their influence. Concomitantly, the Soviets suffered damage to their political reputations by not being able to achieve victory on any of the three continents where their own forces or those of their proxies were engaged. U.S. counterinsurgency support for the El Salvadoran government also helped stem a seemingly inexorable tide of radical revolutionary successes.

Finally, low-intensity contingency operations such as Urgent Fury and the raids against Libya in 1986 highlighted the relative strength of U.S. conventional force-projection against the inability of the Soviets to protect clients or project their own force. In all, this was not a bad job of maintaining focus and applying strength to weakness. On the other hand, fairly tight control over such operations was maintained by policymakers who could not simply "let slip the dogs of war" to accomplish general missions any way the dogs saw fit. The policymakers were correct to do so.

## OPERATIONS, LIC, AND MANEUVER WARFARE

The operational level of conflict is that level in between the strategic and the tactical. For the military, "operational art is the employment of military forces to attain strategic goals in a theater of war or theater of operations through the design, organization, and conduct of campaigns and major operations."[28] Furthermore, "its essence is the identification of the enemy's operational center of gravity."[29] Hence, the operational level is geographically bounded by the concept of the "theater," such as the European or China-Burma-India theaters in World War II. FM 100-5 also indicates that the operational level normally occurs above the level of corps-sized units, but this is dependent on the situation in any given theater. Politically, it is sufficient to think in geographical terms.

Lt. Gen. Victor H. Krulak, USMC (ret.) has stated that "each guerrilla conflict is a tactical, not a strategic undertaking."[30] While most of the army's institutional focus has been on the tactics of LIC, one cannot simply characterize such conflicts as essentially tactical, whether they be of the contingency, peacekeeping, or insurgency varieties. All such operations happen in a larger theater. Each occurs as part of a larger strategic plan. Surprisingly, though, the army and air force manual on LIC, FM 100-20, has little in it about the operational level. The manual addresses "the same logic process commanders use in campaign planning during conventional war." This process revolves around three questions: (1) "What conditions must be produced to achieve the strategic goal?" (2) "What sequence of events will most likely result in the desired conditions?" (3) "How should resources be applied to produce that sequence of events?"[31] Although FM 100-5 and FM 100-20 do not coincide at this point, by answering the second question a campaign planner can discover the enemy's center of gravity.

As with the strategic level, the *Maneuver Warfare Handbook* has little to say about the operational level. Lind is perhaps more succinct than FM 100-5 when he says, "The operational art is the art of using tactical events . . . to strike directly at the enemy's strategic center of gravity."[32] To Lind, though, this usage of tactical events within the concepts of maneuver warfare would allow smaller forces to defeat larger forces, because, it seems, larger forces tend to want to offer tactical battle whenever and wherever they can. By doing this, the larger forces are engaging in nothing more than "attrition warfare on the operational level."[33] On the other hand, smaller forces must choose their battles much more carefully—ones that have the maximum opportunity to contribute to the achievement of their strategic goals. Hence, forces must adhere to maneuver concepts not only at the tactical level but at the operational level, too, lest they find themselves the victor in many battles, but the loser of the war.

Logically, if smaller forces can defeat larger forces by using maneuver warfare, larger forces can win conflicts at much lower costs by using the same concepts. Since the United States has been the stronger force in most of its recent low-intensity operations, and we have an historic aversion to casualties, this point is particularly apt. Unfortunately, Lind provides little on how this is done.

The maneuver warfare concepts of focus of effort and surfaces and gaps are particularly relevant here. At the operational level, they correspond to the idea of the center of gravity and the application of strengths against critical weaknesses. The center of gravity is defined as "the hub of all power and movement, on which everything depends."[34] If we realize that low-intensity conflicts can function as an operational tool to attack an adversary's weakness at the strategic level, then what is the best method to employ that tool in a particular instance?

Contingency and antiterrorist operations are often short in duration and violently executed. The operational focus here is probably quite clearly connected to a strategic goal, but applied in a particular theater: for example, "prevent the expansion of Soviet influence in the Caribbean, and reduce if possible." Or, "prevent further terrorist attacks against US citizens in Europe." In peacekeeping and insurgency operations of long, indeterminate duration, the strategic goals may be much more general: promote stability of a given region.

Thinking in theater, or geographical, terms, what might centers of gravity be in LIC operations? In peacekeeping operations, "the hub" might be a disputed border region, such as the southern border zone in Lebanon. In contingency operations such as Urgent Fury, the center could be the immediate isolation of the enemy from outside support. In an antiterrorist retaliation raid such as that conducted against Libya in 1986, the center could be the demonstration of the personal and political vulnerability of a key terrorist supporter like Qaddafi. In insurgency operations, the key focus is on establishing legitimacy to rule.[35]

When addressing the application of resources to campaigns in low-intensity conflicts at the operational level, the idea of identifying operational strengths and weaknesses is useful. In contingency and antiterrorist operations, the main resources will probably be military in nature, supported by political initiatives. In counterinsurgency operations and peacekeeping operations, the military resources should remain secondary to political resources. In proinsurgency operations, military resources may initially be more important, but in later stages must be supplanted by political efforts to be truly successful.

Given a focus on the enemy center of gravity and the likely resources, what might be the operational strengths and weaknesses in low-intensity conflicts? In contingency and antiterrorist operations, the operational gaps are recognizable in traditional military terms. Does the enemy have a strong or weak capability to reinforce his troops in the theater? Does his military organization depend on outmoded communications? Or is his intratheater mobility inferior to ours? The last two questions directly apply to the question of whether we can get inside the enemy's operational decision cycle for these operations.

In peacekeeping and insurgency operations, the weaknesses become more political and psychological, and thus harder to nail down. In peacekeeping, what is the situational weakness that we can exploit (passively one presumes) to ensure that no potential belligerent can escalate an incident to combat or war? It might be the need for the parties to the dispute to be seen by the world community or other regional actors as adhering to the letter or spirit of international agreements. It might also be the need for economic or military aid. The identification of such weaknesses and the application of diplomatic, economic, and military resources to exploit them will require a finely tuned creativity. Furthermore, most of these operational decisions will be made not by the military command, but by the diplomats in overall charge of the peacekeeping effort.[36]

In insurgency operations as in the other LIC operations, one must continually search for weaknesses related to the operational center of gravity. In insurgency, this is the struggle for legitimacy to rule. One of the more lucid paradigms constructed to deal with insurgency also indicates four other key dimensions: (1) organization for unity of effort; (2) support to the government battling insurgency; (3) "discipline and capabilities of [the] government's armed forces"; and (4) the "ability to reduce outside aid to the insurgents."[37] Implicit in this paradigm is that these dimensions contain physical, political, and psychological aspects. Physical factors include geography, resources, and societal infrastructure. Political factors could be such things as international standing of the belligerents, availability of sanctuaries in neighboring countries that profess neutrality, or the nature of the government under attack. Psychological factors address intangible, but nevertheless potent, aspects such as the degree of national identity, morale in the armed forces, or the level of dissatisfaction in the population.

To discover operational surfaces and gaps in this environment, one must ask a series of questions. Is the insurgency part of a larger theater problem? An example would be the regional economic and social morass of Central America, which breeds discontent and calls for substantial change in many of the region's countries. Can the insurgency be isolated from the larger theater?[38] What are the grievances that separate a section of the people from the government and prompt the insurgency? What is the capability of the threatened government to provide desired or needed goods or services? Can a counterinsurgency effort seize the key issues from the insurgents? Questions such as these flow from the key dimensions above, and each relates directly to the physical, political, and psychological quest for the legitimacy to rule.[39]

The thought process of maneuver warfare applied to the operational level of insurgency requires a thorough evaluation of such topics, always with the ultimate intent of counterposing the in-theater strengths of our side against the weaknesses of our adversary. If the insurgents are dependent on a sanctuary across an international border, or are dependent on outside supplies that cross an international border, we can, in a counterinsurgency role, bring diplomatic, economic, and military resources to bear to attack this weakness by attempting to seal the border and convert other regional actors to our views of the situation. In proinsurgency, we can seek to enhance the abilities of existing insurgent organizations to exploit local disaffections, perhaps by providing communications capabilities in the form of a portable AM radio transmitter, or by securing a site for such a transmitter in a location outside the threatened government's territory. Or, as we did in Nicaragua, we can further weaken the adversarial government through an economic boycott.

Thus, at the operational level of LIC we have not so much the province of the military, but of integrated methods: civil affairs and civic action, public affairs, economics, diplomacy, and appropriately tailored military operations. As such, we must be as skeptical at this level of maneuver warfare's emphasis on mission orders as we were at the strategic level, and for the same reasons. In contingency and antiterrorist operations it may be sufficient to issue a "what" order, leaving the "how" to the executing commanders and diplomats in the area. In insurgency, though, the political authorities will place broad constraints on mission execution across all methods at the theater level. Since the operational center of gravity is the battle for legitimacy, the execution of any of the programs must be accomplished such that no damage is done to our side in this battle.

A fair argument against this concept is that such political constraints are true of all levels of war. The differences between LIC and higher-intensity conflicts, though, turn on the question of which resources predominate. In LIC, nonmilitary resources tend to have primacy. This argues for much stronger control over execution than the maneuver warfare principles, which flow from an intellectual concern for higher-level conflicts, imply. In peacekeeping, for example, the orders are likely to be highly detailed and restrictive.

## TACTICS, LIC, AND MANEUVER WARFARE

Contingency operations and counterterrorism strikes are indistinguishable in most tactical aspects from normal military operations. Just Cause, on its own, becomes a contingency operation. Yet it would have been executed essentially the same if it had been part of a larger conflict. The same is true of the counterterrorist strike on Libya in 1986. Peace-keeping operations are unique, but the techniques employed at the tactical level differ little from normal soldier duties of garrisoning observation posts or conducting patrols, except, in peacekeeping, the patrols generally want to be seen.[40] Other authors in this volume cover normal tactical military operations at length. Consequently, this section will deal with the maneuver warfare implications for the special tactical problems of insurgency, and will forgo further discussion of the other missions inherent in LIC.

Supporting insurgents, or countering them, has evolved into its own style of military operations. The term "insurgency" conjures up foot-weary American soldiers on yet another patrol fighting interminably for who-knows-what, hamstrung by reams of political restrictions. Insurgency is not of short duration, and our experiences tell us that forces committed to the operations won't be adequate to cover all areas, thus permitting the enemy some sort of sanctuary. The missions and objectives are defined in ethereal terms ("protect democracy; restore stability"), if defined at all. Whereas contingency missions seem similar to what is expected of regular units in higher-intensity warfare, insurgency missions somehow seem to be in a different category, vested with a life of their own.

Given LIC's disparate missions, what can the concepts of focus, mission orders, and surfaces and gaps tell us? Maneuver warfare, on its face, appears oriented to modern conventional force-on-force operations. The concept of mission orders implies that defeating the enemy's armed forces in the most expeditious and efficient manner is primarily what matters. The central focus, aimed at the most critical gap in the enemy's disposition—"gaps and surfaces" inevitably evokes linear battle images—directs the effort in such a manner as to bring about the desired defeat of the enemy in battle.

Insurgent warfare is quite different from the imagery associated with the normal language of maneuver warfare. Many of the tasks inherent in fostering or countering an insurgency have little to do with actual tactical combat. On the other hand, the threat of combat is inextricably linked to all aspects of insurgency. American military doctrine divides insurgency into three phases: (1) the latent and incipient, (2) guerrilla warfare, and (3) war of movement.[41] The key maneuver warfare concepts will have different meanings and effects in the different phases of insurgency.

In the latent and incipient phase of insurgency, subversion may exist as a potential threat among a disaffected population, or it may actually be underway. Subversive groups form and grow, and may commit acts of terrorist violence. Without large, identifiable forces in the field, how does one apply maneuver warfare to this level of tactics in LIC? Again, if maneuver warfare is a thought process rather than a how-to-do-it checklist, then intellectually we should be able to apply the concepts to any form of conflict, even one where tactical engagements are incidental.

In both proinsurgency and counterinsurgency during the latent and incipient phase, military operations are of secondary importance. Political considerations are primary, as they are at the strategic and operational levels of LIC. Hence the concept of a focus of effort is good. The concepts of surfaces and gaps—strengths and weaknesses—are still useful. Mission orders, or decentralized execution, are still problematic.

In the latent and incipient phase, the focus of effort is the legitimacy of the government in power—its attachment to the people. If the government lacks legitimacy, then subversive groups will grow steadily. In this phase, counterinsurgency operations would seek to address the root causes of the lack of legitimacy. Most of the tools necessary for this will not be military. However, certain military units can aid the process. Most of them will be combat service support units. Engineer, medical, transport, and civil affairs units are the most useful. Signal units can be effective, too, if, for example, the threatened government lacks adequate communications with all regions of the country.

Such units, host nation or foreign, can enhance legitimacy by demonstrating that the current government and its allies are willing to work to improve conditions for the populace. Such military operations can only be effective, though, within a much larger political effort to promote legitimacy. Doctrinally, that larger framework is the internal defense and development program (IDAD).[42]

Proinsurgency operations take the opposite tack. They must seek to take advantage of the disaffection that already exists. Such operations in this phase do not require much in terms of manpower or equipment. Military advisers are helpful in forming and training the nucleus of future guerrilla units. Special operations forces are designed, in part, for such support. Materiel support—the provision of light armaments and communications equipment—may be just as important. The formation of units supported by external forces may prompt more of the disaffected population to take up arms. External support, then, can make the insurgent or subversive groups appear more legitimate.

In the guerrilla war phase of insurgency, the insurgents begin to conduct continuous military operations of increasing magnitude. The focus of all efforts for both sides remains the legitimacy of the ruling government, and the potential viability of the insurgents to rule in its place.

In the guerrilla phase, how does an insurgency attack the legitimacy of the government's efforts? By moving where and when it wants, striking unexpectedly. The insurgency must also build its own legitimacy as an alternate form of government—presumably by treating the people better than the government does, or, at least, promising them that they will be treated better in the future. By doing these things, the insurgents are demonstrating, and attacking, governmental weaknesses.

The maneuver warfare concepts of surfaces and gaps gain in saliency. Politically, the insurgents have to identify those aspects of the ruling government that are vulnerable to political exploitation. Militarily, a similar identification process occurs. Moreover, the two must be linked. What military targets can the insurgents, whom we presume are still militarily the weaker in this phase, attack that would bring discredit on the government and strengthen the insurgents' claims? Generally, insurgents attack outposts or symbols of government—outlying barracks, guard posts, convoys, off-duty soldiers, or military representatives of allied nations. These are weaker areas of governmental control and within the insurgents' capabilities. The manner in which insurgents execute such tactical operations differs little from conventional squad or platoon operations. Again, I would refer readers to other sections of this volume for maneuver warfare applications at this level.

It is also in this phase that mission orders become quite relevant to LIC, whether we are discussing the actions of insurgents or the forces assigned to counter them. We expect insurgents to operate in small groups, away from supplies and reinforcements, and perhaps out of direct communication with superiors. To be effective, the insurgents have to follow a commonly understood intent for their actions, but with a great deal of flexibility of execution. The same is true of the best counterinsurgency efforts, which will be discussed below.

A counterinsurgency effort in the guerrilla phase faces a dual politico-military task. The government must counteract the growing military actions of the insurgents while simultaneously attempting to win back politically the disaffected populace. The former operations are counterguerrilla operations; the latter are IDAD missions.[43] Counterguerrilla operations are conducive to maneuver warfare concepts in much the same manner as military operations in mid-intensity and high-intensity conflicts.

In counterguerrilla operations, an attacking force using maneuver warfare principles seeks the collapse of the enemy's force. The focus of effort remains the enhancement of legitimacy for the ruling government. All military operations against the guerrilla insurgents must be undertaken with this focus foremost in mind. Given this focus, what might destroy the guerrillas' legitimacy? Demonstrating their inability to effectively challenge the government's physical control of the country, primarily. This entails defending the loyal populace and economic infrastructure. It means that the government forces have to be able to operate wherever they please. Most importantly, it means that military forces supporting the government do not do anything in the accomplishment of their missions that might decrease the legitimacy of the government. This places population protection, from the effects of firepower and maneuver as well as from the insurgents, at the top of the list of concerns.

The process of delegitimizing and weakening guerrilla forces in the field requires a detailed analysis of guerrilla strength and weaknesses. The terms "surfaces" and "gaps" are evocative of linear warfare, or, perhaps, of warfare where units are reasonably contiguous. Guerrilla warfare is, though, a continuous process of hide-and-seek. The concept of a strong or a weak point in the enemy's defensive scheme does not mean the same as it does in mid-intensity or high-intensity warfare, simply because the units may spend little time in close proximity to one another. But the extension of these terms, which we have used throughout this essay, to mean merely strengths and weaknesses is appropriate here as well. Insurgent military weaknesses may derive from their dependence on outside support. They may derive from a lack of mobility, firepower, leadership, or cohesiveness. Counterguerrilla forces must conduct tactical operations that directly impact on these identified weaknesses.[44]

It is here that the link between insurgent weaknesses, tactical center of gravity, focus of effort, and legitimacy come together. Any one of the insurgent weaknesses, taken by itself, may not be decisive. But by identifying several weaknesses and focusing counterguerrilla efforts on them, the counterinsurgency effort may delegitimize the insurgency. The tactical center of gravity, then, would be this group of military weaknesses that were directly linked to the insurgency's political legitimacy. In the often-amorphous world of insurgency, it is highly likely that this is the military situation that would present itself.

Conversely, the counterguerrilla forces must be cognizant of their own vulnerabilities, which may be the insurgents' strengths. Historically, such weaknesses have been a lack of intelligence, which is often linked to a lack of contacts among the affected population; a tendency to concentrate in formations or locations that become easily attacked targets; and a tendency to overreliance on firepower, which inevitably affects civilian populations to the detriment of the government's attempts to bolster its legitimacy.

Since counterguerrilla operations are by nature dispersed, mission orders and decentralized execution should be hallmarks of these military actions. Counterguerrilla actions are not won by the big battalions, but by the better platoons and squads. Yet, such flexibility must be conducted within a widely understood framework of limitations that deal directly with the focus on legitimacy. Destruction of guerrilla formations, even their collapse, remains secondary to the legitimacy focus. Consequently, the flexibility available to small unit leaders in their combat with the enemy may be quite circumscribed.[45] It may be

better for the long-term political health of the country to have insurgent units—which are still viable in a military sense, and have not
been physically or psychologically weakened—to give up the military
fight and sue for peaceful integration into an open political system as
a direct result of the politico-military counterinsurgency strategy. Counterguerrilla operations in this scenario would be directed at circumscribing
the activities of the insurgent units without necessarily entailing an
attempt at destroying the guerrilla units, as would be normal in conventional operations.

The third phase of insurgency, the war of movement, involves insurgent units strong enough to engage government forces in direct,
decisive combat. The insurgency in this phase becomes essentially a
mid-intensity conflict between similarly armed units. We can thus treat
it as such in terms of maneuver warfare, and we need not consider it
further here.

## CONCLUSION

The thought process of maneuver warfare is indeed applicable to
low-intensity conflicts. At the tactical level of war, the maneuver warfare concepts and their implementing techniques are most sharply defined. They become less defined and more conceptual at the operational and strategic levels of war. This is consistent with the notion
of a spectrum of conflict. At higher intensities of conflict, military
operations, while subordinate to politics, are almost coequal. At lower
levels of conflict, the role of military operations becomes increasingly
ill-defined.

At the operational and strategic levels of war, no matter what the
intensity, political considerations dominate military considerations. At
the level of tactics in a mid- or high-intensity conflict, military issues
rise dramatically in prominence to be bounded only by the most general of political constraints. This is not the case with LIC; political
considerations continue to maintain a tight hold over even the lowest
level of tactical operations.

The concepts of maneuver warfare stem from the study of mid- and
high-intensity conflicts. Yet, the broadest interpretations of these concepts
(mission orders, focus of effort, and strength and weaknesses) can function
at all levels of LIC. They must, however, be applied in a manner consistent

with an understanding of the differences and similarities inherent in the mission categories composing LIC.

The concept of mission orders suffers the most when applied to LIC due to the constant political constraints involved at all three levels of LIC. Nonetheless, it, too, retains usefulness particularly at the tactical level of a guerrilla phase insurgency. Given the broad understanding of counterterrorist and contingency operations within the military, mission orders can also function well here at all levels.

In summary, the lack of definitional and conceptual clarity present in the bodies of discussion of both LIC and maneuver warfare make a blending of the concepts a daunting task. Yet, by teasing out the underlying essence within both subjects, I hope to have demonstrated that maneuver warfare, a way of thinking about fighting, can apply to LIC, a type of conflict where fighting is not always present, but the threat of it is. Neither subject is likely to go away. We must deal with both.

# Notes

1. Michael T. Klare and Peter Kornbluh, "The New Interventionism: Low-Intensity Warfare in the 1980s and Beyond," in *Low-Intensity Warfare*, eds. Michael T. Klare and Peter Kornbluh (New York: Pantheon Books, 1988), p. 3, 7.

2. Max. G. Manwaring, preface, *Uncomfortable Wars: Toward a New Paradigm of Low Intensity Conflict*, ed. Max G. Manwaring (Boulder, Colo.: Westview Press, 1991), p. xii. And Max G. Manwaring, "Toward an Understanding of Insurgency Wars: The Paradigm," *Uncomfortable Wars: Toward a New Paradigm of Low Intensity Conflict*, ed. Max G. Manwaring (Boulder, Colo.: Westview Press, 1991), p. 19, 20.

3. U.S. Army, FM 100-5, *Operations* (Washington, D.C.: U.S. Government Printing Office, 1986), p. 4 (hereafter cited as FM 100-5).

4. U.S. Army and U.S. Air Force, FM 100-20, *Military Operations in Low Intensity Conflict* (Washington, D.C.: U.S. Government Printing Office, 1990), p. 1-1 (hereafter cited as FM 100-20).

5. I choose to not dwell on whether LIC is just a rehashing of "Unconventional Warfare" from the 1960s. I do so not least because the activities associated with pro- or counterinsurgency occur so commonly that "unconventional" is hardly a fitting description. Likewise, the U.S. has used military force short of war more than 120 times since 1946; for the period 1946–1975, see Barry M. Blechman and Stephen S. Kaplan, *Force Without War: US Armed Forces as a Political Instrument* (Washington, D.C.: Brookings Institution, 1978). Such a frequency of use also defies the description "unconventional."

6. Klare and Kornbluh, p. 7.

7. Col. D. Dennison Lane and Lt. Col. Mark Weisenbloom, "Low-intensity Conflict: In Search of a Paradigm," *International Defense Review*, no. 1, 1990, p. 37.

8. FM 100-20, p. ii.

9. Lane and Weisenbloom make a similar point. They recommend abandoning "LIC" in favor of "small wars" because they believe this term to be more descriptive of the common "manifestations" of LIC. Yet, not all these wars are small, and not all of the operations are wars. See Lane and Weisenbloom, p. 37.

10. Martin Van Creveld, *The Transformation of War* (New York: Free Press, 1991).

11. William S. Lind and Michael Wyly, *Maneuver Warfare Handbook* (Boulder, CO: Westview Press, 1985), p. 7.

12. Lind, p. 7.

13. Carl von Clausewitz, *On War*, eds. and trans. Michael Howard and Peter Paret (Princeton: Princeton University Press, 1976). See his remarks on educating the judgment of commanders, p. 141, and the value of "musty books," p. 147, and "learned monographs," p. 185.

14. Lind actually cites Captain B. H. Liddell Hart's "The 'Man-in-the-Dark' Theory of Infantry Tactics and the 'Expanding Torrent' System of Attack," *Journal of the R.U.S.I.*, February 1921, but his thoughts are consistent with Liddell Hart's views in *Strategy*, 2d ed. (New York: Signet, 1974). Lind cites Col. John Boyd's "Patterns of Conflict" briefing on pp. 4–6 of *Maneuver Warfare Handbook*.

15. Liddell Hart, *Strategy*, pp. 144, 145; Lind, p. 4.

16. For an example of a political science argument on the ways policymakers deal with the stress and confusion inherent in decision making, see Alexander L. George, "Adapting to Constraints on Rational Decisionmaking," in *International Politics: Anarchy, Force, Political Economy, and Decisionmaking*, 2d ed., eds. Robert J. Art and Robert Jervis (Boston: Scott, Foresman and Co., 1985), 491–509. George's discussion deals with high-level policymakers, but could be applied easily to all levels of military decisionmaking.

17. Liddell Hart, *Strategy*, p. xx.

18. Ibid., pp. 407–409.

19. Lind, p. 6.

20. Ibid., p. 7.

21. FM 100-5, p. 9.

22. "The Maneuver Warfare Symposium Quarterly Newsletter," no. 1, 17 January 1991, p. 2.

23. For a standard discussion of this trend in strategic thought, see Abraham F. Lowenthal, "Ronald Reagan and Latin America: Coping with Hegemony in Decline," in *Eagle Defiant: United States Foreign Policy in the 1980s*, eds. Kenneth A. Oye, Robert J. Lieber, and Donald Rothchild (Boston: Little, Brown, 1983).

24. For those who find comfort in quotes from the masters, consider Clausewitz: "To discover how much of our resources must be mobilized for war, we must first examine our own political aim and that of the enemy. We must gauge the strength and situation of the opposing state. We must gauge the character and abilities of its government and people and do the same in regard to our own." Clausewitz, pp. 585, 586. *Schwerpunkt* and surfaces and gaps leap out of this excerpt.

25. FM 100-5, p. 9.

26. FM 100-20, p. 1-2.

27. Ibid., p. 1-5.

28. FM 100-5, p. 10.

29. Ibid.

30. Victor H. Krulak, "Strategic Implications of 'the Little War'," in *Student Text 100-39 Low Intensity Conflict: Selected Readings* (Ft. Leavenworth, Kans.: U.S. Army Command and General Staff College, 1985), p. 84.

31. FM 100-20, pp. 1–7

32. Lind, p. 24.

33. Ibid.

34. From Clausewitz, quoted in FM 100-5, p. 179.

35. Manwaring, p. 20. Or, consider what former TRADOC Commander Gen. John W. Foss has said about the "decisive operations stage" of AirLand Battle-Future as applied to low-intensity conflict: "This could be a national election with the population protected by its military, the insurgents discredited and the government gaining legitimate status." See Gen. John W. Foss, "Advent of the Nonlinear Battlefield: AirLand Battle-Future," *Army*, February 1991, p. 24.

36. According to FM 100-20, the general organization of peacekeeping efforts include a "political council" to function as the negotiating and coordinating center for all activities. See FM 100-20, pp. 4-2, 4-3.

37. Manwaring, pp. 21, 22.

38. Most of these questions are important regardless of whether we function in a pro- or counterinsurgency role. In proinsurgency, we may want or need to capitalize on theaterwide factors that might enhance our chances. Conversely, in counterinsurgency, our efforts may fail if we do not cut the insurgents off from sanctuaries or outside supplies. Further, some insurgencies may not be resolvable absent regionwide solutions to economic, social, and political ailments. Again, Central America comes to mind.

39. Appendix C, "How to Analyze an Insurgency or Counterinsurgency," of FM 100-20 provides a much more detailed list of such topics and questions.

40. One officer who studied LIC suggested that military police units are the best suited for peacekeeping. See Maj. Mitchell M. Zais, "LIC: Matching Missions and Forces," *Military Review*, August 1986, pp. 90, 91.

41. The discussion on the characteristics of insurgency comes from U.S. Army, FM 90-8, *Counterguerrilla Operations* (Washington, D.C.: U.S. Government Printing Office, 1986) pp. 1-3, 1-4.

42. FM 90-8, p. 1-5.

43. Ibid.

44. When counterguerrilla forces find insurgent units in defensive positions, or vice versa, then the conventional notion of surfaces and gaps applies. On the other hand, such operations tend to resemble more assaults on a circular

strongpoint with easily obtained routes of escape. Then, the attacking force is left with the difficult task of rapidly concentrating enough force to encircle the enemy. Simply flanking the enemy and getting in his "rear" may not have much meaning. For a discussion of encirclement tactics in Vietnam, see Robert A. Doughty, *Evolution of U.S. Army Tactical Doctrine 1946-1976* (Leavenworth Papers, No. 1) (Ft. Leavenworth, Kans.: U.S. Army Command and General Staff College, 1979), p. 36.

45. See FM 90-8, p. 1-6. Minimizing usage of force and damage are heavily emphasized.

# Defeating the Enemy's Will: The Psychological Foundations of Maneuver Warfare

## David A. Grossman

> The will to fight is at the nub of all defeat mechanisms. . . .
> One should always look for a way to break the enemy's will
> and capacity to resist.
>
> Brig. Gen. Huba Wass de Czege

Defeating the enemy's will. That is the essence of maneuver warfare, that you defeat the enemy's will to fight rather than his ability to fight. But how do you defeat a man's mind?

We *can* measure and precisely quantify the mechanics of defeating the enemy's ability to fight, and it is this tangible, mathematical quality that makes attacking the enemy's physical *ability* to fight so much more attractive than attacking the enemy's psychological *will* to fight. At some level none of us can truly be comfortable when we dwell on the fact that our destiny as soldiers and military leaders ultimately depends on something as nebulous and unquantifiable as an enemy's "will," and we are tempted to ignore such aspects of warfare. But somewhere in the back of our minds, a still, small voice reminds us that ultimately the paths of victory run not through machinery and material, but through the hearts and minds of human beings.

So what is the foundation of the will to fight and kill in combat, and what are the vulnerable points in this foundation? In short: what are the psychological underpinnings of maneuver warfare? To answer these questions, students of maneuver warfare must truly understand, as we have never understood before, the psychological responses of that hungry, frightened, cold individual soldier in combat. "Of the maimed, of the halt and the blind in the rain and the cold, of these must our story be told."[1]

S. L. A. Marshall, John Keegan, Richard Holmes, and Ardant du Picq are but a few of the perceptive individuals who have made significant contributions to the enormous task of piecing together a host of individual observations into a coherent fabric, but the work of most observers and researchers has the flavor of the reports made by the proverbial blind men groping at the elephant. Past observers have identified many important and valid aspects of the beast, but a consistent shortcoming seems to have been their inability to integrate their own observations with those of others. Thus, while one grasps a leg and declares the creature to be a tree, another finds a flank and calls the beast a wall, and still another proclaims the trunk to be a snake. In a way, all are correct, but the magnitude of the beast we call "war" is even greater than the sum of its parts.

The analogy of blind men is really quite appropriate, for we are all truly blinded when we attempt to look too closely into the searing flames of pain and denial that surround combat. Many observers have noted the millennia-old institution of repression and denial which makes understanding the psychological responses to combat so difficult. "There is," wrote the psychologist-philosopher Peter Marin, "a massive unconscious cover-up in which both those who fought and those who did not hide from themselves the true nature of the experience."[2] And, based on his own self-observation, the philosopher-soldier Glenn Gray concluded that: "few of us can hold on to our real selves long enough to discover the real truths about ourselves and this whirling earth to which we cling. This is especially true of men in war. The great god Mars tries to blind us when we enter his realm, and when we leave he gives us a generous cup of the waters of Lethe to drink."[3]

Thus, in its horrified and revolted response to the enormity of war, the human consciousness has traditionally scattered and buried the pieces of the beast that we seek. Like archaeologists, we must exhume each piece from whence it has been entombed in layers of denial. Like paleontologists, we must piece together each fragment brought out into the bright light of understanding and comprehension, and carefully fit it with all the others so as to understand fully the magnitude of the beast.

The task is daunting. We human beings are extraordinarily complex creatures, and when considered in groups, our potential complexity grows exponentially. And the numbers of the pieces of our collective psyche that lie buried in the minds of living veterans—and in the fields of military science, history, psychology, sociology, and philosophy—are legion. One veteran I interviewed referred to such scientific study of men in combat as "A world of virgins studying sex, with nothing to go on but porno films." British Gen. Shelford Bidwell comes to the same general conclusion when he states that the union of soldier and scientist must always lay on "dangerous ground."[4] The objective of this study is to form such a union, to tread that dangerous ground and apply the skills of a soldier, a historian, and a psychologist in order to form a first, tentative framework of understanding that others may build upon.

## THE PSYCHOLOGICAL PRICE OF WAR

Nations customarily measure the "costs of war" in dollars, lost production, or the number of soldiers killed or wounded. Rarely do military establishments attempt to measure the costs of war in terms of individual suffering. Psychiatric breakdown remains one of the most costly items of war when expressed in human terms.

Richard Gabriel
*No More Heroes*[5]

Defeating the enemy's will is not too far removed from the process of inflicting psychiatric casualties on the enemy's soldiers. In fact, it would come very close to the mark to say that maneuver warfare (as opposed to attrition warfare) seeks to inflict psychic as well as physical damage upon the enemy, and a brief examination of the psychological price of modern war would be an appropriate place to begin our study of the psychological underpinnings of maneuver warfare.

In his book, *No More Heroes*, Richard Gabriel outlines the staggering "psychic" costs of war. "In every war in which American soldiers have fought in this century, the chances of becoming a psychiatric casualty . . . were greater than the chances of being killed by enemy fire."[6] In World War II, America's armed forces lost 504,000 men from the fighting effort because of psychiatric collapse—enough to man fifty divisions! We suffered this loss despite efforts to weed out those mentally and emotionally unfit for combat by classifying 970,000 men as unfit for military service due to psychiatric reasons.[7] At one point in World War II, psychiatric casualties were being discharged from the U.S. Army faster than new recruits were being drafted in.[8] Swank and Marchand's World War II study determined that after 60 days of *continuous* combat, 98 percent of *all* surviving soldiers will have become psychiatric casualties of one kind or another.[9] (Swank and Marchand also found that the 2 percent who are able to endure sustained combat had as their most common trait a predisposition toward "aggressive psychopathic personalities." The importance of this statistic will be addressed later.)

In order to fully understand what it is that unravels the "will" of the individual fighting soldier and turns him into a psychiatric casualty, we need to identify *all* of the major factors that interact to cause this tremendous psychic burden.

### The Soldier's Dilemma: Dogged by Shadows on Either Hand

> The man who ranges in No Man's Land
> Is dogged by the shadows on either hand
> "No Man's Land"[10]
> James H. Knight-Adkin

Observers who have reported on the nature of the psychological trauma associated with combat keep coming up with different answers. Each of these observers seems to have come up with a piece of the truth, but the full magnitude of the physiological and psychological impact of war is greater than the sum of its parts, and the soldier is dogged by shadows at every turn. Some of the diverse factors that need to be incorporated into a complete understanding of the combat soldier's circumstance are outlined below, and all of these factors add relentlessly to the burden of that horrible Catch-22 at the core of combat, that heart of darkness at the center of all combat processes: to kill or not to kill . . . and the price thereof.

• The impact of physiological arousal and fear. Appel and Beebe[11] are but a few of many, many observers in the field of the behavioral sciences who hold that fear of death and injury is the primary cause of psychiatric casualties. Richard Gabriel is among many who make a powerful argument for the impact of physical exhaustion caused by extended periods during which the sympathetic nervous system is activated in a continuous "fight or flight" response.

• The weight of exhaustion. Among actual veterans, many accounts seem to focus on the fatigue and exhaustion they experienced in combat. The psychologist Bartlett states definitively that "there is perhaps no general condition which is more likely to produce a large crop of nervous and mental disorders than a state of prolonged and great fatigue."[12] The British General Bernard Fergusson stated that "lack of food constitutes the single biggest assault upon morale."[13] And Guy Sager, a German veteran of the eastern front in World War II, is one of the many veterans who learned that cold was the soldier's first enemy. "We urinated into our hands to warm them, and, hopefully, to cauterize the gaping cuts in our fingers ... each movement of my fingers opened and closed deep crevices, which oozed blood."[14]

• The stress of uncertainty. The initial results of extensive research on the 1991 Gulf War indicates that one of the major stressors on individual combatants was the tremendous uncertainty of war.[15] This constant state of uncertainty, which is a major part of what Clausewitz referred to as the "friction of war," destroys the soldier's sense of control over his life and environment, and eats away at his limited stock of fortitude.

• The burden of guilt and horror. Richard Holmes, on the other hand, spends a chapter of his superb book, *Acts of War*, convincing us of the horror of battle, and the impact of the guilt associated with it: "Seeing friends killed, or, almost worse, being unable to help them." And Peter Marin accuses the field of psychology of being ill prepared to address the guilt caused by war and the attendant moral issues. He flatly states that, "Nowhere in the [psychiatric and psychological] literature is one allowed to glimpse what is actually occurring: the real horror of the war and its effect on those who fought it."[16]

• An aversion to hate and killing. In addition to these more obvious factors of fear, exhaustion, uncertainty, guilt, and horror, the less obvious but absolutely vital factors represented by the average human being's aversion to hate and killing have been added here. These two factors are the most difficult to observe, but the very fact that they are not intuitively obvious makes them in many ways more important. These interpersonal aggression processes are the riddle that lies deep in the heart of darkness that is war.

For the purposes of a study of maneuver warfare, let us gain perspective by looking first at the impact of physiological arousal and fear on the battlefield, and then contrast this with the impact of being confronted with manifest, close-range, interpersonal hatred on the battlefield. The rest of this study will then focus on the dilemma associated with killing circumstances in combat—i.e., the average human being's powerful resistance to killing and those processes and circumstances that can be manipulated to enable aggression in combat.

## The Role of Physiological Arousal and Fear: "Sarge, I've Pissed Too"

And then a shell lands behind us, and another over to the side, and by this time we're scurrying and the Sarge and I and another guy wind up behind a wall. The sergeant said it was an .88 and then he said, "Shit and shit some more."

I asked him if he was hit and he sort of smiled and said no, he had just pissed his pants. He always pissed them, he said, just when things started and then he was okay. He wasn't making any apologies either, and then I realized something wasn't quite right with me, either. There was something warm down there and it seemed to be running down my leg. I felt, and it wasn't blood. It was piss.

I told the Sarge, I said, "Sarge, I've pissed too," or something like that and he grinned and said, "Welcome to the war."

A veteran's account of World War II,
as recorded by Barry Broadfoot
*Six War Year*, 1939–1945[17]

To comprehend fully the intensity of the body's physiological response to the stress of combat, we must understand the mobilization of resources caused by the body's sympathetic nervous system, and then we must understand the impact of the body's parasympathetic "backlash," which occurs as a result of the demands placed upon it.

## Sympathetic and parasympathetic processes: cooks and clerks in the front line

The sympathetic nervous system mobilizes and directs the body's energy resources for action. It is the physiological equivalent of the frontline soldiers who actually do the fighting in a military unit.

The parasympathetic system is responsible for the body's digestive and recuperative processes. It is the physiological equivalent of the cooks, mechanics, and clerks that sustain a military unit over an extended period of time.

Usually these two systems sustain a general balance between their demands upon the body's resources, but during extremely stressful circumstances the "fight or flight" response kicks in and the sympathetic nervous system mobilizes *all* available energy for survival. This is the physiological equivalent of throwing the cooks, bakers, mechanics, and clerks into the battle. In combat this very often results in nonessential activities such as digestion, bladder control, and sphincter control being completely shut down. This process is so intense that soldiers very often suffer stress diarrhea, and it is not at all uncommon for them to urinate and defecate in their pants as the body literally "blows its ballast" in an attempt to provide all the energy resources required to ensure its survival.

It doesn't take a rocket scientist to guess that a soldier must pay a heavy physiological price for an enervating process this intense. The price that the body pays is an equally powerful backlash when the neglected demands of the parasympathetic system become ascendant. This parasympathetic backlash occurs as soon as the danger and the excitement are over, and it takes the form of an incredibly powerful weariness and sleepiness on the part of the soldier.

## The criticality of the reserve

> He, general or mere captain, who employs every one in the storming of a position can be sure of seeing it retaken by an organized counterattack of four men and a corporal.
>
> Ardant du Picq[18]

Napoleon stated that the moment of greatest danger was the instant immediately after victory, and in saying so he demonstrated a remarkable understanding of the way in which soldiers become physiologically and psychologically incapacitated by the parasympathetic backlash that occurs as soon as the momentum of the attack has halted and the soldier briefly believes himself to be safe. During this period of vulnerability, a counterattack by fresh troops can have an effect completely out of proportion to the number of troops attacking.

It is basically for this reason that the maintenance of an "unblown" reserve has historically been essential in combat, with battles often revolving around which side can hold out and deploy their reserves last. The reserve has always played a vital role in combat, but du Picq was one of the earliest advocates not only of "holding out a reserve as long as possible for independent action when the enemy has used his own," but he also insisted on the revolutionary concept that this process "ought to be applied downward" to the lowest levels. He also perceived the technological process of increasing lethality on the battlefield which continues today. "There is more need than ever to-day, for protecting . . . the reserves. The power of destruction increases, the morale [of human beings] stays the same." Clausewitz further understood and put great emphasis on the danger of reserve forces becoming prematurely enervated and exhausted when he cautioned that the reserves should always be maintained out of sight of the battle.

These same basic psycho-physiological principles explain why successful military leaders have historically maintained the momentum of a successful attack. Pursuing and maintaining contact with a defeated enemy is vital in order to completely destroy the enemy (the vast majority of the killing in historical battles occurred during the pursuit, when the enemy turned his back), but it is also valuable to maintain contact with the enemy as long as possible in order to delay that inevitable pause in the battle which will result in the "culmination point." The culmination point is usually caused as much by logistical processes as anything else, but once the momentum of the pursuit stops (for whatever reasons) there are severe physiological and psychological costs to be paid, and the commander must realize that his forces will begin to immediately slip into a powerful parasympathetic backlash and become vulnerable to an enemy counterattack. An unblown reserve force ready to complete the pursuit is a vital aspect of maneuver warfare and can be of great value in ensuring that this most destructive phase of the battle is effectively executed.

### Fear and loathing in the bomb shelter

In continuous combat the soldier roller-coasters through a seemingly endless series of these surges of adrenaline and their subsequent backlashes, and the body's natural, useful, and appropriate response to danger ultimately becomes extremely counterproductive. Unable to flee, and unable to overcome the danger through a brief burst of fighting, posturing, or submission, the bodies of modern soldiers quickly exhaust their capacity to rejuvenate and slide into a state of profound physical and emotional exhaustion of such a magnitude and dimension that it appears to be almost impossible to communicate it to those who have not experienced it. As Gabriel puts it, "A soldier in this state will inevitably collapse from nervous exhaustion—the body simply will burn out."[19]

Most observers of combat lump the impact of this physiological arousal process under the general heading of "fear," but fear is really a cognitive or emotional aspect of nonspecific physiological arousal. The impact of fear and its attendant physiological arousal is significant, but the part it plays in creating psychiatric casualties needs to be placed in perspective.

The "role" of fear on the battlefield would be held by many researchers to be more appropriately termed the "reign" of fear, since their sole explanation for combat psychiatric casualties is fear of death and injury in combat. But is fear (and its attendant physiological arousal) the only or even the most important factor in the causation of combat psychiatric casualties? Although fear of death and injury is undoubtedly a significant factor, I submit that it is *not* the only and possibly not even the most significant factor. This becomes most evident if we examine the results of strategic bombing in World War II.

Consider the carnage and destruction caused by the months of continuous "Blitz" in England or years of Allied bombing in Germany during World War II. Day and night, in an intentionally unpredictable pattern, for months and even years on end, relatives and friends were mutilated and killed all around these people, and these civilian populations suffered fear and horror of a magnitude few humans will ever experience. This unpredictable, uncontrollable reign of fear is exactly what most experts hold responsible for the tremendous percentages of psychiatric casualties suffered by soldiers in battle. And yet, incredibly, the incidence of psychiatric casualties among these individuals was very similar to that of peacetime. The Rand Corporation Strategic Bombing Study published in 1949 found that there was only a very slight increase in the psychological disorders in these populations as compared to peacetime rates, and that these occurred primarily among individuals already predisposed to psychiatric illness. Psychologically, these bombings appear to have served primarily to create a loathing for the enemy: to harden the hearts and increase the willingness to fight among those who endured them.

The impact of fear and physiological arousal in combat should never be underestimated, but it would appear that something more than just fear is required to defeat the enemy's will. Close examination indicates that we can identify several other factors that add to the psychological burden of the soldier in combat. For the purposes of maneuver warfare, one of the most important of these is the role of interpersonal hatred manifested in the enemy's close-range, aggressive actions on the battlefield.

## The Role of Hate

> My first reaction, rooted in the illusion that anyone trying to kill me must have a personal motive, was: "Why does he want to kill *me*? What did I ever do to *him*?"
>
> Phillip Caputo
> author and Vietnam veteran[20]

Through roller coasters, action and horror movies, drugs, rockclimbing, whitewater rafting, scuba diving, parachuting, hunting, contact sports, and a hundred other methods, our society pursues danger. Danger in and of itself is seldom a cause of trauma in our everyday peacetime existence, but facing aggression and hatred in our fellow citizens is a horrifying experience of an entirely different magnitude.

The ultimate fear and horror in most modern lives is to be raped or beaten, to be physically degraded in front of our loved ones, to have the sanctity of our homes invaded by aggressive and hateful intruders. Death or debilitation is statistically far more likely to occur by disease or accident than by malicious action, but the statistics do not calm our basically irrational fears. More than anything else in life, intentional, overt *human* hostility and aggression assaults our self image, our sense of control, our sense of the world as a meaningful and comprehensible place, and (ultimately) our mental and physical health.

The soldier in combat is no different. He resists the powerful obligation and coercion to engage in aggressive and assertive actions on the battlefield, and he dreads facing the irrational interpersonal aggression and hostility embodied in the enemy soldier.

## Maneuver Warfare Applications of the Role of Hate

If we understand the role of hate in the soldier's dilemma then we can use it to obtain a greater understanding of the psychological underpinnings of maneuver warfare. Airpower advocates persist in their support of strategic bombing campaigns (which are rooted in an attrition warfare mentality), even in the face of evidence such as the post–World War II Strategic Bombing Survey, which, in the words of Paul Fussell, ascertained that: "German military and industrial production seemed to increase—just like civilian determination not to surrender—the more bombs were dropped."[21] Historically, aerial and artillery bombardments *are* psychologically effective, but *only* in the front lines when they are *combined* with the Wind of Hate as manifested in the threat of the physical attack that usually follows such bombardments.

This is why there were mass psychiatric casualties resulting from World War II artillery bombardments, but World War II's massed bombing of cities was surprisingly counterproductive in breaking the enemy's will. Such bombardments without an accompanying close-range assault, or at least the threat of such an assault, are ineffective and may even serve no other purpose than to stiffen the resolve of the enemy!

This is why putting friendly troop units in the enemy's rear is infinitely more important and effective than even the most comprehensive bombardments in his rear, or attrition along his front. This argues strongly for a doctrine similar to the World War II German principle of the *Kesselschlacht* (i.e., a constant striving for decisive action in the enemy rear) as an essential element in obtaining decisive victory. In this doctrine the *Aufrollen* (i.e., rolling up the flanks after making a penetration) becomes a secondary operation which is conducted solely to support the *Schwerpunkt* or the main thrust, which is flexibly directed into the enemy's center of gravity by the commander's intent.

In the Korean War the U.S. Army experienced the psychological effectiveness of an enemy who directed penetrations and surprise attacks behind our own lines. During the early years of that war, the rate of psychiatric casualties was almost seven times higher than the average rate for World War II. Only after the war settled down, lines stabilized, and the threat of having enemy forces in the rear areas decreased did the average incidence of psychiatric casualties go down to slightly less than that of World War II.[22] Later, when U.N. forces were able to penetrate and threaten the enemy's rear area during the Inchon landing, these same processes began to work in their favor.

Even in the ideal bombing grounds of the barren deserts of the 1991 Gulf War, where for over a month the full weight of American, British, French, Canadian, and Italian airpower was brought to bear on the conscript soldiers of a Third World despot, enemy units did not and would not surrender in large numbers until faced with maneuver units on the ground and in their rear. (In fact, recent evidence indicates that these bombings were significantly ineffective. Initial reports were of more than 100,000 Iraqi casualties inflicted in the war, the vast majority from air strikes. But recent, authoritative reports indicate that "as few as 8,000 Iraqi soldiers may have been killed in the Kuwait Theater of operations during the 43 days of combat."[23] If all of these casualties were inflicted from the air, that would be less than eight deaths resulting from each sortie of a multi-million-dollar aircraft loaded with the latest in multi-million-dollar smart munitions.) The simple, demonstrable fact is that the *potential* for close-up, *inter*personal hatred and aggression is more effective and has greater impact on the will of the soldier than the *presence* of *im*personal death and destruction.

## THE EXISTENCE OF THE RESISTANCE

Studies by Medical Corps psychiatrists of the combat fatigue cases in the European Theater . . . found that fear of killing, rather than fear of being killed, was the most common cause of battle failure in the individual.

S. L. A. Marshall[24]

Having established a foundation for an understanding of the dilemma that faces the soldier in combat, we must next look at the nature of the individual combatant's responses to his environment (Figure 1). In the animal world, when two creatures of the same species come in conflict, their combat is almost never to the death. Rattlesnakes use their poisonous fangs on other creatures, but they wrestle each other; piranha fish bite anything that moves, but fight each other with flicks of their tails; and animals with antlers and horns attempt to puncture and gore other species with these natural weapons, but meet their own species in relatively harmless head-to-head clashes. Against one's own species the options of choice in nature are to "posture" before and during mock battle, to "submit" by making oneself harmless or exposing oneself to a killing blow, or to take "flight" from the aggressor. The "fight" option is almost never used, thus ensuring the survival of the species.

It is widely held that only man has no such resistance to killing. But does he? World War II Gen. S. L. A. Marshall, veteran and the Official Historian of the European Theater during World War II, first brought to the attention of the world the fact that only 15 to 20 percent of the riflemen in combat would fire their weapons at an exposed enemy.[25] Marshall was the first person in history to conduct systematic interviews with individual soldiers immediately after combat, and, although his methodological procedures have recently been reexamined, his basic concept of a majority of soldiers failing to actively pursue the "fight" option withstands close scrutiny.

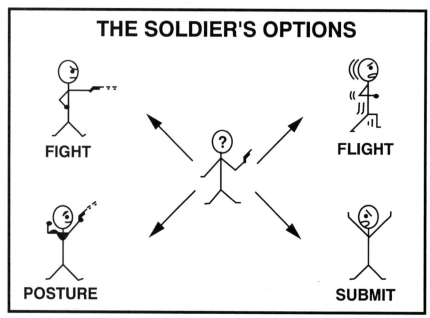

Figure 1: The soldier's response options upon being confronted with interpersonal aggression

### "Posturing"

Man does not enter battle to fight, but for victory. He does
everything that he can to avoid the first and obtain the second.

Ardant du Picq[26]

The anthropologist Irenaus Eibl-Eibesfeldt tells us that: "One threatens
[postures] by making oneself bigger—whether by raising one's hack-
les, wearing combs in one's hair or putting on a bearskin . . ."[27] Such
plumage saw its height in modern history during the Napoleonic era,
when soldiers wore high, uncomfortable shako hats that served no purpose
other than to make the wearer look and feel like a taller, more dangerous creature. In the same manner, the roars of two posturing beasts
are exhibited by men in battle. For centuries the war cries of soldiers
have made their opponents' blood run cold. Whether it be the battle
cry of a Greek phalanx, the "Hurrah!" of the Russian infantry, the wail
of Scottish bagpipes, or the rebel yell of our own Civil War, soldiers
have always instinctively sought to daunt the enemy through nonvio-
lent means prior to physical conflict, while encouraging one another
and impressing themselves with their own ferocity, and simultaneously
providing a very effective means of drowning the disagreeable yell
of the enemy.

With the advent of gunpowder, the soldier has been provided with
one of the finest possible means of posturing. Paddy Griffith points
out that soldiers in battle have a desperate urge to fire their weapons:

Time and again we read of regiments blazing away uncontrolla-
bly, once started, and continuing until all ammunition was gone
or all enthusiasm spent. Firing was such a positive act, and gave
the men such a physical release for their emotions, that instincts
easily took over from training and from the exhortations of officers.[28]

Ardant du Picq became one of the first to document the common
tendency of soldiers to fire harmlessly into the air simply for the sake
of firing. Du Picq made one of the first thorough investigations into
the nature of combat with a questionnaire distributed to French officers in the 1860s. One officer's response to du Picq stated quite frankly
that "a good many soldiers fired into the air at long distances," while

another observed that "a certain number of our soldiers fired almost in the air, without aiming, seeming to want to stun themselves, to become drunk on rifle fire during this gripping crisis."[29]

Lt. George Roupell encountered this same phenomenon while commanding a platoon in World War I. He stated that the only way he could stop his men from firing into the air was to walk down the trench, "beating the men on the backside and, as I got their attention, telling them to fire low."[30] And the same trend can be found in the firefights of Vietnam, where, according to one congressional report, over 50,000 bullets were fired for every enemy soldier killed.

### "Submission" and "Flight"

> It is to be noted that when a body [of troops] actually awaits the attack of another up to bayonet distance (something extraordinarily rare), and the attacking troop does not falter, the first does not defend itself.
>
> Ardant du Picq[31]

A quest for further understanding of this process brings us to an examination of those individuals in combat—80 to 85 percent of the individual riflemen, according to S. L. A. Marshall's research—who would not kill or even "posture" in combat. Griffith states that:

> Even in the noted "slaughter pens" at Bloody Lane, Marye's Heights, Kennesaw, Spotsylvania and Cold Harbor an attacking unit could not only come very close to the defending line, but it could also stay there for hours—and indeed for days—at a time. Civil War musketry did not therefore possess the power to kill large numbers of men, even in very dense formations, at long range. At short range it could and did kill large numbers, *but not very quickly* (emphasis added).[32]

Griffith estimates that the average musket fire from a Napoleonic or Civil War regiment firing at an exposed enemy regiment at an average range of 30 yards would usually result in hitting *only one or two men per minute!* Such firefights "dragged on until exhaustion set in or nightfall put an end to hostilities. Casualties mounted because the contest went on so long, not because the fire was particularly deadly."

This does not represent a failure on the part of the weaponry. John Keegan and Richard Holmes in their book, *Soldiers*, tell of a Prussian experiment in the late 1700s, "in which a battalion of infantry fired [smoothbore muskets] at a target one hundred feet long by six feet high, representing an enemy unit, resulted in 25 percent hits at 225 yards, 40 percent hits at 150 yards, and 60 percent hits at 75 yards." This represented the potential killing power of such a unit. The reality is demonstrated in their account of the battle of Belgrade in 1717, during which "two Imperial battalions held their fire until their Turkish opponents were only thirty paces away, but hit only thirty-two Turks when they fired and were promptly overwhelmed." Sometimes the fire was completely harmless, as in Benjamin McIntyre's observation of a totally bloodless nighttime firefight at Vicksburg in 1863:

> It seems strange however that a company of men can fire volley after volley at a like number of men at not over a distance of fifteen steps and not cause a single casualty. Yet such was [sic] the facts in this instance.[33]

(Cannon fire, like machine-gun fire in WWII, is an entirely different matter, sometimes accounting for over 50 percent of the casualties on the blackpowder battlefield, and artillery fire has consistently accounted for the majority of combat casualties in this century. There is reason to believe that this is as much due to the enhanced psychological effectiveness of these systems—due to group accountability processes at work in a cannon, machine gun, or other crew-served weapons firing—as it is to their increased mechanical killing potential, i.e., their contribution to what artillery officers like to call the "metal density of the air." This critical point will be addressed in detail later.)

Recent historical reenactments also verify this trend. A 1986 study by the British Defense Operational Analysis Establishment's field studies division used historical studies of more than 100 19th- and 20th-century battles, and test trials using pulsed laser weapons to determine the killing effectiveness of these historical units. The analysis was designed (among other things) to determine if Marshall's non-firer figures were correct in other, earlier wars. A comparison of historical combat performances with the performance of their test subjects (who were not actually killing anyone with their weapons and were not in any physical danger from the "enemy") determined that the killing potential in these circumstances was much greater than the actual historical casualty rates. The researchers' conclusions openly supported S. L. A. Marshall's World War II findings, pointing to "unwillingness to take part [in combat] as the main factor" which kept the actual historical killing rates significantly below the laser-trial levels.

In addition to the obvious options of firing over the enemy's head (posturing), or simply dropping out of the advance (a type of flight), and the widely accepted option of loading weapons and otherwise supporting those who were willing to fire (a compromise between the demands of submission and fighting), evidence exists that during blackpowder battles, thousands of soldiers elected to passively "submit" to both the enemy and their leaders through "fake" or "mock" firing. The best indicator of this tendency toward mock firing can be found in the salvage of multiply loaded weapons after Civil War battles. According to Lord, after the battle of Gettysburg, 27,574 muskets were recovered from the battlefield; of these, 24,000 were loaded. Twelve thousand of these loaded muskets were found to be loaded more than once, and 6,000 of the multiply loaded weapons had from three to ten rounds loaded in the barrel. One weapon had been loaded 23 times.[34]

The practical necessity for muzzleloaders to be loaded from a kneeling or standing position, combined with the shoulder-to-shoulder massed firing line of this era, presents a situation in which—unlike that studied by Marshall—it was very difficult for a man to disguise the fact that he was not shooting, and what du Picq called the "mutual surveillance" of authorities and peers must have created an intense pressure to fire in this type of battle. Many leaders took advantage of the endless training hours their soldiers had spent in firing drill by having the men fire "by the numbers" in a volley fire in which every man fired and loaded together. There was not any of what Marshall termed the "isolation and dispersion of the modern battlefield" to hide nonparticipants during volley fire. Their every action was obvious to those comrades who stood shoulder-to-shoulder with them. If a man truly was not able or willing to fire, even to fire over the enemy's heads as we have seen is so common, the only way he could disguise his lack of participation was to load his weapon (tear cartridge, pour powder, set bullet, ram it home, prime, cock), bring it to his shoulder, and then *not actually fire*, possibly even mimicking the recoil of his weapon when everyone else fired.

Here was the epitome of the industrious soldier. Carefully and steadily loading his weapon in the midst of the turmoil, screams, and smoke of battle, no action of his could be criticized by his superiors and comrades. But secretly, quietly, at the moment of decision, just like the 85 percent observed by Marshall, he finds that he is unable to pull the trigger and kill his fellow man.

The Battle of Cold Harbor deserves a close look here, since its instance of "thousands" of casualties occurring in mere "minutes" is the example most casual observers of the American Civil War would hold up to refute the assertions made by Griffin. Bruce Catton, in his definitive, multivolume account of the Civil War, debunks the very common misconception that 7,000 casualties occurred in "Eight Minutes at Cold Harbor." It is quite correct that most of the isolated, disjointed Union charges launched at Cold Harbor were halted in the first ten to twenty minutes, but once the attackers' momentum was broken, the attacking Union soldiers did not flee, and the killing did *not* end. Catton notes that:

> . . . the most amazing thing of all in this fantastic battle is the fact that all along the front the beaten [Union soldiers] did not pull back to the rear. They stayed where they were, anywhere from 40 to 200 yards from the confederate line, gouging out such shallow trenches as they could, and kept on firing . . . all day long the terrible sound of battle continued. Only an experienced soldier could tell by the sound alone, that the pitch of the combat in mid-afternoon was any lower than it had been in the murky dawn when the charges were being repulsed.[35]

Actually, it took up to eight *hours*, not eight minutes, to inflict those horrendous casualties on U. S. Grant's Union soldiers. And, as in most wars from the time of Napoleon to today, it was not the infantry but the *artillery* (in this case firing grapeshot at close range) that inflicted most of these casualties.

### Maneuver Warfare Applications of the Soldier's Options

If we can clear away the fog of the battlefield and grasp the concept that the average soldier in combat has a strong predisposition toward the options of posturing, submission, and flight, and a powerful resistance toward engaging in killing activity, then we have gained vital knowledge about the nature of the individual on the battlefield. And, more so on the battlefield than anywhere else in life, knowledge is power.

## Developing superior posturing

[T]here is in every one an animation, a natural ardor that
is instilled by the onset of combat. Generals ought not to check
but to encourage this ardor. It was for this reason that, in older
times, troops charged with loud shouts, all trumpets sounding,
in order to frighten the enemy and encourage themselves.

Ardant du Picq[36]

If we accept that the ultimate objective of combat should be to break the enemy's will, then it can be more specifically stated that, within the framework of the "Soldier's Options" model, the objective is to foster submission or flight responses in the enemy. In conflicts in the animal kingdom, this is usually accomplished through superior displays of posturing.

Noisemaking is probably one of the most important aspects of posturing. Griffith quotes an account of yelling in its finest form in the thick woods of the American Civil War's Wilderness Battle:

. . . the yellers could not be seen, and a company could make itself
sound like a regiment if it shouted loud enough. Men spoke later
of various units on both sides being "yelled" out of their positions.[37]

In these instances of units being "yelled" out of positions, we see posturing in its most successful form, resulting in the opponent's selection of the flight option without even attempting the fight option. And, of course, this is the biological objective in posturing during intraspecies conflicts: it prevents the males of a species from killing themselves off during ritualistic confrontations.

As soldiers we posture primarily through firepower, and the value of artillery as a means of psychological domination should not be underestimated by the maneuverist. Firepower *can* have a psychological effect that is far greater than the physical attrition it inflicts upon the enemy, but such firepower-based posturing *must* be accompanied by a physical manifestation of close-range, human aggression in order for it to cause the enemy to submit or flee.

If we consider firepower to have a significant psychological or "posturing" value, then we may need to carefully consider such factors as the decibels put out by our artillery rounds and our close-support weapon systems (i.e., is it a good idea to replace 7.62mm, M60 machine guns—a truly daunting noisemaker—with the 5.56mm Squad Automatic Weapon in the light infantry platoon?), the realism of the volume put out by blank adapters (could it be that part of the initial resistance to the M16 vs. the M14 was the "wimpy" way it sounds when fired with its distinctive blank adapter?), and the nuances of using a new generation of electronic hearing protection on the battlefield. That is, is it feasible to build an ear plug–type device that would make it possible to hear friendly commands while shutting out most of the sounds of the enemy's fire, and still have the soldier feel that his fire is a daunting presence on the battlefield? An important element in such a decision may be the degree to which the concussion of a weapon's firing signature can be "felt" by the firers; anyone who has fired an M60 or has been next to one when it is firing will understand what I mean by "feeling" a weapon fire.

**Fostering flight and submission**

> Xenophon says . . . "Be it agreeable or terrible, the less something is foreseen, the more does it cause pleasure or dismay. This is nowhere better illustrated than in war where every surprise strikes terror even to those who are much stronger . . ."
>
> A man surprised, needs an instant to collect his thoughts and defend himself; during this instant he is killed if he does not run away.
>
> Ardant du Picq[38]

Superior posturing, however, is not always the most effective means of daunting an opponent in the animal world. Indeed, too much investment in face-to-face, ceremonial posturing confrontations can simply result in a stylized, set-piece approach to warfare. A more applicable approach to conflict in nature would observe the circumstances in which a small assailant can catch a larger, more powerful opponent by surprise and thereby cause it to submit or flee by virtue of the unexpected ferocity of its attack.

Human beings generally need to be emotionally prepared in order to engage in aggressive behavior. The combat soldier, in particular, needs to be "psyched up" for a confrontation. An attack launched at a time and place when the soldier thought he was safe takes advantage of the stress of uncertainty, destroys his sense of being in control of his environment, and greatly increases the probability that he will opt for flight (i.e., a rout) or submission (i.e., mass surrender). A highly mobile, fluid enemy who can launch surprise attacks in what the enemy believes is his rear area is particularly daunting and confusing, and the presence of such interpersonal hostility can be disproportionately destructive to the will to fight.

Viewed in another way, attacking at an unexpected and unprepared location results in the defender's inability to orient himself. The defender's observation-orientation-decision-action cycle, or his "OODA Loop," has thus been stalled, and he cannot respond. Having been caught off balance, the defender panics and attempts to gain time by fleeing, or simply submits by surrendering in confusion to his assailant.

Psychological research in the area of information processing and human decision making has established a broad base of understanding of normal psychological responses to an "information overload" environment. As too much information comes in, the typical reaction is to fall back initially on heuristic, or "rule of thumb," responses. These heuristic responses involve processes such as: "anchoring" on early information to the exclusion of later, possibly conflicting, or more accurate data; making decisions based on their "availability" or the ease with which a particular response comes to mind (e.g., repeating a recently executed maneuver); or falling into a "conformational bias" in which only information that confirms or supports the current working hypothesis is processed and contrary information is filtered out of consciousness. If these heuristic responses fail (as they are quite likely to), then the normal human response is to become trapped into a "cascading effect" in which he reacts with increasingly inappropriate actions and either fails completely (i.e., is destroyed by the enemy) or completely stops trying and falls into a paralyzed state sometimes referred to by psychologists as "learned helplessness" but always referred to by soldiers as "surrender."

A classical example of this kind of maneuver warfare operation can be observed in Nathan Bedford Forrest's campaign against William Tecumseh Sherman's forces during Sherman's march to the sea in the American Civil War. Forrest, with only a few thousand cavalry, forced Sherman to leave more than 80,000 men to guard his supply centers and his 340-mile-long supply line. On several occasions Forrest fell on unprepared units three times his size and inflicted disproportionate casualties upon his hapless enemies. His primary weapon was surprise. The rear-echelon units he was attacking were not humanly capable of maintaining a fighting pitch at all times, while Forrest's troops entered battle having already attained "morale superiority" since they had plenty of time to prepare themselves emotionally prior to launching their surprise attacks.[39]

### Enabling killing

The final, and perhaps most obvious, application of our understanding of the average soldier's aversion to close-range killing is to manipulate the soldier's training and the variables of his combat environment in such a way as to psychologically "enable" him to kill the enemy. This "killing enabling process" is essential to the understanding of what is happening to the soldier on the battlefield, and is therefore the next area to be examined as we look at how to defeat the enemy's will.

## THE PROCESS OF "ENABLING KILLING"

> I shot him with a .45 and I felt remorse and shame. I can remember whispering foolishly, "I'm sorry" and then just throwing up . . . I threw up all over myself. It was a betrayal of what I'd been taught since a child.
> William Manchester, novelist and World War II veteran describing his response to killing a Japanese soldier[40]

The magnitude of the trauma associated with killing became particularly apparent to me in an interview with one old soldier. He was the commander of a VFW Post where I was conducting some interviews, and had served as a sergeant in the 101st Airborne Division at Bastogne in World War II. He talked freely about his experiences and about comrades who had been killed, but when I asked him about his own kills he stated that usually you couldn't be sure who it was that did the killing. Then tears welled up in his eyes and after a long pause he said, "But the one time I was sure . . ." His sentence was stopped by a little sob, and pain wracked the face of this noble and respected old gentleman. "It still hurts, after all these years?" I asked in wonder. "Yes," he said, "after all these years." And he would not speak of it again.

The next day he told me, "You know, Captain, the questions you're asking, you must be very careful not to hurt anyone with these questions. Not me you know, I can take it, but some of these young guys are still hurting very badly. These guys don't need to be hurt any more." And I was profoundly struck by the certainty that I was picking at the scabs of terrible, hidden wounds in the minds of these kind and gentle men.

Killing in close combat is, unquestionably, a profoundly traumatic experience. Years of research in this field have convinced me that there is a powerful resistance in most individuals to killing their fellow human beings. I have become equally convinced that there is a set of circumstances and pressures that can cause most human beings to overcome this resistance.

Having established the nature of the soldier's dilemma, and having established the presence of the soldier's natural, preferred responses to aggression, the next and most important step is to understand the circumstances and pressures that can be brought to bear on the individual soldier to "enable" him to overcome this reluctance to killing. The objective of this study is to attempt to understand the psychological underpinnings of maneuver warfare, and I submit that these factors are the basic, underlying psychological forces which are effectively manipulated in maneuver warfare to: (1) empower the will of one's own forces and (2) undermine or attack the enemy's will to fight.

### The Milgram Factors: The Killer's Relationship to Group, Authority, and Victim

I observed a mature and initially poised businessman enter the laboratory smiling and confident. Within 20 minutes he was reduced to a twitching, stuttering wreck, who was rapidly approaching a point of nervous collapse . . . At one point he pushed his fist into his forehead and muttered: "Oh God,

let's stop it." And yet he continued to respond to every word
of the experimenter and obeyed to the end.

Stanley Milgram[41]

In the 1960s, Dr. Stanley Milgram's famous studies of obedience
and aggressive behavior under laboratory conditions at Yale University found that, in a controlled, laboratory environment, over 65 percent of his subjects could be readily manipulated into inflicting a lethal
electrical charge on a total stranger. The subjects sincerely believed
that they were causing great physical pain to a total stranger whom
they had just met. Despite their victim's pitiful pleas for them to stop,
65 percent continued to obey orders and increase the voltage and inflict the shocks until long after the screams stopped and there could
be little doubt that their victim was dead.[42] This research by Milgram
(which has since been replicated many times in half a dozen different
countries) combines with that of other psychologists to identify the
three major interactions incorporated in Figure 2 as (1) the Distance
from the Victim, (2) the Demands of Authority, and (3) Group Absolution. Analysis indicates that each of these variables can be further
operationalized into subcategories as indicated in Figure 2.

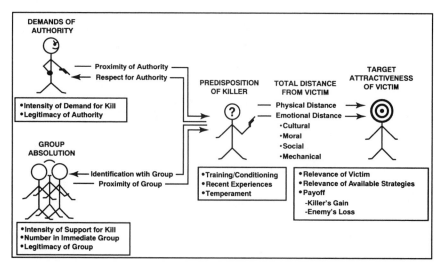

Figure 2: Killing enabling factors

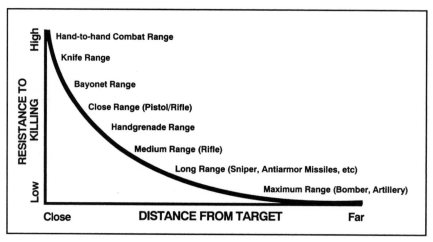

Figure 3: Relationship between distance from target and resistance to killing

## Physical distance

> To fight from a distance is instinctive in man. From the first day
> he has worked to this end, and he continues to do so.
>
> Ardant du Picq[43]

The physical distance between the actual aggressor and the victim
was created in Milgram's studies by placing a barrier between the subject
and the individual he was shocking. This same process can be generalized to and observed in historical combat circumstances, as portrayed
in Figure 3. John Keegan in *The Face of Battle* notes that "only a fraction
of one per cent of all wounds" at the Battle of the Somme in World
War I were inflicted with edged weapons—and most of those in the
back.[44] Interviews and research reveal countless incidents in which
combatants confronted with an enemy soldier at close range did not
fire, but when faced with an enemy who could be attacked with a hand
grenade, or who could be engaged at medium range or long range, the
incidence of nonfiring behavior goes down significantly. At the greatest
range, among high-altitude bombers or artillery crews, incidents of refusal
to fire are extraordinarily rare.

Units with a history and tradition of close-combat, hand-to-hand killing inspire special dread and fear in an enemy by capitalizing upon this natural aversion to the "hate" manifested in this determination to engage in close-range interpersonal aggression. The British Gurkha battalions have been historically effective at this (as can be seen in the Argentineans' dread of them during the Falklands War), but any unit that puts a measure of faith in the bayonet has grasped a little of the natural dread with which an enemy responds to the possibility of facing an opponent determined to come within "skewering range."

What these units (or at least their leaders) must understand is that actual "skewering" almost *never* happens; but the powerful human revulsion to the threat of such activity, when confronted with superior posturing represented by a willingness or at least a reputation for participation in close-range killing, has a devastating effect upon the enemy's morale. This powerful revulsion to being killed with cold steel could be observed when mutinous Indian soldiers captured during the Sepoy Mutiny "begged for the bullet," pleading to be executed with a rifle shot rather than the bayonet.

The combination of closeness with uncertainty (especially at night) helps explain why flank and rear attacks shatter the enemy's will to fight. The assumption that the enemy is *very* close raises the level of uncertainty. This closeness and uncertainty combine and conspire with the darkness's lack of mutual surveillance in such a manner as to erode and destroy the enemy's will to fight.

### Emotional distance: blindfolds and bayonets in the back

> Combat at close quarters does not exist. At close quarters
> occurs the ancient carnage when one force strikes the other in
> the back.
>
> Ardant du Picq[45]

One of the more interesting processes to occur in the area of emotional distance is the psychological leverage gained by not having to see the victim's face. Israeli research has determined that hooded hostages and blindfolded kidnapping victims have a significantly greater chance of being killed by their captors.[46] This demonstrates the difficulty associated with killing an individual whose face you can see, even when that individual represents a significant threat by being able to later identify you in court.

This same enabling process explains why Nazi, communist, and gangland executions are traditionally conducted with a bullet in the back of the head, and individuals being executed by hanging or firing squad are traditionally blindfolded or hooded. Not having to look at the face of the victim provides a form of psychological distance which enables the execution party and assists in their subsequent denial and/or rationalization and acceptance of having killed a fellow human being.

In combat the enabling value of psychological distance can be observed in the fact that casualty rates increase significantly *after* the enemy forces have turned their backs and begin to flee. Clausewitz and du Picq both expound at length on the fact that the vast majority of casualties in historical battles were inflicted upon the losing side during the pursuit that followed the victory. In this vein du Picq holds out the example of Alexander the Great, whose forces, during all his years of warfare, lost fewer than 700 men "to the sword."[47] They suffered so few casualties simply because they never lost a battle and therefore had to endure only the very minor casualties inflicted by reluctant combatants in close combat and never had to suffer the very significant losses associated with being pursued by a victorious enemy.

The killing during the pursuit has also traditionally been conducted by cavalry, chariot, or tank units, and these have their own form of psychological distance, which enables their killing activity. In combat a good horseman becomes one with his mount and is transformed into a remarkable new species. He is no longer a man, but is instead a ten-foot tall, half-ton, four-legged, centaur-like "pseudospecies" that has no hesitation to slay the lesser creatures that scurry about beneath him—especially if these lesser beings are being pursued and have their backs turned.

The category of emotional distance also addresses such processes as:

• Cultural distance, such as racial and ethnic differences, which permits the killer to dehumanize the victim.
• Moral distance, which takes into consideration the kind of intense belief in moral superiority and vengeful/vigilante actions associated with many civil wars.

• Social distance, which considers the impact of a lifetime of practice in thinking of a particular class as less than human in a socially
stratified environment.
• Mechanical distance, which includes the sterile "Nintendo Game"
unreality of killing through a TV screen, a thermal sight, a sniper sight,
or some other kind of mechanical buffer that permits the killer to deny
the humanity of his victim.

## The demands of authority

> The mass needs, and we give it, leaders who have the firm-
> ness and decision of command proceeding from habit and an
> entire faith in their unquestionable right to command as
> established by tradition, law and society.
>
> Ardant du Picq[48]

In Milgram's study the demands of authority were represented by
an individual with a clipboard and a white lab coat. This authority figure
stood immediately behind the individual inflicting shocks and directed
that he increase the voltage each time the victim answered a series of
(fake) questions incorrectly. When the authority figure was not personally present but called over a phone, the number of subjects who
were willing to inflict the maximum shock dropped sharply. This process
can be generalized to combat circumstances and operationalized into
the following sub-factors:

• Proximity of the authority figure to the subject. Marshall noted
many specific World War II incidents in which almost all soldiers would
fire their weapons while their leaders observed and encouraged them
in a combat situation; when the leaders left, however, the firing rate
immediately dropped to 15 to 20 percent.
• Killer's subjective respect for the authority figure. To be truly effective,
soldiers must bond to their leader just as they must bond to their group.
Compared to an established and respected leader, an unknown or discredited leader has much less chance of gaining compliance from soldiers
in combat.
• Intensity of the authority figure's demands for killing behavior.
The leader's mere presence is not always sufficient to ensure killing

activity. The leader must also communicate a clear expectancy of killing behavior.

• Legitimacy of the authority figure's authority and demands. Leaders with legitimate, societally sanctioned authority have greater influence on their soldiers; and legitimate, lawful demands are more likely to be obeyed than illegal or unanticipated demands. Gang leaders and mercenary commanders have to work carefully around their shortcomings in this area, but military officers (with their trappings of power and the legitimate authority of their nation behind them) have tremendous potential to cause their soldiers to overcome individual resistance and reluctance in combat.

### Groups: accountability and anonymity

> Whenever one surveys the forces of the battlefield, it is to see that fear is general among men, but to observe further that men commonly are loath that their fear will be expressed in specific acts which their comrades will recognize as cowardice. The majority are unwilling to take extraordinary risks and do not aspire to a hero's role, but they are equally unwilling that they should be considered the least worthy among those present.
>
> I imagine that those versed in the sciences would see in these statements simple proof that the ego is the most important of the motor forces driving the soldier, and that if it were not for the ego, it would be impossible to make men face the risks of battle. From that point, one could go on to say that social pressure, more than military training, is the base of battle discipline, and that when social pressure is lifted, battle discipline disintegrates. But I would prefer the simple statement that personal honor is the thing valued more than life itself by the majority of men.
>
> S. L. A. Marshall[49]

In the area of group processes, a tremendous volume of research indicates that the primary factor that motivates a soldier to dangerous and difficult deeds during combat is not fear of death, but a powerful sense of accountability toward his comrades on the battlefield. Ardant du Picq referred to this as "mutual surveillance." It is this process of mutual surveillance that ensures that crew-served weapons such as cannon or machine guns will almost always fire effectively in combat.

Marshall noted that a single soldier falling back from a broken and retreating unit will be of little value if pressed into service in another unit, but if a pair of soldiers, or the remnants of a squad or platoon, is put to use, they can generally be counted upon to fight well.[50] The difference in these two situations is the degree to which the soldiers have "bonded" or developed a sense of accountability to their comrades. Du Picq sums this matter up when he says that "Four brave men who do not know each other will not dare to attack a lion. Four less brave, but knowing each other well, sure of their reliability and consequently of mutual aid, will attack resolutely. There," says du Picq, "is the science of the organization of armies in a nutshell."[51]

One of the important things that occurs in groups is the empowering of killing processes. Conrad Lorenz tells us that "Man is not a killer, but the group is." Psychologists have long understood that a "diffusion of responsibility" can be caused by numbers. It has been demonstrated in literally dozens of studies that bystanders will be less likely to interfere in a situation in direct relationship to the numbers who are witnessing the circumstance. Thus, in large crowds, horrendous crimes can occur with low likelihood of a bystander interfering, but if the bystander is alone, faced with a circumstance in which no one else shares the responsibility, then the probability of intervention is very high.

In the same way, groups can provide a diffusion of responsibility or a kind of anonymity that will enable mobs to commit acts they would never dream of doing as individuals. Among groups in combat, this same combination of accountability and anonymity is a significant factor in enabling killing.

These group factors are a key part of the process that has made chariots and tanks so effective on the battlefield. Chariots and tanks engage in the same form of pseudospeciation as cavalry, but they are also a crew-served weapon and are enabled by the same group processes that have made artillery and machine guns the major killers on so many battlefields for so many years.

## The Shalit Factors: Victim Characteristics and
## Tactical Circumstance

> Man taxes his ingenuity to be able to kill without running the
> risk of being killed.
>
> Ardant du Picq[52]

Israeli military psychologist Ben Shalit has developed a model revolving around the nature of the victim, which has been modified slightly
and incorporated into this model. The Shalit factors consider the
nature of the victim and the tactical circumstances associated with a
combat kill.[53] On this level the soldier conducts a personal assessment
of his available options and their potential "payoff" in terms of the
relevance of the victim and the relevance and effectiveness of available strategies for killing the victim.

Although somewhat obvious, such factors as, "Will I do the enemy
any harm by killing this poor slob, and will I be able to get away with
it without getting killed myself?" should not be overlooked as critical factors in the potential killer's decision to engage in a specific killing
circumstance.

## The Predisposition of the Killer:
## Training/Conditioning of the Soldier

Marshall felt that his contributions to the U.S. Army's training program
increased the firing rate of the individual infantryman from 15 to 20
percent in World War II to 55 percent in Korea[54] and 80 to 95 percent in Vietnam.[55] The way he did this was by making a simple application of operant conditioning to the training of the soldier. Although
he might not have called it such, there is little doubt that this is what
was happening.

World War II–era training was conducted on a grassy firing range
(a known-distance or "KD" range) on which the soldier shot at a bull's-
eye target. After he fired a series of shots, the target was checked and
he was then given feedback telling him where he hit. Modern training uses what is essentially operant conditioning techniques to develop
a firing "behavior" in the soldier.

When operant conditioning is taught to psychology students at West
Point, the modern army marksmanship range is used as a classical example

of "Skinnerian" operant conditioning. In this training, or "shaping," process everything comes as close as possible to simulating actual combat conditions. The soldier stands in a foxhole with full combat equipment, and man-shaped, pop-up targets appear in front of him, becoming "discriminative stimuli." The "target behavior" is to immediately and unhesitatingly shoot those pop-up targets, and "positive reinforcement" is given in the form of immediate feedback when the target drops if it is hit. In a form of "token economy" these hits are then exchanged for marksmanship badges which usually have some form of privilege or reward (praise, public recognition, three-day passes, etc.) associated with them. Several independent studies indicate that this powerful conditioning process has dramatically increased the firing rate of American soldiers since World War II. We can't be sure that the *killing* rate has gone up, since much of the increase in firing may be "posturing," but the powerful impact of modern training/conditioning techniques is a major factor in enabling aggressive behavior on the battlefield.

Richard Holmes has noted the ineffectiveness of an army trained in traditional World War II methods as opposed to an army whose soldiers have been "conditioned" by modern training methods. Holmes interviewed British soldiers returning from the Falklands War and asked them if they had experienced any incidence of non-firing similar to that observed by Marshall in World War II. They replied that they had not seen any such thing in their soldiers, but they most definitely had observed it in the poorly trained Argentineans, whose only effective fire had come from machine guns and snipers.[56] [Modern snipers are enabled by group processes since they are almost always teamed with a "spotter" who provides mutual accountability and turns the sniper into a crew-served weapon. In addition, snipers are enabled by: (1) the physical distance at which they fire, (2) the mechanical distance created by viewing the enemy through a scope, and (3) the fact that they are predisposed by temperament due to their careful selection by command and "self-selection" through their willingness to volunteer for the job.]

### The Predisposition of the Killer: Temperament
Swank and Marchand's World War II study noted the existence of 2 percent of combat soldiers who are predisposed to be "aggressive

psychopaths" and apparently do not experience the normal resistance to killing or the resultant psychiatric casualties associated with extended periods of combat. The negative connotation associated with the term "psychopath" or its modern equivalent, "sociopath," is inappropriate here, since this behavior is a generally desirable one for soldiers in combat, but there does seem to be some foundation for a belief that a very small percentage of all combatants are doing a tremendously disproportionate amount of the killing.

The *Diagnostic and Statistical Manual* (DSM-III-R) of the American Psychiatric Association (APA) indicates that the incidence of "antisocial personality disorder" (i.e., sociopaths) among the general population of American males is approximately 3 percent.[57] Armies over the centuries have become very good at utilizing such highly aggressive individuals during wartime, so if only a third of this 3 percent were compatible with military life, a hypothetical 1 percent of soldiers would, by the APA's DSM-III-R definition, "have no remorse about the effects of their behavior on others."

Like most personality disorders, this one is a continuum which contains many individuals who, while not meeting the full diagnostic criteria, are on the "borderline" of antisocial personality disorder. The DSM-III-R tells us that some individuals "who have several features of the disorder [but not enough to be diagnosed with it] achieve political and economic success," and it may be that this small percentage also needs to be taken into consideration.

But this is not a complete answer, and as a psychologist I believe that we have just begun to come to the nub of this matter. There is strong evidence that there exists a genetic predisposition for aggression. In all species the best hunter, the best fighter survives to pass on his biological predispositions to his descendants. There are also environmental processes that can fully develop this predisposition toward aggression; when we combine this genetic predisposition with environmental development we get aggression. But there is another factor, and that factor seems to be the presence or absence of empathy for others. Again, there may be biological and environmental causes for this empathic process, but whatever its origin, there is undoubtedly a division in humanity between those who feel and understand the pain and suffering of others, and those who cannot. The presence of aggression, combined with the absence of empathy, results in sociopathy.

The presence of aggression, combined with the presence of empathy, results in an individual completely different from the sociopath.

One veteran I interviewed told me that he thought of most of the world as sheep: gentle, decent, kindly creatures who are essentially incapable of true aggression. In this veteran's mind there is another human subspecies (of which he was a member) that is a kind of dog: faithful, vigilant creatures who are very much capable of aggression when circumstances require. But, according to his model, there are wolves (sociopaths) and packs of wild dogs (gangs and aggressive armies) abroad in the land, and the sheepdogs (the soldiers and policemen of the world) are environmentally and biologically predisposed to be the ones who confront these predators.

I have met these men, these "sheepdogs," over and over again as I interviewed veterans. They are men, like one U.S. Army lieutenant colonel, a Vietnam veteran, who told me: "I learned early on in life that there are people out there who will hurt you if given the chance, and I have devoted my life to being prepared to face them." These men are quite often armed, and always vigilant. They would not misuse or misdirect their aggression any more than a sheepdog would turn on his flock, but in their hearts many of them yearn for a righteous battle, a wolf upon whom to legitimately and lawfully turn their skills.

Some may think of them as sheepdogs, and that is a good analogy, but I prefer another term, another analogy. There is a model, an "archetype," which, according to Jung, exists deep in the "collective unconscious"—an inherited, unconscious reservoir of images derived from our ancestors' universal experiences and shared by the whole human race. These powerful archetypes can drive us by channeling our libidinal energy. They include such Jungian concepts as *the mother, the wise old man,* and *the hero.* I think that Jung might refer to these people as heroes not as sheepdogs.

According to Gwynne Dyer, United States Air Force research concerning aggressive killing behavior determined that 1 percent of USAF fighter pilots in World War II did nearly 40 percent of the air-to-air killing, and the majority of their pilots never even tried to shoot anyone down.[58] This 1 percent of World War II fighter pilots, Swank and Marchand's 2 percent, Griffith's low Napoleonic and Civil War killing rates, and Marshall's low World War II firing rates can all be at least partially explained if only a small percentage of these combatants were actually willing to actively kill the enemy in these combat situations. Call them sociopaths, sheepdogs, or heroes as you please, but they exist, they are a distinct minority, and in time of war our nation needs them desperately.

### Application to Maneuver Warfare

In terms of maneuver warfare this model permits us (among many other things) to understand the psychological value of maneuver over firepower, and the enabling processes that are created through granting discretion and authority to subordinates in an *Auftragstaktik*, or "mission orders," environment.

### Maneuver

> Frederick liked to say that three men behind the enemy were worth fifty in front of him.
>
> Ardant du Picq[59]

One of the most powerful forms of "distance" on the battlefield is created by placing subordinates between the subject and the victim. Thus, a leader who does not have to do the killing himself is enabled (by physical and psychological distance) to "demand" aggressive behavior of his subordinates, and subordinates are enabled by the leader's demands. A commanding general is just one more individual, a human being who is subject to the same stresses and demands as the rifleman, and he is equally susceptible to empowering or undermining through manipulation of the variables outlined in this model. The leader may have training, experiences, and predispositions, which differentiate him from his subordinates, and we can and should attempt to influence those on the battlefield, but what we must also always strive to influence (through maneuver) is the leader's links to his higher authority and group absolution processes.

Within this model it can be observed that maneuver can be psychologically more effective than firepower since maneuver cuts off or threatens to cut off the enemy's source of legitimacy and authority by isolating large elements from their link to group and authority enabling processes. Firepower can kill members of the group, but the group is still in contact and the group still enables its members. Firepower can kill leaders but the leader's subordinates and staff can leap into the breech, and the chain of command, *and* its vital link to the legitimacy of the soldier's society, still exists. As a corollary to maneuver, we can note that the objective of maneuver should ultimately be the pursuit, and can establish a psychological explanation for the tremendous increase in killing that occurs during the pursuit and rout, which *usually has resulted from maneuver.*

### Auftragstaktik

> Today there is a tendency . . . on the part of superiors to infringe on the authority of inferiors. . . . It goes very high and is furthered by the mania for command. . . . It results in lessening the authority of subordinate officers. . . . The tendency is to oppress subordinates; to want to impose on them, in all things, the views of the superior. . . . A colonel . . . thus takes all initiative from subordinate officers, and reduces them to a state of inertia. . . .
>
> [When] this firm hand which directs so many things is absent for a moment . . . subordinate officers are like a horse, always kept on a tight rein, whose rein is loosened or missing. They cannot in an instant recover that confidence in themselves, that has been painstakingly taken from them.
>
> Ardant du Picq[60]

With *Auftragstaktik*, or "mission orders," the leader disseminates his authority with the mission, and the piece of authority that is passed down with the mission empowers subordinates at all levels. Patton understood this concept when he directed his subordinates to tell their men *what* to do but not *how* to do it, and then to "let them amaze you with their ingenuity." A subordinate leader who is told precisely *how* to do something no longer has any obligation, accountability, or even legitimacy in accomplishing the task by an alternative method when the initial plan becomes impractical. *Auftragstaktik* empowers aggressive behavior by:

• Increasing the proximity and number of authority figures. Ideally, under *Auftragstaktik*, every soldier becomes an obedience-demanding authority. The last line of the U.S. Army Ranger Creed is "I will go on to accomplish the mission, though I be the lone survivor." That mentality, and the cultivation of subordinate leaders and soldiers who can make it come alive, is the ultimate objective of *Auftragstaktik*.

• Increasing a subordinate's subjective respect for the authority figure, since the authority and initiative of the highest commander have been passed to the lowest subordinate.

• Increasing the authority figure's demands for killing behavior. Since the subordinate leader becomes the originator of his own set of mission orders, which are built upon the framework of his superior's mission orders (as opposed to being an errand boy simply passing down messages from on high), he accepts ownership of the mission and becomes strongly invested in demanding mission accomplishment from his subordinates.

• Increasing the legitimacy of the authority and the demands of subordinate leaders by institutionalizing a process in which it is the norm for subordinates to assume broad discretion and flexibility. Only then will you have a true, pervasive, mission orders environment.

### The Last Three Inches:
### The Battle within the Mind of the Commander

Ultimately, the final and most important battle takes place, not in the last 300 meters, nor even in the last 30 meters, but in the last three inches: inside the mind of the commander. Maneuver warfare, a "thought process" directed at the enemy's "mind," must win that battle above all others, and this study of the psychological underpinnings of maneuver warfare would be deficient if it did not examine those psychological factors that can constrain the commander from using maneuver-oriented operations.

### The Quest for Order

There are plenty of small-minded men who in time of peace are inexorable in matters of equipment and drill, and perpetually interfere in the work of their subordinates. They thus acquire an unmerited reputation, and render the service a burden, but above all do mischief in preventing development of individuality, and in retarding the advancement of independent and capable spirits.

Archduke Charles

What the Archduke is talking about here, and what Ardant du Picq was talking about in the quote at the beginning of the earlier section on *Auftragstaktik*, is recognized today as an overwhelming desire for control, practitioners of which are sometimes referred to as having a "controlling" personality. There is in every human being a need for order, and each of us continually strives to maintain order in our environment so as to maintain the necessary degree of control over our lives. When faced with stress and loss of control, we all have an inclination toward a particular response. Some respond with direct aggression, others by becoming passively aggressive (the Mahatma Gandhi approach), or by becoming overly dependent upon and submissive to higher authority, or by becoming "histrionic" with great displays of emotion and posturing, or by becoming avoidant and withdrawing within themselves. And some respond by compulsively seeking control of every aspect of their environment.

All of us generally have an inclination toward one or another of these responses, and by training and through pure force of intellect we usually channel it into a pool of various responses from which we can select the appropriate one for each situation. The "controlling" response is very common in the military because it is so effective in peacetime, and those who are good at it seldom learn to constrain it until it is too late.

It is essential to note that this is *not* an "obsessive compulsive" or an "anal retentive" individual. At its greatest extreme, when it has caused someone's interaction with their daily environment to become completely dysfunctional, this controlling tendency may manifest itself as an obsessive compulsive personality disorder, just as a preference for direct, overt, aggressive responses, when taken to the extreme, can manifest itself as an antisocial personality disorder—i.e., a sociopath. What we are discussing here is a normal personality type which has an inclination toward a specific type of response.

Individuals too closely attached to other types of responses to stressful situations (e.g., aggression, passive aggression, dependence, histrionics, avoidance, etc.[61]) are generally weeded out by the demands of the military system, but a good, hardworking micromanager can flourish. While these commanders can overcontrol in garrison and in training and will generally prosper in doing so, in the swirling maelstrom of the battlefield such micromanagement becomes impossible. In combat these individuals may respond to stress and loss of control in the only way they know, in the same manner that has been so successful for them in the past: by taking an ever tighter grip on the reins of command. If you tighten the reins on a "beast" (in this case the military organization), it simply slows down and is increasingly unable to respond to the demands of its environment. More stress is responded to with more control, which results in less responsiveness to the demands of combat, which creates more stress, which is responded to with even more draconian control measures . . . and so on, in an ever tightening cycle of inappropriate responses that can ultimately lead to defeat and despair.

The motivation for overcontrol is not always rooted in a controlling personality. Sometimes it is motivated by a kind of narcissism or egoism. These individuals are driven by their ego to centralize control. Narcissism is quite common in professions such as politics and the military. The perks, the awards and decorations, and the "ruffles and flourishes" that come with military rank are a major source of reward for the commander (we sure don't do it for the money), and all good commanders probably have a healthy vein of narcissism, but the true narcissist is driven by this as his only motive. His ego can sometimes motivate him to achieve tremendous deeds on the battlefield, but he is generally not capable of receiving vicarious reinforcement from the autonomous achievements of his subordinates. In the eyes of a narcissist, the achievements of an autonomous subordinate are not his achievements. To him his force is an extension of his ego, and he derives great power from that fact; but to release control of any element is to diminish himself, and the very thought of decentralized, maneuver-based operations is abhorrent.

Whether motivated by narcissism or by a need to micromanage, these "controllers" are absolutely and unequivocally opposed to maneuver warfare and its decentralization of command; they sense that within an army that has truly internalized maneuver warfare doctrine, their *modus operandi* would have to be modified into a more well-rounded pool of responses, or else they will soon go the way of the mighty megalosaurus.

The forces of egoism and micromanagement have worked for many leaders for their entire military careers, and when faced with a doctrine that looks like an invitation to chaos, they can become quite hostile. But maneuver warfare is not chaos; it is simply decentralization guided by the intent of the commander and intelligently executed by carefully trained subordinates. In this synergistic effort there is greater "control" than any one human could ever achieve. Sun Tzu wrote of the deceptive appearance of chaos that occurs when a commander who is "skilled in war" executes maneuver warfare. "In the tumult and uproar," he said, "the battle seems chaotic, but there is no disorder; the troops appear to be milling about in circles but cannot be defeated. Apparent confusion is a product of good order."[62]

## The Quest for Honor and Glory

When you subdue your enemy without fighting who will pronounce you valorous?

Sun Tzu[63]

In the same passage quoted at the end of the last section, Sun Tzu goes on to say that in warfare "apparent cowardice [is a product] of courage; apparent weakness of strength." Herein lies another psychological cause for opposition to maneuver warfare: to the warrior motivated by a desire for honor and glory, this "dancing around the enemy" smells of weakness and cowardice.

While getting my graduate degree in psychology, I fulfilled my practicum requirement by serving as a junior high school counselor. I worked in group sessions with many troubled young men, and one thing they consistently wanted from me was help in getting their way with the adults—parents, teachers, and others—whom they saw as "the enemy" on their adolescent battlefields. I told them that I knew a way to increase their "charisma," a "charm spell" that was guaranteed to increase the probability of having things go their way by 10 to 20 percent or more.

They were eager, they were excited. "Charm spells" and "charisma" were terms from "Dungeons and Dragons–type role-playing and video games, and they wanted to learn this piece of psychological magic. The trick is, I told them, to appropriately use the magic words "please, sir, and ma'am."

A few were excited and convinced by this mercenary and manipulative application of the old "magic word," but most were disgusted. They would never do such a thing. They could never debase themselves in such a weak and cowardly manner. Their self-esteem, their image, was so weak that they could not permit themselves to say these hateful words of appeasement. They wanted the "enemy" to submit before the superior force of their will power, but they did not have sufficient will to use the means available to them. The only method they could conceive of using was some form of physical posturing or brute strength: to outyell, outpout, or outhit their opponents. But in this as in all human interactions, the victory goes most often not to the strong, nor to the swift, but to the sly.

We must never underestimate the power of the desire to maintain one's self-image. In the case of these children (and of many adults), it prevents them from using simple courtesy as a social stratagem. In combat, the desire not to be seen as a coward in the eyes of others is the single most powerful motivating force on the battlefield, a force sufficient to overcome the instinct for self preservation and make men face certain death without wavering. But, in addition to sustaining men on the battlefield, the demands of the self-image also have a long history of constraining combatants.

A friend of mine was the sponsor for a visiting Central African officer who was attending the U.S. Army's Infantry Officer Advance Course. This experienced, intelligent, and articulate African officer almost failed the tactics portion of the course because he could not and would not devise any plan nor select any answers that involved a flank or rear attack. To even imagine doing so would be profoundly dishonorable and was simply unthinkable.

It is easy to feel superior to such an officer today, but he is only an obvious aspect of a long heritage. From the ancient Greeks, who preferred "manly" face-to-face combat and refused to use projectile weapons, to the French, who were offended and shocked that the Germans refused to meet them in honorable World War I–style combat and came around their Maginot line, history is full of sacrifices made on the altar of the "warrior" self-image. Today that legacy of self-inflicted constraint can be seen in the resistance to the use of maneuver concepts.

The ancient Chinese soldier-scholar, Sun Tzu, recognized this problem almost two and a half millennia ago in *The Art of War*. "Generally," wrote Sun Tzu,

> in war the best policy is to take a state intact; to ruin it is inferior to this. Do not put a premium on killing. To capture the enemy's army is better than to destroy it . . . for to win one hundred vic-

tories in one hundred battles is not the acme of skill. To subdue the enemy without fighting is the acme of skill.[64]

Who can argue with this as a goal? To do this is the true mark of "a master of war." But, adds Sun Tzu,

The victories won by a master of war gain him neither reputation for wisdom nor merit for valor. A victory gained before the situation has crystallized is one the common man does not comprehend. Thus the author gains no reputation for sagacity. . . . When you subdue your enemy without fighting who will pronounce you valorous?[65]

This is the problem. There is no glory, certainly not glory as Americans perceive it, in an ideal maneuver victory. There is a real reluctance to drive around the enemy and have a bloodless victory. It seems contrary to the warrior mentality that resides in all of us. It's just not "cricket."
"Therefore," concludes Sun Tzu,

the general who in advancing does not seek personal fame, and in withdrawing is not concerned with avoiding punishment, but whose only purpose is to protect the people and promote the best interests of his sovereign, is the precious jewel of the state.

But, adds Tu Mu, an ancient commentator on Sun Tzu of over a thousand years ago, "Few such are to be had."
Americans in particular are inclined to deify the brand of glory personified in the prizefighter or the football team. These precisely measured and matched activities exemplify the American concept of "glory" in a "fair fight." To such individuals maneuver warfare can seem like "dancing around the enemy," and those who practice or promote it are thought of in the same way that old-fashioned boxing fans considered the "float like a butterfly, sting like a bee" style of Muhammad Ali: "What's all this 'science' baloney? Stand up and fight, ya coward!" But maneuver warfare has absolutely no intention of fighting fair and will "stand up and fight" only as a last resort. Maneuver warfare is not an old-fashioned prizefight, but a bullfight in which the bull, a huge and deadly opponent, is first worn down and confused by oppo-

nents with superior mobility—the picadors—before the matador finally comes in and, with grace and skill, pierces his opponent's heart with one, single, clean sword thrust. But Americans are repulsed by bull-fighting. And perhaps it is appropriate to leave it behind us as a form of entertainment; as a form of warfare, however, when we face an opponent intent on killing our sons and daughters, nothing else is acceptable. The military leader who eschews the matador's coup de grace in an endeavor to attain the "glory" and "honor" of a boxer's toe-to-toe slugfest must never be given responsibility for American lives.

This does not mean that there will never be times when we must meet the enemy head-on in equal combat. Far worse than a leader who has no spirit for maneuver is a leader who has no stomach for fight-ing at all. In the American Civil War, McClellan seems to have suf-fered from such a character flaw. Sun Tzu recognized a need for "or-dinary" units that would hold the line while "extraordinary" units would maneuver to unhinge the enemy. At least U. S. Grant had the spirit to grapple with his opponent in order to apply his superior numbers and industrial resources to crush his opponent—and he was, arguably, capable of some pretty fair maneuvering upon occasion. A true "master" of war, in the sense of Sun Tzu and in terms of maneuver warfare, is one who can use both attrition and maneuver, both the ordinary and the extraordinary, and, most importantly, who knows how to properly balance the two.

MacArthur had to fight bloody, sustained battles in New Guinea in order to lay a base for his "island hopping" maneuver campaign of bypassing enemy strong points in the Pacific, and in Korea MacArthur had to fight a desperate holding battle at the Pusan perimeter in order to execute the decisive maneuver operation at Inchon. Someone has to, in Patton's colorful words, "Hold 'em by the nose" while the ma-neuver element "kicks 'em in the ass." The leader responsible for American lives must be the matador who distracts and frustrates the enemy with an elusive and flexible cape while striving for the opportunity to not just "kick" the enemy but quickly and cleanly pierce deep into his heart. But he must also be *capable* of courageously facing the enemy in mortal combat, while not preferring to do so.

There is in each individual who holds himself to be a warrior an atavistic, primal force that craves a special kind of domination glory, a force that desires to grapple with and best the enemy. It can be seen in those teenage boys who could not say please; it can be seen in the ceremonial, head-butting combats of goats and other horned and ant-lered creatures during mating season; and it can be seen in even the greatest of maneuverists when their will power runs low and the hind-brain gains control over the intellect.

When worn down and exhausted deep in the enemy's country, Napoleon and Robert E. Lee, two great maneuverists, both hit a point at which they seemed to be no longer willing to maneuver, no longer able to fight with the intellect. In a kind of moral exhaustion, like a weary Muhammad Ali in the fifteenth round of a hard match, Napoleon at Borodino and Lee at Gettysburg could not bring themselves to "will" their forces into one last flanking movement and seemed to almost fatalistically, unconsciously decide that "Today is the day I will come to grips with my enemy, today is as good a day as any to die." Lee, without Stuart and his cavalry "eyes," and deep in enemy territory, resigned himself to a blind grappling with the enemy at Gettysburg. Napoleon, his forces eroded by the long march deep into Russia, and frustrated by his inability to decisively defeat his elusive enemy, did the same at Borodino. And in both cases, when they stopped maneu-vering they lost.

Future commanders, exhausted and frustrated by seemingly endless maneuvering against their enemy, will reach the point at which they cannot go on and come to feel that they must risk all on one last roll of the dice. In their staff and amongst their subordinates are the Picketts and the Murats: clamoring for glory, eager to lunge into the jaws of death, lusting for the honor of coming to grips with the enemy. These valuable and aggressive subordinates may give unspoken or even spoken messages of frustration or thinly veiled contempt and disgust for the failure of their leader to come to grips with the enemy. They are pis-tols full of impotent rage quivering in the commander's hand. At some point their moral force may outweigh that of the commander, and he can no longer hold them back. He lets slip his dogs of war in equal battle, and the victory goes, not to the sly, nor to the swift, but to the strong in a bloody battle on equal terms.

## Winning the War in the Commander's Mind

If maneuver warfare is "a thought process which seeks to pit strength against weakness to break the enemy's will," then, as a thought pro-cess, it must exist first and foremost in the mind of the commander, and it is there that it must be nurtured and supported. What we must ask ourselves is, how can this thought process, as manifested in an organization that has embraced maneuver warfare as a fundamental doctrine, provide psychological support mechanisms that will develop and sustain the commander's moral force, his "will to maneuver"?

This question is deserving of another paper completely, one focusing on the potential contributions of: (1) the military education and officer development system, and (2) the staff system. Suffice it to say here that the education and professional development system should nurture subordinates who have the capacity for both aggression action *and* maneuver. These subordinates, who will later become commanders, must become Longstreets who encourage their commander to maneuver and who envision for themselves the glory of the matadors first, and that of the prizefighting "slugger" only as a last resort. And their reading and study of the military arts must support a world view; it must enable a *Weltanschauung*, which believes, as Sun Tzu put it, that "the best policy is to take a state intact; to ruin it is inferior . . . To capture the enemy's army is better than to destroy it. . . . To subdue the enemy without fighting is the acme of skill."

In the same way, the staff system must develop and nurture professional staff officers who are imbued with the spirit of maneuver and will put aside aspirations for command and the direct glory of physical confrontation. This was the strength of the German general staff in World War II, and there is a desperate need for those who would be von Mellenthins to future Balcks. The subordinate and the staff officer, combining to support the moral force of the commander in maneuver as well as in direct, bloody confrontation, can be a vital source of support for the battle that is constantly being waged in the commander's mind.

## SEEING THE ELEPHANT

Battle is the final objective of armies and man is the fundamental instrument in battle. Nothing can wisely be prescribed in an army—its personnel, organization, discipline and tactics, things which are connected like fingers of a hand—without exact knowledge of the fundamental instrument, man, and his state of mind, his morale, at the instant of combat.

Ardant du Picq[66]

During the American Civil War the soldier's first experience in combat was called "seeing the elephant." Success in future wars may depend on our not just seeing, but knowing, controlling, and directing the beast called war. Centuries of soldiers and scholars have been like the proverbial blind men groping at the elephant. When any of us examines the individual's response to war our gropings will probably be equally blind, for we do truly wander in a land where "the great god Mars tries to blind us when we enter" and "gives us a generous cup of the waters of Lethe" when we leave. But by having collected and assembled the reports of those who have gone before us, we can come to a deeper understanding of the nature of the beast and the underlying psychological processes associated with maneuver warfare.

Warfare is the ultimate "survival of the fittest" environment, and the evolution of warfare within this environment has traditionally occurred through a kind of unconscious, Darwinian, natural selection. Today we have, perhaps for the first time, the capacity to begin to understand, anticipate, and consciously control that evolutionary process in one very important way.  That is what maneuver warfare is all about.

# Notes

1. This is a paraphrasing of John Masefield's great poem, "A Consecration." John Masefield, *Poems* (New York: Macmillan, 1947), p. 1.

2. Peter Marin, "Living in Moral Pain," *Psychology Today,* November 1974, p. 72.

3. J. Glenn Gray, *The Warriors: Reflections on Men in Battle* (London: Frank Cass and Co., 1970), p. 16. Lethe is the mythical river of forgetfulness in Hades.

4. Shelford Bidwell, *Modern Warfare* (London: 1972).

5. Richard A. Gabriel, *No More Heroes: Madness and Psychiatry in War* (New York: Hill and Wang, 1987), p. 88.

6. Gabriel, p. 77.

7. Ibid., p. 72.

8. Richard Holmes, *Acts of War: The Behavior of Men in Battle* (New York: Free Press, 1985), p. 260.

9. R. L. Swank and W. E. Marchand, "Combat Neuroses: Development of Combat Exhaustion," *Archives of Neurology and Psychology,* vol. 55, pp. 236–247.

10. This is an excerpt from WWI veteran James H. Knight-Adkin's "No Man's Land," a powerful poem which does a superb job depicting the horror of the soldier's dilemma. James H. Knight-Adkin, "No Man's Land," in *A Treasury of War Poetry: British and American Poems of the World War 1914–1917,* ed. George Herbert Clarke, (New York: Houghton Mifflin Co., 1917), pp. 158, 159.

11. J. W. Appel and G. W. Beebe, "Preventive Psychiatry: An Epidemiological Approach," *Journal of the American Medical Association,* vol. 131, August 18, pp. 1469–1475.

12. Holmes, p. 115.

13. Ibid., p. 126.

14. Ibid., p. 235.

15. Presented by representatives of the Walter Reed Army Institute for Research at the Inter-University Seminar on Armed Forces and Society, Baltimore, Md., October 11–13, 1991.

16. Marin, p. 68.

17. In Paul Fussell, *The Norton Book of War* (New York: Norton & Company, 1991), p. 466.

18. Ardant du Picq, *Battle Studies* (Harrisburg, Penn.: Military Service Publishing Co., 1946), p. 167. Col. Charles Ardant du Picq is arguably the earliest and greatest of those soldier/scholar/psychologists upon whose shoulders modern soldiers and scholars have the privilege to stand. Du Picq was killed in the Franco-Prussian war in 1870, and his book, *Battle Studies,* was published in France after his death. His "Studies" are based on the personal knowledge and keen observations of a career soldier, a firm understanding and study of the classics, and an extensive survey (probably the first of its kind) soliciting observations and input from his fellow officers in the French Army.

19. Gabriel, p. 80.

20. Holmes, p. 147.

21. Paul Fussell, *Wartime: Understanding and Behavior in the Second World War* (New York: Oxford University Press, 1989), p. 16.

22. Gabriel, p. 75.

23. *U.S. News and World Report,* January 20, 1992, p. 44.

24. S. L. A. Marshall, *Men Against Fire: The Problem of Battle Command* (Glouchester, Mass.: Peter Smith, 1978), pp. 78, 79.

25. Ibid., p. 54.

26. du Picq, p. 43.

27. Irenaus Eibl-Eibesfeldt, *The Biology of Peace and War: Men, Animals, and Aggression* (New York: Viking Press, 1975), p. 32.

28. Paddy Griffith, *Battle Tactics of the Civil War* (New Haven, Conn.: Yale University Press, 1989), p. 112.

29. Holmes, p. 173.

30. Ibid.

31. du Picq, p. 125.

32. Griffith, p. 149.

33. Ibid., p. 121.

34. F. A. Lord, *Civil War Collector's Encyclopedia* (Harrisburg, Penn.: Stackpole Company, 1976), p. 86.

35. William B. Catton, *Bruce Catton's Civil War* (New York: Fairfax Press, 1984), p. 556.

36. du Picq, p. 21.

37. Griffith, pp. 159, 160.

38. du Picq, pp. 43, 82.

39. William McElwee, *The Art of War: Waterloo to Mons* (Bloomington, Ind.: Indiana University Press, 1974), pp. 156, 157.

40. William Manchester, *Goodbye, Darkness* (London: Penguin Books, 1981), p. 366.

41. Quoted in Camille B. Wortman and Elizabeth F. Loftus, *Psychology,* 3d ed. (New York: Alfred A. Knopf, 1981), p. 508.

42. Stanley Milgram, *Obedience to Authority* (New York: Harper and Row, 1974).

43. du Picq, p. 112.

44. John Keegan, *The Face of Battle* (New York: Viking Penguin, 1976), pp. 278, 279.

45. du Picq, p. 149.

46. Ben Shalit, *The Psychology of Conflict and Combat* (New York: Praeger Publishers, 1988), p. 56.

47. du Picq, p. 133.

48. Ibid., p. 95.

49. Marshall, p. 149.

50. Ibid., p. 151.

51. du Picq, p. 110.

52. Ibid., p. 46.

53. Shalit, p. 56.

54. Marshall, p. 9.

55. Holmes uses the figure of 80 percent (p. 325). A recent survey of veterans by R. W. Glenn ("Men and Fire in Vietnam," *Army*, April, 1985, pp. 18–27), indicates a 95 percent firing rate.

56. Holmes, p. 326.

57. American Psychiatric Association, *Diagnostic and Statistical Manual of Mental Disorders, Third Edition, Revised* (Washington, DC: APA, 1987), pp. 342–345.

58. Gwynne Dyer, *War* (New York: Crown Publishers, 1985), p. 22.

59. du Picq, p. 114.

60. Ibid., p. 210.

61. For an excellent study of these basic personality disorders (including the narcissistic personality mentioned later) see Theodore Millon, *Disorders of Personality: DSM-III, Axis II* (New York: John Wiley and Sons, 1981). Of particular interest is Millon's concept that everyone has an inclination toward one or another of these responses, but it is only in their more severe manifestations of these that they become true personality disorders.

62. Sun Tzu, *The Art of War* (New York: Oxford University Press, 1971), p. 92.

63. Ibid., p. 87.

64. Ibid., p. 77.

65. Ibid., p. 87.

66. du Picq, p. 39.

# PART 2

# INSTITUTIONALIZING MANEUVER WARFARE

To date, most of the work appearing in professional military journals and other published sources on maneuver warfare has focused on its definition and explication as a body of thought. While advocates and critics contest its validity and potential applicability for the U.S. military, there has been little or no discussion of the institutional issues that go hand in hand with important organizational change.

Adoption of maneuver-oriented battle doctrine involves much more than a revision of current operations manuals. Command and control, senior/subordinate relationships, leader development, individual and collective training, and the unit environment will be affected significantly when, for example, military organizations attempt to shift from a centralized to a decentralized system of command, or from a linear to a nonlinear battlefield orientation.

Organization theory teaches that large institutions have their own distinct cultures and operating routines, and that innovation and change are typically resisted because they challenge these defining characteristics and modes of behavior. These essays suggest that ideas may be less important than the strategies used to implement them. For maneuver warfare to realize its potential, it must become part of the institutional and organizational culture of the U.S. military, and not a rival culture imposed by force from outside.

# Institutionalizing Maneuver Warfare: The Process of Organizational Change

### Michael J. Meese

## INTRODUCTION

An adage among inventors says: "If you build a better mousetrap, people will beat a path to your door to buy it." The other essays in this volume describe maneuver warfare in all of its dimensions, and it is up to the reader, and ultimately the army, to determine if the maneuver warfare mousetrap is superior to the AirLand Battle mousetrap that it would potentially replace. This essay does not specifically promote maneuver warfare; rather, it describes the long path of innovation that maneuver warfare will have to traverse for the army to adopt it as doctrine.

The development, adoption, and implementation of any form of institutional change is difficult in any large organization. This is especially true in the army. To be successful in promoting a better doctrine, maneuver warfare proponents must understand fully the process of doctrinal innovation, the factors that affect it, and the strategies that facilitate successful organizational change. To support this thesis, I have examined much of the literature on business innovation, public sector innovation, and military history, and will draw on those sources to outline my view of the military innovation process.

I first examine why doctrinal innovations take place and explain why maneuver warfare is an example of such an innovation. Second, I describe a model of the innovation process in the army. Third, I address factors that influence the process of military innovation and the problems with implementing changes in the army. In the final section of this essay, I use the model of military innovation developed in the previous sections to recommend strategies that maneuver warfare proponents should use to facilitate the implementation of new doctrine in the army.

## WHY INNOVATE?

The proper doctrine is critical to the military in particular and to the nation in general. Although debates over doctrine have increased since the development and publication of the 1976 version of FM 100-5, *Operations*,

> the Army should never forget that the best weapons can be rendered useless by improper employment, and the material and organizational developments cannot [or at least should not] occur without doctrinal development.[1]

Indeed, the doctrine that the military adopts and continuously updates increases or decreases the options available to national policymakers. The ability of states to provide for their own defense and influence international relations may be significantly degraded if military doctrine is not sufficiently innovative. As Barry Posen writes in *The Sources of Military Doctrine*,

> A military doctrine may also harm the security interests of the state if it fails to respond to changes in political circumstances, adversary capabilities, or available military technology—if it is insufficiently innovative for the competitive and dynamic environment of international politics. If war comes, such a doctrine may lead to defeat.[2]

While this shows the significance of doctrine and the importance of appropriate innovation, how does one distinguish innovation from normal organizational change?

The question of terminology is not just an academic one. It determines the way the army considers maneuver warfare. The best description of innovation is in the classic theory text, *Organizations*, by James March and Herbert Simon:

> Initiation and innovation are present when change requires the devising and evaluation of new performance programs that have not previously been a part of the organization's repertory and cannot be introduced by a simple application of programmed switching rules.[3]

This definition implies that some portion of the previous organizational routine is replaced by new procedures, tactics, or strategy. If old strategy can coexist with a change, that change is not an innovation. If army leadership perceives that maneuver warfare is a new concept that the army cannot incorporate without jettisoning some existing organizations and procedures, then it is an innovation and will be responded to as such.

As the other essays in this volume indicate, maneuver warfare includes changes in all forms of doctrine, training, and education of officers and noncommissioned officers, and ultimately it affects the entire culture of the United States Army. Even if proponents could infiltrate portions of maneuver warfare into current army procedures, it would not be advantageous for either the army or maneuver warfare proponents to do so. Such a piecemeal approach would prevent a thorough evaluation and approval of maneuver warfare as a concept, and without such approval it would just be another set of buzz words competing for attention among the students and practitioners of Army doctrine.[4] By competing for and achieving approval as an innovation in the way that the army thinks about warfare, maneuver warfare can lead to the changes necessary to implement it successfully.

## THE PROCESS OF DOCTRINAL INNOVATION

Several authors have developed theories that have explained military innovation, but only a few authors have hypothesized about the process that military innovation takes.[5] This is inherently a difficult task, because by the definition above, innovation forces an organization to operate in a way that is different from its standard operating procedures. Hence, military organizations do not often record the way that innovations successfully alter routine operations.

Successful corporations, however, try to include internal innovation as a matter of policy, and there is a substantial body of literature that addresses corporate innovation. Many of the attributes and procedures of business are endemic to all large, hierarchically structured organizations. I have drawn on that literature and expanded and adapted a model of corporate innovation to analyze internally generated innovation within the military. Figure 1 graphically depicts this model. Robert Burgelman originally developed the structure of the model after ex-

| | Initiating Processes | | Implementing Processes | | |
| --- | --- | --- | --- | --- | --- |
| | Definition | Impetus | Strategic Context | Structural Context | Diffusion |
| Department of the Army | Monitoring | Authorizing Deciding | Rationalizing Disseminating *Organizational Championing* | Restructuring *Selecting* | Promoting Enforcement |
| Doctrine Managers (TRADOC, CAC) | Coaching Stewardship | *Organizational Championing* Strategic Building *Doctrinal Championing* | Delineating Defining the Domain | Negotiating | Training |
| Doctrine Writer/ Proponent | Doctrine technical need/threat linking | Strategic Forcing, Coordination | Gatekeeping Idea Generating Bootlegging | Inspecting, Questioning, Line Running | Inspecting Refining |

Figure 1: Doctrinal Innovation Model

tensively observing private and public sector internal innovation and then attempting to model it.[6] While there are differences between military and other organizations, the model makes sense because it reflects the logical stages through which any doctrinal innovation would have to pass. When I applied this framework to other authors' discussions of military innovation, I found that the model is entirely consistent with historical examples of military innovation. I identify those similarities throughout the rest of this essay. It is also consistent with the Army's own publications that describe the Army Life Cycle Model and the Life Cycle System Management Model.[7]

The model concerns internal innovation: changes that organizations create from within, rather than those that outsiders impose on the organization. This is the proper model to use because, as I will argue below, that is the source of most innovations in the military. Moreover, impetus for maneuver warfare doctrine is primarily coming from within the army rather than being imposed upon it.

The model itself identifies core processes based upon corporate experience. (The double lines on Figure 1 outline the core processes.) These essential processes are the focus of the innovation effort during each phase. They start at the level of the doctrine proponent, move to the army management level as organizational structure is altered, and then move back down the army hierarchy as the doctrinal innovation is implemented.

## Initiating Processes

### Definition

The beginning of an internal innovation is the first core process in the lower left corner of Figure 1. The doctrinal proponent is not necessarily someone assigned the job of developing doctrine. Rather, it is people who recognize that the fundamental way that the army is conducting warfare is not appropriate for the current missions, threats, soldiers, and equipment. Stephen Peter Rosen describes military innovation as an ideological struggle, and the first step is specifying the nature of the ideology. As he puts it, "this ideology must be *a new theory of victory*, an explanation of what war will look like and how it will be won [emphasis in original]."[8] The details of this new way of war include two sets of linkages. The first is that doctrinal proponents link capabilities—technology and materiel, command and control, personnel and training—to form a new doctrine. Simultaneously, proponents link that doctrine to a potential enemy to test its military effectiveness.

In this phase, doctrinal managers provide stewardship, coaching, and shielding as necessary to allow the creative process of doctrine initiation to take place. Higher-level authorities, to the extent that they are aware of any innovations, simply monitor the proceedings.

### Impetus

The second part of the initiation process is moving the embryonic doctrine into the mainstream thought of doctrinal managers, and ultimately, to the Army Staff. This is probably where maneuver warfare is in the U.S. Army today. At this stage, doctrinal proponents conduct *strategic forcing*. This is the process of achieving and reporting consistent, impressive results, thereby demonstrating that senior leadership cannot ignore the innovation. Included in this process is coordination with others, partially to consult and improve the doctrine, but mostly to coopt their support and demonstrate that the new doctrine is viable as the potential new ideology for the organization.

Another core process in this phase is *strategic building*. At the level of the doctrine manager, new ideas are discussed with other branches and agencies so that proponents can improve them and ensure that the innovation process has not taken place within a vacuum. In his study of innovation in the navy, Vincent Davis describes strategic building as innovation proponents developing "horizontal and vertical alliances" with their contemporaries and eventually with flag officers.[9] For maneuver warfare, this process of *doctrinal championing* includes evaluating the innovation and building support for it throughout the Army. It only takes a minor translation of business terms from this extensive quote to understand the role of a doctrinal champion in the army:

> This kind of championing is largely a political activity. The head of new business development [doctrine manager] often has to commit his or her judgement (in terms that can be verified as being right or wrong) and put his or her reputation on the line in saying that a particular venture [doctrine] will be successful if it is properly supported. Cautious but astute organizational champions make sure that the causes they sponsor are consistent with the existing predispositions of top management [the army]. More brilliant or perhaps more risk-prone executives seek to change the disposition of top management and get them to accept a new business field as legitimate for corporate development. Part of their success is probably simply a function of personality and persistence, of being able to be enthusiastic and appearing confident and articulate in explaining and justifying one's position. But there is also an intellectual component, as we have seen: successful organizational champions are able to devise a suitable overall long-run strategy for a business and perceive new ventures in strategic terms, in contrast to the technical terms used by product champions.[10]

Doctrinal champions are the bridge between the interests of technically oriented proponents and the strategic goals of the army as an institution. One good example of strategic building is Sir Burnett-Stuart's championing of British Armored Doctrine before World War II. Burnett-Stuart "carefully analyzed the implications of the new military technology and showed how it could be adapted to meet the demands of the British army. He also painted a clear and convincing picture of the nature of future war to a rising generation of professional soldiers."[11] This building process is one of the most important for an innovation because it is at this stage that organizations eliminate many innovations.

At this point in the model, the initiation process leads to a decision at the Army Staff level to authorize the new doctrine within the entire army. The decision, of course, may not be a single one, depending upon the nature of the innovation. When the army approves a change, at least conceptually, then the implementing processes begin.

## Implementing Processes
### Strategic Context
The remaining phases are best analyzed from the Army Staff down. The strategic context phase identifies where the new doctrine fits within the army and which existing doctrine and procedures the new doctrine will alter or replace. At the highest level, the Army Staff rationalizes, explains, and sells the innovation to all interested parties, both inside and outside of the army. In both this phase and the next, *selecting* is a core process at the Army Staff level. Selecting involves the articulation of the details of what was meant by the approval decision that initiated implementation.

The doctrine manager qua organizational champion is critical to the selection process because he can shape the institutional interpretation of the innovation. He delineates all the details of the new plan, many of which may have (intentionally or unintentionally) been tentative before the approval of the doctrine. It is important to note his perspective and dual focus. He needs to consider the advancement of pure doctrine with the selective application of new concepts in support of the army as an organization. In this role the doctrine manager may have to make tradeoffs between being *right* doctrinally so that he remains *relevant* organizationally.

The delineation procedure also identifies the domain of the innovation—exactly what other areas of the army this change will affect. Some analysts feel "the domain problem is most crucial in the innovation process because defining the domain indicates what part of the environment the organization must consider relevant in its decision making."[12] This domain must be as large as necessary, but no larger, so that implementation and selling of the innovation can be as concentrated as possible.

Simultaneously, proponents work feverishly to flesh out their newly approved doctrine. The tasks listed in Figure 1 are normal staff procedures that facilitate the execution of any major decision. Many of the details of an innovation may not be specified exactly until this time.

This is where proponents develop what Rosen calls the "concrete new tasks" associated with an innovation.[13]

## Structural Context

The structural context translates the ideas of where the innovation fits in strategically into faces and spaces on organization charts. Again, the army leadership has the core process of restructuring to implement the new doctrine. The doctrine manager delineates and negotiates the specific details with major commands throughout the army. Proponents attempt to monitor implementation through "running the lines" out to the lowest affected unit to determine how units in the field actually execute the intent of the innovators and the army.

## Diffusion

Burgelman's model of business innovation stops with structural context, because after a company sells a product, it is not as interested in whether consumers believe in it. Public sector innovations, from practicing maneuver warfare to wearing seat belts, are only as successful as the degree to which the last soldier or citizen believes in them.[14] Diffusion throughout the organization is the phase that determines the permanence of the organizational change.

At the Army Staff level, senior leadership promotes the innovation and enforces it. This includes adjusting the institutional rewards system, especially the promotion and command selection system, to recognize and support the innovation. In Rosen's terminology, "the new theory of victory must be reflected in the change in the distribution of power."[15] In the case of maneuver warfare doctrine, the army would recognize and reward officers who adhere to the new concepts as opposed to those officers who are dogmatic adherents to firepower as the sine qua non of battle.

The doctrine manager's level is also a core process, because training at the individual, collective, and leader levels facilitates the diffusion of new doctrine throughout the army. A study of the public sector indicates that diffusion is easier depending upon five characteristics: relative advantage over the old system; compatibility with existing values; simplicity; trialability (can the average person test it); and observability (can the average person see that it is superior).[16] Because of the complexity of maneuver warfare and the inherent difficulty in testing, observing, and demonstrating success, it may be difficult for the army to internalize maneuver warfare even after the army leadership adopts it. Simultaneously, proponents are continually evaluating the doctrine and refining it.

The processes that I described in this model are all interrelated. Actions taken at different points have implications that constrain future decisions and feed back to prior ones. The advantage of using this model is that it allows the maneuver warfare proponent the opportunity to see the stages and levels through which a doctrinal change in the army takes place. With this model of the process of innovation, I now turn to the factors that affect innovation and strategies to support the implementation of maneuver warfare.

## THE FACTORS THAT AFFECT INNOVATION

Scores of factors affect military innovation. In describing the many innovations in German infantry tactics before and during World War I, for example, Bruce Gudmundsson concludes:

> If there is a single thesis to this book, it is that there is no single explanation for the transformation of the German infantry that occurred during World War I. . . . A large number of personalities, ideas, situations, and organizational forces interacted to push the German Army towards the 'infiltration' tactics that won the spectacular tactical victories of late 1917 and early 1918.[17]

This section of the paper will briefly review four areas that affect doctrinal innovation and evaluate their potential impact on the propensity for the army to adopt and implement maneuver warfare. Those areas are organizational structure, organizational culture, organizational stress, and civilian influence.

### Organizational Structure

The hierarchical structure of the army has a different effect on innovation depending upon whether the innovation is in the initiation or implementation phase. In the initiation phase, the army's hierarchical structure is part of a vicious circle that is the Catch-22 of doctrinal innovation. The innovation will not receive support without demonstrating that it can be successful, and it cannot demonstrate success without receiving support. In business terms, "new knowledge or innovations can disrupt the equilibrium and tend therefore to be blocked by various mechanisms."[18] The resistance to change is particularly evident in the military, whose structure provides many levels of approval before an idea can be legitimized.[19]

While the hierarchical nature of the military makes the initiation process more difficult, it may actually make the implementation process somewhat easier. Harvey Sapolsky describes the converse of this point when he writes, "The factors that increase the probability that organizational participants will devise and present innovation proposals are precisely those factors that decrease the probability that the organization will adopt the proposals."[20] Since maneuver warfare is an actual, defined, developed idea, the stifling nature of the military organization has been overcome, at least in this instance. The role of organizational structure reinforces the implications of the model above: proponents of new doctrines should now focus their energy on cultivating champions and support among doctrinal managers and the Army Staff.

## Organizational Culture

Several studies of the organizational culture of the military have identified the problems of developing and advocating radical changes. The collective, formal, and sequential nature of military socialization leads to an organizational culture that fosters what John Van Maanen and Edgar H. Schein call a custodial, as opposed to an innovative, organizational culture.[21] The potential deleterious consequences of being wrong reinforce this resistance to change. Whereas a business may not be able to pay a high quarterly dividend if it improperly innovates, the army has much more at stake. Timothy Lupfer identified this characteristic in the German army in World War I: "The Germans always remained very conscious of their army's ability to perform. An army that adopts tactical doctrine that it cannot apply will greatly multiply its misfortune."[22]

At the levels of senior army leadership, however, resistance to change becomes almost a moral dilemma. Since senior leaders have vociferously advocated current doctrine as Truth (capital T) to officials within and outside the army, it is difficult and requires great courage to explain that the army was not lying; rather, the Truth changed. As Doughty observed,

> If the three major periods of doctrinal change have a consistent theme, it is the earnest and sincere objection by individuals in and out of the system that the envisioned changes were tampering with the sacrosanct and should be halted or greatly modified.[23]

From both an organizational culture, a mission-oriented, and a moral perspective, it will be extremely difficult to develop and maintain support for any new doctrine, irrespective of its superiority over current doctrine.

### Organizational Stress

Some analysts have hypothesized that organizations only innovate after the ultimate stress—massive defeat.[24] In fact, both business theory and military history tend to refute that point. In business, extreme distress occasionally leads to radical (usually unsuccessful) attempts at solvency, but usually firms become more conservative and less innovative as they move toward failure.[25] Similarly, it is not clear that military organizations innovate after defeat either. In his incisive study of the army in Vietnam, Andrew Krepinevich concludes that, despite the magnitude of the defeat, "the Army made little effort to preserve the learning that had occurred during the war; rather, it expunged the experience from the service's consciousness."[26]

Most studies have concluded that moderate innovation is most successful at times of moderate organizational slack or moderate organizational distress. Slack facilitates innovation because it provides resources to develop, test, and implement new ideas. During the relative slack of the early 1980s, for example, the army did innovate with new concepts, with varying degrees of success. These included the following changes, most of which did not radically alter traditional army routines: the light divisions, the motorized division, the national training centers, the new manning system, the regimental system, the J-series Tables of Organization and Equipment (TO&E), the AirLand Battle doctrine, and the Center for Army Lessons Learned.

The army today is characterized by what theorists would call moderate organizational distress. In spite of budget stringency and an uncertain threat, success in Desert Storm, Just Cause, and numerous humanitarian missions have lead to an institutional belief that, while the army is not in danger of collapsing, the exact shape of the army of the future is unclear. This would seem to facilitate moderate innovation. In other words, "new goals, values, and supporting power structures are necessary."[27] Jay Stone demonstrates that military organizations can successfully innovate after victory by his study of the British after the Boer War. In fact, the following paragraph in the 1902 *Combined Training* manual, written based upon British experience in the Boer War, is equally applicable for the American army today:

> Success in war cannot be expected unless all ranks have been trained in peace to use their wits. Generals and commanding officers are, therefore, not only to encourage their subordinates in so doing by affording them constant opportunities of acting on their own responsibility but, they will also check all practices which interfere with the free exercise of the judgement, and will break down, by every means in their power, the paralyzing habit of an unreasoning and mechanical adherence to the letter of orders and to routine, when acting under service conditions.[28]

Defeat is clearly not necessary to facilitate reforms, and the moderate distress that the army faces in the 1990s may lead to searching for ways to maximize military effectiveness with the army's limited resources. The answer to that search may be through improving doctrinal effectiveness through maneuver warfare.

### Civilian Influence

Barry Posen hypothesized that civilian intervention was necessary to cause military innovation. Again, most studies of public sector innovation and military history tend to reject that hypothesis.[29] In his study of corrections systems' management, George Downs observes, "environmental groups rarely possess strong, programmatically specific priorities. They may possess strong correctional [or doctrinal] ideologies, but they are uncertain about how to operationalize them . . ." or achieve their ends.[30] Even the president's influence is limited. This was reflected during the Vietnam War in the lack of response by the army to President Kennedy's and later President Johnson's Special Group (Counterinsurgency):

Unable to fit the President's prescriptions into its force structure oriented on mid- and high-intensity conflict in Europe, the Army either ignored them or watered them down to prevent its superiors from infringing upon what the service felt were its proper priorities.[31]

Civilian leadership can certainly stop programs altogether, but it is difficult for it to promote a specific type of innovation without leadership coming from inside the army. Although external forces may be helpful in the exploration of ideas and the definition of maneuver warfare, it is unlikely that they will have a strong effect on innovation of military doctrine. Moreover, the recent success in Desert Storm and the high level of support for army leadership provide a fair degree of shielding from external forces that might otherwise oppose doctrinal changes.

### Technology

Technology has a similar effect on doctrine as civilian intervention. By itself, it does not drive doctrinal innovation, and military history is replete with volumes that document the advance of technology without regard to doctrine.[32] After his review of 30 years of doctrinal changes in the Army, Robert Doughty concludes, "Intellectual changes can sometimes be more difficult to achieve than materiel changes."[33] Since maneuver warfare does not specifically advocate the increased application of new technology, it is doubtful whether outside support of technology producers and managers—defense contractors and the Army Material Command—will have an impact on the adoption of maneuver warfare. It may, however, be a useful strategy to emphasize that maneuver warfare is a better doctrine to exploit the capabilities of the Abrams tank and the Bradley Infantry Fighting vehicle, since their development did not include a concomitant full-scale revision of army doctrine.[34] Moreover, as the Army decides how to use its precious procurement dollars in the next decade, a clear doctrinal view, potentially emphasizing maneuver warfare, is essential so that those dollars are spent optimally.

## STRATEGIES TO IMPLEMENT MANEUVER WARFARE

Several implications flow from the model and discussion above. While there is no one step that can be taken to assure the implementation of maneuver warfare, I have made several generalizations below and categorized them roughly into "dos and don'ts" for implementing maneuver warfare.

## Things to Do
### Understand the process

It is necessary for maneuver warfare proponents to recognize important characteristics about the model of doctrinal innovation. First, doctrinal innovation is a long process involving many people at different levels. Proponents often abandon innovations due to lack of interest or persistence rather than being rejected outright. Second, there are differences in perspective between the levels. While proponents thrive on the details, the army as a whole views doctrinal innovation as only one way to better accomplish national goals. Third, major arguments over specific aspects of maneuver warfare will be made several times throughout the model, but they need not be. For example, it is not essential to specify the type of examination that War College students will take under a maneuver warfare doctrine during the definition part of the process, since that decision will not ultimately be made until the diffusion stage. While it is worth thinking about, it is not worth losing political support early in the innovation process over relatively insignificant issues.

### Choose analogies and simplifications carefully

Because of the length of the process and the size and hierarchical organization of the army, simplified concepts (sometimes called "bumper stickers") are essential to convey the essence of the maneuver warfare doctrine. Proponents should select these simplifications carefully because they will determine the institutional perception of maneuver warfare. The perception may become reality in spite of detailed explanations to the contrary.

### Focus on organizational champions

The affiliation and cultivation of organizational champions are particularly important to the process. Champions span the phases of initiation and implementation and can provide useful supportive perspective to doctrinal proponents. This begs the question of how maneuver warfare proponents can cultivate champions of their doctrine.

Although I have not found definitive research on the subject, it is likely that champions must first intellectually affiliate with maneuver warfare; then they can help facilitate the implementation of a new doctrine.

As an intermediate step, maneuver warfare proponents should wholeheartedly support an informed evaluation of tactics, doctrine, and warfare. As Harold R. Winton pleads at the conclusion of his book,

> The complexity of this task [articulating a vision of the nature of future war] places great demands on military leaders. It dictates intellectual mastery of the nature of war in general as well as the various forms that war assumes in a given era. Such mastery requires firm grounding in the theory of war, informed historical study, close analysis of contemporary developments, and an ability to project trends into the future in order to anticipate requirements. Such intellectual mastery also demands an inquisitional ethos of argument and analysis in which the best ideas about how to fight ultimately win out based on logical examination of objective evidence.[35]

If maneuver warfare is a better mousetrap, then a rigorous analysis of all aspects of army doctrine will lead informed doctrinal managers to champion it. Maneuver warfare should support rather than avoid critical evaluation of all army doctrine.

### Be cautious of evaluations

In the impetus phase, a core process is strategic forcing—demonstrating success so that the organization must deal with the innovation. In essence, the proponent has to prove that he does in fact have a better mousetrap. For military doctrine, unbiased measures of assessing effectiveness are elusive. War is the ultimate test, but even with combat experience, one cannot categorically reject the hypothetical. For example, would the army have lost fewer lives or taken less risk and still accomplished the mission of Desert Storm if it had used Active Defense instead of AirLand Battle doctrine? This is especially problematic, since assessments of doctrine in peacetime consist of battle simulations or exercises at the National Training Center. The parameters for those evaluations are established by the army's senior leadership, who, because of the understandably conservative biases discussed above, can establish apparently "objective" evaluations that doom maneuver warfare to failure. This is particularly true if the standard for objectivity comes from the preexisting Truth—AirLand Battle doctrine.

## Support complements to maneuver warfare

Even if the process of doctrinal innovation is slow, certain actions taken by the army in other areas can support or impede the eventual implementation of maneuver warfare. First, *high-quality, ready, disciplined soldiers* are essential to the future of maneuver warfare. Since an evaluation of the appropriate doctrine includes consideration of troops available, the current emphasis that the Chief of Staff, General Sullivan, has placed on maintaining high-quality soldiers is a necessary precondition to the implementation of maneuver warfare. If the quality in the army erodes to the conditions of the late 1970s, then it is unlikely that the army could implement maneuver warfare, even if it was superior from a theoretical or doctrinal perspective. Second, increased *decentralization* within the army is both a feature of maneuver warfare and an independent action that could be taken without the adoption of a new doctrine. As the army reorganizes in the next several years, maneuver warfare proponents should support changes that "power down," shifting responsibility to leaders at lower echelons.

Third, increased *officer and senior noncommissioned officer self-education* complements the eventual implementation of maneuver warfare. The belief of the German army in World War I should be incorporated as army service schools revise their curriculum for the 1990s: "the vast majority of German officers believed that Germany's fate depended directly upon their tactical competence."[36] Increased study of history, wargaming, tactics, and professional development is important irrespective of doctrine, but is an essential element of maneuver warfare doctrine. This support of complements is not the same as the piecemeal infiltration of maneuver warfare that I discouraged above. Maneuver warfare itself will remain a major innovation; these changes just make the eventual adoption and implementation of maneuver warfare substantially easier.

## Things to Avoid

### Piety in ideas

Implementing concepts is essential to the articulation of any doctrine. In the formation and articulation of maneuver warfare doctrine, proponents should identify, prioritize, and pursue specific essential characteristics of their new way of warfighting. Not every idea is of equal importance, and emphasis on every aspect of maneuver warfare means that proponents cannot give any single area special focus. As doctrine evolves, decision makers may eliminate some aspects proponents strongly believe in because they do not serve the broader mission of the army or cannot be broadly supported at this time. Unless a particular idea is absolutely central to the essence of maneuver warfare, proponents should be willing to compromise and negotiate rather than continually fight over low-priority issues.

### Piety in individuals

Champions of innovation are not usually mavericks, because the description of a champion given above includes an individual who has a dual focus: he or she is concerned with both the advance of doctrine and the needs of the army. If maneuver warfare becomes synonymous with any person, then its fate rests on the nation's collective opinion of that person, rather than on a careful evaluation of the doctrine itself. Indeed, Stephen Peter Rosen observes that military mavericks "were all ineffective in promoting innovation, despite strong external support. Their behavior and the outside intervention they solicited aroused the hostility of the military establishment, which therefore became *less* receptive to change [emphasis in original]."[37] Champions must always remember that the message is more important than the messenger.

Examples of this type of champion exist, even if their unpretentious style makes them less well known. In the development of British armored warfare, General Burnett-Stuart represented the established British army to the reformers and represented the voice of reasoned reforms in armored warfare to the British army. While this may not be an enviable position, it is exactly the role that a courageous, intelligent doctrinal champion should play. In the German army during World War I, the organizational champion was Lt. Gen. Erich Ludendorff, the first quartermaster general of the German Army High Command. As Lupfer describes, Ludendorff recognized his role and played it well:

The importance of Ludendorff's personality, however, was that it fostered the corporate spirit, encouraging several German officers to participate in the collective effort and not allowing his own ego to interfere. His personality did not monopolize the effort.[38]

Successful doctrinal champions will not become living legends in the style of Adm. Hyman Rickover or Gen. Billy Mitchell. If they are successful at selling a better doctrine to the army and the nation, however, they will have contributed more than they could if they assumed the role of an isolated and masterless maverick.

## Skunkworks

One of the strategies of innovation that has become popular through its promotion in *In Search of Excellence* is the use of skunkworks— small semi-autonomous units of large organizations that are designed to promote innovation. While these may work in limited cases where they have explicit approval and access to senior leaders, they are often counterproductive to innovation. The problem is that skunkworks are often so isolated that, as Rosabeth Moss Kanter argues, they fail to approach change integratively:

> To see problems integratively is to see them as wholes, related to larger wholes, and thus challenging established practices—rather than walling off a piece of experience and preventing it from being touched or affected by any new experiences.[39]

Doctrinal innovation isolated in an office may develop concepts that are theoretically elegant but of little practical use to the army as a whole.

Skunkworks also may signal the tacit rejection of innovation by an organization. During the impetus phase of the initiating process, the opposite of strategic forcing and strategic building is *strategic neglect*. Pigeonholing maneuver warfare innovation into an obscure office on a TRADOC organization chart may appear to address the issue, but it may also be a way of isolating it from the rest of the army. This process of isolation is poignantly described in the following extensive quote:

> Thus when innovation intrudes, the structure responds with various strategies to deal with the threat; it might incorporate the new event and alter it to fit the preexisting structure so that, in effect, nothing has really changed. It might deal with it also by active rejection, calling upon all of its resources to "starve out" the innovator by insuring a lack of support.

The most subtle defense, however, is to ostensibly accept and encourage the innovator, to publicly proclaim support of innovative goals, and while doing that to build in various controlling safeguards, such as special committees, thereby insuring that the work is always accomplished through power structure channels and thus effecting no real change. This tactic achieves the nullification of the innovator while at the same time giving the power structure the public semblance of progressiveness. The power structure can become so involved in this pose that the lower-line personnel come to honestly believe that they are working for the stated ideals . . . while in reality they labor to maintain the political power of the status quo.

Hence while the power structure continues to proclaim innovation, it expends great energy to insure, through its defensive maneuvers, the maintenance of the status quo. Innovation is thus allowed, and even encouraged, as long as it remains on the level of conceptual abstractions, and provided that it does not, in reality, change anything![40]

Obviously, the creation of maneuver warfare offices does not automatically signal the strategic neglect of the innovation. If doctrinal innovators do not have the capacity or opportunity to develop new ideology of warfare for the army as a whole, however, it is unlikely that the army will implement maneuver warfare successfully.

## CONCLUSION

Innovation in military organizations is a long process. Proponents of maneuver warfare need to understand the process described above and the factors that can affect the implementation of a new doctrine. Although some of the characteristics of the army, including organizational structure and culture, resist innovations, the moderate distress that the army is undergoing may provide a window of opportunity for organizational change.

The first step is to make the mousetrap as perfect as possible before trying to sell it to the army. This volume is an important contribution in that regard, because it allows the proponents of maneuver warfare to define and refine the doctrine. As the essential elements of maneuver warfare take shape and are translated into accurate, simplified descriptions, they can be promoted throughout the doctrinal managers of the army. Then specific steps can be taken to cultivate champions and use those champions to secure approval for doctrinal change. After the army leadership decides to adjust its ideology of warfare, more of the details can be delineated as the army defines the strategic and structural context in which maneuver warfare will be used. Unlike the adage of the mousetrap, the army will not beat a path to the maneuver warfare proponents' door. In the final analysis, the process of selling maneuver warfare doctrine to the army may be far more difficult than the development of the doctrine itself.

# Notes

1. Robert A. Doughty, "The Evolution of US Army Tactical Doctrine, 1946–76," Leavenworth Papers, No. 1 (Fort Leavenworth, Kans.: U.S. Army Command and General Staff College, 1979), p. 48.

There are several works that trace the evolution of FM 100-5. In Michael W. Cannon, "The Development of FM 100-5," masters thesis, University of Iowa, 1984, the author describes the ignorance and the importance of doctrine prior to 1976. Cannon writes: "The trend that links all the FMs together is that until the mid-1970s, FM 100-5 was largely ignored by the Army leadership. The FM was never treated seriously as a manual for use in the field and was looked upon with disdain by the majority of the military." (p. 84)

2. Barry R. Posen, *The Sources of Military Doctrine: France, Britain, and Germany between the World Wars* (Ithaca, N.Y.: Cornell University Press, 1984), p. 16.

3. James G. March and Herbert A. Simon, *Organizations* (New York: John Wiley and Sons, 1958), pp. 174, 175.

4. Indeed, with the complexity of modern warfare, piecemeal changes cannot change the character of battle. Peter Paret says that since the Napoleonic wars, "what differentiated the new wars from their predecessors was not a new weapon, a different tactic, or fresh strategic insights, but the integration of these and other factors in the matrix of a new political reality." See Peter Paret, *Innovation and Reform in Warfare* (Colorado Springs: U.S. Air Force Academy, 1966), p. 5.

5. One important exception is Timothy J. Lupfer, "The Dynamics of Doctrine: The Changes in German Tactical Doctrine During the First World War," Leavenworth Papers, No. 4 (Fort Leavenworth, Kans.: U.S. Army Command and General Staff College, 1981). He describes wartime innovation as a nine-step process: perception of a need for change; solicitation of ideas, especially from combat units; definition of the change; dissemination of the change; enforcement throughout the army; modification of organizations and equipment to accommodate the change; thorough training; evaluation of effectiveness; and subsequent refinement. I have used many of his nine steps in the development of the model listed in this section and have tried to associate them with the applicable levels of organization.

6. See Robert A. Burgelman, "A Process Model of Internal Corporate Venturing in the Diversified Major Firm," *Administrative Science Quarterly,* June 1983, pp. 223–244.

7. The reason why I do not just use the army's published models is that they are even more general than this model and do not distinguish between actions taken by actors at different levels. For a description of the army's view of how it conducts force integration, see "How the Army Runs," ST 25-1, *Resource Planning and Allocation* (Fort Leavenworth, Kans.: U.S. Army Command and General Staff College, 1992), chapter 4.

8. Stephen Peter Rosen, "Understanding Military Innovation," *International Security*, vol. 13, no. 1 (Summer 1988), p. 141.

9. Davis's examination of three specific navy cases of innovation revealed that middle grade officers (Lieutenant Commander to Captain in the Navy) were the ones who were most likely to be the champions of innovations. See Vincent Davis, *The Politics of Innovation: Patterns in Navy Cases* (Denver, Colo.: University of Denver Press, 1967).

10. Robert A. Burgelman and Leonard R. Sayles, *Inside Corporate Innovation: Strategy, Structure, and Managerial Skills* (New York: Free Press, 1986), pp. 142, 143.

11. Harold R. Winton, *To Change an Army: General Sir John Burnett-Stuart and British Armored Doctrine, 1927–1938* (Lawrence, Kans.: University Press of Kansas, 1988), p. 236.

12. Gerald Zaltman, Robert Duncan, and Jonny Holbek, *Innovations and Organizations* (New York: John Wiley and Sons, 1973), p. 116.

13. Rosen, pp. 141, 142.

14. Few studies of military innovation stress the diffusion after the innovation has overcome the internal and external obstacles. One useful study that emphasizes it is Carl-Axel Gemzell, *Organization, Conflict, and Innovation: A Study of German Naval Strategic Planning: 1888-1940* (Stockholm, Sweden: Scandinavian University Books, 1973).

15. Rosen, p. 142.

16. Everett M. Rogers and Joung-Im Kim, "Diffusion of Innovations in Public Organizations," in *Innovation in the Public Sector*, eds. Richard L. Merritt and Anna J. Merritt (London: Sage, 1985), p. 88.

17. Bruce I. Gudmundsson, *Stormtroop Tactics: Innovation in the German Army, 1914–1918* (New York: Praeger Publishers, 1989), p. xv.

18. Zaltman, Duncan, and Holbek, p. 86.

19. An extreme case of hierarchical organization inhibiting the initiation of innovation is the structure that existed in the former Soviet army. In one study, innovation only survived if there was a substantial negative effect of not innovating and, especially, if there was limited time available to seek and

receive guidance from higher authority. See Mary Zey-Ferrell, Arlene Parchman and Jerry Gaston, *Initiative and Innovation in the Soviet Military* (College Station, Tex.: Center for Strategic Technology, The Texas Engineering Experiment Station, Texas A&M University, 1984).

20. Harvey Sapolsky, "Organizational Structure and Innovation," *Journal of Business*, vol. 40, no. 4 (1967), p. 497.

21. For a detailed discussion of the socialization processes that retard innovation, see John Van Maanen and Edgar H. Schein, "Toward a Theory of Organizational Socialization," *Research in Organizational Behavior*, vol. 1, pp. 209–264. In their six dimensions of socialization, the military is clearly near the stifling or custodial end of the spectrum (as opposed to the innovative end) in five of the six. The only positive aspect of the military is fixed boundary switching, i.e. roughly fixed promotion scheduling. This facilitates innovation because, when individuals are away from critical boundary changes and socialization settings (such as when they are at nominative assignments at service academies), they can be innovative without worrying that it will alter their selection for promotion.

22. Lupfer, p. 56.

23. Doughty, p. 47.

24. The theory that defeat is one of the key reasons for military reform is argued by Barry R. Posen, *The Sources of Military Doctrine*, p. 47.

25. Kenneth E. Knight, "A Descriptive Model of the Intrafirm Innovation Process," *Journal of Business*, vol. 40, no. 4 (1967), p. 485.

26. Andrew F. Krepinevich, Jr., *The Army and Vietnam* (Baltimore, Md.: The Johns Hopkins University Press, 1986), p. 260.

27. Zaltman, Duncan, and Holbek, p. 20.

28. From Great Britain War Office, *Combined Training (Provisional)* (London: Harrison and Sons, 1902), p. 4, quoted in Jay Stone and Erwin A. Schmidl, *The Boer War and Military Reforms* (New York: University Press, 1988), p. 117.

29. Stephen Peter Rosen specifically addresses Barry Posen's theory that civilian intervention is a necessary condition for doctrinal innovation. Upon a further study of similar cases, he concludes that "military innovation in peacetime is a long-term process over which civilian government officials have, at best, limited and indirect influence." Rosen, p. 167.

30. George W. Downs, Jr., *Bureaucracy, Innovation, and Public Policy* (Lexington, Mass.: D.C. Heath, 1976), p. 86.

31. Krepinevich, p. 37.

32. For a trenchant study of technological advancements without doctrinal advancements see Robert Seney Ballagh, Jr., "The Development of French Field Artillery Doctrine, 1870–1914," masters thesis, Duke University, 1971.

33. Doughty, p. 47.

34. In Daniel J. Kaufman, *Organizations, Technology, and Weapons Acquisition: The Development of the Infantry Fighting Vehicle*, Ph.D. dissertation, Massachusetts Institute of Technology, 1983, Kaufman argues that the infantry fighting vehicle was developed with very little regard to the doctrine with which it would be employed.

35. Winton, pp. 239–240.

36. Gudmundsson, p. 174.

37. Rosen observed the innovations promoted by Captain B. H. Liddell Hart, Colonel Charles de Gaulle, and General Billy Mitchell. See Rosen, p. 139.

38. Lupfer, p. 8.

39. Rosabeth Moss Kanter, *The Change Masters: Innovations for Productivity in the American Corporation* (New York: Simon and Schuster, 1983), p. 27.

40. This article discussed mental health innovation in the 1960s, but as reflected in the excerpt above, its observations are just as relevant to the army of the 1990s. Anthony M. Graziano, "Clinical Innovation and the Mental Health Power Structure: A Social Case History," *American Psychologist*, vol. 24, no. 1 (January 1969), p. 16.

# Implementing Maneuver Warfare

## Richard D. Hooker, Jr.

Important changes in the way an army fights cannot be implemented merely by rewriting doctrine. The AirLand Operations doctrine which is now in the workup stage incorporates many maneuver warfare concepts, but more is needed besides a new operations manual. Because a philosophy of warfighting requires an army that can implement it, written doctrine is necessary but not sufficient to implement a maneuver-based AirLand Operations doctrine servicewide. Institutional change must follow and support doctrinal change if new doctrine is to be fully realized in action. This paper suggests some institutional changes that might improve our army's ability to fully exploit the maneuver potential of AirLand Operations.[1]

Institutional change is always difficult and can often engender resistance.[2] Calls for change can be interpreted as criticism of institutional norms and values and of service traditions and service culture. To some extent, senior leaders may feel vested in a system they understand, were raised in, and which nurtured and prepared them for command. They may interpret pressures for change as criticism of the institution, and attack the credentials and qualifications of juniors and outsiders.

Often they will be right. Self-styled "reformers" can have many different agendas, which may or may not coincide with a bona fide interest in improving national security or the performance of the institution. From an organizational viewpoint, externally driven change which does not embody the expertise unique to the organization and which neglects the normal processes of consensus building will often fail.

A healthier perspective is to look at institutional change as a normal, evolutionary process leading to a better, more effective military. Acceptance is more likely when change develops internally and consensually. Although this approach may be incremental, not radical, it is more likely to take hold and become imbedded in service doctrine and culture. Ultimately, the idea itself may not be as important as the techniques used to introduce and implement it. Maneuver warfare, to be accepted and embraced servicewide, must be perceived internally as a sound, effective, evolutionary step leading to a more capable army. Viewed in this light, institutional changes needed to complement evolutionary changes need not be interpreted as challenges to the status quo. Instead, they should be seen as opportunities to build upon existing strengths to improve the deterrent and warfighting capabilities of the force.

## A BLUEPRINT FOR CHANGE

Broadly speaking, implementing maneuver warfare demands a re-examination of the processes we use to train leaders and units. For leaders serving in administrative or support posts, required skills and abilities will differ from those needed in the maneuver arms. In combat support and service support branches, leaders may serve in the combat zone where their duties require them to support but not conduct the fight. To identify and develop leaders in maneuver units, the most important step is to address squarely the fact that some individuals will be able to grasp and execute a maneuver warfare thought process, but many will not. Everything depends upon identifying and preparing a relatively small pool of leaders and placing them in unit environments where their skills and talent will have the greatest impact. As a point of departure, we can look at leader selection, training and education, the leadership evaluation and assignment system, and the unit environment as places to begin shaping an army capable of maneuver warfare.

Our current system does a good job of identifying and recruiting potential leaders, but it does not discriminate by personality type or psychological aptitude. Officers are assigned to the various branches of the service based on their standing in precommissioning training, but without any particular attempt to identify psychological compatibility with the assigned branch. Enlisted soldiers receive no special screening or testing to match them by skills or temperament for promotion to leadership positions in the maneuver arms. The system does not identify the most intelligent, most aggressive, most confident, most physically fit, or most innovative and direct them to the sharp end of the force where these characteristics are most in demand.

In contrast, the Israeli Defense Forces conduct three days of exhaustive physical and psychological screening and intelligence testing for all recruits to match them to the appropriate job. Recruits are classified into 15 categories. This classification combines raw intelligence, educational level, and a "motivation-to-serve" index. Only soldiers in the top six categories are permitted to go on to NCO training, and officers are taken from the top two only. Top officer candidates are assigned to the Air Force, armored forces, paratroop units, and the infantry in that order. The great majority of top-scoring candidates are assigned to maneuver combat specialties.[3]

While these policies do establish a pecking order of sorts among branches, they serve to concentrate talent and ability in branches where the need is demonstrably the greatest. At the same time, individuals with technical, administrative, or managerial skills and abilities are given the opportunity to pursue rewarding and satisfying careers of service to the nation in the support and technical branches. In this system, organizational and individual concerns for prestige, influence, and promotion potential are consciously subordinated to the goal of putting the right person in the right job.

A system like this is not necessarily incompatible with our service culture or values. On the contrary, the service ethic demands subordination of personal or group interests to the interests of the institution as a whole. To do this, it is first necessary to come to grips with our traditional aversion to elitism.[4] Our system of leader selection, promotion, evaluation, and assignments is based on the fundamental premise of fairness—the idea that every leader must be provided the maximum exposure to schooling, competitive assignments, and a fair opportunity to compete for command and promotion.

The fly in the ointment is that all leaders are not equally endowed with talent and ability. While it is difficult to argue with "fairness," it makes little sense to strive for uniform selection, schooling, and assignment patterns for the aggregate if leaders of real merit and potential are thereby denied opportunities to hone their skills.

One example of this philosophy is the practice, common in larger branches, of providing company command opportunities to virtually every officer. Because command is a crucial requirement for subsequent promotion, fairness demands that all will have their chance. But some leaders clearly outperform their peers. Second and even third command tours would develop deeply experienced troop leaders who would be more effective in positions of greater responsibility in later years. The interests of the organization would be better served, albeit at the expense of some individuals not judged suited for command. Today, repetitive command tours are rare because they restrict the number of command openings available for officers waiting in line.

Another example of the principle of fairness in action is the practice of evenly distributing "high performers" across the force. Such a policy ensures that competing commands get their fair share of top-quality leaders, and that no single organization is markedly advantaged over others. As junior officers complete company command and become "branch-qualified," they are sent to nominative assignments at the Military Academy, in ROTC Cadet Command, Recruiting Command, or Reserve Component advisory duty. Each command insists on a proportional share of the best leaders. These pressures ensure that many top-shelf troop leaders will never go to follow-on troop assignments to build on their initial command experiences, but will instead fill billets away from troops in a wide variety of service commands.

This principle is almost universal. Support branches insist on a fair distribution of top-third officers in the Conditional Voluntary Indefinite branch redesignation process. Utility aviation commands insist that the attack helicopter community not monopolize top performers in flight training. The training base demands its fair share of the best talent available. So do overseas commands, major service staffs, joint staffs, and functional area managers. Within each service, there are scores of organizations determined to ensure their continuing influence and prestige. None of them can afford to be deprived of the best available leadership.

These examples demonstrate how "fairness" permeates the force to prevent the concentration of the very best talent in operational units. Arguments to the contrary are often dismissed as elitist. If defined as advancement by favor, influence, or selfish ambition, elitism must of course be shunned. Too often, however, any special treatment of individuals—even (or perhaps especially) individuals selected purely on the basis of proven merit—is harshly criticized as elitism. When used in defense of mediocrity, such criticism is worse than self-serving. It is dangerous. Leadership in democratic armies implies an exchange of privilege for merit, not mediocrity. To achieve this ideal the able and talented must be identified and encouraged to develop their special skills for the good of the service.

An alternative approach would be to place every maneuver arms officer in a troop assignment following the officer advanced course, without a guaranteed expectation of command. Battalion and brigade commanders would assign these officers to staff positions and evaluate them for command, but there would be no pressure to find command positions for every officer. Some officers would serve extended command tours or have multiple company commands based on demonstrated potential and performance. Others would serve their tour with troops as staff officers, or command only once, and depart to fill requirements for nominative assignments. A few officers of proven troop-leading ability, perhaps 15 percent, could be offered a follow-on troop assignment, perhaps with a year off in between for schooling, in lieu of a nominative assignment. Under this system, an officer approaching promotion to major might well have led two or three platoons, served as a company executive officer and staff officer, and commanded two or even three companies in ten years' time.

## EVALUATING EXCELLENCE

At first glance it might appear that selecting the best qualified leaders for promotion is the whole point of the officer and noncommissioned officer personnel management process. But if the goal is to identify and prepare the relatively few who show real promise of mastering the art of maneuver warfare, we might well establish markedly different criteria to assess future leaders and to educate and train them.

For example, statistical and administrative indicators of success are often weighted more heavily in the evaluation process than tactical performance or innate leadership ability. Inspection results, maintenance figures, property accountability, disciplinary incidents—anything that can be quantified and used to quickly assess a unit's posture—carry more weight than a commander's tactical proficiency or his unit's ability to perform mission-essential tasks. Of course, these are important performance indicators. But they are not what matters most, and frequently they will have little to do with combat readiness. In many cases, an absence of safety violations, good accountability of sensitive items, completing assigned training missions on time, and adherence to prescribed checklists ("checking the block on the ARTEP Training and Evaluation Outline") for basic missions will define a successful unit and commander. Yet a commander may excel in all these and lack any particular aptitude for combat leadership.

This critique may sound unfair. Clearly the army has made great strides in training in the last decade, and tactical proficiency in units has improved. But trying to assess the difference between a talented leader and an earnest and well-drilled one requires a different approach.

One way is to impose stress by rapid changes in the situation to evaluate the thought process used to respond to these changes. Junior leaders can replace commanders at critical times. Times, objectives, missions, and the enemy situation can be manipulated to increase uncertainty, stress, and friction. There may be resistance to these practices in training because they impair a unit's subjectively evaluated performance or because they could upset the timing of a densely packed training schedule. But these are poor reasons to miss an opportunity to identify and train leaders for combat.

The problem of how to measure performance under these conditions is more difficult because it cannot really be quantified. It does not lend itself to checklists. But it is measurable by asking questions such as: How did this leader arrive at a decision? Does it conform to the commander's intent? Does it reflect patterned behavior? How well are friendly and enemy strengths and weaknesses assessed? Can this leader think and act quickly and decisively? Can he defend his decision? Of course, senior leaders must be able to recognize and apply this way of thinking before they can evaluate it in others, which lends strength to the conclusion that more is required than rewriting the manuals.

Many leaders, otherwise gifted and competent, will have difficulty when evaluated against these criteria. This is particularly true when juniors otherwise excel in quantifiable areas that traditionally define success. But battlefield leadership cannot be measured by AWOL rates, maintenance scores, or successful file keeping—as important as those may be. We must look beyond these criteria to the realm of the intangible and the hard-to-measure. In centrally directed command hierarchies, conformity and risk aversion are highly prized. In an army capable of maneuver warfare fighting, originality and daring are encouraged and rewarded.

In keeping with this philosophy, we might reexamine the formal evaluation process for leaders in troop-leading positions. To supplement the observations of superiors, aggregated profiles of peer and subordinate ratings would yield a much more rounded picture. The views of these groups often differ markedly from those of senior raters.

Good leaders have little to fear from these ratings. If applied with common sense (by screening for soldiers soured by disciplinary action, for example), such a system would not, as many critics assert, degenerate into a popularity contest. Soldiers and peers know capable leaders when they see them. And leaders who lead by creating relationships based on trust and confidence will be known by their character and loyalty, not only to their superiors but to their soldiers and peers as well. In our professional literature one finds strong opposition to alternate rating regimes that incorporate input from peers and subordinates. But should we really advance leaders who consistently impress their superiors while consistently failing in the eyes of their soldiers and comrades? A revised leader evaluation schema might give us a better capability to identify truly talented practitioners of maneuver warfare.

## BUILDING A BATTLE FOCUS

A reevaluation of how combat training is actually practiced in maneuver units may also improve the army's ability to execute an AirLand Operations doctrine based on maneuver precepts. Unit training must embrace a true multi-echelon approach before units can attain true proficiency in maneuver warfare. Individual *and* collective training must take place simultaneously and continuously. Lower-level commanders must be relieved of some of the crushing administrative burdens they now bear. Soldiers must primarily know fundamentals, but they must know them exceedingly well. This argues for repetitive training to high standards, led by first echelon leaders with plenty of opportunities for live firing and hands-on training. Tasks that are only tangentially related to combat skills must be ruthlessly suppressed. Time is too precious to squander on the peripheral.

Leaders must be trained to operate within the framework of the commander's intent to achieve a desired result. Commanders should never insist on rigid adherence to prescribed format or method, but they should demand results and regularly critique a subordinate's decision process. Aggressiveness, risk taking (as distinct from foolhardiness), initiative and innovation should be rewarded, not punished. Wisdom will come with age and experience, but the willingness to shoulder responsibility and act decisively can be fragile. Commanders must encourage, not discourage, young leaders with these traits.

As a rule, commanders should personally conduct leader training, which will often take place while individual- or squad/crew-level training is in progress. Lieutenants should be trained in battalion-level operations so they can understand and react to the tactical situation two levels up. Historical or actual contingency scenarios should be used to lend realism and immediacy. In every conceivable way, every leader must be imbued with the fundamentals of maneuver warfare: commander's intent, focus of effort, mission orders, and the use of strength against weakness to destroy the enemy's will to resist. Leaders at every level must understand that what matters most is results.

When leaders and soldiers come together for collective training, commanders should begin with the ideal, then build in the friction of war with faulty or incomplete intelligence, leader changes, poor communications, logistics failures, and so on. Free-play, force-on-force exercises should be the norm, not the exception, followed by rigorous and objective critiques which begin with the commander and his performance. Battlefield conditions can be simulated with taped combat sounds, smoke, pyrotechnics, and live and blank ammunition.

Soldiers should train when cold, wet, and hungry. Casualty evacuation and NBC events should be part of every training exercise at platoon level and above. Tactical concepts should be simple, original, and varied. Leaders should never apply the same solution to the same problem twice. Finally, leaders, soldiers, and units must be committed to train to standard, not to time. These principles will ensure that realism and stress are part of every training event, and that units will conclude training only when the training standard has been achieved.

## TEACHING A MANEUVER THOUGHT PROCESS

In the "schoolhouse," the officer and noncommissioned officer professional education system, a number of steps could be taken to improve how we identify and develop maneuver leaders. Leader education should challenge, and so it is important to set tough standards and require all students—not just the bottom percentiles—to reach to meet the standard. Leader courses that have failure rates of 2 percent or less probably do not challenge the average student. Clearly they do not do much for the most talented and motivated. And high performers in the educational process should be rewarded with first pick of assignment to the most challenging units and command and staff positions in troop units.

The focus of instruction should be on two things: battle and how to think. Subject areas not directly related to these should not dominate the process. Techniques and tactics are important, but they should be taught within the context of a thought process. We should not be concerned with standard responses to standard situations. Methods of instruction and evaluation should force the student to come to a decision and defend it, not memorize masses of data; if students are not familiar with basic information such as weapons ranges, movement rates, or terminology, it will be apparent in their classroom performance. Currently most army leadership courses place heavy emphasis on school solution, fill-in-the-blank or multiple-choice examinations that do little or nothing to develop analytical ability or verbal and written skills.

An examination designed to test a student's decision process might look like the following:

You occupy a village overlooking a ford with a Bradley infantry company, engineer platoon, and attached tank platoon. The ford is one mile north of the town. The road runs through the town, which is surrounded by woods and low, marshy ground. In four hours you expect an enemy tank regiment to cross. The brigade commander's intent is to delay the enemy for 12 hours to cover the disengagement of the division. Your battalion's mission is to defend three crossing sites stretched along ten kilometers of riverline. Your mission is to defend the ford site until further orders. There is air parity and you have priority of fires from one divisional artillery battalion. The time is now 1800. You have fifteen minutes to prepare your concept. Begin work.

There are many possible solutions here. Much important information is omitted and planning time is short. The tactical problem presents very unfavorable force ratios. The student is under real pressure, which can be intensified as the course progresses by allowing less time and introducing sudden changes in the enemy and friendly situation.

Whether or not the student employs a standard tactical response is not important. What does matter is the thought process—more specifically, the *decision* process—used to arrive at the answer. In this scenario an average student might elect to fight for the riverline from the town, hoping to keep the enemy on the far bank. He might issue detailed instructions for firing positions, fire control measures, and so on. But this solution is linear, predictable, and unimaginative. It posits essentially an attritional exchange: "We will fight for the river; failing that we will fight for the town."

It is reasonable to assume that a tank regiment will destroy a mechanized infantry company team relatively quickly if confronted with a conventional defense. The enemy possesses mobility and firepower advantages so great that the destruction of the friendly force is likely. The odds are good that the brigade's 12-hour delay will be a good deal shorter.

A talented and imaginative student might reason that the enemy is coming on without advanced reconnaissance elements, with little supporting infantry, at night. Speed is important to him since the enemy is clearly trying to regain contact and disrupt the disengagement. These weaknesses are counterbalanced by the friendly force's advantages of surprise, concealment, and favorable terrain. The possibility exists to destroy a large part of the enemy force outright with a skillful plan, boldly executed. The student should think not in terms of "how can I hold out as long as possible?", but "how can I shape the battle to achieve a decisive result and still be here tomorrow morning?" A good solution, pitting strength against weakness to break the opponent's will, could look like this:

> My intent is to use the river to separate the enemy to destroy him piecemeal. We will let the enemy come on, to cross the ford and enter the town. The advance guard will be permitted to pass through. At that point the enemy should have one battalion in the built-up area, one crossing the ford, and one on the far bank. I will hit the enemy throughout the depth of his formation all at once. The lead unit will be cut off by scatterable mines and destroyed

by dismounted infantry and mines in the town. The fording unit will be hit by command-detonated mines, tank and TOW fires from the flanks, and an air strike. The destruction of the fording unit is the focus of effort. The trail battalion will be suppressed by field artillery fires. Tanks and Bradleys will constitute the mobile reserve. If the plan fails, they will hang on to the flanks and fight a running battle while the infantry strongpoints the town. The brigade reserve will then have an opportunity to hit the weakened enemy in the flank and finish him off.

A good presentation will satisfy the brigade commander's intent, express the concept clearly using mission orders, designate a focus of effort, use strength against weakness, and attack the will of the opponent. Whenever possible, real historical scenarios should be used because they stimulate interest and provide actual decisions to evaluate and discuss.

Here, the opposing commander is not met with the response he expects. When he is hit it is everywhere at once. He is unable to identify exactly what he is facing and will have difficulty responding to all the simultaneous threats directed against him. He may well lose a significant part of his force. The plan is simple, bold, energetic, and maximizes the capabilities of a small force.

This approach to leader education does not focus on amassing knowledge, but insists on the ability to assess, decide, and act. Emphasis is placed on the result achieved, not on adherence to prescribed format. In the modern German Armor Officer's Advanced Course, students are required to brief their solutions to boards of field grade officers, who force them to defend their decisions and the thought process by which they are derived.[5] This technique descends directly from the traditions of the *Generalstab*, the German General Staff, and its famous *Kriegsakademie* (War College). There, only two sins were considered unforgivable: the failure to make a timely decision, and the inability to make a reasoned defense of one's solution.

Wargaming is one way to sharpen these skills. Leader education programs now devote only a fraction of available classroom time to combat simulations which force students to solve challenging battlefield problems and defend their solutions. Many of the simulations employ an attrition-based schema which rewards the simple massing of combat systems to "service" target arrays, without adequately addressing the importance of deception, uncertainty, the personality of the opposing commander, surprise, or fatigue. Hermann Balck captured the essence of what is missing from most battle simulations by observing that even the loss of a single subordinate commander might dictate a wholly different tactical response because of the changed personality, character, and abilities now introduced into the battle. One way to capture this dimension is to use recently retired senior officers as controllers and umpires. Their broad knowledge and experience are invaluable assets that could make purely technical simulation exercises live and breathe with the friction and drama of battle. Above all, battle simulations must replicate the uncertainty, conflicting and incomplete information, rapidity and stress of decision making under combat conditions.

The army should seriously consider two additional innovations which will improve its ability to conduct maneuver warfare at all levels. One is a general staff system. The other is a regimental system that provides for personnel stability and recurring assignments to the same unit.

## INSTITUTIONALIZING EXCELLENCE

A true general staff is a necessity because without one the army will find it difficult to truly implement a shared doctrine servicewide. We have already observed that much of what is so effective about maneuver warfare lies in the realm of what can only be described as "art." Only a relative few will possess the intuition, intelligence, and insight to master it. Younger officers with special talents and abilities should be identified early on, perhaps as senior captains or young majors, through rigorous examination based solely on demonstrated merit and character (ideally through a stressful series of interviews and blind-graded analytical essays based on historical scenarios).[6]

After selection, the general staff aspirant would attend a special two-year course leading to an advanced degree (similar to the current School of Advanced Military Studies program), followed by field grade service on division and corps operations staffs as a member of the Field General Staff. Key positions on these staffs would be coded for general staff officers only.

At the senior field grade level, general staff officers selected to attend the War College would compete for selection to an Army General Staff, again going on for a second year of intensive study after the War College course. To preclude "crowding" these officers because of their extensive schooling requirements, their assignments should be managed on an individual basis within the General Staff, permitting them to focus exclusively on their duties as operators. These officers would form an even smaller group intended to serve as principal staff officers for operations in all division, corps, field army, joint task force, and major unified commands (where joint organizations require an army representative as operations officer).

Army General Staff officers would not be excluded from command, but the operative principle is the institutionalization of operational excellence in the principal combat units. Ideally, every senior army and joint commander would have an operations officer of uncommon ability and experience, trained to an extraordinarily high level in the planning and conduct of combat operations at the tactical, operational, and strategic levels according to a shared doctrine based on maneuver warfare precepts.

Standards for general staff officers should be high, competition stiff, and the size of the general staff corps should be kept small. The German example of anonymity for general staff officers—to "be more than you seem"—would go far to prevent the growth of professional enmity or resentment between line and general staff officers. As nowhere else, character embodied in selflessness, professionalism, and a self-effacing manner would be an absolute requirement in an American General Staff. Intellectual arrogance on the part of general staff officers would ensure the early death of any general staff initiative.

Meaningful incentives would be needed to attract the best possible talent, perhaps in the form of early promotion for those few officers selected to join the Field or Army General Staffs. While these officers might continue to compete for command selection as line officers, they should not monopolize available command positions and their subsequent promotion should be based on outstanding performance as masters of the operational art. To be truly effective, a general staff must provide opportunities for promotion to general officer based solely on excellence as a staff officer. Uniform career patterns might well dilute or degrade the development of the kind of innovative, original, uncommon personalities and intellects which may often permit an army to reach for true excellence. Merit and ability as an operational expert—with or without complementary abilities as a troop leader—must be the exclusive criteria.

General staff officers would not as a rule command divisions or corps (at least, not solely because of their status as members of the general staff) or dominate the army leadership. They would not usurp the legitimate prerogatives of commanders they support. Conceptually, a general staff exists for one purpose and one purpose only: to institutionalize operational excellence at every level of the fighting force from division to theater command. In this way a shared approach to combat operations—an intuitive feel for doctrine and how it can be applied to the current situation—becomes possible. In short, the organization begins to think on the same wavelength and use the same thought process. One way to think of this is to picture commanders as the fighting heart of the combat organization, with the handful of General Staff officers in the division or corps functioning as the thinking brain.

It is important to stress what such an organization should *not* be. It should not constitute a corporate decision-making body chartered to monopolize the decision/policy process. It should not, as an organizational entity, span the civil-military interface. It should not preempt or appropriate the legitimate prerogatives of commanders, or "share" their command authority in a joint decision-making process. It need not be called a "General Staff" if the term carries troublesome connotations. What *is* important is that we institutionalize our doctrine in our commanders and principal operational officers to enable the service to function in combat in accordance with a uniform, shared operational vision. This may require special treatment for individuals with unique talents and abilities.[7]

## BUILDING UNBREAKABLE UNITS

Still, it will not be enough to institutionalize excellence at top levels. At the sharp end of the force, those small units who do the fighting, killing, and dying must be capable of shouldering the greater demands of maneuver warfare. They must think and act faster. They must approach infiltration and penetration into rear areas, night operations, decentralization, and the increased friction and uncertainty of the nonlinear battlefield with confidence and resolve. This cannot be achieved in units composed of transient strangers. To "do" maneuver warfare, soldiers must know and trust each other and their leaders. One way, perhaps the only way, to build the kind of morale, esprit, and cohesion needed to employ maneuver warfare is to stabilize soldiers and leaders in units through a working regimental system.

The concept is simple. Soldiers and officers join a regiment when they enter the service. When serving subsequently with troops, they return to the regiment, an organization of three operational battalions, possibly with a fourth serving overseas, and a fifth, manned only by officers and NCOs from the regiment, which trains all combat replacements at branch training centers. To avoid staleness, units can rotate overseas or to other duty stations periodically (perhaps as companies to keep disruption manageable). Individuals will leave periodically to serve as instructors, recruiters, advisers and so on. But always, career soldiers and leaders will return to the regiment, to serve with comrades who know each other well.

Within the regiment, soldiers and leaders are stabilized for lengthy periods to build cohesion at the crew, team, and squad level. Leaders stay with their units; they do not flit from job to job to "build experience." Soldiers will typically serve a complete enlistment tour of three years before promotion to sergeant, and promotion to NCO rank confers special standing and respect and is accompanied with appropriate ceremony and emphasis.

To replace departing soldiers, the regiment does not request individual replacements. Instead, it receives replacement "packages" at regular intervals from the training battalions, ensuring that new soldiers arrive with ready-made friendships and firm socialization into the customs, traditions, history, and standards of the regiment. These steps will produce an order-of-magnitude improvement in vertical and horizontal cohesion, esprit, and morale. Regiments will become more than "units." They will take on many of the aspects of a large extended family, and like families they will foster an environment of mutual trust, confidence, and protectiveness against outside threats.

In the early 1980s, the Army made a serious attempt to implement a working regimental system. That attempt failed badly due to opposition from senior army leaders. To succeed today, two institutional norms must be met head-on and overcome. The first is the army's emphasis on generalized officer development. The second is the opposition of the personnel bureaucracy to any changes that might complicate its "efficient" management of personnel resources.

The typical officer career pattern exposes the individual officer to a diverse set of professional experiences. In the infantry, for example, an officer may serve in mechanized, light, and air assault assignments, the training base, a high-level staff billet, and several lengthy periods of schooling in a twenty-year career. In some cases this principle is so strong that brigade and even assistant division commanders are assigned to certain types of maneuver units they have never served with before.

In theory this system provides a well-rounded pool of officers who can competently lead in any environment. In practice, it prevents the development of real expertise, which can only come from long experience and association. Light infantry units, as one example, have a distinctive ethos and operate differently. They depend heavily on infiltration tactics and not on rapid movement and firepower. When staffed with officers with no particular light infantry perspective, experience, or focus, light infantry units may fail to realize their real potential. The same is true of cavalry units or Bradley units led by officers who are "new to the game" or who have been away for many years.

A partial explanation for the prevalence of the "generalist" approach to personnel management is its ease of operation. From the standpoint of pure efficiency, it is easier to assign and manage infantry or armor officers than light and heavy infantry or cavalry and tank officers. When readiness is defined in terms of percentage of leader and personnel fill—not how cohesive, expert, or experienced soldiers, leaders, and units are—we can expect personnel managers to favor a systems approach that responds to quantifiable indicators of success or failure. The result is very high personnel readiness rates armywide—and personnel turbulence at the small unit level, which by some estimates approaches 150 percent annually.

The Army can come to grips with the problem by realizing that high levels of cohesion, esprit, and morale can be achieved—for all that they are difficult to measure precisely—by implementing a personnel management system that is *less* efficient from a systems point of view but *more* efficient from a capabilities perspective. Cohesive units have fewer disciplinary problems, happier families, higher retention rates for quality soldiers, and more soldiers who complete their initial terms of enlistment. In short, they are much more capable.

Initiative and intelligent, decentralized execution requires trust and intimate knowledge of the strengths, weaknesses, and personalities of soldiers and leaders. This in turn requires the stability and supporting environment provided by a regimental system. And in a smaller, "poorer" army, that is a powerful strategy for success.

## SUMMARY

These recommendations suggest a course by which the army can move toward implementing the doctrine it is writing for itself. It will not be easy; changing large institutions never is. But the U.S. Army is not just another bureaucratic organization. It is made up of many thousands of soldiers who share a common goal: to be ready to fight and die in defense of American values and ideals. As soldiers we share an ethic that puts the nation and the common defense above questions of narrow self-interest or bureaucratic convenience. If these ideas are found to be valid, if they stand up to the scrutiny of the professional soldier, they will be given a fair hearing. No army can afford to stand still. It's unlikely this one will.

# Notes

1. For a discussion of maneuver warfare and its relation to AirLand Operations, see the author's "21st Century Doctrine and the Future of Maneuver," *AUSA Institute of Land Warfare Paper No. 8*, October 1991; "Commander's Intent and the Art of Maneuver," *Army Aviation*, December 1992; and "Redefining Maneuver Warfare," *Military Review*, February 1992.

2. For a classic discussion of institutional change see Colonel Huba Wass de Czege, "How To Change an Army," *Military Review*, November 1984.

3. Reuven Gal, *A Portrait of the Israeli Soldier* (NY: Greenwood Press, 1986), pp. 76–96.

4. de Tocqueville identified this characteristic trait as early as the 1830s: "the passion for equality [in America] penetrates on every side into men's hearts, expands there and fills them entirely. . . . their passion is ardent, insatiable, incessant, invincible." In the military, this powerful cultural norm contributes to a reluctance to markedly favor individuals, organizations, or branches of the service. Thus, for example, we see the practice of apportioning quotas to the Command and General Staff College by branch rather than on the basis of individual performance. See Alexis de Tocqueville, *Democracy in America*, ed. Richard D. Heffner (New York: New American Library, 1956), pp. 191, 192.

5. Interview with Capt. Frederick Karl Hellwig, USA, a 1987 graduate of the course, 3 August 1991.

6. It is necessary to make this evaluation process as objective and comprehensive as possible. In the Austrian army, candidates are subjected to a grueling five-day examination that tests the subject's knowledge of current events, tactics, general military topics, military history, and a foreign language. The essay format is used throughout, and each examination is graded by a panel of senior general staff officers. The identity of the candidate is not revealed to the grading team. Successful candidates attend a three-year War Academy course and are awarded the military equivalent of the Ph.D. (the coveted "dG" designation) and immediately advanced in grade several years ahead of their contemporaries. Interview with Oberst (Colonel) Gunter Hoffler, Austrian Army, 28 June 1991.

7. The modern Bundeswehr approximates this system in that it selects, trains, assigns and promotes general staff officers, but has no formal General Staff

as such. See Oberst Norbert Majewski and Lt. Col. John H. Peyton, "German Army General Staff Officer Training," *Military Review*, December 1984. The best and most accessible study of the history of the German General Staff—the model for all others—remains Col. Trevor N. Dupuy's *A Genius For War: The German Army and General Staff 1807–1945* (Fairfax, Va.: Hero Books, 1977).

# *Auftragstaktik:* Mission Orders and the German Experience

## Franz Uhle-Wettler

Command and control of highly mobile forces on a modern, fluid battlefield is a challenging task indeed. For many years, armed forces have searched for a methodology adequate to this task. The study of the system used by the Prussian and German armies of the 19th and 20th centuries received a powerful impetus in the mid-seventies when a prominent American scholar, Trevor N. Dupuy, argued that the German armies between 1807 and 1945 consistently outperformed their opponents due to their system of command.[1] A follow-on study by Israeli scholar Martin Van Creveld supported Dupuy's findings.[2] Thus, various experts recommended adoption of the German system, which soon came to be called *Auftragstaktik* (literally, mission tactics).[3]

Obviously, if there is any substance to the assertion of superior German battlefield performance, it is useful to study its cause. This cause certainly has not been superior courage. Many nations fielded forces of admirable gallantry, including the Russians, the chief opponents of the German army in World War II. Also, there is no such thing as an inborne German combat efficiency; history shows how quickly the quality of a nation's forces can change. For instance, in the mid-18th century wars, German and Prussian forces easily defeated superior French forces. In 1806 and 1807 the French easily defeated the Prussians wherever they met them. In 1813 and 1815 the Prussians again defeated the French. It seems that any nation's forces will fight courageously when a few basic conditions are fulfilled: a valid cause to fight for, unit cohesion, officers and NCOs whom the troops trust, and tolerable weaponry.

## ROOTS OF BATTLEFIELD EFFECTIVENESS

So much for what makes an army fight. But that does not mean it will fight effectively. Often, effectiveness is the result of superior tactics.

236

But tactics is not the only cause. This is illustrated by the German airborne assault on the Mediterranean island of Crete in 1941.

At Crete, virtually the only German asset was air superiority. The British and Greek defenders had much more powerful assets, including superior naval forces, great numerical superiority[4] and prepared positions. In those days, airborne attackers could take along only hand-held weapons, so the first waves had at best a few light mortars and a few radios. Only after capture of an airfield could light artillery be delivered, and delivery of tanks or motor transport, such as were available to the defenders, was impossible.

The worst drawback was that the defender knew the German radio code ("Ultra"). Thus he knew every detail of the attacker's battle plan, including drop zones and drop time. The assaulting force parachuted or glider-landed with hand-held weapons right into the positions of a vastly superior defender who was waiting for them, guns and rifles cocked and pointed. But the assaulting force won, capturing an island of strategic importance and causing losses to the defender that far exceeded their own.[5] Tactics cannot have produced that victory, because in the prevailing circumstances tactics were immediately reduced to the attempt of small, isolated units fighting desperately to survive. The assaulting force could not offer a battle of combined arms with major units fighting in a coordinated manner, with tactics as an important force multiplier. There must have been something else powerful enough to outweigh the disadvantages the assaulting force had to face.

British Field Marshal Lord Carver, who saw much of the British-German fighting in World War II, has thrown some light on the search for this "other" source of battlefield efficiency.[6] As he argued, time and again British units were destroyed within eyesight of other units who remained inactive since they waited for orders or for approval of what they intended to do. This suggests that an army will fight effectively when its courage is multiplied by two related factors: good tactics and initiative, i.e., by the readiness of officers, NCOs, and soldiers to act on their own, possibly even disregarding their mission.

The importance of initiative stems directly from the basic characteristics of war. War is the domain of the uncertain, of friction, and often of chaos. It will likely remain so, since war is fought not by machines but by soldiers using machines. Thus it is a contest between opposing wills and minds whose reaction in an environment of danger and death cannot be predicted. Managerial planning and meticulous execution cannot guide units and soldiers through such friction, chaos, and uncertainty. Therefore, when the unexpected intervenes, those who wait for new orders will lose. Those who react faster than their opponent will win. They will be like chess players who move two pieces while their opponent moves only one. Unless history deceives us, *Auftragstaktik* has been one means to generate that initiative.

## THE DEVELOPMENT OF *AUFTRAGSTAKTIK*

Unfortunately, there are few books or articles to tell us how *Auftragstaktik* was developed and what it means. It seemed to have evolved in a natural way, not as something that required specific explanation, theory, and terminology. Even the term is new: it was first used after World War II, when the circumstances it denoted had already passed away. The term *Auftragstaktik* was soon translated as "mission-type orders," since some writers believed that its essence was the conscious effort to give a subordinate only a (general) mission, leaving him maximum freedom as to how to execute the mission.

However, a comparison of Allied and German World War II operations orders reveals few differences and certainly none that are large enough to explain differences in force efficiency. Consequently, change in the format or phrasing of combat orders will not produce a revival or an adoption of *Auftragstaktik*. Since there is no underlying philosophy, it may be useful to examine the ground out of which *Auftragstaktik* grew and was developed. Perhaps this will show what its preconditions and its essence are.

*Auftragstaktik* was created in the kingdom of Prussia, the foremost of the states that later made up Germany. Throughout most of the 18th century, Prussia was ruled by two kings only, both of whom personally ruled their kingdom, including its commerce, finances, laws—and army. For instance, both kings personally inspected all regiments every year, and the protocols show that they inspected even those details that other armies considered the petty business of noncommissioned officers. As one of the kings, who preferred French to German, instructed his officers: *Soignez les détails, ils ne sont pas sans gloire; ils sont le premier pas qui mène à la victoire.* (Attend to the details. They are not without glory. They are the first step to victory.)

This was unique in the 18th century, when aristocrats usually considered soldiering very much a gentleman's sport, not to be taken too seriously in peacetime. But Prussia was not a compact nation-state like Britain, Austria, or France. She was spread out in more than a dozen bits and pieces over the whole of northern Germany, as the vagaries of feudal inheritance had created her.

Thus her precarious security situation had produced a unique outlook upon soldiering, vividly illustrated by an official report to the king of France by the French Field Marshal, the Count of Belle-Isle:

> The King of Prussia exercises command not only in the major issues, but in the small ones also. Always, he has his tent pitched in the center of the army camp. He issues all orders. He rises every morning at four o'clock, mounts his horse and personally inspects all outposts. He is fully dressed from morning to bedtime, wearing the ordinary blue uniform, distinguished from other officers by one medal only. The Duke of Holstein, the oldest lieutenant general of the army, spends eight months of the year with the regiment he is honorary colonel of. He arrived here having marched 600 kilometers . . . with his regiment like any ordinary colonel. Even the royal princes and the king's brother serve as ordinary officers and wear the normal uniform. Since all senior officers act as described, you may imagine the attention to duty common among the junior officers. Thereby, the training standard of the army has been raised to a level simply incredible.[7]

This training standard, which the French marshal called "incredible," must have instilled some of the pride and self-confidence that are indispensable for independent action and initiative. This self-confidence was enhanced by a second feature: as the French marshal noted, the Prussian army of the 18th century probably was the only European army that had no insignia for officers.[8] This is indicative of the way the Prussian army tried to reconcile subordination with pride and self-esteem.

On duty, of course, subordination was paramount. But off duty, all officers were equal. Significantly, the Prussian army had considerable differences with those senior officers who had started their careers serving other sovereigns, as was possible in those days. Many of them had great difficulties with this system and had to be reprimanded more than once. But the system was indispensable for the preservation of self-esteem and for the preservation of that basis upon which initiative can grow.

Important and less known (sometimes even concealed), these deliberate attempts to preserve the dignity of man were extended to the sergeants, soldiers, and the lower classes of the civil population as well. By way of illustration, torture was banned in Prussia in 1740, many decades before it was banned in most European states. Primary education was made obligatory in 1717 (163 years before it was in Britain). Universal manhood suffrage, though census-based, was introduced in 1794, when in the U.S. slavery was still legal. Universal equal manhood suffrage was introduced in the whole of Germany in 1871, when in Britain only about 15 percent of the male population had the right to vote.[9]

The unusual respect for the lower classes is also reflected by the disciplinary system. In the 18th century, flogging in the Prussian army required a sentence by a court composed of a legal advisor, three senior officers, three junior officers, three NCOs, and three other ranks—all of whom had equal votes, whereas in the British army only an informal decision by a body of officers was sufficient. In 1807 Prussia forbade corporal punishment almost completely, at a time when the British army limited flogging to 1,000 strokes—which meant almost certain death. By mid-1840, Prussia abolished the few remaining cases when an extremely light form of corporal punishment could still be ordered by a court. At the same time, the British Royal Navy sentenced 2,150 sailors per year to flogging.[10] In the Union and Confederate armies during the Civil War, corporal punishment was banned in 1861 and 1862, but such measures as "bucking and gagging" and wearing a barrel as punishment remained—unthinkable in the army of the kingdom of Prussia.

## FOUR CONTEMPORARIES ASSESS *AUFTRAGSTAKTIK*

By the mid-19th century, Prussia and the Prussian army had a long tradition of unusual devotion to professionalism and devotion to duty. They had an equally long tradition of unusual respect and good treatment of the lower classes. This was the basis for the natural growth of *Auftragstaktik*. It was a command and control system not created, not deliberately developed out of whatever philosophy or necessity. It grew naturally, by itself, and therefore it was considered the natural way of battlefield command.

The results of this system of command are seen in statements by observers from four different nations. In 1860 a cousin of the king, a field marshal not only by rank but a true soldier, wrote:

> It seems that among the Prussian officers developed an unusual feeling of independence towards superiors and a readiness to accept responsibility as can be found in no other army. The Prussian officers would not suffer restrictions by rules and regulations as are customary in Russia, Austria, England. With our officers we could not fight a defensive battle according to regulations as Wellington did, binding the individual by methodology and rules. We allow more freedom for the decision of the individual . . . and support success independently even where it would be against the battle plan of a supreme commander such as Wellington.[11]

Thirty years later, an English author finds: "Nowhere in this world is independence of thought and freedom of decision as much groomed and supported as in the German army, from the corps commanders down to the last NCO."[12] A Russian general who had been an observer of the Franco-German war arrived, in his two-volume account of the war, at the following conclusion: "At the root of the German victory is an unbelievable readiness to act independently, a readiness displayed at all levels down to the very lowest and displayed on the battlefield as well as in other matters."[13] Finally, shortly after the Franco-German war, a French lecturer told the students of the *École Supérieur de Guerre*, all of whom must have participated in the war:

> Common among the (German) officers was the firm resolve to retain the initiative by all means . . . NCOs and soldiers were exhorted, even obligated to think independently, to examine matters and to form their own opinion. These NCOs were the backbone of the Prussian army . . . their special role, supported by a respect for them unknown in other armies, secured them an honorable and envied position. The Prussian army was proud of them.[14]

This may suffice to illustrate that the system of *Auftragstaktik* had not and could not be grafted ready-made on whatever basis. Rather, it grew out of many decades of education of the masses, of respecting the individuality and dignity of junior officers, sergeants, and soldiers. Last but not least, it was the result of a relentless pursuit of professionalism, out of which grew self-assurance and self-confidence.

## *AUFTRAGSTAKTIK:* PRUSSIAN BATTLE PROCEDURES

At first sight, it seems that battle procedures in the German army were not dissimilar to the procedures of other armies: the commander appreciated the situation, and developed a decision (battle plan), on the basis of which he stated the mission of subordinate commanders. The subordinates received their commander's intent (battle plan), and their mission, appreciated their situation, and developed their intent, on the basis of which they stated their subordinates' mission—and so on, down the line.

This procedure is the same in all armies. But in the Prussian and later the German armies there seems to have been a difference: the importance of the mission (in whatever way it may have been stated and phrased) was reduced. The importance of the commander's intent was very much more emphasized. At first look, this seems rather innocent and inconsequential. But it was not. When an unexpected situation sprang up, commanders could more easily act on their own—as long as they stayed within their commander's intent.

Thus, if there is any single feature that is the core of *Auftragstaktik*, it is *not* a specific way of stating missions. The decisive feature is the high emphasis placed on commander's intent and the low emphasis placed on the mission received. When around 1860 a major was reprimanded by a Prussian prince and field marshal, the major pleaded that he had acted upon strict orders. The field marshal's response ("the king made you a major because he believed you knew when *not* to obey") may not be remarkable. But perhaps it is remarkable that even semiofficial publications often mentioned this response as a model. Thus it is not surprising that in 1906 a paragraph was inserted in the chief manual which *obliged* officers to disobey their mission if there were any doubt that the mission was appropriate to the battlefield situation. Similarly, out of a random sample of 22 map exercises conducted in the mid-thirties of this century and examined by the author, only four tasked the participants to examine how to execute a given mission. Eighteen of the exercises placed the participants sooner or later in a situation where they first had to determine if their mission could still be considered valid, if they should disobey it—and which mission they then should give themselves.

## REVIVAL OF *AUFTRAGSTAKTIK?*

*Auftragstaktik*, or what was left of it, died when Germany collapsed in 1945. Two or three decades later, interest in it revived, possibly because NATO nations were looking for a powerful force multiplier that could assist in offsetting the quantitative superiority of the Warsaw Pact. Also, there may have been a second reason: a future war between high-technology forces may be dominated by electronic warfare as much as World War II was dominated by armor. Battlefield commanders will then be faced again with rapidly changing situations and obsolete missions—and will be unable to refer to higher authority because their radios are jammed.

Therefore, in future wars initiative and independent action may be even more important than in past ones. Ultimately, this raises the question of whether it is possible to create a corps of officers, NCOs, and even soldiers who are up to the essence of *Auftragstaktik*. This means that when facing an unexpected situation, they must think: "When my boss gave me my mission, he cannot have anticipated this situation. Therefore, I shall disregard my mission and shall act within my boss's intent." If the situation changed completely, it may even be mandatory to have soldiers of all ranks who think "when my boss developed his intent and battleplan, he did not anticipate this situation. Therefore, I must disregard my mission and my boss's intent and must do what I believe my boss would want me to do if he saw this situation."[15]

Obviously, such a system will lead to general chaos, unless all participants are very highly trained. Independent action can only be a principle when it is based on sound professionalism—the first prerequisite for *Auftragstaktik*. The second prerequisite is a good, possibly even cocky, sense of self-confidence. *Auftragstaktik* will grow only among soldiers who consider themselves masters of their trade, who are proud to be with the troops, who love a command job and do not hanker after the next desk job, close to the Almighties in the service staffs and the joint staff.

The third precondition is a difficult one. It concerns the supervisors and sometimes even the political masters. They will foster the growth of *Auftragstaktik* only when they accept, even applaud, subordinates who solve a problem in a way the supervisor did not expect and considers best. When the supervisor intervenes too often and too early, and especially if he intervenes too forcefully, he may prevent a momentous mistake. But it is he who commits a stupid blunder, because he prevents the rise of initiative—the key to success in war. Supervisors must recognize that besides discourtesy and indiscipline there is only one thing that justifies a sharp reprimand: inaction, waiting for orders and waiting for approval. Anyway, introduction or revival of *Auftragstaktik* primarily means educating supervisors, not subordinates. Unfortunately, for supervisors "it is easier to shepherd sheep than lions, but with the latter one has more effect on the enemy."[16]

Finally, the last prerequisite: the army's life-style. There seem to be armies today that determine the daily life of their units by SOPs, statistics, inspections, and tests, and whose activity centers around rules, regulations, and manuals. Some of their senior commanders seem to be so busy evaluating the reports and statistics of their subordinates and so occupied preparing reports and statistics for their supervisors that they have little time left to go out to the troops—not to supervise them once more, but to do their primary job: to see, to talk, to help.

All this may be justified. But officers thus educated are unlikely on the day of battle to be the bold risk takers, ready to put initiative and their own judgement in the forefront. An army that wants to have risk takers with initiative will have to foster them in peacetime by appropriate selection, promotion, education, and assignment, and especially by an appropriate life-style and daily routine. To do so, however, is a responsibility of the senior and the most senior officers, and even of the political masters.

This leads to the conclusion already suggested: introduction or revival of *Auftragstaktik* primarily means educating supervisors, not subordinates. The supervisors, the highest army officers, have to create the fertile soil from which the tactics they desire can grow. If they do so, they may almost forget deliberate actions to introduce *Auftragstaktik*. It will grow by itself. If they don't create that soil but talk about *Auftragstaktik*, exhorting their subordinates to practice it, they will be like those who order sheep to behave like lions.

Where do these conclusions lead? Perhaps to the following: *Auftragstaktik* means the readiness to act independently and the capability to do so sensibly. If you try to introduce *Auftragstaktik,* you will be like a farmer who sows wheat in an arid desert. You are bound to fail. There is only one sure way to succeed: if you want *Auftragstaktik,* forget about it. Instead, create an army in which independence has become a life-style, and in which a high level of professionalism prevails as well as a cocky, well-founded self-confidence. If you create such an army, independent action and *Auftragstaktik* will follow naturally. Sounds easy, doesn't it?

# Notes

1. Trevor N. Dupuy, *A Genius for War: The German Army and General Staff 1807-1945* (Fairfax, Va.: Hero Books, 1977).

2. Martin Van Creveld, *Fighting Power: German and US Army Performance 1939-1945* (Westport, Conn.: Greenwood Press, 1982).

3. Richard Simpkin, *Race to the Swift: Thoughts on Twenty-First Century Warfare* (London: Brassey's Defense Publishers, 1985); John Vermillion, "Tactical Implications of the Adoption of Auftragstaktik for Command and Control on the Airland Battlefield," unpublished paper, School of Advanced Military Studies, Ft. Leavenworth, Kans., 1985; J. Nelson, "Where to Go from Here? Considerations For the Formal Adoption of Auftragstaktik by the US Army," unpublished paper, School of Advanced Military Studies, Ft. Leavenworth, Kans., 1986; Martin Van Creveld, "On Learning from the Wehrmacht and Other Things," *Military Review* vol. LXVIII, no. 1, 1985, pp. 62–71.

4. About 42,000 defenders (British, Greek, Australian, New Zealander). On the first day about 5,500 German airborne troops attacked, reinforced day by day to about 18,000.

5. German losses were 2,071 killed, 1,888 missing (almost all killed), and 2,594 wounded. British losses were 3,723 killed (including 2,011 Royal Navy), 1,737 wounded, and 11,836 prisoners. Greek losses were about 1,500 killed and about 5,000 taken prisoner. One hundred forty-nine German aircraft were destroyed. Three cruisers and six destroyers of the British Royal Navy were sunk.

6. Lord Michael Carver, *Dilemmas of the Desert War* (London: 1986).

7. Quoted by G. Mendelssohn-Bartholdy, *Der Konig*, 16th ed. (Bielefeld: 1954), p. 139.

8. Christian Duffy, *Friedrich der Grosse und Seine Armee* ("The Army of Frederick the Great") (Stuttgart: 1978), pp. 27, 55. Only general officers were allowed a small feather at their cap.

9. Hans Setzer, *Wahlsystem und Parteienentwicklung in England* ("Electoral System and Development of Political Parties in England") (Frankfurt: 1973), p. 87.

10. H. Hopkins, *The Strange Death of Private White* (London: 1977), pp. 12–21, 228–245. The figures for army flogging, probably even higher, are unknown.

11. Field Marshal Prinz Friedrich Karl von Preussen, quoted by D. Ose, "Der Auftrag," *Europaische Wehrkunde,* June 1982, p. 264.

12. S. Whitman, *Imperial Germany: A Critical Study of Fact and Character* (London: 1889), quoted by F. Doepner, *Bundeswehr and Armeereform* (Dorheim: 1969), p. 67.

13. Woide, *Die Ursachen der Siege und Niederlagen im Kriege 1870,* deutsch von Klingender, 2 vols. (Berlin: 1894 and 1896), II, p. 88; also I, pp. 56, 154 and 368, II, p. 5.

14. L. Rousset, *Histoire Generale de la Guerre Franco-Allemande* (Paris: 1886), pp. 21, 34.

15. For examples in military history see Franz Uhle-Wettler, *Hohe und Wendepunkte Deutscher Militargeschichte* (Mainz: 1984), pp. 143–150, 155 ff., 180 f., 215 f., 225 ff., 274 ff.

16. General W. von Blume, quoted by Dr. Daniel Hughes (Army Combined Arms Center, Fort Leavenworth, Kans.) in a yet unpublished article on *Auftragstaktik.* The author is indebted to Dr. Hughes for valuable information.

# Teaching Maneuver Warfare

## Michael Duncan Wyly

Teaching maneuver warfare places new and different demands on the teacher. Interestingly, the contrast in methodology between teaching the old and the new parallels the contrast between the two styles of fighting. For instance, before 1989, the U.S. Marine Corps doctrine called for *methodical battle*: a set-piece, closely orchestrated, slow-moving battle, tightly controlled from a highly centralized command. Instruction was also methodical. Today, U.S. Marine Corps doctrine calls for *maneuver warfare*: a fast-paced battle, loosely controlled and decentralized, highly responsive to a changing situation. The new teaching techniques are also less controlled and highly responsive—responsive to the understanding of the students.

The imperative of my message here is that the old style of teaching will not work anymore. Maneuver warfare cannot be taught through methodical teaching. I have watched instructors try it in the Marine Corps for nearly two years and witnessed its failure. At the same time, I have watched others in the Marine Corps teach in a different style that is suited to the subject matter, and seen the results: enthusiastic students who can talk the language and understand combat in a context of maneuver. The new style of teaching that I shall describe is mandatory if the new style of fighting is to be learned.

Before 1989, Marines learned methodical battle from an instructor who stood on a stage with a pointer and lectured to one or two hundred men at a time. He began by giving them definitions to learn. He introduced them to the old control measures that defined linear battle: the inevitable box formed by a *line of departure* at one end and the inevitable *FSCL (fire support coordination line)* at the opposite end, and a boundary on each side. A piece of terrain, almost always a hill, but occasionally a town or a bridge, or maybe even a treeline, occupied the center of the box and was designated the *objective*. An oval-shaped line was drawn around it and this became the end towards which the battle was fought. The enemy became an inanimate object that sat immobile on the objective waiting to be defeated, shown graphically as a box colored red, in contrast to the blue friendly forces whose predictable courses were drawn with straight arrows, reflecting the certainty with which commanders expected to seize their terrain objectives. Seizing objectives was what the methodical battle was about, never defeating the enemy. In Vietnam we made a subtle shift from seizing terrain to counting bodies. We went back to terrain after the war. But while we were counting bodies we were no closer to an understanding about defeating the enemy. The war's having ended with the enemy in control of Ho Chi Minh City is proof enough of that.

Field exercises eventually followed the lectures. Yet they, too, were set pieces. Most of the students filled the ranks of platoons and companies, and few were exposed to learning about making decisions save those designated platoon leaders, company commanders, and the like. Even then, leaders did not learn to make decisions so much as they were taught a decision-making *process*, a methodology outlined step by step in a book that no commander is ever known to have actually followed in a real war.

Methodical battle was taught in an orderly sequence. *Order*, after all, was the hallmark of methodical battle. After definitions and control measures, it was time to lecture the students on a limited repertoire of attacks: frontal assault, envelopment, and a thing called penetration, which was really a frontal assault that had somehow managed to smash its way through.

The defense was introduced later and was often taught as a separate course. Defensive battle had its own definitions, control measures, and rules. There were the FEBA (*Forward Edge of the Battle Area*), the *Security Area, Battle Area*, and *Reserve Area*, all neatly laid out in an orderly schematic. Instructors quizzed students to trip them up on the fine points like the subtle differences between the *Combat Outpost Line* and the *General Outpost Line*. Lines provided a pervasive structure that defined defensive warfare, and left their imprints forever in students' minds. The student could pick from a narrow repertoire of defenses that included such imaginative choices as the linear defense (keep the enemy on *his* side of the line) and the perimeter defense (circle the wagons). As in the attack, little or no thought was given to destroying the enemy unless it could be assumed he would commit his forces in a suicidal—yet orderly—attack into our *Final Protective Fires*.

Orderliness dominated everything. Lectures were scheduled in 50-minute blocks, each governed by an approved outline that dictated to the instructor what he was to cover from beginning to end. If he didn't finish in 50 minutes, the instructor had to embarrass himself by running overtime and disrupting a carefully orchestrated schedule by encroaching on the next instructor's time. The alternative was to deprive the students of the information.

Teaching maneuver warfare is like doing maneuver warfare. When the teacher begins, he does not know how far he will go in an hour or how many turns he will take in how many different directions. His mission, after all, is to teach students to think, to exercise judgment. It is not to teach a repertoire of attacks or formulistic procedures, as it was in the Marine Corps before 1989.

Distinctions between offense and defense tend to merge in practice and in teaching. The idea is to defeat and destroy the enemy, however best. Whether through a lightning attack or a deceptive ambushlike defense, the goal is the same. Transition from offense to defense is rapid, almost instantaneous. Sometimes both are conducted simultaneously, or an operation has the characteristics of both at once. The teacher cannot discuss offense in isolation from defense, because in maneuver warfare the two are so closely tied.

The content of the maneuver warfare course cannot be neatly divided into 50-minute blocks, each predisposed to cover a given outline. Instead, the class will meet biweekly or more, and each session will take up where the other left off. It cannot be accurately predicted at the beginning of the semester exactly where students will be in the middle. The *teacher* governs the content of each session, not the central institution. Only the teacher is "at the front," i.e., on the ground on the spot and able to know. The teacher must proceed at whatever pace will keep his students challenged and exercising their minds. The course is not about imparting knowledge. It is about teaching judgment. There are no rules or formulas.

Maneuver warfare is fighting without formulas. Therefore there are none to teach. The teacher feels and probes his students as the soldier in combat feels and probes his enemy in maneuver warfare. He seeks opportunities, isolates resistance, and exploits breakthroughs. He decides how fast to go, what examples to use, and how much depth to go into, all based on what he learns about his students as he goes along. When a student grasps an idea and develops it in open discussion, the teacher acts like a fisherman, playing out line, letting him run. The student might, after all, possess genius. He might form ideas the teacher has never dreamed of. The classroom is not a place to limit thought.

Maneuver warfare is decision making; that is, the application of mission tactics. So the teacher must equip his students to make decisions. Mission tactics are the tactics of employing the mind of every Marine in the battalion and turning him loose to think and to make decisions. Given this, it is decision-making ability that, in maneuver warfare, determines whether or not the unit is successful. Therefore, it is the maneuver warfare teacher's task to develop judgment: judgment that can be applied in decision making. More than content, methodology, or procedures, the task at hand is teaching the student to make decisions.

And what better way to teach decisions is there than to require the student to *make* decisions? He must make them repeatedly and often, under a multitude of circumstances, subject to the harshest criticism of his teacher and his peers. Several settings should be used. Students should be taken to the field and be called upon to make decisions there. They should gather around a sand table to make decisions while viewing the whole battle graphically. They should be brought to the classroom where they can get more map exercises and more varied, short, simple scenarios with greater frequency, free from the overhead of terrain models and limitations imposed by the scale of the sand box.

I prefer to start beginning students in the field. Though the student might get a better picture in the classroom or around the sand table, it is in the field that the student experiences the atmosphere most like that which will prevail when he leads in combat. Therefore it is most productive for him to begin making his decisions in this environment. Yet, he will need to get a picture of the battle at some point and see it graphically, as he only can around a sand table or on a map in a classroom. But this can come a little later. In combat he will not have such a clear picture. Why mislead him in the beginning? Show him as much as you can from the beginning what it will really be like. Then the whole picture will be more meaningful when you show it to him in the classroom. He will have a better appreciation for what you are talking about. Fewer of your words will be wasted.

An expedient terrain model can be made in the field. When we do get to sit in the classroom, one of the things we will call on the student to do is to imagine himself on that piece of terrain depicted on a map sheet or sand table. He has to think of himself as being there on the ground, bearing the elements, making decisions. He will have difficulty doing that if he has never been in the field.

Field work can be a combination of exercises where students (1) play the part of riflemen and actually participate in a sham battle and (2) take terrain walks where the teacher calls upon individuals to make decisions. In the sham battle the student experiences the requirement for teamwork and coordination. In the terrain walk, he is called upon to exercise his hand at making decisions under the close scrutiny of teacher and peers.

An ideal teacher-to-student ratio in a terrain walk is about one to twelve. Field work of this nature should not be restricted to wilderness settings. Battles are more often than not fought in and around populated areas. That means the student should be called upon to consider roadways, bridges, railroads, houses—all the things he will very likely have to contend with when he faces combat.

A three- to five-day period in the field doing terrain walks is ideal. He learns something of the field skills essential to maneuver warfare while he is studying decision making. Though he should travel to populated areas and make decisions among man-made features, he will probably need to spend his nights on some government reservation—very likely in a wilderness setting. This is not counterproductive. All the time he does this he is developing his field skills.

Indoor sessions are valuable, too, for reasons already expressed. The view of the whole battlefield is important, even though the commander in a real situation who leads from the front, as maneuver warfare demands, will seldom have the luxury of seeing the whole battle laid out so nicely. In combat, he nevertheless must be able to visualize the whole battlefield. It is important that he begin making this connection while a student.

But whatever the setting, the function of the teacher who is working with students on decision making in maneuver warfare is the same. He must make his students commit themselves. He poses a problem and he asks the student, "What are you going to do?"

The student is allowed to answer only that question: "What are you going to do?" His answer must describe *action*. And he must answer quickly. He is allowed to make no other remark except to answer the question, "What are you going to do?" He must not be allowed to "feel the teacher out" by suggesting various possible answers, seeking eye contact from the teacher that will hint the "right" course. He must not be allowed to fall into the mode that he learned in college philosophy or sociology classes, where all kinds of academic suppositions are encouraged and everything is acceptable. Warfare, after all, is not an academic exercise and it is not a game of words. Warfare is action. Decisive action. The student's mind must be trained to act.

The student will certainly want more information then you have given him upon which to base his decision. If you have given him as much information as he feels he needs, then you have given him too much. Combat decision making is decision making with incomplete information. It is dealing with uncertainty and thriving on chaos. In Vietnam we never knew what was really happening. I, myself, am guilty of telling students, "You must attack command and control—the brains of the opposing force," and it is good if you can do that. But in Vietnam we had no way of knowing whom we were attacking. I never knew if I was fighting command and control people, logisticians, infantrymen, privates, majors, colonels, or what. Suddenly someone was there. Was it even the enemy? How could we be sure? We could never be sure. We had to be careful. But we also had to be bold. And we had to make the right decision. It was life and death. There was no room for error. But errors would occur. The teacher needs to give the student an appreciation for this feeling. Only then is it meaningful when the student gives his answer to "What are you going to do?"

Rationale will be discussed later—only *after* the student commits himself to a decision. Why? Because this is how it must be done in combat, where time is always of the essence. And in maneuver warfare, time is even more critical.

This is not to suggest that the rationale for the student's decision is not important to the teacher. It is crucially important. It is so important, in fact, that the teacher should refrain from criticizing the student's decision until the student has been given the opportunity to explain why he did what he did. The teacher may question the student about his decision before he presents rationale. This is to test his resolve.

He may even goad the student, to test his confidence. But in so doing, the teacher begins the process of drawing out the rationale. It is through assessing the rationale that the teacher will determine whether or not the student is developing judgment, whether his course of action was wise or unwise. In discussing rationale, examples from combat history may be evoked. So may capabilities of weapons, the intent or presumed intent of the enemy, weather, morale, terrain—all the variables.

The principle that has been applied here is that combat decision making must be done implicitly if it is to be effective. The demands of combat simply do not allow for passage of time between deciding and acting. Acting now is nearly always better than acting later, even if the later action might have been better thought out. In a contest between two opposing wills, much can be gained through catching one's opponent off guard. When the goal is to shatter the enemy's cohesion, as it is in maneuver warfare, catching the enemy off guard is among the greatest of opportunities likely to come your way.

Sound rationale is no less important in maneuver warfare. But one's ability to apply it must be developed so that it becomes instinctive. Thus the importance of exercises such as described here—making decision upon decision in a multitude of varying situations, different terrain, different kinds of enemy. The more you do it the better you get, like calisthenics. The teacher should put his students in one jam after another and make them decide how to get out of it.

There is a danger here for the teacher. He can go overboard in this direction and teach the wrong lesson. If the message becomes "Anything you do is going to get you in trouble" then the lesson the student may erroneously carry away is likely to be "Don't make decisions—they get you in trouble." For example, if the teacher's response to an attack in one direction is "You've hit a minefield, now what do you do?" and as soon as the student changes direction, it is "You're in an ambush," then when he decides to bypass the ambush site with his reserves, his reserves get hit in the rear with a tank attack supported by air. Everything he does is wrong. The lesson inadvertently taught is to do nothing.

Instructors err just as frequently at the opposite end of the spectrum, however, when they fall into the "everything's OK" syndrome. Everything's OK can make for happy students and a relaxed life for the instructor, but not much is taught. There *are* wrong answers. Wrong answers in a maneuver warfare course do not include any specific action. Unlike the old methodical battle courses, teaching maneuver warfare allows the student to do anything: he can decide to attack, defend, go right, left, backward or forward, use his supporting arms or not use them, go in stealthily without preparation fire or blow everything up before he moves. Any of these actions is fine. Where he can go astray is in the realm of *how* he does things.

For instance, the student might disperse too much or not enough. Here the teacher is called upon to know his stuff—not just a bunch of rules. He also must make provision for the student to justify what appears to be an error in judgment when he gives his rationale. Dispersing too much is a common error made by the student without combat experience. He has dispersed too much if he loses focus and can no longer realistically bring his unit together and employ it decisively against the given enemy. Admittedly, this is a subjective call for the teacher. But this is why teachers need to be well schooled in combat history and, whenever possible, have combat experience. (Combat experience without knowledge of combat history is not of much value for the teacher, however, as I shall soon show.)

Overdispersement to the detriment of focus was a common error in Vietnam. When I was a company commander in that war, I found that I could preside over a firefight very effectively against pretty much anything the North Vietnamese could throw at me if I had my whole company together. Two firefights I also could handle, but it was difficult and taxed all my faculties. Three firefights and I was not a company commander anymore; my company degenerated into three platoons engaged in three separate, unconnected battles. This was fine if the enemy we confronted was weak enough that our platoons could do what was necessary to win. Otherwise, however, it was a case of overdispersement and lost opportunity to win. When I was working an area where the enemy was tough, I wanted to have my whole company close enough so its elements could work together toward a single end. I wanted to have what it took to win a firefight decisively, no questions asked.

An equally common error is not to disperse enough. There was plenty of that in Vietnam, too. Keeping your Marines too close together can lead to disasters, a recent and classic case in point being the 1983 Beirut bombing of the Marine barracks which cost over 240 lives, with no payback to the enemy. But disasters measurable in high casualties are not the only consequences of underdispersement. Missed opportunities are another. In Vietnam, when units "holed up," husbanding forces together for protection, the enemy was able to run roughshod over the civilian population. Concentrated U.S. units were visible to the North Vietnamese and could be avoided.

Another common student error to which the maneuver warfare teacher must be alert is the tendency to close out options. Maneuver warfare is a style of fighting that keeps options open, recognizing the unpredictability of combat. It would be futile to try to list here all the ways a commander can inappropriately close out options in combat. A few examples would include failure to keep a large enough reserve, not dispersing enough, using a single route of advance when multiple routes are available, defending in isolated areas, holding one side of a river and letting the enemy have the other, and the classic mistake of blowing or burning bridges behind you.

As students progress, the teacher will be able to transition from demanding a simple statement of what action they will take to having them actually issue the order they would give to their subordinates in the situation postulated. Emphasis must remain on action, however, reminding students that combat is an action thing and not wordsmithing. Orders given in class should predominantly be oral because the oral order is preferred in maneuver combat, written orders being slow and cumbersome. This is not to say that the written order does not have a certain utility in the classroom on occasion. It does, as long as the requirement is only to write brief renditions of what would be communicated orally—not the lengthy formatted documents that typified study of methodical battle in the past. The value in the classroom of committing the decision to writing in the form of a brief order is that it forces the student to make a commitment. When the class is large, it becomes difficult for the teacher to put all the students on the spot as much as he might. By demanding that they write their orders down and hand them in, the teacher forces them to make a commitment, which is difficult for many people. This ability to commit decisively is, after all, the rare quality we seek in combat leaders. Then, after the written work is handed in, the teacher can call on students to give supporting rationale for their decisions. Because the teacher now has the written commitment in hand, the student cannot revoke or withdraw his decision as he begins to feel pressure, especially when he realizes that his fellow students had ideas quite different than his own, which may, by the time he is called on, make his own look foolish.

Another technique in demanding student decisions is to use a stopwatch. Give them ten minutes, five minutes, or ten seconds—whatever is appropriate and reasonable in the situation.

In requiring students to give their orders, de-emphasize format. Once again, combat is an action thing. Too often in the classroom and in the bureaucracy, I have seen Marines—especially senior Marines—wanting to make it a game of words. The instructor who feels insecure about his background in tactics seeks refuge in criticism of words. In the days of methodical battle, Marines insisted on using the five-paragraph format for orders. Too often I have seen Marines rejecting good tactical ideas because they could not fit them into the format. Too often I have heard squad leaders stutter through the format of the five-paragraph order and then, afterward, say, "Alright, guys, now, here's what we're going to do . . ." and proceed in their own words and with no set format to give a clear, concise imperative statement of what needs to happen.

Now that we have rejected the format, let us discuss two elements that really ought to be in the order somewhere. Or if they are absent in words, the student must be able to show that they are implied so clearly that no words are necessary. These are intent and focus of effort.

The student must know what his intent is, and he must convey it clearly, remembering that in maneuver warfare it falls upon his subordinates and his subordinates' subordinates to know the commander's intent two echelons up. They cannot know it if he does not express it clearly. He has no requirement to restate his senior's intent and his senior's senior's intent every time he issues an order; however, he must be aware and must keep his subordinates aware as appropriate. The teacher should query the student about his intent whenever the student gives an order. He should ensure that the intent focuses on the enemy—on what the student intends to do to the enemy.

Focus of effort—*Schwerpunkt*—is the richest of all the maneuver warfare concepts. Without this, the commander is less than a commander. His subordinates are left without focus, unsure of how their leader envisions the battle. The teacher who hears a student's order and cannot quickly identify his chosen *Schwerpunkt* needs to interrogate the student until it becomes clear.

Teaching maneuver warfare stresses judgment more than knowledge, but this does not mean that the teacher can be void of knowledge. In fact, he needs more knowledge than the teacher of methodical battle did. The teacher of methodical battle needed knowledge about, obviously, *methodology*. The teacher of maneuver warfare, i.e., the teacher of judgment, needs knowledge of war.

Combat experience on the teacher's part is extremely valuable. It allows him to criticize and lend insights he otherwise could not possibly have. It also gives him credibility with the students. But this credibility becomes dangerous if the teacher has not studied combat history. There might be an exception if the veteran-teacher had experienced several wars. The problem emerges at its worst when he has only experienced one. When I was a lieutenant in Vietnam, we all despised majors. The common criticism that every Marine lieutenant in combat in Vietnam seemed to have of majors was "He thinks he's still in Korea." I promised myself that when I became a major, my lieutenants would never say of me, "He thinks he's still in Vietnam." Successive wars tend to be different. The most common criticism of the military mind is that it gravitates to the war already fought and is insensitive to the demands of the present. Professional warriors, if they are equivalent to professional physicians who can treat pain and even cure patients of disease not heretofore encountered, must be able to respond to war situations that are completely new. To do this requires an in-depth understanding of war itself. It requires answers to such questions as: What are the enemy's real strengths and where are his vulnerabilities? What is the importance of speed? What is the meaning of speed in combat, and how can I achieve it? What will constitute this enemy's defeat? Where can I take risks?

So the study of history becomes important to everyone who would presume to teach warfare. One war is insufficient. He needs to know the degree to which wars have differed and how they have differed, because the war he is preparing his students for is likely to be vastly different than the last one. How else to know that except to study a whole range of wars and how they have differed; to know how the Greeks and Romans fought and contrast this early Western thinking with Genghis Khan's revolutionary style, yet be able to draw comparisons between Genghis Khan and Xenophon? Why did the United States do so well in World War II and so poorly in Vietnam? What was so different? Or did we do so well in World War II? Why did the Germans lose? The instructor who finds himself out of his depth when confronted with such questions is ill equipped to prepare students for a future war, the nature of which no one can predict with accuracy.

Military history is an unfortunate term because in the minds of would-be warriors it conjures up the image of arrogant students and professors, idly speculating about things they never will be called upon to do and couldn't if they had to. It conjures images of school days and academic questions, such as why Roosevelt did what Stalin wanted and not Churchill, or why Marines wear red stripes on their blue trousers. It is for this reason I so often say "combat history" instead of "military history." What I really mean is war: the study of war. Our profession's discipline has simply not enjoyed much respectability, and no wonder! Our fixation on methodical battle deserved no respect. The study of the old khaki-covered FMFMs, which were so prolific in the U.S. Marine Corps in the 1960s, had little relevance to the demands of Vietnam. The same manuals in the 1970s had even less relevance to the future. By 1980 we should have known better. By 1989 we did.

But any profession, art, or science studies its history. They call it something else. We do not learn physics without an awareness of Newton, Faraday, and Einstein. The psychologist needs to know who Freud and Jung were and what they thought and did. A lawyer studies his profession largely through precedents set in the past. The maneuver warfare teacher should use historical case studies in much the way that business case studies are used at Harvard Business School. That is, in advance of a decision-making exercise, students study historical material relative to an actual engagement. They are called upon in the classroom or in the field to make decisions and support them with rationale. The availability of information about the actual outcome and the knowledge that the event actually happened keep the exercise in touch with reality. In this way the students are studying human behavior, which is the essence of the determinant in battle. They are not simply theorizing.

No one expects that the historical event being studied will somehow be repeated. Even if it is, the outcome is likely to be different. Changed technology is but one of many variables, and even if all else stayed the same, the mere fact that different human beings would be making the decisions and doing the fighting would likely lead to a different outcome. What the student gains from the case study is not a formula for achieving success, but a look at human behavior in combat, an understanding of the many variables involved, an appreciation of which variables weigh more under different circumstances, and some additions to his "bag of tricks" for application in real war.

Furthermore, it was through the study of combat history that we derived the various concepts that, taken together, define what we now know as maneuver warfare. It is important that students understand these concepts; not only how to apply them, but where they came from. That is, they need to know and be confident that maneuver warfare is not somebody's new theory, but rather a style of fighting that has been proven very powerful again and again.

There is a temptation to teach the concepts of maneuver warfare by selecting a number of historical examples, at least one for each concept, and then showing the student an example of that concept in action—surfaces and gaps in the German Operation Michael, April 1918, for instance. But there is a problem with this method because it misuses history. I am unimpressed with the student whose thinking starts and stops with what the professor tells him ("Operation Michael is an example of surfaces and gaps," for instance) and even less impressed with the professor who teaches that way. We have already established that teaching maneuver warfare is teaching people to think. If we are indeed interested in teaching soldiers and Marines to think, then let's not tell them "Here is what you are to get out of studying this battle." That equates to "Here is what I want you to think." Instead, have them read about Operation Michael, give them the German doctrine that was published in January 1918 and applied for the first time in that operation (*Angriff im Stellungskriege*) and have them study it. Expose them to how the Germans prepared and trained for the operation. Study the British and French reactions to it. Then, ask the students what *they* discover from the operation. The teacher may be surprised: maybe there is more than surfaces and gaps in that example. A student may see the key to the whole thing as being integration of the light machine gun in German assault squads. Low-level integration of combined arms and decentralized command are important innovations to understand, so teacher and student together should make the most of such observations when they come up in class. The teacher need not always have the last word.

Use historical cases together with hypothetical cases to put students' minds to work making decisions. Then bring out the concepts as they come up in class discussion or in the field during the exercise or terrain walk. Let the ideas flow as they will, as Sun Tzu's army was likened to flowing water. A student solution to a map exercise may be to issue new orders to a reserve platoon to go through a recently discovered gap. Another student may point out that this may be unnecessary. You may want to hold your reserve in case of an even greater opportunity, he points out. In a unit that is actually practicing maneuver warfare and demanding high initiative at low levels, nearby units would go through the gap without orders, based on the first intimation from lead units that the gap exists. So no new order need be issued. The initiative of the soldiers in lead units may be depended upon. The commander may hold on to his reserve for a future opportunity. Here is *reconnaissance-pull*. An alert teacher will point this out while it is relevant to the discussion. This leads to discussion of the effect created on the enemy when your forces get inside and behind his men. Now the teacher introduces concepts of *infiltration attack,* and *isolation and penetration*. As students weigh various courses of action, some emerge as slower than others. Now the teacher mentions the value of *high tempo* and *security in speed.*

All these points would likely come out in a discussion of 1st Marine Division's invasion of Kuwait in Desert Storm, 1991. Other case studies will introduce other concepts, though with different groups of students, different case studies will introduce different concepts just as different bodies of individuals and different leaders will influence battles differently, even though they are fought under otherwise similar circumstances. The German crossing of the Meuse, May 1940, will likely evoke discussion about *multiple thrusts* and *der Schwerpunkt.* Discussion of the U.S. Army's crossing the Rhine at Remagen bridge demonstrates the wisdom of *"don't wait for orders."* Napoleon's decision making at Austerlitz may be the perfect vehicle to introduce discussion of the *reserve.* The skilled teacher would have in his repertoire the ability to demonstrate how Hermann Balck used reserves repeatedly to good effect on the eastern front in 1943.

The thought of building such a repertoire of historical knowledge may seem intimidating at first. It need not be so. Out of the thousands of engagements that can be drawn upon for teaching, a small number are used repeatedly, knowledge of which constitutes a cultural literacy in the subject through which one can communicate relatively well with most anyone who has acquired a background in combat history. Any teacher ought to be conversant in all of these before he teaches a fundamental course in tactics:

Desert Storm, 1991
Beirut, 1983
Grenada, 1983
Falkland Islands, 1982
Golan Heights, 1973
Dewey Canyon, 1969
Khe Sanh, 1968
Israel's Six-Day War, 1967
Ia Drang Valley, 1965
Inchon, 1950
Normandy, 1944
Kursk-Orel, 1943
Stalingrad, 1941–1943
Germany's defeat of France, 1940
Operation Michael, 1918
Tannenberg, 1914
First Marne, 1914
The Schlieffen Plan, 1905
Sedan, 1870
Königgrätz, 1866
Cold Harbor, 1864
Gettysburg, 1863
Vicksburg, 1863
Jena-Auerstädt, 1806
Leuthen, 1757
Cannae, 216 B.C.
Leuctra, 371 B.C.

These are not uniquely maneuver battles. They are simply battles one should know in order to study, draw comparisons, and discuss warfare intelligently with others. Students should become familiar with them.

It is of utmost importance that students be made to read. Since developing military judgment requires studying war, students need to read about battles. Because our society, including our colleges, has deemphasized reading in the past twenty years, it is important that the maneuver warfare teacher both give reading assignments and ensure his students are doing them. He will quickly discover that many college graduates are apt to neglect reading; they have learned in American colleges that no one really expects them to read. Written work, including "pop" essay quizzes, and graded classroom discussion of assigned reading will help ensure that students are doing their reading. They must read if they are to learn to analyze and make connections between battles of the past and battles of the future, and to conceptualize in order to deal with the unknown.

One of the things that fascinated me when I taught tactics in the Marine Corps—years before there was any official encouragement to read—was how quickly students who had not been reading discovered that they enjoyed it. Getting the hook in students to read about warfare is one of the easiest tasks the maneuver warfare teacher has. Warfare is probably the most exciting activity that one can read about. What we had done in the post–World War II Marine Corps was to take the most exciting subject in the world—tactics—and make it boring. By neglecting decision making and, in its place, teaching methodology, by removing the account of human experience from the course of studies, we had managed to make our Marines' lives as dull as possible.

Of course, the argument that this discussion inevitably evokes is the argument for teaching procedures and definitions first. Definitions and procedures have their place and they are important. Whether definitions ought to be "taught," however, is a legitimate question. I think people can learn definitions without a teacher. The teacher can demand their use. He probably should. But somehow this seems outside the realm of teaching and more a matter of maintaining discipline. Procedures, such as how to employ weapons, how to communicate, how to request air support, are indeed important also. Many require rote memory and should be applied instinctively. Training and discipline are required to instill them, and I have no argument against them. What we have done in the past, however, is to emphasize procedures, and so surround them by bureaucratic trivia that we lose focus and miss completely the main task at hand: making sure our warriors are up to the harshest intellectual demands of combat—making tough decisions under stress.

But the question remains: What do we do about definitions, procedures, and weapons capabilities? The answer is that we demand our soldiers and Marines know these things so well that they do not need to stop and think about them. How do we do that?

Step number one is to distill the essential from the nonessential. We cannot fool the troops. If it's unimportant, they know it's unimportant, and we become laughingstocks. Step number two is to identify where this essential information is available. Definitions, procedures for requesting needed support in combat, coordination, and capabilities of weapons are in most cases already set down. Many need streamlining. That which is not set down or needs to be streamlined must be put into its most useful form and printed. For the most part it need not be taught or lectured about. It is best assimilated through study and hands-on experience. In fact, study and hands-on experience are the only ways that students are ever going to assimilate, and apply quickly enough, things like picking up a radio and communicating with it, laying a machine gun, calling an artillery mission, or providing for logistical needs. But none of these things can be done well or appropriately by anyone who does not know about tactics. Tactics in maneuver warfare is decision making and speed. Everything else must follow the tactics. Tactics are not built around radio procedures. Radio procedures should be built around tactics. The same applies with all other procedures. Therefore, the first step is to make sure our soldiers are competent tacticians. That is what makes soldiers soldiers: being tacticians—being warriors. Understanding tactics makes them able to use radios, machine guns, artillery, airplanes, supply trucks, and spare parts, both conventionally and in all kinds of innovative ways that speed up the process and make this equipment so much more relevant to maneuver warfare. So let us leave definitions and procedures to book study followed by field application. Recognize that adequate coaching in the field can be gotten from good NCOs. Let us not neglect the discipline of definitions and procedures, but let us not get so fixated on them that we neglect teaching tactics. Tactics come first.

So the answer to the question of whether to teach definitions or tactics first is *teach tactics first*. No procedure irrelevant to tactics is relevant to the battle. If it is not relevant to the battle, it is not relevant to war and not relevant to the profession. So teach tactics first.

I have made a bold statement here. Carried to the extreme, it bypasses the whole concept of operational art and could be misinterpreted to mean that the sole object of war is to engage in battle. That would be wrong. Wars *can* be won without decisive battle. Napoleon's Ulm maneuver was decisive even without engagement. But the army that is not competent to win in battle is unlikely to intimidate its adversary as Napoleon's did Mack's in 1805. So I stand on my bold statement. No tactical competence means no credibility, and therefore no relevance to war.

Regarding teaching maneuver warfare, if a student can learn decision making at the tactical level and apply it to maneuver, he is well on the way to learning to apply maneuver at the operational and strategic levels also. He will need to study at these levels eventually, and be exercised at these levels, but tactics is the foundation.

Recognizing, then, that definitions and procedures are important, but only relevant if they are relevant to tactics, let us return to how to teach tactics, this most fundamental of military subjects.

I taught an evening course at Quantico when I was vice president of the Marine Corps University. I opened it to all ranks and used it to experiment with ways of teaching maneuver warfare. I taught it five successive semesters and it was never the same twice. It helped me to develop some of my thoughts on the subject and helped a number of Marines gain an appreciation for what these so-called maneuver tactics were all about. I called the course "Contemporary Tactical Thought." I did not call it "Maneuver Warfare" because, deep in my heart, I feel there are only two kinds of tactics: good tactics and bad tactics. In developing maneuver warfare, very simply, we tried to adopt that which was good and reject that which was bad about tactics. Maneuver warfare has been a fitting name because it restored maneuver to tactical thinking, maneuver having fallen by the wayside in the technology explosion that accompanied the aftermath of World War II and development of the atomic bomb.

In "Contemporary Tactical Thought" I usually began by requiring reading of Lupfer's *Dynamics of Doctrine* and Lind's *Maneuver Warfare Handbook* as prerequisites, so that we could start right out discussing battle with an understanding of the fundamentals presented in those two books.

In order to immerse students immediately into the solving of combat problems, I gave them the first four chapters of William Glenn Robertson's "Counterattack on the Naktong" (*Leavenworth Papers*, No. 13), a well-documented study, including superb maps, on the very early days of U.S. involvement in the Korean War. I had a number of reasons for selecting this study. It involves defense of a river line, and rivers make nice, clear issues of contention, besides presenting the temptation (especially for the defender) to become linear and to orient on a terrain feature (the river) instead of the enemy, which is exactly what the Americans did in August 1950. Also, I wanted my students to see how bad we had gotten during just a few years of peace, and how quickly we had put all thought of maneuver aside in deference to firepower, especially once we were able to rest our minds under the false security blanket of the atomic bomb. I like studying the Korean War because it is so heavy with lessons for us *today* and because it tends to be neglected. Had we paid attention to what was happening in Korea, we might have been prepared for Vietnam and able to cope with it. Furthermore, the problems introduced to us in 1950 have yet to be played out. It was in Korea that a low (*very* low) technology army, the Chinese, did relatively well against the highest technology army (including Marines) in the world. In fact, the Naktong study shows also that the North Korean Army was doing quite well, at least for a while. Students of maneuver warfare need to consider why that was and what it augurs for the future.

Now that we have Desert Storm to consider as history, we have an example of a Third World country trying to resort to high technology and discovering that it was not a good way to confront the United States. Even now I am not comfortable that either the U.S. Army or Marine Corps has faced up to the problem of preparing their "warriors." Our adversaries in the Far East had to be warriors; that is, they had to apply the art of war because they had no other option. I am neither holding them (North Koreans, Chinese, North Vietnamese) to be the premier soldiers of the world, nor am I condemning technology. I am simply pointing out that for years we neglected the essence of good tactics, that it hurt us, and that even though we do have the best technology in the world, there is nothing wrong with being the best tacticians in the world as well. In fact, the U.S. Army and Marine Corps have a responsibility to the eighteen-year-olds of this country to be the best tacticians in the world. In Vietnam, I saw starkly the price of neglecting that responsibility.

So, in "Contemporary Tactical Thought," we studied the early stages of Korea. I let my students' minds run free so they could make the decisions they thought ought to have been made by American commanders fighting North Korean infiltrators. I did not restrict them to the training inadequacies or military inadequacies of the 1950s American military. They supplemented their readings in Robertson's book with Max Hastings's *Korean War* and Russell Spurr's *Enter the Dragon*.

We did decision-making exercises in class, and soon left the Korean War behind as we tackled John English's *On Infantry*, chapter by chapter. This is an important book and it never works as a prerequisite. People don't really read it. They say they do but they don't. Perhaps it's the misguided emphasis on speed-reading in this country. Many officers told me they have read the book but then they can't discuss it in class. So I made them go through it, and we discussed it, applied its concepts in decision exercises, and wrote about it in essay quizzes.

After this we tackled the German stuff. In the early days of maneuver warfare I was shocked by the prejudice against Germans. It is simply a hurdle we have to overcome. I know they lost two world wars, but suffice it to say, one of the reasons they lost was not bad tactics. Their tactics, in fact, were so powerful that the entire world had to go to war against them. Hitler, Nazism, and all kinds of evils spelled their doom, but if we ignore the intellectual breakthroughs in tactics that they made in a century and a half of unprecedented military study, then we are indeed neglectful. So, in "Contemporary Tactical Thought," we read Rommel's diary, Gudmundsson's *Stormtroop Tactics*, and some chapters out of Manstein and von Mellenthin.

I must mention at this point another book I used in the course, *Infantry in Battle*, tactical problems compiled by the U.S. Army Infantry School in the 1930s. The book serves throughout any modern tactics course for a number of reasons. Its combat examples cross cultural lines to include U.S., British, French, and German so it helps a little with the prejudice problem. It is one of those rare books, along with Lupfer's, Rommel's, and English's, that takes you down to the tactical level and poses questions relevant to the squad leader and platoon leader. Furthermore, the book is extremely well done. It is an excellent text and workbook for a tactics student who is curious to learn about how to maneuver on the battlefield and concerned about learning good tactics as opposed to bad.

This takes us into yet another dimension. In the 1930s, the U.S. Army Infantry School was doing it right. I own a copy of the post–World War II version of *Infantry in Battle* and it is decidedly inferior. Somewhere we lost the way. The Marines were teaching it right in the '30s also.

I have investigated the archives at Quantico and discovered old problem exercises that are very similar to those presented in *Infantry in Battle*. In the 1930s the Army and Marine Corps were teaching their students what we now call the case study method. They were giving their students real-world cases and demanding that they make decisions with incomplete information. They placed heavy emphasis on maneuver along with firepower, and did not fall into the post–World War II trap of neglecting maneuver and considering firepower almost exclusively. They followed the philosophy I am trying to restore. The evidence is that I am offering little new here, but a return to some valuable lessons of the past. Where and why we lost the way raises other questions I will not endeavor to answer in this essay.

One of the best experiences I had with "Contemporary Tactical Thought" was the semester I did the exam in the field. Because it was given as an evening course—and maybe also because of my overwillingness to compromise with work schedules—I did not conduct the course according to my ideal, which would have meant beginning in the field. As an alternative, I finished in the field by giving the exam orally outdoors. It was not difficult to get permission from students' commanding officers for them to be with me during daylight working hours on the last day of class. I was already getting favorable comments about the course, and commanders were understanding. There is something about the idea of an exam in the field that seems fitting for Marines. Should any Marine be allowed to stay in the Corps if he does not periodically go into the field and submit himself to a test of his tactical decision-making ability? Is it right to release the private from boot camp if we have not personally quizzed him about what he would do on a given spot of ground if he were in a tactical crisis upon which his life depended—and his fellow Marines' lives? Should the gunnery sergeant be a gunnery sergeant if he has not been taken outdoors and tested, made to think on his feet about combat? How can the major be given a certificate that says he is a graduate of the Command and Staff College if he has not demonstrated in the field that he can make tactical decisions and deal with the unexpected at the battalion and regimental level?

In "Contemporary Tactical Thought" I took a group of young NCOs to the field for their final exam. We talked frankly about tactics, Vietnam, and wars of the future. They shared with me afterward (in fact, after their grades were awarded and they were "safe"!) that it was during this session that tactics became real to them for the first time and that their confidence grew like never before. Of course we should have done it during the *first* meeting of the class, and in many more sessions. Without any doubt, the field is the place to begin. All my best experiences have occurred when I have done it that way. Not only were the sessions in the field among the most instructive, but the classroom periods that followed "took" in a way they never would have with students who had not yet gone outdoors. But it is important to do the exam at the end of the course in the field, too. That was a major lesson I carried away from "Contemporary Tactical Thought."

Overall, we find that a great deal more is expected of the maneuver warfare teacher than was of the instructor of methodical battle. The teacher of maneuver warfare must study war and be able to discuss on his feet real issues of decision making. To be bound to the structure of schedules and lesson plans is to demonstrate the modus operandi that is counter to maneuver warfare. Maneuver warfare is a style of operating as well as a style of fighting. The adage "how we operate in peace is how we will operate in war" applies here. We can hardly hope to conduct business in peacetime along the old bureaucratic lines that typified the days of methodical battle, and then suddenly, in time of war, switch successfully to high-tempo maneuver thinking, demanding the highest initiative at the lowest level and focusing on the enemy's moves instead of a preordained plan.

The up side is that teaching maneuver warfare is more interesting to the student, more exciting, and it better prepares him for combat. The down side is that it requires a lot more work and study on the part of the teacher. But the down side has an up side. The teacher who has labored to equip himself to handle the new demands of teaching maneuver warfare is a better soldier—better prepared for war and better prepared to lead.

# PART 3

# THE HISTORICAL BASIS OF MANEUVER WARFARE

Maneuver warfare is firmly rooted in the study of military history, the common data base and wellspring of our understanding of the military art. While the attempt to explain maneuver warfare as a theory or model is relatively recent, military history is replete with examples of commanders who understood and applied what could be called a maneuver thought process.

Maneuver warfare, which has been defined as "a thought process which seeks to pit strength against weakness to break the enemy's will," can be contrasted with methodical or "attrition" warfare which seeks advantage through cumulative tactical engagements leading to the weakening and ultimate physical collapse of the enemy. These two contending schools can be thought of, not as polar opposites, but rather as cultural and organizational predispositions that dominate the doctrine and operations of armies. The following case studies contrast these competing doctrines or styles of war.

# Maneuver Warfare: The German Tradition

## Bruce I. Gudmundsson

To modern American maneuverists, the fact that the German army had no word for "maneuver warfare" presents a number of problems. From the point of view of public relations, this "dog that failed to bark" leads to the superficial but powerful argument that, since the Germans had no word for maneuver warfare, they did not practice it. This, in turn, leads quickly to the accusation that maneuver warfare is little more than a gleam in the eyes of contemporary reformers who have mapped their own prejudices onto selected anecdotes from German military history.[1]

A far more pressing problem exists for the professional soldier who wishes to imitate the tactical and operational virtuosity of his counterparts who served in the armies of the Kaiser, the Weimar Republic, and the Third Reich. Do the tenets of maneuver warfare as promulgated by today's reformers bear any practical relation to the German tradition of military art? Did the Germans win so many battles and campaigns because they were concerned about OODA loops, mission orders, tempo, focus of effort, and the like, or was there some other secret to their military success?

The purpose of this essay is to answer both sets of questions. It will attempt to describe, in rough outline, the development of the German maneuver warfare tradition. Because this tradition did not arise like Athena from the head of Zeus, fully grown and armed for battle, this essay will also attempt to show where the various elements of the German maneuver tradition emerged. In the course of doing this, the essay will also sketch the outlines of the larger German military tradition and place the maneuver tradition within the context of that larger tradition.

Before moving on, it is important to explain the term "tradition." As used in this essay, tradition refers to a set of values, attitudes, teachings, and techniques passed down from one generation to the next. Over the course of time, the contents of the set may change. New elements are added and some old elements fade away. These changes notwithstanding, there is enough in common between adjacent generations to allow the diligent researcher to trace a clear path from the present to the past and back again.

Separating the German maneuver warfare tradition from the larger German tradition is important because, even though its influence was considerable, the maneuverist viewpoint never managed to completely dominate the German army. In the 19th century, it had to contend with both the extreme formalism of theorists such as Heinrich von Bülow[2] and the anti-intellectualism of "practical soldiers." In the 20th century, the German maneuverists again faced serious competition from German advocates of methodical battle, Erich von Falkenhayn's strategy of attrition,[3] and the fixation on real estate that Falkenhayn shared with Adolf Hitler.

## THE OPERATIONAL TRADITION

Because a tradition, like a river, is fed from a number of tributary streams, it is often hard to determine where it begins. Any explorer trying to trace the German maneuver tradition back to its source, however, cannot avoid running into Frederick the Great. Largely because his position as the ruler of an archipelago of provinces rising out of a sea of enemy states gave him little other choice,[4] Frederick based his campaigns on two insights that would later become key elements of maneuver warfare: a keen appreciation for the importance of operational tempo, and a willingness to take risks in order to be strong at the decisive place and time.[5]

With his isolated possessions spread over much of what is now Germany and Poland, Frederick knew that "he who defends everywhere defends nowhere" and that the defense of one province, however successful, merely guaranteed the loss of all others. This, combined with the fact that Frederick's relatively small army was often threatened by two or more hostile countries, led Frederick to advise concentration of forces and rapid movement against one enemy contingent before other hostile forces got close enough to cooperate.

While Frederick often failed to take his own advice, the most notable instance where he acted in accordance with his own precepts was
his campaign of 1757 against the Austrians, the Russians, and the French.
While the French were mobilizing and the Russians making the long
march from their homeland, Frederick struck first at the Austrians. Two
bloody battles, one of which (Prague, 6 May 1757) was counted a victory
for Frederick and the other (Kolin, 18 June 1757) for the Austrians,
failed to knock the Austrians out of the conflict. The latter's own timidity and a small Prussian contingent, however, were enough to keep
them at bay while Frederick turned against the French.

Frederick's decisive victory at Rossbach, 5 November 1757, eliminated
the French threat for a year, and he was free to march once more across
Germany to face an Austrian counterattack. This Austrian resurgence
was stopped by Frederick's most famous victory, his envelopment of
the Austrian line at Leuthen, 6 December 1757. The year ended with
two of three enemy armies driven away. The price of the concentration of forces that allowed Frederick to accomplish this, however, was
high. In October, while Frederick and his army were far away, an Austrian
raiding force was able to plunder Frederick's capital at Berlin, and
the Russians were allowed free rein in Frederick's detached province
of East Prussia for close to a year.[6]

The next five years of the Seven Years' War saw a repetition of
this pattern. Frederick concentrated against one enemy, fought a battle
or two, and swiftly marched across Germany to concentrate against
another enemy. And while we cannot forget his English and Hanoverian
allies who kept the French busy throughout this time, the fact that Frederick
was never decisively defeated by either the Austrians or the Russians
must be credited to the speed with which he marched and the ruth-
lessness with which he stripped his provinces in order to maintain his
main striking force.[7]

Unfortunately for Prussia, Frederick the Great's art of war was not
inherited by his immediate successors. While much was made of the
more retrograde aspects of Frederick's military system—the impractical uniforms, the parade ground tactics, and the nobility's monopoly
on commissioned service—the key to Frederick's success was soon
forgotten. For while Prussian tactics were slowly changing for the better,[8]
Prussian movement off the battlefield became ponderous, Prussian

leaders displayed great indecision, and Prussian campaign plans gave far more importance to the defense of Berlin and its associated lines of communication than the defeat of the enemy. It was not until the upheavals that followed the disaster of Jena-Auerstädt (1806) brought a group of self-conscious and deliberate reformers into positions of authority that the maneuverist aspects of Frederick's system were revived.

Students of both Frederick the Great and Frederick's French disciple Napoleon Bonaparte, the reformers realized that the Corsican had taken the ideas of tempo and focus of effort one step further. Fighting enemies (the Russians, the Prussians, and the French) with far greater resources that, to add insult to injury, often acted in concert against him, Frederick had to be satisfied with incomplete victories. Thus, while he was often able to use battle to blunt an enemy's advance in a certain theater, or knock a relatively small force out of the contest, he never found himself able to disarm a major adversary to the point where he could dictate peace terms in the enemy capital.

Napoleon, on the other hand, could fight battles of "annihilation" (*Vernichtung*). That is to say, in a single battle or closely related series of battles (such as Austerlitz or Jena-Auerstädt), he was able to kill, wound, capture, or disperse enough of the enemy's main army that further resistance became futile. Strengthened by the raising of a national militia (the *Landwehr*), bolstered by the arrival of substantial allied contingents, and motivated by an ambitious policy that included driving Bonaparte from Europe, the reformers made the "annihilation concept" (*Vernichtungsgedanke*) a key part of their style of war.[9]

The second major innovation of the reformers was the transformation of the General Staff from a unitary headquarters into a complete system for operational command and control. Both Frederick and Napoleon were themselves integral parts of their armies' ability to conduct high-tempo operations.[10] The reformers replaced this single weak link with a collective "brain" in the form of a network of bright, well-trained (but never irreplaceable) operations officers. Assigned as the chief advisors to corps and army commanders, these staff officers had a strong enough sense of both the common goal and each other's peculiarities to induce their nominal masters to cooperate effectively.

The campaign that culminated in the Battle of Leipzig, 16–19 October 1813, shows how the reformers were able to use the General Staff to focus the efforts of a number of national contingents in a campaign aimed at a battle of annihilation. Of particular note was the way in which the leaders of the Alliance coordinated the actions of three separate armies composed of the troops of four major powers and a host of minor states.[11] "They never made the attempt at wishing to regulate the movements of the three Armies minutely in advance for every day and place, or even to direct them continually by orders from head-quarters. They had rather settled in broad outline, on a simple and clear general idea of operations, and left it to the three Commanders-in-chief to act according to circumstances."[12]

Unfortunately for the reformers, the glory they had earned at Leipzig and other battles of the "Wars of Liberation Against Napoleon" would not last for long. Napoleon had barely landed on St. Helena when an ungrateful Prussian government began undermining the very military reforms that had enabled it to stay in power. In the dark age that fol-lowed, the tradition of operational maneuver was all but forgotten. What need was there, after all, for a grand outflanking movement or a maneuver on interior lines when the only visible enemies of the Prussian state were the urban middle classes and an ever-rebellious Polish gentry?

By the middle of the 19th century, conditions were once again ripe for a revival of the Prussian tradition of operational maneuver. The long peace between monarchs who feared their own people more than they feared each other began to break down. Beginning with the French campaign in Italy in 1859, war on a Napoleonic scale pursued with Bonapartist vigor became once more the dominant feature of Euro-pean military life.

This explosion in the "demand" for operational maneuver was met, on the "supply side," by Helmuth von Moltke. Like Frederick, Napo-leon, and the Prussian reformers, Moltke had a strong inclination to-ward the life of the mind. His studies of military history, European geography (to include recent improvements in roads and railroads), politics, and recent developments in military technology such as easily loaded rifles, all combined to convince him that victories of the type enjoyed by Napoleon and the Prussian reformers were still possible.

Moltke's contribution to the widening stream of operational maneuver went far beyond the innovations with which he is usually credited. Moltke's exploitation of the railroad, the telegraph, and an improved road network to operate on "external lines" has for generations been part and parcel of most surveys of military history. And even the least enthusiastic staff college student can contrast Moltke's practice of uniting his army during a battle with Napoleon's habit of assembling his forces before any significant clash of arms. What is less well known is Moltke's continuation of the work begun by the giants of the Prussian reform movement, Gerhard von Scharnhorst and Neidhardt von Gneisenau.

Like Scharnhorst and Gneisenau, Moltke knew that he could not micromanage army and corps commanders who were, at the very least, his social and military equals. It is not surprising, then, that Moltke wrote orders in a manner strongly reminiscent of that of the reformers—painting a broad picture of what he desired to accomplish and relying on those officers of his General Staff serving on army and corps staffs to do what was necessary to transform that vision into reality.

Of course, Moltke's directives would have little effect on those who were strangers to the world of ideas. For this reason (if not because of a strong natural inclination), Moltke became a teacher as well as a practitioner of the art of war. The main vehicle for Moltke's teaching was the "applicatory method." First formalized by the Swiss educator Johann Heinrich Pestalozzi (1746–1827), the applicatory method sought to teach practical arts—to include the art of war—by means of problems to be solved rather than precepts to be remembered. The direct line of transmission of the applicatory method was from Wilhelm zu Schaumberg-Lippe's experimental military academy to Scharnhorst (who had been a student of Schaumberg-Lippe) to the Prussian *Kriegsakademie* (War Academy) reformed by Scharnhorst to Moltke.[13] Additional impetus for the method came, no doubt, from a rage for Pestalozzi's methods that was going on in civilian educational circles in Moltke's time.

The forms used in the applicatory method varied. One-sided tactical decision games (*Planspiele, Planübungen*, or *Planaufgaben*) were the simplest. All that was required was a teacher, a sketch map, and a simple scenario that put the player in a position where he had to make a decision. Staff rides (*Stabsreise*) were more complicated. Usually involving more senior officers, they consisted of solving problems of the kind that might be faced by large units on ground that armies were expected to use in actual war.[14] Later in the century, two-sided, double-blind, refereed wargames (*Freikriegspiele*) provided an intermediary between the two extremes.

The common denominator of these exercises was the stress that they put on rapid decision making. Although the student was expected to give a rationale for his decision, sound judgment was not enough. Under strict time pressure, the student had to consider the general situation, absorb information about what was going on in his immediate surroundings, make a decision, and then give orders to his unit. In the terminology of modern American maneuver warfare, he was expected to observe, orient, decide, and act more quickly than his opponent.

Aided by collaborators such as Julius von Verdy du Vernois and Jacob Meckel, Moltke oversaw the spread of the applicatory method throughout the German army. In the 1850s, tactical decision games started to appear as a regular feature in the *Militärwochenblatt,* a semiofficial newspaper with strong connections to Moltke's General Staff. Books of map problems started to appear, followed by wargame sets and descriptions of staff rides.[15] The greatest engine for the expansion of the applicatory method, however, was Moltke's General Staff itself.

Officers who wished to attend the *Kriegsakademie* had to pass an entrance exam, the military portion of which consisted largely of tactical decision games. Those officers who passed the test spent much of their time at the *Kriegsakademie* doing simple map problems, playing two-sided wargames, and participating in staff rides. Those who failed cannot have avoided absorbing a good deal of both the techniques of particular exercises and the underlying philosophy. This was particularly true as the prestige of the General Staff grew and ambitious officers made correspondingly greater efforts to prepare themselves for the examination.[16]

Most students at the *Kriegsakademie* would never serve on the General Staff. Those that did were exposed to even more of the applicatory method, often by means of exercises conducted by Moltke himself. These "demigods" not only kept the tradition strong, but spread the practices when they served their periodic command tours with troop units. Those who returned to regimental duty after one, two, or three years at the *Kriegsakademie* also contributed to the spread of the applicatory method.

By the end of the 19th century the applicatory method was part and parcel of the German way of war at all echelons from the General Staff down to platoons. Nonetheless, had it been the only "maneuverist" aspect of German military culture, it probably would have degenerated into the type of map problem that predominated in the English-speaking world—an exercise in which a group of students was given a great deal of time, not to solve a tactical problem, but to divine, individually or collectively, a school solution devised at leisure by the instructor.[17]

The applicatory method thrived in Germany because it coexisted with a cult of decisiveness that grew stronger throughout the hundred years that preceded World War II. With its origins no doubt in the essentially feudal worldview and chivalric fantasies of the German officer, this cult fostered an attitude that valued a quick decision arrived at on the spot even if it required deviation from explicit orders. "Prince Carl of Prussia once pregnantly summed up this Prussian conception of obedience to an over-servile Staff officer. The King, he said, had put him on the Staff, because he had expected him to know when to disobey."[18]

Just as the campaign of Leipzig was the fruit of the reformers' efforts, the fruits of Moltke's work were the two victorious "seven weeks'" campaigns of 1866 (against Austria) and 1870 (against France). Indeed, as late as 1917, German armies led by Moltke's disciples continued to win victories reminiscent of Moltke's battles of annihilation. These victories—against the Russians in 1914, against the Serbs in 1915, against the Romanians in 1916, and against the Russians again in 1917—could, however, be won only as long as the two essential preconditions enjoyed by Moltke in 1866 and 1870 continued to hold. On the eastern front of World War I, where all of these German victories were won, there were open areas in which corps and armies could maneuver. In the rear areas, moreover, there was a rail system that allowed the Germans to move units and supplies to various parts of the theater far faster than the enemy could move his resources.

In the West, however, these conditions no longer existed. In 1914, France and her allies were able to do what France had not been able to do in 1870—form a continuous front. Even if this front was temporarily pierced—as it was at Soissons in 1915—the highly developed French network of railroads and motor routes allowed the French to move reinforcements to the breech far faster than the Germans could move through the hole they had made.

This change in the operational environment made the war of "grand maneuvers" as obsolete as the battle tactics of massed battalions that had coexisted with it. If the Germans were to win victories of the type won by Napoleon, the Prussian reformers, and Moltke, they would have to find ways of overcoming these operational disadvantages. Their first attempt to regain operational mobility—the stormtroop tactics of World War I—failed. Their second attempt—the mechanization of stormtroop tactics that we now know as the Blitzkrieg—succeeded. Neither of these attempts would have been possible, however, without another major element of the German maneuver warfare tradition.

## THE *JÄGER* TRADITION

The origins of the second major tributary of the German maneuver tradition—the light infantry tradition—are harder to trace than those of the stream that passes through Frederick the Great. Frederick, after all, was not only a king but a man of considerable culture. A ready pen enabled him to record his thoughts, a small army of contemporaries proved willing to record his deeds, and eight generations of posterity have seen fit to preserve every scrap of paper relating to his reign. The same cannot be said for the uncouth foresters who filled the ranks of German *Jäger* units or their largely unlettered officers. Because of their reluctance to write, we have little documentation of the deeds of men whose virtuosity in the field of small unit tactics matched the skill of their royal contemporary.

The exception to this general rule of silence—and the instrument by which we are able to pierce the veil that has so long covered the German *Jäger* tradition—was a young Hanoverian veteran of the Seven Years' War (1756–1763) named Johann Ewald. In a remarkable pamphlet first published in 1763, Ewald described an approach to the "small war"—the "war of posts" of *Jäger* detachments and hussar patrols—that still has much to teach the would-be guerrilla or light infantry-man of today.[19]

Ewald went on to serve, on the British side, in the American War of Independence. As his diary attests, that conflict provided forest fighters of various types—German *Jäger* and Loyalist Rangers as well as British and Patriot Light Infantry—ample opportunity to prove their superiority over their counterparts of the line.[20] This clear lesson notwithstanding, the idea that infantrymen could be trusted to move rapidly through the woods without deserting, to make individual use of cover without sitting out the battle, and to aim a well-sighted rifle without aiming it at one of his own officers did not easily take root in Prussia.[21]

The one exception to this rule was found in the two *Jäger* companies formed by Frederick the Great in 1744. Recruited, as far as possible, from the sons of gamekeepers and other forest dwellers, these units were distinguished not merely for the marksmanship and stalking skill of the individual *Jäger*, but also for their loyalty. At a time when the ranks of the line infantry battalions were full of foreigners tricked, coerced, and even kidnapped into lifetime enlistments, the *Jäger* were native Prussians who could look forward to retiring to positions of responsibility on royal and private hunting grounds. In an era when the discipline of other infantrymen was maintained by extensive corporal punishment, the greatest punishment for a *Jäger* was transfer to a line unit.[22]

By 1806, the year of the catastrophic defeat of the Prussian army at the twin battle of Jena-Auerstädt, there were about 2,000 *Jäger* in the service of the King of Prussia. Parceled among the various detachments of the Prussian army for service as scouts or military policemen, they were, however, unable to do much to prevent the disaster. As a result, the battle of Jena-Auerstädt is chiefly remembered for the pathetic spectacle at the village of Vierzehnheiligen, where Prussian line infantry in close order stood in an open field and fired ineffective volleys at sharpshooting French infantrymen protected by stone walls.

In the vigorous French pursuit that followed the battle, the bulk of the Prussian army added disgrace to their defeat when scores of officers surrendered perfectly defensible positions and thousands of individuals deserted the colors. One of the few bright spots in this catastrophe was the loyalty and skill of the *Jäger*. In small groups and even as individuals, large numbers of *Jäger* fought their way through French-controlled territory and reported for duty.[23]

## THE FIRST SYNTHESIS

In the reform of the Prussian infantry that followed Jena-Auerstädt, the tactical lessons taught by the French infantry during the battles, and the proof of loyalty provided by the *Jäger* after battles, had a great impact. The same reform movement so active in the realm of operational maneuver was able to rewrite key manuals, cause an increase in the number of light troops, and retrain the entire Prussian infantry in a system of tactics that borrowed heavily from the *Jäger* tradition.[24]

When, in a series of campaigns that Germans often call the Wars of Liberation, the reformed Prussian infantry took the field again against Napoleon, it was sufficiently flexible to provide the Prussian commanders with the teeth that they needed to carry out the campaigns of operational maneuver of Scharnhorst and Gneisenau. In the brigade and division battles that preceded Napoleon's encirclement at Leipzig, Prussian infantry fighting in open order were so consistently superior to their French counterparts that the latter were repeatedly pushed back into the main body of their army.[25]

In the years that followed the defeat of Napoleon, the formalism of the late 18th century once again reared its ugly head. Though vestiges of the reforms of 1806–1815 remained, each passing year saw the line infantry move further and further away from the methods that had brought victory in the Wars of Liberation. The *Jäger* tradition, however, found safe haven in the *Jäger* battalions of the growing Prussian-German army.

Two factors preserved this haven. First, the game preserves of the aristocracy—those great nurseries of the German hunter—continued to supply trained woodsmen to *Jäger* units. Indeed, for most of the 19th century only those men who had, after their two or three years of mandatory military service, reenlisted for an additional term of service, were allowed to be gamekeepers on public lands.[26] Second, the *Jäger* battalions were organized into a separate branch, with their own drill regulations, their own weapons, and, most important of all, their own inspector general.[27]

In many armies the introduction of rifled firearms to the entire infantry served to deprive units raised as light infantry or rifle troops of their special role on the battlefield.[28] This happened to some degree in Germany. German *Jäger* units took part in a number of the less subtle frontal attacks of the Franco-Prussian War. Alien customs such as marching in step and the carrying of battleflags were introduced. Nonetheless, the twin facts of separate inspectors and special recruitment preserved German *Jäger* from amalgamation into the line.

In the first decade of the 20th century, the German *Jäger* were once more involved in the "war of posts." Large battalions of four rifle companies, a bicycle company, and a machine-gun company were attached to cavalry divisions and corps. As the latter formations rode ahead of the main body of the army, the *Jäger* units would seize and control those terrain features—woods, villages, bridges, and defiles—whose possession might prove useful in the battle to sweep away the eyes and ears of the enemy army. In a development that foreshadowed the Second World War, some of these *Jäger* units were carried in trucks.[29]

## THE SECOND SYNTHESIS

When in October and November of 1914 the German armies in the West stopped moving and the war of grand maneuvers gave way to position warfare, the *Jäger* battalions proved far more useful than the cavalry divisions they had supported. Although the German armies had been deprived of their power of maneuver by the lack of open flanks, the *Jäger* found the no-man's-land between the two opposing forces to be a natural arena for their abilities. This was especially true in heavily forested areas such as the Argonne.

If the unit histories of *Jäger* battalions are any guide, German *Jäger* lost no time in dominating no-man's-land—aggressively patrolling, setting ambushes for enemy patrols, and even raiding the enemy's trenches. In all of these activities, the *Jäger* tradition of trusting individual riflemen and junior leaders with a great deal of tactical responsibility was the key to success. Already accustomed to operating in small groups and using accidents of terrain too small to be of use to larger units, having long possessed great skill in moving quietly and invisibly, *Jäger* had a huge advantage over line infantrymen who had been taught to think in terms of movement by platoon or company and volley fire.[30]

In the course of the first year of trench warfare these skills were combined with new weapons introduced by German combat engineers— the hand grenade, the flamethrower, and mortars of various sizes— to form the first units of trench warfare specialists, the famous Assault Battalions (*Sturmbataillone*). The founder of these units, Capt. Willy Martin Rohr, had spent a good part of his long peacetime career in command of or in the company of *Jäger*. In the summer of 1915, Rohr's track record of success in applying *Jäger* tactics in conditions of trench warfare brought him command of a special unit of combat engineers formed to experiment with ways of solving the "riddle of the trenches."[31]

The techniques developed by Rohr and his storm troopers were various. As the war went on and conditions changed, moreover, some techniques were discarded and others were added. The common denominator to all these techniques, however, remained the same—the intensive training of individuals and small groups followed by battlefield reliance on the courage, initiative, and tactical judgement of NCOs and private soldiers.

This ability to work in small groups—then known as *Stosstrupps* ("penetration teams") allowed Rohr's storm troopers to take maximum advantage of suppressive fire (particularly that provided by organic heavy weapons), to exploit "micro-terrain" and stealth to get close to the enemy, and to rapidly penetrate deeply into a trench system by "bombing along" communication trenches. On a small scale, this meant a high success rate for trench raids and terrain-oriented "attacks with limited objectives." On a larger scale, this ability to "infiltrate" into an enemy position promised to allow the German army as a whole to undertake an offensive in the West.

The importance of this capability for the development of the German art of war cannot be overstated. For over a hundred years, the German art of war had been based on the exploitation of open flanks. From the Seven Years' War to the World War I campaigns (against Russia, Serbia, Romania, and Italy) that Germany won, the German ability to strike the enemy with speed and violence from an unexpected direction had been their key to victory. As a result, the chief consideration in the planning of campaigns had been setting up situations where this sort of attack could take place.

The situation on the western front—where the Allied position was anchored on one side by the North Sea and on the other by the muscular neutrality of the Swiss Confederation—denied the Germans the flank that was so necessary for their art. Stormtroop tactics, which would replace the great open flank exploited by a field marshal with a thousand little flanks exploited by corporals, promised to restore to the Germans the possibility of offensive action at the operational level.[32]

In the spring and summer of 1918, the German Supreme Command made five attempts at using stormtroop tactics to restore mobility to the western front. While each attempt but the last were masterpieces of tactical execution, and while the British and French armies on the receiving end of the offensives came close to collapse, the inability of the German armies to rapidly exploit the holes that they had chopped in the French and British lines gave the latter time to move, by truck and by rail, fresh divisions and corps to the threatened sectors.

## THE THIRD SYNTHESIS

As is often the case, the lessons learned in the stormtroop experiment bubbled under the surface of the German peacetime army for half a generation while the men who had learned those lessons as young men rose to positions of prominence in the military hierarchy. Only then, when the Rommels, Guderians, and Balcks rose to the surface and began the task of adapting stormtroop tactics to the new technologies of the tank and the airplane, were the techniques and attitudes so expensively acquired in the First World War put to full use.

Some parts of the stormtroop tradition—particularly as they related to the small unit tactics of infantry and combat engineer units—were restored with little change. This gave the units that constituted the bulk of the German army—"walking" infantry supported by horse-drawn artillery—a superiority in "retail" combat that, while hard to quantify, is obvious to all who take the time to study company, battalion, and regimental engagements of World War II.

The crowning glory of German military achievement in World War II, however, was not gained at the "retail" level. Rather, the wonders achieved by German armies in that conflict, whether they resulted in victory—as in 1939, 1940, and 1941—or merely the postponement of an inevitable defeat—as in 1943, 1944, and 1945—were achieved at the "wholesale" level. That is to say, the Germans were able to so effectively upset the peace of Europe because they had found a way to fight campaigns at a Napoleonic tempo despite a dramatic change in the strategic environment.

Part of the credit for this must be given to the internal combustion engine. Tanks, trucks, and ground attack aircraft allowed the Germans to exploit rapidly, at the operational level, gains made at the tactical level in ways that would not have been possible in World War I. Such means alone, however, were not enough. After all, in many campaigns Germany's enemies had more tanks, trucks, and combat aircraft. What brought the German army such resounding success was the application of the essence of stormtroop tactics—ruthless concentration of effort and rapid exploitation of success by leaders who knew their business—at the higher tactical and operational levels.

Some of those who were best at these "stormtroop tactics on wheels" were, interestingly enough, officers who had the strongest ties to the older parts of the German maneuver warfare tradition. Hermann Balck, for example, had started his career as a *Jäger*, as had Guderian. As his World War I diary attests, Rommel had a good dose of *Jäger* tactics during his service with the Württemberg mountain troops. All three were deeply steeped in the applicatory method—Balck as the son of Wilhelm Balck, a published authority on the subject, Guderian as a top student at the *Kriegsakademie*, and Rommel as the author of a book of tactical problems.[33]

This is not to say that the maneuver warfare tradition was a closed club. Proof of this comes from the obvious talent of Erich von Manstein and Ewald von Kleist. Manstein began his career in a grenadier regiment of the Prussian Guard, one of the least maneuverist enclaves in the German army. Kleist was a cavalryman. Nonetheless, both managed to excel at maneuver warfare at the higher tactical and operational levels.

## THE IMPACT OF THE TRADITION

One of the most frequently heard arguments against maneuver warfare is the assertion that the Germans were "zero for two in two world wars" and, as a result, their methods have no value. While this argument is most often put forward by those who are arguing not merely against maneuver warfare but also against the serious study of military history, it is a powerful one and must be dealt with. For while the scoffers (whose real message is "don't worry, be happy") will probably not be convinced by any counterargument, there is much to be gained by settling the issue.

The first step toward this goal of repudiating the arguments of the "zero for two" school is to separate the maneuver warfare tradition of the German army from the German army itself. For while the concepts, habits, and prejudices of maneuver warfare grew to maturity within the ranks of the German army, and while the German army has beer infused with the spirit of maneuver warfare to a degree attained by few other armies (notably those of the Finns and the Israelis), maneuver warfare never completely dominated the tactics, was but one of many influences on the campaigns, and but rarely determined the strategy of the German army.

Thus, for each instance where German storm troopers infiltrated through an enemy position to "collapse it from within," there was an occasion where a German battalion walked into rifle fire as if on parade at Potsdam. For each mobile defense, where German defenders adroitly sidestepped a bombardment and then returned to smash the exhausted attackers in a surprise counterattack, there were times when a German unit was ordered to hold a piece of militarily insignificant terrain "to the last man and the last bullet." In short, for each "Cut of the Scythe" there was a Stalingrad, for each "Battle of the Frontiers" there was a Verdun.[34]

More importantly, the level at which maneuver warfare was least applied, that is to say, strategy, was the most important one. As a result, much tactical and operational virtuosity was wasted in battles and campaigns that did little to improve Germany's strategic position. Rommel's brilliant victories in Africa, for example, may have helped the Japanese by weakening Commonwealth garrisons in the Far East. They did little, however, to help the overall German war effort. The same might be said for the invasion of the Balkans. Militarily, the conquest of Greece and Yugoslavia was brilliant. In the long term, however, it provided little more than an additional breeding ground for partisans.

## LESSONS LEARNED

Looking at maneuver warfare as a tradition within the German army, rather than the property of all German soldiers, gives modern maneuverists an important perspective on both the art of war as a whole and their position within military institutions. The first lesson to come into view is the primacy of strategy. Inspired tactics can do little more than win the wrong battle at the wrong time and place. Brilliant campaigning can rarely, if ever, salvage a poor choice of theaters or enemies.

The second lesson, which is of far more immediate use to most military professionals, is the slow pace of any far-reaching institutional reform. While the Prussians got some immediate benefits from the *Jäger* units that they raised in the middle of the 18th century, the big payoff did not come until the Napoleonic Wars. While the Allied victory over

Napoleon at Leipzig can be largely credited to the work of the Prussian reformers, the military views of the reformers were not institutionalized until the second half of the 19th century. And while the stormtroop tactics of World War I brought the Germans close to victory in 1918, it was not until the German army was recreated on the eve of World War II that the complex combination of organization, attitude, and armament that we have come to call "infiltration tactics" became part and parcel of every German infantry squad.

The third lesson, however, is perhaps the most important. If we recognize that maneuver warfare was a tradition within the German army rather than the common possession of the institution as a whole, we will have a far better sense of what in the armies that served the Kingdom of Prussia, the German Empire, and the Third Reich is worthy of emulation. Thus, rather than asking "What did the Germans do?" we can say "How would the *Jäger* solve this tactical problem?" "How would Frederick have dealt with this strategic dilemma?" "How would Scharnhorst have run his staff?" and "How would Moltke have trained his subordinates?"

# Notes

1. See, for an example of this point of view, Daniel J. Hughes, "The Abuses of German Military History," *Military Review*, December 1986.

2. For a thorough discussion of Bülow and other theorists who influenced 19th-century German military thought, see Rudolf von Caemmerer, *The Development of Strategical Science During the 19th Century*, trans. Karl von Donat (London: Hugh Rees, 1905).

3. Falkenhayn's attrition concept was a theory of victory quite separate from any tradition in the German army. Indeed, Falkenhayn's biggest difficulty at Verdun was failure to convince his subordinates to act in accordance with his idea. For a brief description of this problem, see chapter four of the author's *Stormtroop Tactics: Innovation in the German Army, 1914-1918* (New York: Praeger Publishers, 1989). For a more extensive treatment, see Hermann Wendt, *Verdun 1916, Die Angriffe Falkenhayns im Maasgebiet mit Richtung auf Verdun als strategisches Problem* (Berlin: E. S. Mittler, 1931), *passim*.

4. Christopher Duffy put it elegantly when he wrote, "Frederick's way of war was greatly influenced by the vulnerability of the Brandenburg heartland." *The Military Life of Frederick the Great* (New York: Atheneum, 1986), p. 90.

5. Duffy, *The Military Life of Frederick the Great*, p. 302.

6. Ibid.

7. The greatest proof of this was his willingness to abandon Berlin in 1760 rather than disperse his forces; see Duffy, *The Military Life of Frederick the Great*, pp. 208, 209.

8. See Peter Hofschröer, *Prussian Light Infantry, 1792 to 1815* (London: Osprey, 1984).

9. At this point, the terminology gets tricky. In the literature of 18th- and 19th-century military theory, the term "maneuver" is used to describe the formalistic, geometric approach to campaigns advocated by theorists such as Heinrich von Bülow and is often contrasted with the far more vigorous Napoleonic style. It is important to stress that in this essay (and throughout the literature of modern American military reform), the term "maneuver warfare" refers to an approach that is diametrically opposed to the military minuet so beloved in the Age of Reason. See, for an example of this other use of the term "maneuver," Gordon Craig, *The Politics of the Prussian Army, 1640-1945* (New York: Oxford University Press, 1955), pp. 28, 29.

10. For details on Napoleon's personal "OODA loop," see Martin Van Creveld, *Command in War* (Cambridge, Mass.: Harvard University Press, 1987).

11. The four major powers were Russia, Sweden, Prussia, and Austria. Although a small British contingent (six infantry battalions and half of the Rocket Troop) served in the campaign, the contribution of Great Britain came mostly in the form of cash. H. W. L. Hime, "The British Army in Germany, 1813," *Journal of the Royal Artillery*, vol. XLIII, no. 11, p. 433.

12. Caemmerer, p. 50. Caemmerer refers to this approach as command by instructions (*Directive* in the original German) rather than dispositions (*Disposition*). Rudolf von Caemmerer, *Die Entwickelung der strategischen Wissenschaft im 19. Jahrhundert* (Berlin: Wilhelm Baensch, 1904), p. 40.

13. For Wilhelm zu Schaumburg-Lippe's influence on Scharnhorst, see Charles Edward White, *The Enlightened Soldier: Scharnhorst and the Militärische Gesellschaft in Berlin, 1801–1805* (New York: Praeger Publishers, 1981). For his life and military ideas, including his enthusiasm for light troops, see Hans H. Klein, *Wilhelm zu Schaumburg-Lippe, Klassiker der Abschreckungstheorie und Lehrer Scharnhorsts* (Osnabrück: Biblio Verlag, 1982).

14. The German staff ride was very different from a modern American staff ride. Whereas American staff rides are battlefield tours with the immediate aim of bringing military history to life, a German staff ride was usually conducted in terrain that seemed to be a likely site for a future battle. Thus, the question was not "Why did Lee decide to split his forces at Chancellorsville?" but "What would you do if you received a report that an enemy corps had occupied those heights over there?"

15. In the last two decades of the 19th century, many of these books were translated into English by both expatriate Prussians and Americans.

16. Many of the surviving examples of 19th-century German tactical decision games were published for the use of officers preparing for the *Kriegsakademie* entrance exam.

17. The reader interested in the degeneration of the applicatory method should carefully read Timothy Nenninger's *The Old Army and the Leavenworth Schools* (Westport, Conn.: Greenwood Press, 1987).

18. Walter Goerlitz (Brian Battershaw, translator), *History of the German General Staff, 1657–1945* (New York: Praeger Publishers, 1954), p. 76.

19. Johann Ewald, *Abhandlung über den Kleinen Krieg* (Kassell: Johann Jacob Cramer, 1785). This is available in an excellent English translation by Robert A. Selig and David Curtis Skaggs as *A Treatise on Partisan Warfare* (Westport, Conn.: Greenwood Press, 1991).

20. Close to twenty years before J. F. C. Fuller resurrected the British light infantry tradition for English-speaking readership, Wilhelm Balck was aware,

not only of the tactics of British light infantry of the late 18th and early 19th centuries, but also of their similarities to those of Prussian *Jäger*. Wilhelm Balck, "Die Entwickelung der taktischen Anschauungen in der englischen Armee nach dem Burenkrieg," *Viertelsjahresheft für Truppenführung und Heereskunde*, March 1906, pp. 450, 451.

21. Frederick's fear of his fight troops shooting their officers and deserting was well founded. For examples of this, the ultimate indiscipline, see Christopher Duffy, *The Army of Frederick the Great* (New York: Hippocrene, 1974), pp. 76, 77.

22. Transfer from a Jäger battalion to a line unit not only resulted in an immediate loss of status, but also cost the malefactor his employment as a gamekeeper upon leaving the colors. Peter Paret, *Yorck and the Era of Prussian Reform, 1807–1815* (Princeton: Princeton University Press, 1966), pp. 29, 30. For a detailed picture of life in the Prussian *Jäger* Regiment at the end of the 18th century, see Wilhelm von Voß, *Yorck* (Oldenburg: Gerhard Stalling, 1906), pp. 9–17.

23. Paret, pp. 114, 115.

24. Ibid., pp. 147–153.

25. Ibid., 210, 211.

26. Paul Pietsch, *Die Formations und Uniformierungs-Geschichte des preußischen Heeres 1808–1914* (Hamburg: Verlag Helmut Gerhard Schulz, 1963), pp. 176–178.

27. Curt Jany, *Geschichte der Preußischen Armee vom is Jahrhundert Bis 194* (Osnabrück: Biblio Verlag, 1967), p. 133, and Pietsch, *Die Formations und Uniformierungs-Geschichte,* p. 165.

28. For a discussion of this tendency, see Wilhelm Balck, *Modern European Tactics*, trans. Louis R. M. Maxwell (London: Sands and Company, 1899), vol. I, pp. 33, 34; von Gottberg, *Geschichte des Hannoverschen Jäger Battalions Nr. 10* (Berlin: E. S. Mittler, 1903), pp. 349, 350; and Freiherr von Hagen, *Geschichte des Königl. Sächsischen 1. Jäger Battalions Nr. 12,* (Freiburg in Sachsen: Verlag von Craz und Gerlach, 1909), pp. 203, 204. For an example of an argument in favor of "Einheitsinfanterie," see Paulus, "Einheitliche Waffengattungen," *Militärische Rundschau*, 1896, pp. 265–267.

29. For details of this, see the author's "The German Army of World War I: The 1st Cavalry Corps," *Tactical Notebook*, April 1992.

30. The most detailed in this regard is H. H. Alten und Andere, *Geschichte des Garde Schützen Battalions 1914–1918* (Berlin: Gerhard Stalling, 1928). For additional examples, see Alexander von Bülow, *Die Jäger Vor* (Leipzig: F. A. Brockhaus, 1917).

31. Unless otherwise noted, all material on German stormtroops in World

War I is from my *Storm Troop Tactics: Innovation in the German Army, 1914-1918* (New York: Praeger Publishers, 1989).

32. In an attempt to keep this piece short, I have paid far too little attention to the role played by artillery in stormtroop tactics. Please see the extensive treatment of the subject in my *On Artillery* (New York: Praeger Publishers, 1993).

33. Wilhelm Balck, *Kriegspiel und Übungsritt als Vorschule für die Truppenführung* (Berlin: R. Eisenschmidt, 1913) and Erwin Rommel, *Aufgaben für Zug und Kompagnie (Gefechtsaufgaben, Gefechtsschießen, Geländebesprechung), Ihre Anlage und Leitung* (Berlin: E. S. Mittler, 1940).

34. The "Cut of the Scythe" (*Sichselschnitt*) was the German plan of operations against France in 1940. Its defining feature was the decision to put the *Schwerpunkt* against the weak French forces in the Ardennes. The "Battle of the Frontiers" is the name given by the French to the encounter battles that took place in the month of August 1914. In these engagements, which were, in terms of numbers of men, technology, and the advantages of terrain, among the fairest fights in history, the Germans almost always got the better of their adversaries because of their willingness to concentrate, the speed with which their officers at all levels made decisions, and their fondness for envelopment. In 1932 and 1933, the British magazine *Fighting Forces* published a series of articles by A. H. Burne that described, at the rate of one engagement per article, a number of the division actions of the "Battle of the Frontiers."

# From the *Offensive à Outrance* to the Methodical Battle

## Robert A. Doughty

During World War I, the French made dramatic changes in their doctrine, shifting from a preparation to fight highly mobile battles in 1914 to a preparation for methodical battles in 1918. The French entered the war expecting a war of maneuver, and during the first few months of fighting participated in numerous mobile battles. New weapons and methods, however, quickly transformed the conflict into a struggle dominated by trenches, barbed wire, and lethal firepower. As the French adapted to the unanticipated battlefield conditions, they went from one extreme, which placed strong emphasis on the offensive and mobility, to the other extreme, which prized firepower more than anything else. French infantry units prepared to fight as if they were part of a gigantic machine, moving from phase line to phase line and responding to shifts of artillery fire in an almost mechanical fashion. In contrast to the frivolous wasting of lives and materiel in the beginning of the war, methodical battles in the final phases of the war enabled the French to save lives and concentrate overwhelming materiel superiority against the enemy. From their perspective, the methodical battle seemed to be the perfect solution to what had been an unsolvable battlefield problem.

Although the roots of French doctrine in 1914 reach deep into the military experience of France, the period prior to World War I included numerous technological and institutional advances that affected strategy, tactics, organizations, and equipment. The introduction of rapid-fire artillery, breech-loading rifles, and machine guns occurred at the same time as the scale and scope of warfare expanded and as the corps and field army became standard institutions for most armies. As the French debated the effects of these important changes, most theorists foresaw highly mobile battles in which the offensive reigned supreme. Many drew their ideas from an intense study of Napoleonic battles; others analyzed more recent wars, such as the Russo-Japanese War of 1904–05, but failed to recognize the changing nature of warfare. Despite a great deal of reflection and analysis, France prepared to fight mobile battles in August 1914 that bore little resemblance to the static warfare that characterized most of the fighting during the next four years.

In explaining the origins of the *offensive à outrance*, historians have often noted the influence of lecturers at the *École Supérieure de Guerre*, who emphasized the importance of the offensive and who focused primarily on wars of maneuver.[1] Lt. Col. (later Marshal) Ferdinand Foch was one of the most influential members of the faculty at the *École Supérieure de Guerre* and argued in 1903 that improvements in firearms favored the offensive. He calculated how an attack with two battalions against one battalion would result in the attacking troops firing some 10,000 more bullets than the defenders. By comparing this to the smaller advantage provided by earlier rifles, Foch confidently predicted that increases in firepower favored the attacker and would enable him to gain "moral superiority."[2] Nonetheless, he concluded that "central attacks" such as those previously launched by Napoleon had been "given up," and that flank attacks were necessary to gain "superiority of fire" against an enemy.[3] In a later work that first appeared in 1904, Foch observed: "In strategy as in tactics, one attacks. But the attack is not simple. It is accompanied constantly by maneuver seeking, in strategy, the adversary's line of communications, [and] in tactics, the envelopment of the enemy's flank to destroy him or to reach his line of communications." He concluded that industrial advances had modified the "forms of war" but not the "fundamental principles about the conduct of war."[4]

Another important contributor to French thinking was Col. Louis Loyzeaux de Grandmaison, who is often accused of being the main author of the *offensive à outrance* of 1914. He was an articulate, influential officer who was chiefly concerned with the employment of large formations,[5] and who contributed significantly to the development of the infamous Plan XVII. Many of those who died in 1914 had been weaned on some of Grandmaison's phrases, such as, "To fight means to advance despite enemy fire."[6] Most had paid little or no attention to the careful qualification he had made to the notion of infantrymen always advancing. In 1910, for example, he wrote, "In open terrain, a frontal infantry attack is impossible. During the attack, it is the role of the artillery to establish the superiority of fire needed to suppress the enemy. . . ."[7] Despite these careful qualifications, Grandmaison's ideas had an unintended and disastrous effect, particularly in 1914 when French soldiers tried to advance in the face of determined enemy fire.

The ideas of Col. Ardant du Picq contributed significantly to the tendency of French officers to dismiss the effects of firepower. More than any other theorist, his ideas about "moral ascendancy"[8] permeated the entire French army and provided the inspiration for the *offensive à outrance*. According to Colonel du Picq, the side with the superior "resolution to advance" would prevail, even if his weapons and equipment were equal to or inferior to those of his opponent.[9] Though a victor could suffer more casualties than his opponent, victory would come to the unit whose morale and confidence were superior to that of its adversary. Du Picq argued that an advancing force could "dominate" a defender, and optimistically forecast that an entrenched defender could lose his confidence and flee in terror before a resolute attack.[10]

Colonel du Picq, nevertheless, recognized that increases in firepower had affected the conduct of battle. He advised commanders about the importance of launching carefully prepared attacks and said, "With good troops on both sides, if one does not prepare an attack, there is every reason to believe it will be repulsed."[11] He warned that attacking troops would suffer more than defenders, and that their morale would be weakened because of losses from the defenders' fires. When a defender demonstrated a strong will to fight, the attacking troops could become "demoralized."[12] Despite these warnings, du Picq concluded, "Bayonet charges (even if a bayonet thrust never occurs) or forward movement under fire will have a great effect on [both sides'] morale, and victory will go to the one who provides the greatest order and the most resolute spirit to his advances."[13] While such assertions stirred the emotions of readers sitting quietly in warm, quiet rooms, their faults became very obvious to the French soldiers lucky enough to escape alive from such charges in 1914.

French preparations and thinking were obvious in the 1913 *Regulation on the Conduct of Large Units*, which stated, "Battles are above all moral contests. Defeat is inevitable when hope for victory ceases. Success will come, not to the one who has suffered the least losses, but to the one whose will is the steadiest and whose morale is the most highly tempered."[14] To win the "moral contest," the *Regulation* emphasized using the offensive to seek decisive battle. The *Regulation* explained, "Only the offensive leads to positive results." It added, "Decisive battle . . . is the only means of breaking the will of an adversary. . . ."[15] To achieve such destruction, a commander had to launch violent attacks in the beginning of a war and thereby force an enemy to remain on the defensive. If an adversary seized the initiative with an offensive, a commander had to launch a "violent and energetic" counteroffensive to create a more favorable situation. Though the *Regulation* paid only slight attention to the effects of firepower, it did warn that against a well-prepared enemy with strong supporting arms, an attacker would have to proceed in a "methodical" manner.[16] The *Regulation* developed the idea of maneuver more completely by explaining the importance of a plan of maneuver. The emphasis on moral factors remained supreme, however, and the *Regulation* concluded: "Success in war depends more on perseverance and tenacity in execution [of a concept] for maneuver than on the quality of the concept [itself]."[17]

The French did not ignore technological developments before 1914, for one of the most important reasons for the army's faith in its doctrine was its faith in its main artillery piece, the 75mm cannon. In 1914, the French army possessed 4,268 pieces of field artillery, 3,840 of which were 75mm cannon.[18] As far as the French were concerned, the best use of these fine artillery pieces was to provide "curtains" of fire. The prewar artillery regulations noted:

Artillery fire has only a very limited effect against an enemy protected by shelter; to force such an enemy to uncover himself, he must be attacked by the infantry. Therefore preparation of attacks by the artillery cannot be carried out independently of infantry action. The cooperation between the two arms must, therefore, be constant. The artillery no longer prepares attacks; it supports them.[19]

Thus, instead of softening an objective prior to an attack, artillery provided fires during an attack to suppress the enemy and to disrupt his defensive efforts.

The failure to recognize the increasingly significant link between infantry and artillery and the importance of preparatory fires stemmed from the French overlooking how extensively the battlefield had changed due to the introduction of indirect-fire artillery, rapid-fire rifles, and machine guns. In particular, the French misunderstood the effect that highly lethal firepower would have on the progress of an attack. They mistakenly believed that soldiers' morale could be sustained despite significant losses inflicted by modern weaponry. In short, the French army prepared to use "curtains" of artillery fire and energetic infantry charges to win decisive battles.

After Germany declared war on France on 3 August, the French error became apparent in the first weeks of fighting. As Field Marshal Joseph Joffre, commander of French forces on the western front, prepared his army to fight in accordance with Plan XVII, he planned on launching his main attack on 14 August. To demonstrate to the French people the readiness of their army, however, Joffre launched a small offensive on 7 August into German-held Alsace. The offensive included two infantry divisions and one infantry brigade, with one of the first actions occurring at Altkirch, which is about 15 kilometers south of Mulhouse. With little or no reconnaissance or preparation, one of the regiments fixed bayonets and launched an energetic assault against the small German elements in the town. The regimental commander personally led the assault, sitting astride a handsome white horse. Although he was wounded in the battle, his regiment finally managed to secure the small town.[20] Despite the initial wave of joy throughout France at the news of the victory, indications of future difficulties appeared when the small force failed to make further advances and was finally driven back by the Germans on 10 August.

On the morning of the 14th, Joffre's main attack began with the First and Second Armies advancing on his right flank toward the east. As part of this advance, the 26th Division launched an attack against the village of Cirey. The after-action report of the division explained what happened:

> The attack seemed close to success when a bugle unwisely sounded the charge around 1845 hours. . . . On this signal, the infantry leaders launched their assault. . . . They crossed an area covered by enemy artillery and machine guns. Officer losses were such that the attack failed . . . , and the reconstitution of units became ex-

tremely difficult. All the energy of the officers and men was devoted to [reconstituting the unit]. . . . The exhaustion of the men is extreme. The division is incapable of undertaking an offensive tomorrow.[21]

As Joffre's main attack proceeded, an early report from the Second Army about the 29th Division suggested the extent of the difficulties confronting the French army: "Our infantry attacked with élan, but they were halted primarily by enemy artillery fire and unseen enemy infantry hidden in trenches." By 0900 hours the Second Army had suffered more than one thousand wounded and an unknown number killed.[22] The VIII Corps reported 50 percent casualties among its infantry in the first few days of fighting.[23] A division commander reported that one of his units had been "annihilated by a rain of large caliber shells."[24] By 20 August, the attacks by the First and Second Armies had halted.

After launching the right prong of his attack, Joffre launched the second prong on his left. It was no more successful than the first. Following numerous disastrous attacks, the French forces began withdrawing, often in a "disorderly" fashion.[25] After futile attempts to renew the attack, Joffre reluctantly permitted the French forces to return to the defensive positions they had occupied before the launching of the offensive. Having suffered some 300,000 casualties, Joffre informed his army commanders on August 24 that the infantry should attack only after artillery preparation. He explained, "Every time an infantry attack is launched over a long distance before the artillery has an effect, the infantry is hit by machine-gun fire and suffers losses that could have been avoided."[26] German artillery, machine-gun, and rifle fire had made a mockery out of unrealistic predictions of "resolute advances" against prepared defensive positions.

Despite numerous difficulties and heavy losses, the French and British managed in the Battle of the Marne in early September to halt the massive German attack through central Belgium toward Paris. In the subsequent "race to the sea," both sides frantically sought to outflank the other in a series of battles that gradually extended defensive lines toward the west. By the middle of October 1914, a long line of trenches extended from the English Channel to Switzerland. Open warfare had ended, and static, position warfare had begun. For a short while, Joffre put off a large offensive until he could assemble sufficient assets for a breakthrough. In the interim, however, he had his forces nibble away at the Germans,[27] while the French army worked desperately to modify its combat methods.

Of the areas requiring improvement, one of the most important was the frequent lack of coordination in the employment of the artillery and infantry. During the first battles of the campaign, German machine gunners extracted a high toll from the French infantry, which often failed to coordinate its actions with those of the artillery and to suppress machine-gun fire before advancing. Charging forward in their dark blue overcoats and red trousers and caps as if they were on peacetime maneuvers, the infantrymen tried to dig out the Germans with bayonets but were mowed down by machine guns and artillery fire.[28] French commanders advanced as quickly as they could and usually refused to prepare trenches and strong points for their troops to fall back on if the attack failed. When the suicidal charges did collapse, the French had nothing behind them to halt the counterattack, and some units collapsed completely, their withdrawals sometimes becoming routs.

The longer range of German artillery and the lack of heavy French artillery contributed to the French tactical defeats. German long-range howitzers, aided by aerial spotters, often silenced the shorter range 75mm batteries early in the fighting. Unlike German howitzers, which could shoot highly effective, plunging fire from defilade positions, the French 75mm cannon had less effect on entrenched positions and had to fire from more exposed positions because of the flat trajectory of their shells. Other problems also appeared. On 22 September 1914, the French High Command noted, "The insufficient number of long-range cannon in our [field] armies in comparison to similar pieces in the German [field] armies compels our artillery units in many cases to fire the 75[mm] cannon and the 155[mm] cannon for long distances under conditions that causes metal fatigue [in the tubes] and results in a large consumption of ammunition without significant results."[29] Before the war, some French officers had criticized the addition of heavy artillery, since it would limit the mobility essential to a sharp offensive. Confident that their 75mm cannon was the finest artillery piece in the world, and restrained by limited finances, the French had neglected the development of heavier pieces, and in 1914 the Germans had more than twice the heavy artillery of France.[30] The initial battles of 1914, however, quickly convinced the French that they desperately needed additional heavy artillery.

Doctrine for the employment of artillery also changed. Notions of the artillery only providing support, and not firing preparatory fires, quickly disappeared. The French High Command concluded, "Every time that a strong point is to be taken, the attack must be prepared by artillery. The infantry should be held back, and it should not deliver the assault until it has moved close enough to the enemy to be certain that the objective can be reached."[31] The French recognized that the battles were far different from the open warfare they had anticipated. A memorandum from the High Command on 18 November 1914 observed:

> The operations undertaken by most [field] armies have taken on the character of siege operations, and the occupied positions in one way or the other bear a strong resemblance to lines of investment. It is necessary to break through them to resume . . . open warfare. To achieve this rupture, it is necessary to employ means peculiar to siege warfare, in particular artillery of large caliber and long range.

The memorandum added, "It is above all by the intervention of a mass of artillery organized as a siege train that one can expect to achieve the concentration of sufficient fires."[32] Given the shortage of heavy artillery in the French army, however, manufacturing and allocating a sufficient "mass of artillery" to units became one of the most difficult challenges of the war.

The French also recognized the need to reduce the vulnerability of their infantrymen, who often exposed themselves to hostile fire unnecessarily or prematurely and failed to wait for adequate artillery support before attacking. As early as 15 August, one field army commander urged his troops to use trenches and covered positions and explained that the use of such protective measures did not indicate an "abandonment of the offensive spirit." He also urged the use of "methodical" techniques for units to move forward.[33] French commanders sought to disperse their infantry in depth and to avoid dense formations. They also rapidly learned how to use field fortifications. Nonetheless, as one officer noted, soldiers often occupied the "natural strong points of the terrain" but failed to organize them properly because they "were so imbued with offensive ideas." As a result, they frequently "provided very visible and very vulnerable targets to the hostile artillery."[34] Despite terrible casualties, it took time for new habits and practices to spread throughout the army.

During the winter of 1914–1915, the French made numerous adjustments in their methods, and on 2 January 1915 Joffre sent a memorandum to his subordinate commanders providing guidance on the methods of conceiving and executing attacks against strong defensive positions. The key point of the memorandum came in the first paragraph when Joffre explained that due to the increased effects of firepower and the strength of organized defenses, operations in the future had to be "slower and more methodical" than those envisaged in the prewar doctrine. If an attack were to succeed, it had to be prepared down to "the smallest detail," and a large amount of artillery fires had to be concentrated on the objective to ensure the enemy was weakened and the infantry could advance. Joffre warned that these fires had to land in depth throughout the enemy position because the Germans tended to pull the bulk of their infantry out of the front line trenches and then to push them back into the front lines when the French artillery preparation had ended. When an attack succeeded, another attack had to be launched to prevent the enemy from reconstituting his defenses or establishing new lines of defenses, but these subsequent attacks would not be launched until preparations were complete.[35]

Joffre also emphasized the importance of preventing the enemy from concentrating all his forces against the area in which the French were attacking. He ordered his subordinate commanders to launch as many attacks as possible in the "zone of attack." The attacks had to occur "simultaneously" to prevent the Germans from concentrating their reserves against the main attack. The attacks also had to occur across a large enough front to prevent the Germans from neutralizing their effects with flanking fires. The key point, nonetheless, was that the artillery had to provide support "not only during the preparation of the attack, but also *during the attack itself and after it succeeds*."[36] Joffre's memorandum clearly established the framework for fighting battles with the artillery and infantry working in close coordination during an offensive. Rudimentary methodical techniques enabled the French to provide some coordination between the artillery and infantry, but ensuring proper coordination remained one of the most complex challenges of the war.

One of the first examples of a more careful method of attack occurred in Champagne in early 1915. This attack signalled the end of Joffre's nibbling at the Germans and began the period that would last from early 1915 through April 1917 in which France would launch numerous offensives. Most of these offensives sought to penetrate German defenses and relied on a massive concentration of men and materiel to get the job done. As the first of these offensives, the French concentrated on 16 February two corps along a narrow portion of the front and on 19 February reinforced them with two additional corps, seeking to rupture the Germans' positions or at least to prevent them from shifting forces to the east. Another corps joined the attack about a week later.[37] The French supported the attack with large artillery barrages, one corps alone being supported by about 46 batteries of artillery.[38] Although the offensive managed to advance about three kilometers into the German positions, the offensive was characterized more by two successive attacks (one with two corps and the other with three) than by any step-by-step, highly synchronized efforts. Much remained to be done to achieve better synchronization.

Despite continued heavy losses, the French did not abandon their hopes of breaking completely through the enemy's defenses. In a long memorandum on 16 April 1915, Joffre explained that he wanted to "eject the enemy from his entire position and to defeat him without giving him time to recover." He added, "The participants at all echelons will be imbued with the idea of penetrating, of going beyond the first trenches conquered, of continuing the attack without halting. . . ."[39] The French increasingly used step-by-step techniques while still attempting to burst through the enemy defenses with a single, continuous thrust. Hopes of punching through the Germans were valid, however, only as long as they had defenses that were no deeper than the range of French artillery.

Joffre's memorandum of 16 April 1915 also provided information on such matters as the proper frontage (1,000–1,200 meters) for a division in the main attack, the maximum density of soldiers (one soldier per meter), the food and ammunition to be carried by each soldier, the proper place for commanders, etc. It included a schematic showing the placement of units within a division in the attack. In a clear demonstration of the French having comprehended the increased importance of artillery, Joffre called for the artillery to fire large preparatory fires before an infantry attack. Heavy artillery would fire three to four hours, while the 75mm cannon's fires would be periodically interrupted and their effects verified. The memorandum concluded, "Preparation should cease only when the necessary results have been obtained."[40] Clearly, the final results being sought were a complete breakthrough of the enemy's position.

Subsequent battles demonstrated the difficulty of achieving a breakthrough. In September 1915 the French launched a large attack in Champagne. The attack was meticulously planned and was preceded by an artillery preparation of three days with more than 1,100 75mm and 872 heavy artillery pieces participating.[41] The artillery fire contributed significantly to the infantry fighting their way through the first belt of German defenses, but the attackers encountered another strong position to its rear. Since this position was beyond the range of French artillery, it had escaped damage during the preparatory fires. The French infantry, which was encouraged by its initial success, unwisely launched an attack against the second position without proper artillery support and suffered heavy losses. After bringing their artillery forward, they attempted another attack, but this one also failed. This bitter experience demonstrated that a single attack could not penetrate a defensive position whose depth was greater than the range of the French artillery. A message from Joffre on 5 December 1915 concluded the Germans had organized a different type of defense than what they had used for the past ten months.[42] Needless to say, this meant that Joffre had to change his methods and abandon notions of a single, continuous thrust driving completely through the German defenses. Joffre was about to take one of the most important steps in the development of the methodical battle.

The first indication of new French thinking appeared in a message from Marshal Joffre on 16 January 1916 that included the concept of "successive stages" of an operation.[43] Another memorandum on 26 January provided additional information. Joffre explained, "A specific number of attack zones will be identified, including clearly specified successive objectives. . . ."[44] Henceforth, an offensive would consist of a series of successive, carefully controlled attacks, advancing from objective to objective after careful preparatory fires by the artillery. As the infantry moved by bounds, artillery batteries would displace forward to ensure continued firing against enemy positions. The memorandum warned, "One should not push partially disorganized troops too far into hostile territory, [for they are] likely to collapse under a counterattack."[45] To ensure the continuation of the attack and to protect the ground gained by the infantry, the artillery had to displace forward rapidly. The launching of successive attacks thus presented the characteristic of preparatory fires, followed by infantry attacks, followed by artillery batteries displacing forward so they could provide preparatory fires against the next German positions, followed by another infantry attack. The French believed carefully controlled, repetitive blows in this manner would enable them to crack the deep German defenses.

Unlike the glorious battles envisaged by Colonel du Picq, however, the pace and power of the attack would be set by the artillery, not the infantry. A memorandum on 8 January 1916 about offensive combat with small units observed:

> The infantry by itself has no offensive power against obstacles defended by fire [and] provided with necessary protection. . . . One should never launch an attack without preceding and accompanying it with effective artillery support. One does not fight with men against materiel.[46]

The reality of the battlefield had forced the French to modify their doctrine substantially and the infantry to cede its principal role to the artillery. It was not long before some officers complained about the loss of aggressiveness among the infantry. In August 1916, the commander of the French Sixth Army criticized infantry officers who believed the infantry had become a "passive instrument that occupied terrain previously cleared by the artillery of every obstacle and even of all enemy."[47]

Other changes continued to occur, but bitter fighting at Verdun in 1916 reinforced France's reliance on artillery and demonstrated clearly the advantages of the methodical battle. Of the several subordinate battles that comprised the larger battle of Verdun, the capture of Fort Douaumont had a special significance. With Gen. Robert Nivelle commanding the Second Army and Gen. Charles Mangin as his major subordinate commander, the French relied on a tightly choreographed operation with two successive objectives being captured en route to the fort. The attack was strongly supported by artillery, with the French using 654 tubes—including long-range fires from the newly manufactured 400mm railway guns—to fire more than 855,000 rounds of artillery between 20–27 October.[48] Following four days of artillery preparation,[49] the attack began on 24 October and, considering the enormous losses of previous months, captured the imposing fortress easily. The methods used in the capture of Douaumont seemed to provide the answer to many difficult questions.

A memorandum from Joffre on 27 November 1916 summarized the lessons from the previous months' fighting. Most of his points were not new, for he emphasized the importance of attacks being launched on as broad a front as possible to prevent the enemy from concentrating his artillery fires against the attack and to decrease the effect of his reserves. He emphasized having the artillery pushed as far forward as possible so it could fire throughout the enemy position. He also called for the "shortest possible delay" between the successive attacks to reduce the amount of time available to the enemy to improve his position.[50] If the delay between the successive attacks dragged on too long, the French could not achieve success, and their attacks would result only in the wasting of thousands of lives and tons of materiel.

Perhaps most importantly, the advantages of tight centralization and intricate coordination had been clearly demonstrated in the fighting to Joffre and other French leaders. For example, the commander of the Sixth Army warned its subordinate units about letting its artillery support "degenerate" into "independent" batteries acting on their own without contributing to the "combined action" of all the artillery.[51] Similarly, the commander of the Second Army complained about an attack failing for a variety of reasons, including "incomplete" artillery preparation and the first wave attacking before H-hour "on the initiative of a lieutenant." It was clear that this lieutenant's "initiative" had warned the Germans and enabled them to use their artillery effectively against the French.[52] As a consequence of these and other lessons, the fighting at Verdun fixed methodical procedures onto French thinking and made strongly centralized, tightly coordinated battles a permanent part of their operations.

The progress being made, however, did not meet the expectations of France's political leaders. Optimistically hoping that General Nivelle may have found the "solution" to France's problems when he captured Douaumont, they removed Joffre from his position as commander of the French armies on the western front and replaced him with Nivelle on 17 December 1916. This began Nivelle's ill-fated attempt to use a gigantic methodical battle to rupture German defenses in one gigantic push.[53] Nivelle had gained a reputation as an innovator in the early years of the war by suggesting technical improvements in the employment of artillery and supposedly creating the rolling barrage. In an era without radios, the rolling barrage proved to be an excellent method for coordinating infantry and artillery and added substantially to the power of the offensive.[54] If the rolling barrage worked perfectly, the infantry would move into the enemy trenches just after the last artillery rounds landed in them. During the bitter fighting at Verdun, he added to the luster of his reputation. By using bounds to control the movement of infantry units, and by accompanying the movement of the infantry with a rolling barrage, Nivelle utilized techniques that had been devised earlier in the war, but he improved these methods by concentrating newly available long-range fires throughout the successive lines of German defenses.[55] The successful capture of Douaumont seemed to be another brilliant achievement in a highly successful career, leading even Joffre later to describe him as the "saviour of Verdun."[56]

After taking command of French forces on the western front, Nivelle responded to the challenges facing France by conceiving a plan for breaking completely through the enemy front. In December 1916, he provided guidance about the conduct of operations in 1917 and wrote, "The objective . . . is the destruction of the main mass of enemy forces on the western front."[57] In a memorandum dated 16 March 1917 he explained that a "constant, ordered, methodical and rapid push" would result in the rupturing of enemy defenses and the resumption of open warfare.[58] To achieve success, he would mass an unparalleled amount of heavy artillery and arrange to have it place fire throughout the enemy's position so he could push his infantry through the German defenses in one rapid, continuous move. He explained that the heavy artillery had to be employed as if it were a 75mm cannon.[59] Nivelle's enthusiasm and confidence infected the entire French army, but the regression to earlier hopes of a single thrust rupturing the German defenses yielded one of the worst disasters of the war and led to a collapse of morale and the outbreak of mutinies in the French army. About the only thing achieved in the offensive was the French demonstration of how the power of their artillery had increased since August 1914.[60]

Following Nivelle's disastrous offensive in April, he was replaced on 17 May 1917 by Gen. Henri-Philippe Pétain, whose first task was to end the mutinies and then to restore the French soldier's fighting spirit. As part of his reforms, Pétain abandoned the notion of breaking through German defenses and began emphasizing limited offensives in which the methodical battle reigned supreme. Pétain had participated in the Champagne offensive of September 1915 and had learned there the advantages of a series of successive battles. While Nivelle's offensive was being planned, he had voiced strong reservations about its chances for success, and after assuming command of the French forces, sought to fight methodical battles in limited offensives to reduce friendly casualties while inflicting larger losses on the Germans. He apparently had given up hope of breaking through the enemy's defenses and awaited the arrival of the Americans and the perfection of the tank before the final battles of the war could be fought.

On 20 August Pétain launched a limited offensive at Verdun and achieved moderate success. As soon as the Germans concentrated their reserves and offered stiff resistance, he halted the attack. At the end of October, he launched a more elaborate offensive at La Malmaison, where his objective was the high ground which supported the German right flank along the Chemin des Dames. With about 1,850 artillery tubes firing support, including three days of preparatory fires, and with 14 tank companies accompanying the infantry, the French advanced about five kilometers. This advance outflanked the Germans on the Chemin des Dames and forced them to withdraw behind the Ailette River. In consonance with the idea of seeking only limited objectives, Pétain consolidated his gains and did not seek to exploit his victory. His successes at Verdun and La Malmaison demonstrated to the entire French army that methodical attacks with limited objectives could seize critical terrain and inflict large casualties on the Germans. Given Pétain's doubts about being able to rupture the enemy's lines, however, it was difficult to formulate a strategy for ending the war. One alternative appeared in October 1917 when a study in the French High Command predicted that 1918 would consist of a "battle of attrition" and would include a series of attacks delivered over a relatively short period to weaken the enemy and force him to withdraw.[61]

The end of the war came more quickly than some French soldiers had dared hope, however, with one of the most important battles occurring at Montdidier in August 1918. Gen. Eugène Debeney commanded a force of 15 divisions (divided into four corps), supported by more than 1,600 artillery pieces and two battalions of light tanks.[62] The mission of the French First Army was to support an offensive by the British Fourth Army under Gen. Sir Henry Rawlinson. The Germans could not respond adequately to the British and French attack, leading to what General Erich Ludendorff termed the "black day" of the war for the German army.[63] Debeney's success inaugurated the form of open warfare that characterized the last months of the war and proved to be the final step in the evolution of the methodical battle in World War I.

Following the war, the battles of La Malmaison and Montdidier became the models of how to conduct a methodical attack. La Malmaison became the model of an attack with a limited objective; Montdidier became the model of an attack with a broader strategic purpose. Nonetheless, each included huge concentrations of men and materiel; each relied on a series of successive attacks against an enemy in prepared defensive positions; and each included successive steps of preparation, attack, and exploitation. Those officers planning the actions of divisions and corps in the battles used several bounds and phases as control measures to facilitate the coordination of artillery and infantry and prevent accidental bombardment of French units by friendly artillery. They planned on step-by-step actions so commanders could manage the flow of units and supplies onto the battlefield and achieve a victory despite being faced with strong German defenses. Some officers recognized that the intricate workings of a methodical attack bore strong resemblance to the workings of a machine in which each part had a precise function and in which the success of the entire machine depended on each part performing perfectly.

Despite the success achieved with the methodical battle in World War I, the French army's reliance on it after 1918 had unanticipated effects, one of the most important of which was the French becoming more rigid in their approach to combat. Centralization and detailed planning became the primary concern of higher commanders, especially as they considered how to direct the methodical battle. The French believed the locus of decision making had to remain at the higher level, because a higher commander had to coordinate the actions of numerous subordinate units properly. Each command level (field army, corps, division, etc.) had less room for improvisation and adjustment than the level immediately above it, for the entire system was designed to be propelled forward by pressure from above, rather than by being pulled from below. Instead of showing initiative and flexibility, lower-level commanders were expected to perform according to the plan and not to do anything unexpected. An unexpected action, such as a lieutenant showing "initiative," could result in an entire operation being disrupted. As a consequence of training their officers and units to perform in a mechanistic fashion, the French could not respond flexibly to unanticipated demands and could hardly capitalize upon an important gain made by a lower level unit.

Another important effect pertained to the eclipse of the French sense of maneuver. In the broadest sense, there was little that was subtle about the methodical battle, for it bore a stronger resemblance to a huge battering ram than to a swift, unexpected strike. Instead of maneuvering units, the methodical battle emphasized the maneuvering of masses of fire. It was the artillery that would shift from one point to another and the infantry that would follow. By maneuvering fires, a commander could concentrate his fires on the decisive point in the battle, but the "decisive point" was one defined by larger unit commanders. And maneuver was viewed in terms of the movement of larger units, rather than smaller ones.[64]

The eclipse of the sense of maneuver and the preference for maneuvering huge masses of fire contributed to France's rejecting such ideas as German "infiltration tactics" or B. H. Liddell Hart's "expanding torrent." From their perspective, notions of infiltration tactics or expanding torrents of infantry sounded too much like the methods that France had tried in 1914, which had yielded such disastrous results. The irony is that a premonition of these concepts appeared in one of Marshal Foch's earliest works. In a book published before World War I, Foch compared frontal assaults to waves breaking against a dam and concluded, "The dam will not be broken." If a crack were discovered in the dam, however, an attacker could rush through the "breach" and "carry the whole obstacle."[65] Clearly, France chose to place massive pressure against a "dam" and rejected the notion of rushing pell-mell forward through a "crack."

Though France made many adjustments in her doctrine from 1914 to 1918, she proved far less adaptable in the years before World War II. The high price she paid in developing the doctrine of the methodical battle and the great victories she won using it made her reluctant to develop something fundamentally different. Additionally, the eclipse of the sense of maneuver, the preference for centralization, and emphasis on rigidity and obedience severely hampered France's attempts to respond to the highly mobile form of warfare practiced by the Germans in May-June 1940. Methods that worked in 1918 did not work in 1940. Ironically, some of the German concepts rested on ideas that had not worked for the French in 1914 and that had been regarded as bankrupt after 1918. Thus, the methodical battle proved to be instrumental to her victory of 1918, as well as to her defeat of 1940.

# Notes

1. The standard reference is: J. Monteilhet, *Les institutions militaires de la France (1814–1932)* (Paris: Felix Alcan, 1932), passim. For a contrasting view, see: Douglas Porch, *The March to the Marne: The French Army 1871–1914* (London: Cambridge University Press, 1981), pp. 213–214.

2. Marshal Ferdinand Foch, *The Principles of War*, trans. Hilaire Belloc (New York: Henry Holt and Co., 1920), p. 32.

3. Foch, *Principles of War*, pp. 349, 350.

4. Maréchal F. Foch, *De la conduite de la guerre, La manoeuvre pour 1a bataille*, 6th ed. (Paris: Berger-Levrault, 1921), pp. XVI–XVII.

5. Col. Louis de Grandmaison, *Deux Conférences faites aux officiers de l'État-Major de l'Armée* (Paris: Berger-Levrault, 1911), *passim*; Joel A. Setzen, "The Doctrine of the Offensive in the French Army on the Eve of World War I," unpublished Ph.D. dissertation, University of Chicago, 1972, p. 99.

6. Commandant Louis de Grandmaison, *Dressage de l'Infanterie en vue du combat offensif* (Paris: Berger-Levrault, 1910), p. 89.

7. Grandmaison, p. 24.

8. Col. Charles J. J. J. du Picq, *Études sur le Combat* (Paris: Berger-Levrault, 1948), p. 92.

9. Du Picq, pp. 91, 92.

10. Du Picq, p. 92.

11. Du Picq, pp. 95, 96.

12. Du Picq, p. 96.

13. Du Picq, p. 96.

14. France, Ministère de la Guerre, *Décret du 28 octobre 1913 portant règlement sur la conduite des grandes unités* (Paris: Berger-Levrault, 1913), p. 7.

15. *Règlement sur la conduite des grandes unités*, pp. 6, 7.

16. *Règlement sur la conduite des grandes unités*, p. 37.

17. *Règlement sur la conduite des grandes unités*, p. 9.

18. Général F. Culmann, *Tactique d'Artillerie: Matériels d'aujourd'hui et de demain* (Paris: Charles Lavauzelle, 1937), pp. 13, 14.

19. Quoted in Lt. Col. Pascal M. H. Lucas, *The Evolution of Tactical Ideas in France and Germany during the War of 1914–1918*, trans. Maj. P. V. Kieffer (n.p., typescript, 1925), p. 10.

20. Ronald Harvey Cole, "'Forward with the Bayonet!': The French Army

Prepares for Offensive Warfare, 1911–1914," Ph.D. dissertation, University of Maryland, 1975, pp. 380–81.

21. Copie du compte rendu par la 26ème division, 14 août 1914, in France, Ministère de la Guerre, État-Major de l'Armée, *Les Armées Françaises dans la Grande Guerre* (hereafter France, M.G., (*Armées Françaises*), vol. I, part 1, annexes, no. 332 (Paris: Imprimerie Nationale, 1922), pp. 330, 331.

22. Capitaine Fétizon, Compte rendu de la situation de 1a IIème armée le 15 août, 15 aout 1914, in France, M.G., *Armées Françaises*, vol. I, part 1, annexes, no. 318, p. 316.

23. Capitaine Pichot-Duclos, Situation de l'armée d'apres les renseignements de la nuit, 22 août 1914, in France, M.G., *Armées Françaises*, vol. I, part 1, annexes, no. 820, p. 696.

24. Général Bajolle, Général commandant 15ème division à général commandant 8ème C.A., 20 août 1914, in France, M.G., *Armées Françaises*, vol. I, part 1, annexes, no. 689, p. 593.

25. Marshal Joseph Joffre, *The Personal Memoirs of Joffre, Field Marshal of the French Army*, trans. Col. T. Bentley Mott (New York: Harper & Brothers, 1932), vol. I, p. 178.

26. Grand Quartier Général, Général Joseph Joffre, Note pour toute les armées, 24 août 1914, in France, M.G., *Armées Françaises*, vol. I, part 2, annexes, no. 158, p. 129; Henri Isselin, *The Battle of the Marne*, trans. Charles Connell (Garden City, N.Y.: Doubleday and Co., 1966), pp. 35–37.

27. Jean-Jacques Becker, *The Great War and the French People* (Dover, N.H.: Berg, 1988), p. 31. Cite provided by James K. Hogue.

28. Cole, pp. 413, 414, 419–429.

29. Grand Quartier Général, Général J. Joffre, Guerre, 3ème direction, Paris, 22 septembre 1914, in France, M.G., *Armées Françaises*, vol. II, annexes, no. 25, p. 16.

30. Cole, p. 461.

31. Quoted in Lucas, p. 25.

32. État-Major Général 3ème Bureau, Général J. Joffre, Note relative à l'organisation d'une réserve d'artillerie de gros caliber, 18 novembre 1914, in France, M.G., *Armées Françaises*, vol. II, annexes, no. 152, p. 182.

33. IIème Armée, Général de Castelnau, Note du général commandant l'armée au sujet de l'attitude à tenir pour attaquer des organisations défensives, 15 août 1914, in France, M.G., *Armées Françaises*, vol. I, part 1, annexes, no. 319, p. 317.

34. Lucas, p. 27.

35. Grand Quartier Général des Armées de l'Est, Général J. Joffre, Note pour les armées, 2 janvier 1915, in France, M.G., *Armées Françaises*, vol. II, annexes, no. 530, pp. 746–747.

36. Joffre, Note pour les armées, pp. 746–747. Emphasis is in original document.

37. Grand Quartier Général, Général J. Joffre, Annexe à la lettre du 17 mars no. 5668, Offensive en Champagne, in France, M.G., *Armées Françaises*, vol. II, annexes, no. 1205, p. 638.

38. IVème Armée, lére Corps d'Armée, Général Deligny, Ordre général No. 287, Journée du 22 février 1915, 21 février 1915, in France, M.G., *Armées Françaises*, vol. II, annexes, no. 963, p. 302.

39. Grand Quartier Général des Armées de 1'Est, Général J. Joffre, But et conditions d'une action offensive d'ensemble, 16 avril 1915, in France, M.G., *Armées Françaises*, vol. III, annexes, no. 52, pp. 94–108.

40. Joffre, But et conditions d'une action offensive d'ensemble, p. 95.

41. Culmann, p. 154.

42. Grand Quartier Général des Armées de l'Est, Général J. Joffre, Note pour les commandants de groupe d'armées, 5 décembre 1915, in France, M.G., *Armées Françaises*, vol. III, annexes, no. 3117, p. 373.

43. France, M.G., *Armées Françaises*, vol. IV, part 1, p. 49.

44. Grand Quartier Général des Armées de l'Est, Général J. Joffre, Instruction sur le combat offensif des grandes unités, 26 janvier 1916, in France, M.G., *Armées Françaises*, vol. III, annexes, part IV, no. 3298, p. 700.

45. Joffre, Instruction sur le combat offensif des grandes unités, p. 690.

46. Quoted in France, M.G., *Armées Françaises*, vol. IV, part 1, p. 47.

47. VIème Armée, Général Fayolle, Note, 6 août 1916, in France, M.G., *Armées Françaises*, vol. IV, part 2, annexes, no. 2769, p. 465.

48. IIème Armée, Groupement D.E., État-Major, État comparatif des munitions demandées et consommées pour l'opération du 24 octobre, 4 novembre 1916, in France, M.G., *Armées Françaises*, vol. IV, part 3, annexes, no. 1502, p. 641.

49. France, M.G., *Armées Françaises*, vol. IV, part 3, p. 382.

50. Grand Quartier Général, Général J. Joffre, Note relative à la préparation et à l'exécution des attaques, 27 novembre 1916, in France, M.G., *Armées Françaises*, vol. V, annexes, no. 183, pp. 329–330.

51. VIème Armée, État-Major, 3ème Bureau, Général Fayolle, Note, 23 août 1916, in France, M.G., *Armées Françaises*, vol. IV, part 2, annexes, no. 3049, p. 858.

52. IIème Armée, État-Major, 3ème Bureau, Général R. Nivelle, Note pour le Groupement E.F., 31 août 1916, in France, M.G., *Armées Françaises*, vol. IV, part 2, annexes, no. 3156, p. 995.

53. Grand Quartier Général, Ordre général no. 69, 16 décembre 1916, in France, M.G., *Armées Françaises*, vol. V, annexes, no. 296, p. 517.

54. James K. Hogue, "Puissance de Feu: The Struggle for a New Artil-

lery Doctrine in the French Army, 1914–1916," unpublished master's thesis, Ohio State University, 1988, pp. 51, 52.

55. Lieutenant Stephen F. Yunker, "'I Have the Formula': The Evolution of the Tactical Doctrine of General Robert Nivelle," *Military Review*, vol. 14, no. 6 (June 1974), p. 17; Alistair Horne, *The Price of Glory: Verdun 1916* (New York: Penguin Books, 1964), p. 307.

56. Joffre, *Memoirs*, Vol. II, p. 492.

57. Grand Quartier Général, Général R. Nivelle, Plan d'opérations de 1917, 31 décembre 1916, in France, M.G., *Armées Françaises*, vol. V, annexes, no. 368, p. 606.

58. Grand Quartier Général, Général R. Nivelle, Note, 16 mars 1917, in France, M.G., *Armées Françaises*, vol. V, annexes, no. 882, p. 49.

59. Nivelle, Note, 16 mars 1917, p. 49.

60. Lucas, p. 103.

61. Grand Quartier Général, Général de Barescut, La bataille de 1918, 9 octobre 1917, in France, M.G., *Armées Françaises*, Vol. VI, Part 1, Annexes, No. 7, pp. 13, 19.

62. Commandant Marius Daille, *The Battle of Montdidier*, Trans. Major Walter R. Wheeler (n.p., typescript, n.d.), passim.

63. Erich von Ludendorff, *Ludendorff's Own Story* (New York: Harper & Brothers, 1919), Vol. I, p. 326.

64. See Robert A. Doughty, *The Seeds of Disaster: The Development of French Army Doctrine, 1919–1939* (Hamden, Conn.: Archon Books, 1985), *passim*.

65. Foch, *Principles of War*, p. 298.

# Maneuver Warfare in the Light Infantry: The Rommel Model

## David A. Grossman

> Given the same amount of intelligence, timidity will do
> a thousand times more damage in war than audacity.
>
> Clausewitz, *On War*

### ERWIN ROMMEL'S IMPACT ON THE GERMAN WAY OF WAR

While most everyone knows that the World War II Panzer leader, Erwin Rommel, was a daring practitioner of maneuver warfare, too few know that he learned and perfected his maneuver warfare skills as a light infantryman in World War I. Indeed, it can be argued that the German way of war in World War II was profoundly influenced by Rommel's World War I light infantry experiences and the book that grew out of those experiences.

Rommel's book, *Attacks*, was first published in 1937 under the title *Infanterie Grieft An*, and was a tremendous success in Germany before and during the war. By 1944 the book had gone through at least 18 printings, and its impact on the German army was incalculable. (As was its impact on Allied leaders such as George S. Patton, arguably the Allies' greatest master of maneuver warfare, who was "electrified" by the book and read and reread it "until he knew it by heart.")[1]

*Attacks* can be seen as a self-promoting book in which Rommel tells how he won the *Pour le Mérite,* Germany's highest award in World War I—also known as the "Blue Max." His book *was* self-congratulatory and it *did* play a major role in placing him on the road to fame and glory—which ended with his forced suicide in 1944 when he was implicated in an assassination plot against Hitler. But *Attacks* was also an evangelical exhortation to a generation of German soldiers (and to any other soldier who will read and learn from it), building on the "Hutier" system of infiltration tactics and the "mission orders" of World War I, and telling of a better way to wage war. Every section ends with a detailed set of "observations" or lessons based upon his experiences, and those lessons, taken to heart by the Wehrmacht, were lessons in maneuver warfare from a true master.

For Germany, *Attacks* was a clarion call to institutionalize the embryonic maneuver warfare doctrine developed by the German army late in World War I. For a student of maneuver warfare, *Attacks* is a basic, fundamental primer. For an American army struggling to determine its fundamental doctrine and the place of light infantry within that doctrine, *Attacks* serves as a superb example of how maneuver warfare can be executed in the light infantry.

## ROMMEL AND THE 12TH ISONZO BATTLE

> To capture the enemy's army is better than to destroy it.
>
> Sun Tzu[2]

The culmination of Rommel's World War I exploits was his decisive light infantry operation during the 12th Battle of Isonzo on the Italian front in World War I. Using a combination of penetration and infiltration techniques conducted in mountainous terrain under adverse weather conditions, he conducted a campaign that was a textbook example of light infantry maneuver warfare operations.

The chief operational objective of the Italian army upon entering the First World War in May 1915 was the capture of the city of Trieste. During the following two years ten battles took place along the lower course of the Isonzo River, during which the Austrian forces defending on that front had been slowly pushed eastward and the attacking Italians approached Trieste. From August to September 1917, during the 11th Battle of Isonzo, the Italian army launched a massive 50-division attack in a narrow sector and succeeded in securing significant footholds across the Isonzo River and in the mountains west of the river. From here the Italians were in an excellent position to finally secure Trieste on their next attack.

Due to the danger this situation presented to their Austrian allies, the German High Command sent an army of seven veteran divisions to assist in a combined Austrian-German offensive to drive the Italians back across the Isonzo River and deep into their own national territory. That the Germans devoted such a large force to this operation shortly after the tremendous expenditure of men and materiel at Verdun and Flanders is an indication of how seriously the German High Command viewed the situation.

The German troops arrived at the front after a series of night marches, spending their days packed into what Rommel called "the most uncomfortable and inadequate accommodations imaginable." This careful operational security campaign was all for naught, since a Czech soldier with maps and orders outlining the offensive deserted to the Italian side. Thus, at dawn on 24 October 1917, after an extensive artillery preparation and under cover of a heavy rainfall, a combined German and Austrian force of approximately 15 divisions attacked against a forewarned Italian force, which was defending in rugged mountainous terrain in a series of three extensively prepared defensive belts.

In Chapter V of *Attacks* Rommel relates how the German and Austrian forces were able to quickly penetrate the artillery-devastated first defensive belt, as "the remnants of the garrison emerged from the ruins [of their positions] and hurried toward us with hands raised and faces distorted with fear." In this mountainous terrain Lieutenant Rommel, in command of a three-company mountain infantry detachment, was able to infiltrate the enemy's second defensive belt quickly, since most of its Italian garrison "had sought shelter in their dugouts from the streaming rain" and did not realize that the first zone had fallen. By working his way around them and approaching the defensive positions of the second zone of defense from the rear, Rommel was able to force the surrender of most of the second zone positions in his sector.

On the next day, 25 October, after extensive night reconnaissance operations, Rommel followed up the previous day's operation with a penetration of the Italian third defensive line. He was a master at maintaining the momentum of the attack by reinforcing and exploiting the success of earlier offensive operations. Time after time in World War I, light infantry elements under his command were able to infiltrate or penetrate enemy front line positions and rapidly move deep into their rear. The farther behind the front lines he went, the more unsuspecting was his enemy, and the more successful his operations. During 28 hours of constant operations on the 25th and 26th of October 1917, Rommel was able to use these tactics to penetrate the Italian third defensive belt, capture Mount Matajur, and secure a key mountain pass that formed the main supply route for the northern portion of the Italian front.

Carrying full combat loads, the mountain infantry troops under Rommel's command "surmounted elevation differences of eight thousand feet uphill and three thousand feet downhill, and traversed a distance of twelve miles as the crow flies through unique, hostile mountain fortifications." During these operations "the heavy machine gunners, carrying loads of ninety pounds, determined the rate of ascent."

It would be difficult to find a finer example of light infantry maneuver warfare operations. The total of prisoners and trophies captured by Rommel's small detachment during the entire 12th Battle of Isonzo amounted to "150 officers, 9000 men, and 81 guns. Not included in these figures were the enemy units which, after they had been cut off . . . voluntarily laid down their arms and joined the columns of prisoners." The orders of the day of the German Alpine Corps stated that the capture of key terrain by Rommel's unit "caused the collapse of the whole structure of hostile resistance . . . [and] initiated the irresistible pursuit on a large scale." Rommel's success on this operation won him the *Pour le Mérite*, the German army's highest award.

During these 52 hours of nearly constant operations, the Rommel detachment suffered only 6 dead and 30 wounded. Their safety lay in the unrelenting momentum of their offensive operations and the Italians' inability to react to the tempo of Rommel's operations.

Rommel's rapid success, his lopsided casualty figures, and the tremendous number of prisoners captured all presage a similar success achieved through the application of the same maneuver warfare principles during the blitzkrieg against France in 1940, and the Allied ground offensive against Iraq in the 1991 Gulf War. A careful analysis of this World War I operation reveals tactical principles that are fully applicable to future maneuver warfare operations, particularly light infantry operations in rugged terrain.

## THE LESSONS

### Gaps and Surfaces, Reconnaissance Pull, and Attack by Infiltration

Now an army may be likened to water, for just as flowing water avoids the heights and hastens to the lowlands, so an army avoids

strengths and strikes weakness. And as water shapes its flow in
accordance with the ground, so an army manages its victory
in accordance with the situation of the enemy.

Sun Tzu[3]

The first step in a maneuver warfare attack is generally to find or
make a "gap" in enemy lines while avoiding or bypassing the "surfaces" (i.e., strengths) in the enemy lines. In rough terrain an infiltration operation (undetected movement through enemy lines), or a penetration operation (creating and exploiting a gap through enemy lines),
and the extensive exploitation operations that should subsequently occur
behind those lines, require a degree of stealth, cross-country mobility, flexibility, independent operations, logistic austerity, and training
that is characteristic of the light infantry. Infiltration operations in particular
are "natural" light infantry techniques which play to the light infantry's
strengths.

At the operational level, good operations security and deception plans
are essential to support penetration operations. Prior to the 12th Battle
of Isonzo the Germans went to great effort to conceal the movement
of their infantry divisions from enemy observation as they conducted
the approach march to the front, moving their forces only at night and
concealing them by day. In a modern operation of this nature such a
deceptive movement would be much easier to accomplish with light
infantry forces (vice armor or mechanized forces) since they can be
so much more easily concealed from satellites, radar, and thermal imagery
devices.

At the tactical level, light infantry penetration and infiltration operations such as Rommel conducted tend to blend into each other. Prior
to any attack, a careful reconnaissance of enemy lines was always
conducted to find gaps or areas where Rommel's forces could closely
approach enemy lines. During the execution of the attack, he always
tried to take advantage of terrain, weather, and weaknesses in enemy
deployment to move his forces through enemy lines with a minimal
amount of contact. In other words, he always tried to infiltrate. If he
could infiltrate without any contact or by quietly surprising and dis-
patching a small enemy position or section of the line, then he did
so. If the infiltration option failed, he was always ready to execute a
penetration by: (l) having a supporting element, usually consisting of

massed machine guns, in position to suppress enemy forces while (2) a small penetration element created and widened a gap and (3) his exploitation element (which usually consisted of the bulk of his forces) passed through the gap and moved deep into enemy lines.[4]

The infiltration or penetration was not the objective, it was simply a means to an end. The objective was to get through enemy front lines in order to get to logistic and command post areas and key terrain in the enemy rear. Rommel's reconnaissances were usually made while the men rested, and were almost always conducted by officers and NCOs. These leaders were more lightly equipped and did not suffer the fatigue that the men did, making them available for scouting missions.

The leaders conducting these patrols were usually given the freedom to make and secure gaps in the enemy lines if possible. If these reconnaissance patrols came across enemy elements that were not sufficiently alert, the recon patrol would capture them and thus create their own gap. Often these recon elements, in the purest form of "recon pull," made the gaps, sent back a runner, and "pulled" the rest of the unit through. Such gaps are a tenuous, ephemeral commodity, and Rommel always took immediate advantage of these opportunities, communicating back to his men a sense of urgency and the feeling that "a second's delay might snatch away victory."

In support of his recon pull, Rommel made extensive use of visual observation, using his binoculars more than any other single piece of equipment. In later operations he made excellent use of a powerful (captured) telescope and an ad hoc observation squad to conduct visual reconnaissance prior to attacking. In similar operations today's light infantry leader must make creative use of all available visual observation assets—such as TOW and Dragon thermal night-vision sights.

During the passage of his forces through three enemy lines of mountain defensive positions, Rommel made repeated use of stealthy approaches to surprise the enemy and to infiltrate into his positions. On several occasions he took advantage of adverse weather, the fog of war, and fluid front line situations to deceive the enemy into believing that his troops were Italians. In one situation he prepared careful fire support and disposed his troops for a penetration operation, but in hopes of taking it by surprise he ordered a select squad under a handpicked leader to "move up the path as if he and his men were Italians returning from the front, to penetrate into the hostile position and capture the garrison. . . . They were to do this with a minimum of shooting and hand grenade throwing. In case a battle developed they were assured of fire protection and support by the entire detachment." In this instance they succeeded in silently capturing a hostile dugout with 17 Italians and a machine gun. The gap was widened as dozens of additional Italians were captured by approaching their positions from the flank and rear, and the way was opened to move even deeper into the enemy positions—all without firing a shot.

The stealth of these attacks was maintained at all cost, and if some enemy soldiers chose to run rather than surrender, Rommel's men "did not fire on this fleeing enemy for fear of alarming the garrisons of positions located still higher up." Rommel found that "The farther we penetrated into the hostile zone of defense, the less prepared were the garrisons for our arrival, and the easier the fighting."

Recent large-scale night infiltration/penetration operations into Kuwait by the U.S. Marine Corps during the 1991 Gulf War have proven again the value of this classic technique. In this operation the 1st Marine Division under Major General Myatt executed a classical light infantry penetration with two regimental task forces (TF Taro and TF Grizzly), with a third, mechanized, task force (TF Ripper) passing through their gap and acting as an exploitation element which didn't stop until it reached Kuwait City. This operation and extensive operations in the 7th Infantry Division (Light), combining infiltration operations with imaginative use of passive night-vision devices and thermal imagery devices in rough terrain, demonstrate the tremendous potential for successful execution of light infantry infiltration operations on future battlefields.

### Penetration, *Aufrollen, Schwerpunkt,* and *Auftragstaktik*

There are occasions when the commands of the sovereign need not be obeyed . . . When you see the correct course, act: do not wait for orders.

Sun Tzu[5]

When the initial passage through enemy lines of defense could not be accomplished solely through stealth, extensive fire support was required.

Rommel was a master at using his machine guns to provide this fire support. He used extreme care in the placement and preparation of his machine guns, siting each gun himself and personally briefing each machine-gun crew on its field of fire and its role in the operation.

The machine guns would suppress the enemy line, and a small penetration element would rupture enemy lines and begin to roll up the flanks. During World War II these side thrusts to exploit the penetration and protect the flanks of the main body were institutionalized in the concept of the *Aufrollen*.

While the *Aufrollen* sealed off and protected the flanks the bulk of Rommel's forces, the exploitation element, would move rapidly through the gap and begin infiltration deep into the enemy rear. In World War II this highly flexible concentration of forces seeking out the weakest point of enemy resistance and driving deep into the enemy's rear would be known as the *Schwerpunkt*, a term first used by Clausewitz, which translates literally as "heavy force." The *Schwerpunkt* was to become such a vital aspect of the Wehrmacht's way of war that Field Marshall von Hindenberg held that "an attack without a *Schwerpunkt* is like a man without character."

Again, the penetration was not the objective; the objective was to get into the enemy's rear. The penetration, the *Schwerpunkt*, and the *Aufrollen* were all a means to an end, and that end was decisive military action in the enemy's rear.

Rommel stated that during operations behind enemy lines he "did not worry about contact to right and left," believing that his element was "able to protect their own flanks" against a confused and unsuspecting enemy and knowing that there were strong reserves behind him. The strong reserve is, of course, an essential element in maneuver warfare. The German High Command encouraged and supported such penetration operations in their attack orders, which in this case stated: "Without limiting the day's activities in space and time, continue the advance to the west, knowing that we have strong reserves near and behind us."

On one occasion Rommel flatly disobeyed a written order from his battalion commander to pull back. Knowing the commander's intent, and knowing that "the battalion order was given without knowledge of the situation," Rommel went on to execute a successful attack and secure Mount Matajur. His relationship with his battalion commander was such that he knew he could do this, and not only was he *not* reprimanded for this action, but both he and his battalion commander received the *Pour le Mérite* for this achievement.

A somewhat similar action occurred during the 1989 invasion of Panama, when an AC-130 gunship crew refused repeated orders to fire on an enemy position, because they had reason to believe there were friendly troops there. It turned out that there *were* friendly troops on that location and the crew of the gunship were decorated for their refusal to obey orders. Commending individuals for refusing to obey uninformed orders is an important step in developing an *Auftragstaktik* environment. Hopefully this incident indicates that the Prussian concept embodied in the classic statement, "The King made you a major because he believed you knew when *not* to obey" exists to some degree in our armed forces. But the real test is in what would happen if Rommel or this AC-130 crew had been wrong. Obviously some form of reprimand is appropriate when initiative results in failure, but if we truly believe in giving subordinates room to make "errors of commission" (as opposed to "errors of omission," which should never be tolerated), then our judgment must be tempered with a desire to continue to nurture the precious flame of initiative in the breasts of subordinates. This is a principle of leader development that is well represented by the defense of a controversial incident involving cadets at the British Royal Military Academy at Sandhurst. "We have learned," responded the authorities at Sandhurst, "that a wild young man can learn wisdom as he grows older—if he survives—but a spiritless young man cannot learn the dash that wins battles."[6]

Throughout the Isonzo operation Rommel demonstrated extraordinary initiative and spirit, but his actions were guided by the overall commander's intent, and the combination of (1) a high command which delegated the highest levels of independence and freedom of action to its subordinates with (2) a subordinate who had the initiative to utilize this freedom was one of the keys to the tremendous German success in that battle. But the repercussions of this success went beyond its operational and strategic impact on World War I. The 12th Battle of Isonzo, and its widespread publication in *Attacks*, set the standard for the *Auftragstaktik*, or mission orders, environment, which was essential to the success of a later generation of German soldiers.

## The Exploitation

When a dam is broken, the water cascades with irresistible force. Now the shape of an army resembles water. Take advantage of the enemy's unpreparedness; attack him when he does not expect it; avoid his strength and strike his emptiness, and like water, none can oppose you.

Sun Tzu[7]

Once he had penetrated the enemy front line, Rommel was repeatedly able to capture units far larger than his simply by approaching them from a direction they had thought to be secure. Rommel's confidence, poise, and audacity were the key elements in convincing the enemy to surrender. When a unit feels itself to be safe behind its own friendly lines, it is particularly vulnerable once it is cut off from the authority of its superiors and the support of its sister units. Rommel often captured hundreds of prisoners with only a few audacious soldiers. Although some potential enemy forces may be somewhat less inclined to surrender than were Rommel's Italians (or Schwarzkopf's Iraqis), all human beings are vulnerable to the same psychological processes when they are surrounded or when they are suddenly confronted with aggressive action at a time when they imagined themselves to be safe. The potential for such mass surrenders is there for any unit that can penetrate the enemy front line and rapidly and audaciously exploit its position in the enemy's rear.

The fact that Rommel was able to surprise so many enemy forces led him to strongly emphasize the importance of 360-degree security by all units, regardless of their proximity to the front, and the requirement for providing adequate patrolling operations. He stated that "it is not enough to have watchful sentries in the main position; the forward area must be constantly surveyed by patrols, especially in bad weather and in irregular and covered terrain." Today a 360-degree application of early warning systems and thermal imagery devices would be an important part of this process.

During these operations behind enemy lines any close-range, chance contacts with moving enemy elements were made on twisty mountain trails and roads. Rommel almost always "got the drop" on the enemy during these chance contacts, since his personnel were alert and expecting contact and the enemy was moving through the (assumed) safety of his own rear lines. One technique used repeatedly and successfully was "holding the enemy, who was [usually] superior in numbers and weapons, frontally and simultaneously attacking him in flank and rear with assault squads." During these contacts in the enemy rear the only fire support available to Rommel was his own internal machine-gun assets. In the absence of artillery support, he was a master at stripping out his detachment's medium *and* light machine guns to place massed fire on the enemy while his troops approached. A modern-day equivalent might be found in massing the grenade launchers and squad automatic weapons of infantry squads.

On one occasion, Rommel took advantage of a bend in a mountain pass (behind the enemy lines on a main supply route) to collect enemy vehicles as they went about their business. At one time they took over 100 prisoners and 50 vehicles. In ambushes against a cautious and deployed enemy, he attacked at maximum effective range. Against an unprepared and undeployed enemy, he waited until they were at point-blank range, usually giving them an opportunity to surrender first.

## Light Infantry Operations in Restrictive Terrain

The wise general sees to it that his troops feed on the enemy, for one bushel of the enemy's provisions is equivalent to twenty of his . . . In transporting provisions for a distance of one thousand *li*, twenty bushels will be consumed in delivering one to the enemy . . . If difficult terrain must be crossed even more is required.

Sun Tzu[8]

One of the most difficult and impressive aspects of this operation was that it was conducted in rugged mountainous terrain. The capability of light infantry to conduct movement of heavily laden soldiers over this kind of terrain is a source of considerable active discussion and concern among soldiers. The fact that Rommel was able to move his command, burdened with loads up to 90 pounds, over this terrain and through "unique, hostile mountain fortifications" is a testimony to the capability of light infantry.

Past experience with ammunition supply problems in mountain operations led the German mountain infantry companies to carry extra ammunition for the machine-gun companies. Although the weight of the machine guns slowed down the rate of movement, they were echeloned far forward so that there was "a strong fire force right at hand" if they met resistance. This was not always the case, and depending on the tactical situation, Rommel sometimes moved forward in an almost helter-skelter fashion to secure deep objectives, leaving slow-moving personnel behind to come up when they could. One interesting point in this mountain movement is the fact that Rommel made extensive use of wire communications, always running wire behind him as he moved forward. Often this wire served as a navigation aid for follow-on elements and runners, who were able to use the wire as a guide during night movements in pouring rain. Today, bad radio communications, poor land navigation, and breaks in contact are some of the recurring problems in the conduct of mountain operations. Combined with this is potential enemy emphasis on radio electronic combat, which can make radio communications an extremely risky business. The fact that Rommel was able to run extensive wire communications in this environment and then use it as a navigational aid is a useful lesson.

In mountainous terrain the resupply of light infantry forces penetrating deep into enemy territory is a another significant problem, but the momentum of his attack made it possible for Rommel's forces to repeatedly partake of the supplies found in the enemy vehicles and positions they captured. In the attack his unit traveled light, knowing that if they were stalled they would be able to bring forward their mess elements, and if they were successful, they would be able to live off of the enemy's supplies. He and his men made good use of captured enemy pack animals and bicycles during attacks. (Had he needed vehicular mobility it would have been readily available to him by using the vehicles captured in his ambushes, but his strength was in his ability to approach from unexpected directions over rough terrain.) In a later operation they were even able to use clean, dry underwear and sleeping gear from a captured Italian laundry depot, and on several occasions they came to rely "on the abundant weapons and stores of ammunition" captured from the Italians. The most common enemy asset, and that which seemed to have given him and his men the most joy, was the enemy's food. "The contents of the [captured] vehicles offered us starved warriors

will reinforce the penetration, but many others will (for a variety of reasons) have to engage in more conventional operations. Sun Tzu referred to this dichotomy between maneuver and attrition forces as "ordinary" and "extraordinary" forces. Sun Tzu's "extraordinary-ordinary" dichotomy is a good way to look at maneuver vs. attrition warfare. The objective is to unhinge the enemy's defense so as to make his positions no longer relevant, ideally defeating him without a fight. But there *are* times when both extraordinary *and* ordinary (i.e., maneuver and attrition) forces are needed, and often the key is in finding the right balance between the two. Brig. Gen. (then Colonel) Huba Wass de Czege made just such a point in a letter to *Army* magazine when he said:

> People who read maneuver warfare advocates as advocating "dancing around the enemy" or "bloodless war" have misread them. Maneuver warfare advocates do say, and I most whole heartedly agree, that defeat mechanisms are not limited to physically killing people and breaking things. The will to fight is at the nub of all defeat mechanisms.
>
> In many instances . . . the only effective way to get at the will is to kill and break in a sustained, pitched fight: to win by direct application of superior force, as Gen. Douglas MacArthur was forced to do at Buna and Gona in New Guinea.
>
> One should always look for a way to break the enemy's will and capacity to resist in other ways, however. If a strongpoint can be passed, invested and reduced on our terms it should be.
>
> Gen. MacArthur bypassed some islands which were later evacuated by the Japanese themselves. This maneuver strategy was the major element of Gen. MacArthur's blueprint for victory.

Sun Tzu presaged the need for maneuver-oriented operations over two thousand years ago, and MacArthur refined them in the Pacific in World War II, but it was the German army in World War II that first began to institutionalize maneuver warfare. The so called "Hutier tactics" used so successfully by Rommel during this battle were named after General Oskar von Hutier, whose German Eighth Army first used these tactics in the attack on Riga on 1 September 1917. The same "storm troop, soft spot" tactics were then used at the 12th Battle of Isonzo (also called Caporetto), where Rommel gained his fame and the Italians lost over 300,000 men and were almost taken out of the war. Hutier tactics were then used for the first time on the western front on 30 November 1917 at Cambrai in response to the British tank attack, thereby successfully responding to a powerful technological innovation with an equally powerful doctrinal innovation. In March 1918 the Germans applied Hutier tactics on a large scale on the western front in one last effort to win the war. These new tactics:

> succeeded far beyond expectation, particularly in the sector of Hutier, "the apostle of the surprise attack," where his army advanced without check. He took 50,000 prisoners, crushed the Fifth British Army, and drove a wedge between British and French forces. Fortunately for the allies, Ludendorff at this point demonstrated a singular lack of strategic grasp. Of the three armies he had employed in the offensive, only Hutier's continued to make progress; yet Ludendorff failed to exploit this success by redirecting the other two along Hutier's axis. Had Ludendorff done so, he could possibly have split the French and British armies and perhaps gained a Sedan 22 years earlier.[11]

But that is not the end of the story for Rommel, or for Hutier tactics. The history of warfare is a record of natural selection in the harshest of all possible environments, and in this "survival of the fittest" environment the army that completes the next evolutionary development will have a significant advantage over its enemies. Germany learned from its defeat and developed a new style of warfare in World War II. Defeat is often a catalyst for change—assuming, of course, that your enemies permit you to remain in existence long enough to learn from your defeat. Just as Germany's defeat and humiliation in World War I forced them to develop a new stage of warfare, so too does America's defeat and humiliation in Vietnam appear to have made possible the reforms that resulted in our own development and our overwhelming victory in Iraq.

Of course, Rommel was *only* fighting the Italians, the Wehrmacht was *only* fighting the French and the Poles, the Israeli Defense Force was *only* fighting the Arabs, and General Schwarzkopf was *only* fighting the Iraqis. And today we downplay the degree to which each of these "classically inept" armies were respected and feared in their time. But the Italians were beating the Austrians quite handily when Rommel's "supple offensive tactics" (i.e., the Hutier, "storm trooper" infiltration tactics that represented embryonic maneuver warfare doctrine) caused the collapse of their entire front. Looking at the numbers, equipment, and the expertise involved, no one in the West dreamed that France (which had numerical superiority in tanks and men[12]) would fall to the Wehrmacht as quickly and easily as she did. The Arabs were equipped with the best and largest armies money could buy when they were beaten by the badly outnumbered Israelis in seven days in 1967, and again in 1973. And does anyone remember the predictions of "thousands" of casualties we would suffer against the "battle-hardened" Iraqi Republican Guard? Was there *any* single major analyst who called that one right?

In every one of these examples we see the same lopsided casualty rate, the same enormous numbers of prisoners, and the same shock and surprise on the part of the "experts" who had failed to take doctrine and human frailty into account. What these cases all have in common is *not* the relative size or technology of the armies involved.

In every one of these cases the key factor is doctrine—a doctrine that is, perhaps, an evolutionary new development in warfare; a doctrine systematically focused on the center of gravity in order to defeat the enemy's *will* to fight rather than his *ability* to fight. Therein lies the path to Mount Matajur, the path to glory, and the path to decisive victory.

# Notes

1. All quotes, unless otherwise noted, are from Erwin Rommel's *Attacks* (New York: Athena Press, 1979).

2. Sun Tzu, *The Art of War* (New York: Oxford Press, 1971), p. 77.

3. Ibid., p. 101.

4. These concepts are Rommel's, but specific organizational terms such as gaps, surfaces, reconnaissance pull, suppression element, penetration element, and exploitation element are all drawn from William S. Lind and Col. Michael Wyly's *Maneuver Warfare Handbook* (Boulder, Colo.: Westview Press, 1985). This excellent book rates with *Attacks* as an essential maneuver warfare primer which provides an organized and systematic set of basic maneuver warfare terms and concepts.

5. Sun Tzu, p. 112.

6. As quoted in John Masters' *Bugles and a Tiger* (New York: Viking Press, 1956), p. 41. Masters' autobiographical account in *Bugles and a Tiger* is an excellent example of light infantry operations in low-density warfare in the British army prior to World War II. His sequel, *The Road Past Mandalay* (New York: Harpers, 1961), tells of his experience with battalion- and brigade-strength Chindit operations behind Japanese lines in Burma during World War II. *The Road Past Mandalay* serves as a superb example of the potential and the limitations associated with light infantry, maneuver warfare operations in mid- to high-density warfare. (I have employed here Lind's terms "low-, mid-, and high-*density* warfare," rather than the currently doctrinally correct terms "low-, mid-, and high-*intensity* warfare." To the soldier getting shot at, it is *all* equally intense; the distinguishing factor is the density of the combatants.)

7. Sun Tzu, p. 89.

8. Ibid., p. 75.

9. Ibid., pp. 69, 73.

10. Ibid., p. 92.

11. See John English's *A Perspective on Infantry* (New York: Praeger Publishers, 1981), pp. 26, 36. English goes on to point out that there is no reason to believe that Hutier was actually responsible for inventing these tactics. "If any one deserves credit," says English, "it is probably Ludendorff."

12. von Mellenthin and Stofli's *NATO under Attack* (Durham, N.C.: Duke University Press, 1984) provides an excellent historical recap:

| Numbers | France | Germany |
|---|---|---|
| Men | 3,500,000[a] | 2,800,000 |
| Tanks | 3,800 | 2,574 |
| Antitank guns | 12,600 | 12,800 |

a. Combines numbers for French, British, Dutch, and Belgian troops.

In addition, von Mellenthin reports that the French are generally accepted to have had technological superiority in tanks (the French SOMUA vs. the German PzKwIII) and antitank guns (47mm vs. 37mm). The only clear-cut numerical and technological superiority the Germans had was in tactical aircraft.

# Maneuver Warfare in the Western Desert: Wavell and the 1st Libyan Offensive, 1940–1941

## Harold E. Raugh, Jr.

German Field Marshal Erwin Rommel, the "Desert Fox," has been recognized and lauded as one of the most successful practitioners of maneuver warfare. As such, military historians have placed great credence in the observation of one of Rommel's key subordinates that "their unwieldy and rigidly methodical technique of command, their over-systematic issuing of orders down to the last detail, . . . and their poor adaptability to the changing course of the battle were also much to blame for the British failures" in the North African war.[1] While there is an amount of validity to this assertion pertaining to British operations conducted after Rommel's arrival in North Africa on 12 February 1941, it fails to consider the highly successful British First Libyan Offensive, 7 December 1940 to 7 February 1941. Known as Operation Compass, this offensive, conceived and directed at the strategic level by Gen. Sir Archibald P. Wavell, Commander-in-Chief, Middle East, and executed at the operational level by Lt. Gen. Richard N. O'Connor (commanding the Western Desert Force), is an outstanding example of the successful application of the tenets of maneuver warfare.[2] The success of Operation Compass directly refutes the aforementioned German statement, and inspired one professional journal of the U. S. Army to note contemporaneously that:

> Generations hence, when the military student or the embryo military leader is looking in the pages of history for examples of leadership calling for thorough preparation, blinding surprise, whirlwind attack, and relentless pursuit [,] he will turn to the Libyan Campaign and need look no further.[3]

This sentiment was echoed by British Prime Minister Winston Churchill, who opined that Operation Compass "will long be studied as a model of the military art."[4]

334

Upon Italy's belated entry on 11 June 1940 into the Second World War, Wavell had a total of some 85,775 soldiers scattered throughout his immense 3.5-million-square-mile theater of operations, with only about 36,000 troops, none of which were organized in complete formations, in Egypt. Against this, the Italians were able to muster about 215,000 Italian and native troops in Libya, and another 290,000 in Italian East Africa, equaling about half a million enemy troops.[5] French forces in North Africa, Syria, and French Somaliland, upon which Allied plans for the defense of the Middle East depended, were effectively neutralized by government intransigence following the French commander-in-chief's 11 June 1940 declaration that it would be necessary for France to cease hostilities.

Wavell had foreseen such circumstances, and had first directed Lt. Gen. Henry M. Wilson (General Officer Commanding-in-Chief, British Troops in Egypt, and later O'Connor's nominal superior) in October 1939 to study the possibilities of an offensive against Italy in the Western Desert. Wavell, who had many years earlier internalized the mind-set, or ethos, of maneuver warfare, wrote again to Wilson on 10 May 1940: "I want a report as early as possible," Wavell instructed, issuing Wilson a precise mission-type order based upon his intent, "on the practicability of taking offensive action against the Italian posts on the Eastern front of Libya as soon as possible after the outbreak of war."[6] Wavell proposed the capture of the Jarabub Oasis and a post at Atseat by a rapid thrust of the 7th Armored Division. Typically, Wavell, who trusted his subordinate and actively encouraged his initiative and innovation, stated he was "ready to accept responsibility for taking a considerable degree of risk, administrative as well as tactical," in order to attempt to gain a moral superiority over the Italians upon the outbreak of war.[7]

Within hours of the Italian declaration of war, actual hostilities began with the British audaciously capturing Italian outposts on the Libyan-Egyptian frontier. Wavell was faced with a marked numerical inferiority in manpower and material. Rather than implement a contingency plan to foster revolt among desert tribes in Libya, Wavell was better able to utilize his scant resources in the establishment of the Long Range Patrols (L.R.P.), later renamed the Long Range Desert Group. Starting in August 1940, the L.R.P. wreaked havoc and psychologically emasculated the Italians out of all proportion to their small numbers. Wavell's adroit employment of his sparse troop assets, which included simultaneous strikes at Italian positions hundreds of miles apart, served as a useful force multiplier, generating fear and uncertainty among the Italians and magnifying the perceived potency of the British threat. From Italian prisoners, the British learned of the exaggerated effects of their raids and patrols: "there were two . . . three . . . five British armoured divisions operating," they exclaimed.[8] Wavell's deception and initial attempts to destroy the enemy's will to resist met with unparalleled success.

While waiting during the latter half of the summer of 1940 for an expected Italian attack to seize the Suez Canal, Wavell did not remain idle, and reconnoitered the newly constructed British defenses in the Western Desert on numerous occasions. On 11 September 1940, Wavell instructed the Joint Planning Staff to prepare for the eventual invasion of Libya, this statement of intent serving as the true starting point for Operation Compass.

The cautious and lethargic Italian advance began on 13 September 1940, and after covering 65 or so miles of barren desert to Sidi Barrani in four days, halted unexpectedly. After returning from another personal reconnaissance in the Western Desert on 19 September, Wavell issued mission-oriented guidance for a counterstroke to be prepared against the enemy when they reached Mersa Matruh. Wilson and O'Connor, knowing they had their superior's trust and confidence, had both, to a degree, anticipated Wavell's new instructions. This was due not only to a 5 September discussion between Wavell and Wilson on the upcoming battle, but also because it was obvious that the Italians were now in a vulnerable position. Wavell emphasized his intent that this proposed battle should "be planned with a view to the enemy's complete destruction, certainly as soon as our armoured reinforcements . . . are in action [;] this should be well within our power."[9]

As British reinforcements arrived in the Middle East, Wavell revised his guidance for the impending attack on the Italian forces. On 20 October 1940 Wavell issued instructions to Wilson to make an attack on the stationary Italian positions in the Sofafi–Sidi Barrani–Buqbuq area: "a short and swift [operation], lasting from four to five days at the most, and taking advantage of the element of surprise."[10] To cover the distances required without enemy detection, Wavell recommended that two night movements of 40 miles each be conducted, followed by an attack early the next day. Wavell envisioned the assault to resemble a double envelopment, with the 4th Italian Division on the right along the coast, and the reinforced 7th Armored Division attacking on the left the Sofafi group of camps. A pincer movement would follow, cutting off the Italian Nibeiwa and Tummar camps. To maintain secrecy, Wavell concluded: "I do not wish the contents of this note disclosed or the plans discussed with anyone except your Brigadier General Staff, General O'Connor and General Creagh."[11] Wilson took this plan to O'Connor, and observed that, "Neither of us liked it" due to the extended and difficult march the 7th Armored Division would have to conduct, and the unreliability of controlling such distant forces with the signal resources available.[12]

O'Connor believed that the key weakness of the Italian camps lay in the fact that they were out of supporting distance of each other, and by using the element of surprise audaciously, the camps could be defeated in detail. The modified general plan was to initially destroy or capture enemy forces in the Nibeiwa and Tummar camps, while the 7th Armored Division conducted a screen to prevent enemy reinforcements coming from the Sofafi area and to protect the left flank of the attacking 4th Indian Division. If successful, the 7th Armored Division would drive northwards to the sea and sever the Italian line of retreat to the west, and the 4th Indian Division would attack the enemy camps around Sidi Barrani. After a small British column isolated the Maktila camp, which would be crushed later, the Armored Division would advance to Buqbuq to cut off all the Italians there from Sollum.[13] Wilson took this revised plan to Wavell in Cairo, who approved it and directed the completion of detailed planning for this coming attack.

Wilson and O'Connor completed the detailed planning and preparations for Compass while Wavell was attending conferences and reconnoitering the terrain in East Africa. Shortly after his return on 2 November 1940, Wavell issued a confirmatory note to Wilson, his only formal written directive for this offensive. Wavell wrote that he recognized the risks involved in such an operation, but was fully prepared to accept them:

> In everything but numbers we are superior to the enemy. We are more highly trained, we have better equipment. We know the ground better and are better accustomed to desert conditions. Above all

we have stouter hearts and greater traditions and are fighting a worthier cause.[14]

Originally it was planned to launch Compass at the end of November 1940, but the drain of resources for Greece (after the 28 October 1940 Italian attack on that country) required a postponement until the first week of December. During November the enemy was further deceived by the Long Range Patrols, which attacked Italian outposts and airstrips incessantly and conducted raids deep inside enemy territory, diverting the Italian commander-in-chief's attention from Wavell's true intentions and giving the impression of "simultaneous appearances at places 600 miles apart."[15]

But this was not the only technique Wavell employed to deceive the enemy. Wavell later wrote cryptically,

> I attempted, through certain channels known to my Intelligence, to convey to the enemy the impression that my forces in the Western Desert had been seriously weakened by the sending of reinforcements to Greece and that further withdrawals were contemplated.[16]

Through Security Intelligence Middle Ease (SIME), a part of the Middle East Intelligence Center (MEIC), Wavell was able to funnel deceptive information through double agents and other operatives whose function was to pass such disinformation to the enemy.[17] Simultaneously, the double-agent network was spreading information on a massive British troop buildup on the Italian right flank in the desert. Italian reconnaissance airplanes produced photographs that confirmed these stories, but these "reinforcements" were actually dummy tanks made of inflatable rubber, heavy field guns composed of logs on supports with a length of drain pipe fitted to the end of each containing chemicals that produced realistic flashes, and lastly "a platoon of natives who drove their camels and horses across the dunes dragging wooden frame devices behind them" which stirred up the desert dust and from a distance gave the appearance of a moving motorized column.[18] These highly effective ruses were almost an exact replication of the ploys implemented superbly by Gen. Sir Edmund H. H. Allenby, which Wavell had a role in conceiving and executing, which permitted the Egyptian Expeditionary Force to break through the Turkish positions in the Jordan Valley in September 1918. Essential logistical and administrative preparations were also completed during this period, with both divisions establishing forward field supply depots.

Training Exercise No. 1 was conducted on 25 and 26 November 1940 near Mersa Matruh; it was in fact a rehearsal for Compass. Camps representing the enemy Nibeiwa and Tummar camps were marked out to scale on the ground, although this fact was known to only the few aware of the upcoming operation. The soldiers thought this to be a routine training exercise, with an intimation that a further exercise would be held at a later date. This exercise was productive, especially in terms of learning lessons about the moonlight approach march and improving the techniques of attacking an enemy camp in the desert. After this exercise, in which live ammunition was used, an after-action review was conducted by the senior and leading participants.

On 28 November 1940, perhaps as a result of the first corps training exercise, perceptions of the efficacy of his deception plans, or an increase in his self-confidence, Wavell issued a directive to Wilson urging a full and bold exploitation of the expected enemy defeat in Compass. Stressing the tactical and administrative requirements of such an exploitation, Wavell desired to "make certain that if a big opportunity occurs we are prepared morally, mentally and administratively, to use it to the fullest."[19]

The final conference for Compass, presided over by Wavell, was held on 4 December 1940. After an introduction and other remarks, O'Connor "explained the stages of this limited three-day operation which, starting with an assault on the Italian armed camps of Nibeiwa and East and West Tummar at dawn on 9 December, would in all probability end with the capture of Sidi Barrani."[20] After the final details were coordinated, Wilson, on Wavell's instigation, issued an operations order to O'Connor on 5 December. This was the only written order to emanate from Headquarters, British Troops in Egypt, for Compass, and confirmed the proceedings of the previous day's conference: "The plans which you have drawn up and which you described . . . are approved."[21]

On the afternoon of Saturday, 7 December 1940, Wavell and his family, with uncharacteristic ostentation, visited the races at Gezira, and throughout that weekend Wavell was observed by local Egyptian society engaging in lavish entertainment. While Wavell appeared to be frivolously enjoying himself, the desert sands were witnessing the stealthy movement of the Western Desert Force to their rendezvous positions.

The total British force consisted of about 31,000 men, 120 guns, 275 tanks, and 60 armored cars against an estimated total Italian strength, situated within the Egyptian border, of some 80,000 soldiers, with 250 guns and 120 tanks.[22]

One of the most crucial yet intricate and delicate aspects of Compass was the preliminary movement of some 75 miles through open desert for the majority of the troops. The entire Western Desert Force was either mechanized or motorized, which greatly facilitated movement. Although the march times and actual distances varied by unit, both divisions were at their first rendezvous point by the evening of 7 December 1940, when most units were issued the orders that Training Exercise No. 2 would in fact be an actual attack on the Italian camps. Both divisions conducted the second phase of the approach march during the daylight hours of 8 December 1940, and by 5:00 P.M., formations had reached their pre-designated rally points.

The last phase of the approach march was conducted under a moonlit sky, with all units arriving undetected in their assembly areas, within striking distance of the enemy, by 1:00 A.M., 9 December 1940. To help conceal the noise of this movement, British planes bombed simultaneously the Italian camps, and flew over the area throughout the night. These sorties had a dual purpose, in that they also kept the Italian pilots grounded, thus prohibiting them from conducting reconnaissance flights. The Royal Navy also provided a monitor and gunboats which bombarded Sidi Barrani and Maktila. Less than four hours later, in the bitter cold, a battalion of the 4th Indian Division opened fire on the Nibeiwa camp from the east, thus diverting the Italians' attention there. After an hour of desultory firing, a deceptive silence again reigned in the desert until 7:15 A.M., when the 72 guns of the division artillery began an intense bombardment, again from the east, supporting the scheme of maneuver.[23] Shortly thereafter the infantry ("I") tanks of the 7th Royal Tank Regiment struck the northwest corner of the Nibeiwa camp, thus surprising the defenders and avoiding a frontal attack, followed by assaulting infantry from the 11th Indian Infantry Brigade. By 8:25 A.M., Nibeiwa had fallen, with over 20 Italian medium tanks and some 2,000 Italian soldiers being captured.[24] That afternoon, following an artillery preparation, the 4th Indian Division captured the Tummar camps, and was directed to push on toward Sidi Barrani.

The 7th Armored Division had effectively screened the left flank of the 4th Indian Division, had captured Azzizaya, and was fully astride the Sidi Barrani–Buqbuq road. Selby Force, which had a few days earlier emplaced a brigade of dummy tanks in the desert,[25] attempted audaciously to prevent the enemy's escape from Maktila, but was unable to do so because of darkness and bad terrain.

Flushed with an indomitable spirit of victory, the Western Desert Force captured Sidi Barrani and destroyed two additional Italian divisions on 10 December 1940, and Selby Force compelled the surrender of two Italian divisions caught in the open between Mersa Matruh and Sidi Barrani. The backbone of Italian resistance was crushed, with the Western Desert Force continuing the pursuit and mopping up the few remaining Italian pockets of resistance the following day. The capture of Sidi Barrani, for all practical purposes, ended the first phase of Compass, and in three days of fighting (9–11 December 1940), O'Connor's Force captured 38,300 prisoners, 73 tanks, and 422 guns, at a cost of 133 killed, 387 wounded, and 8 missing.[26] The number of enemy soldiers captured was so great that on the night of 10 December one battalion headquarters reported that it was impossible to count the unexpectedly large number of prisoners, and that "there were about five acres of officers and two hundred acres of other ranks."[27]

Amidst competing demands on his meager resources, Wavell was able to continue Operation Compass, and from the numerically superior enemy capture Bardia (4 January 1941), Tobruk (22 January 1941), and Beda Fomm (7 February 1941). After the Battle of Beda Fomm, O'Connor signaled Wavell, "Fox killed in the open . . ." O'Connor, typically understating this achievement, observed, "I think this may be termed a complete victory, as none of the enemy escaped."[28]

"The entire campaign [Compass]," commented insightfully one U.S. Army journal, "was nothing short of miraculous."[29] During the two months from 7 December 1940 to 7 February 1941, Wavell's "Army of the Nile" advanced over 500 miles. It totally destroyed the Italian 10th Army of 9½ divisions and captured some 130,000 prisoners, 400 tanks, and 1,290 guns, at a cost of only 500 British and Dominion soldiers killed, 1,373 wounded, and 55 missing.[30] Throughout Compass, the British never employed a force of more than two divisions, or about 31,000 men.

With the capture of Sidi Barrani, the objectives of Compass had been achieved. Furthermore, the operation is a superb example of the tremendous potential of maneuver warfare. Wavell, Wilson, and O'Connor had been deeply imbued with this thought process, this approach to warfare, early in their careers. All three had studied at the Staff College the American Civil War campaigns of Lt. Gen. Thomas J. "Stonewall" Jackson, and were thus well versed with directive control, the necessity to attack the enemy's weakness and avoid his strength, the need for mutual trust and respect throughout the chain of command, and the importance of maneuver in relation to speed. In addition, whereas all three had participated in futile frontal assaults against an entrenched enemy during the Great War, Wavell had learned the nuances of maneuver warfare while serving under Allenby in Egypt and Palestine in 1917–1918, and O'Connor had commanded troops in the relative fluidity of the Italian front in 1918. Thus, by experience, training, and temperament, these three officers understood and were predisposed to practice maneuver warfare.

Wavell regularly issued, based upon his intent, mission-type orders to his subordinates. There was mutual trust and respect throughout this chain of command. Wavell also gave the authority and responsibility to Wilson and O'Connor to conduct the detailed planning and coordination and to use their own good judgment, intelligence, and initiative in the process. Innovation and flexibility were encouraged at the lowest level.

Since Wavell could not rely on either a manpower or material superiority, he had to pit the British strengths—to include the Long Range Patrols and other deception measures—to achieve a psychological ascendancy over the Italians and instill fear, anxiety, and uncertainty into the enemy soldiers. In the plan for Compass itself, the British, having demoralized the Italians throughout the preceding months, realized they would have to attack the enemy's weaknesses, and by skillfully using the element of surprise, took advantage of the fact that the Italian camps were out of supporting distance from each other. This was the initial focus of effort for Compass, where it was believed a decision could be forced. The British combined arms attack began violently, after a previous feint, early on 9 December 1940, using the naval gunfire and field artillery's firepower to support the scheme of maneuver.[31] As analyzed earlier, the initial phase of Compass was over two days later, and the entire campaign was brought to a successful conclusion on 7 February 1941.

Wavell, at the strategic level, was responsible for the Compass plan's initiation and concept and for the overall direction of the offensive, whereas O'Connor, as his subordinate and commander of the Western Desert Force, was properly responsible for its detailed planning and coordination and its execution at the operational level of war.

Wavell's generalship throughout Compass was outstanding. He continually oversaw the direction of the offensive, and personally visited the commanders and soldiers on a frequent basis. Whenever possible, usually in conjunction with his visits to the "front," he reconnoitered the terrain and areas of operations. He planned the extent of the different phases of Compass, and personally issued his commander's intent and guidance before a significant attack, such as the attacks on Bardia and Tobruk. He then gave his subordinate commanders the authority and responsibility, and full support, to accomplish those objectives. When success was achieved, he ensured his subordinate commanders and units received the recognition commensurate with their contribution. Operation Compass, as a result, was highly successful, and demonstrates the great potential of maneuver warfare.

Wavell, whom Rommel believed was the only British general "who showed a touch of genius,"[32] was an innovative, progressive, and farsighted soldier throughout his long career. He was convinced that the "ideal officer must be afraid of nothing—not even a new idea."[33] Wavell's realistic admonition is especially applicable to those who doubt the efficacy and viability of maneuver warfare.

# Notes

1. Lt. Gen. Fritz Bayerlein, quoted in B. H. Liddell Hart, ed., *The Rommel Papers,* trans. Paul Findlay (1953; reprint, New York: Harcourt, Brace, n.d.), p. 184. General Bayerlein served as chief of staff of the Afrika Korps during the winter campaign of 1940–1941.

2. For a detailed assessment of Wavell's generalship as Commander-in-Chief, Middle East, which includes Operation Compass, see the author's *Wavell in the Middle East, 1939–1941: A Study in Generalship*, with a foreword by Field Marshal Lord Carver (London: Brassey's Defense Publishers, 1991). Interestingly, the entry for "Wavell, Sir Archibald," in *Current Biography 1941* notes that Wavell "is variously called 'The Fox', 'The Wizard', 'The Mediterranean Magician' and 'The Bloodhound'." *Current Biography 1941* (New York: H.W. Wilson, 1941), p. 902.

3. "Britain's Soldier of the Hour," *Military Review*, March 1941, p. 8.

4. Winston S. Churchill, "Give Us the Tools and We Will Finish the Job," in *The War Speeches of Winston Churchill*, vol. II, *The Unrelenting Struggle*, comp. Charles Eade (London: Cassell, 1942), p. 57.

5. Gen. Sir Archibald P. Wavell, Despatch: "Operations in the Middle East from August, 1939 to November, 1940," third supplement to *The London Gazette*, 13 June 1948, pp. 2998, 2999.

6. Letter, "Secret and Personal," Gen. Sir Archibald P. Wavell to Lt. Gen. H. M. Wilson, C.B., D.S.O., General Officer Commanding in Chief, British Troops in Egypt, 10 May 1940, General Headquarters, Middle East, Cairo, ref. C.R.M.E./525/G, WO 201/152, Public Record Office, Kew Richmond, Surrey, England (hereafter cited as PRO).

7. Ibid. For additional details of mission-oriented command and control, called *Auftragstaktik* in the German army, see Richard E. Simpkin, *Race to the Swift: Thoughts on Twenty-First Century Warfare* (London: Brassey's Defense Publishers, 1985), pp. 12, 13, 227–240; Lt. Col. Knut Czeslik, "*Auftragstaktik*: Thoughts of a German Officer," *Infantry*, January-February 1991, pp. 10, 11; Lieutenant Colonel J. L. Silva, "*Auftragstaktik*," *Infantry*, September-October 1989, pp. 6–9; and Major K. N. Stacey, "An Alternative Approach to Battlefield Decision-Making," *British Army Review,* August 1990, pp. 11–16.

8. Quoted in Alan Moorehead, *The March to Tunis: The North African War, 1940–1943* (1943; reprint, New York: Harper & Row, 1965), p. 23.

9. Appendix 196, (memorandum, "Secret," "Note to General Wilson," 21 September 1940), p. 1, to *War Diary of General Headquarters, Middle East*, Vol. 14: G(O) Branch, September 1940, WO 169/13, PRO.

10. Appendix C (memorandum, "Secret," "G.O.C-in-C., British Troops in Egypt," 20 October 1940), p. 1, to Enclosure A (memorandum, "Operations in Western Desert, October to December 1940 [Notes on Genesis and Working Out of 'Compass' Plan]," 15 December 1940), ref. CRME/1553/G(O), to [U.S.] Military Intelligence Division, War Department General Staff, Military Attache Report Great Britain, Subject: "British Campaign in the Western Desert," Report No. BES-134, 1 May 1941, File No. 2017-744/26, Records of the War Department General and Special Staffs, Record Group 165, National Archives Building, Washington, D.C. [hereafter cited as NA].

11. Ibid., p. 2. Maj. Gen. Michael O'Moore Creagh was commander of the 7th Armored Division.

12. Field Marshal Lord Wilson of Libya, G.C.B., G.B.E., D.S.O., *Eight Years Overseas, 1939–1947* (London: Hutchinson, 1948), p. 47.

13. Lt. Gen. Sir Richard N. O'Connor, "Report on Operations in Libya from September 1940 to April 1941," pp. 3, 4, Folder 6312/29, O'Connor Papers, National Army Museum, London (hereafter cited as NAM).

14. Appendix D (memorandum, "Personal and Most Secret," "G.O.C.-in-C., B.T.E.," 2 November 1940), to Enclosure A, BES-134, RG 165, NA.

15. Quoted in John W. Gordon, *The Other Desert War: British Special Forces in North Africa, 1940–1943*, Contributions in Military Studies, No. 56 (New York: Greenwood Press, 1987), p. 58.

16. Enclosure A, p. 3, to BES-134, RG 165, NA.

17. See David Mure, *Master of Deception* (London: William Kimber, 1980), pp. 65–71.

18. Seymour Reit, *Masquerade: The Amazing Camouflage Deceptions of World War II* (London: Robert Hale, 1978), pp. 135, 136. See also Mure, p. 63. Mure has concluded that "Deception in warfare is, of course, nothing new and the father of the particular kind employed in World War II was none other than General Sir Archibald Wavell." Ibid., p. 16.

19. Appendix F (memorandum, "Most Secret," "Lt-General Wilson: Compass-Exploitation," 28 November 1940), p. 2, to Enclosure A, BES-134, RG 165, NA.

20. Miles Reid, M.B.E., M.C., D.L., *Last on the List* (London: Leo Cooper, 1974), p. 83. Reid attended this conference.

21. Appendix G ("Most Secret," "H.Q., B.T.E. Operation Instruction No. 17," 5 December 1940), p. 1, to Enclosure A, BES-134, RG 165, NA.

22. Gen. Sir Archibald P. Wavell, Despatch: "Operations in the Western Desert from December 7th, 1940, to February 7th, 1941," supplement to *The London Gazette*, 26 June 1946, p. 3262.

23. Variations exist in the different accounts of the opening engagements of Compass; some of this information has been derived from John Connell (John Henry Robertson), "Wavell's 30,000," *History of the Second World War* vol. 1, no. 15 (1967): p. 399. This source provides an overview of Compass.

24. War Diary of Headquarters, 4th Indian Division: "G" Branch, entry for 9 December 1940, p. 2, File No. 601/221/WD/Pt.A3, Historical Section, Ministry of Defense, New Delhi, India [hereafter cited as HS].

25. D. W. Braddock, *The Campaigns in Egypt and Libya, 1940–1942* (Aldershot: Gale and Polden, 1964), p. 12.

26. Wavell, Despatch: "Operations in the Western Desert from December 7th, 1940, to February 7th, 1941," p. 3264.

27. Quoted in Winston S. Churchill, *The Second World War*, vol. II, *Their Finest Hour* (Boston: Houghton Mifflin, 1949), p. 611.

28. O'Connor, p. 26.

29. Lt. Richard J. Riddell and Lt. Harvey S. Ford, "The War in North Africa," *Field Artillery Journal*, November 1941, p. 838.

30. Wavell, Despatch: "Operations in the Western Desert from December 7th, 1940, to February 7th, 1941," p. 3268.

31. Of related interest, see Lt. Col. D. J. Richards, "The Era of Manoeuvre Warfare and Its Impact on the Royal Artillery," *British Army Review*, August 1990, pp. 4–10.

32. Rommel, quoted in Liddell Hart, ed., *The Rommel Papers*, p. 520.

33. Brig. Archibald P. Wavell, C.M.G., M.C., "The Training of the Army for War," *Journal of the Royal United Service Institution,* May 1933, p. 260.

# The Wehrmacht Approach to Maneuver Warfare Command and Control

## John F. Antal

> The first demand in war is decisive action. Everyone, the highest commander and the most junior soldier, must be aware that omissions and neglects incriminate him more severely than the mistake of choice of means.
>
> *Heers Dienstvorschrift 300 Truppenführung*
> (German Army Regulation 300, Command of Troops), 1936[1]

Decisive action is central to the concept of maneuver warfare. As shown above, the German army's command and control process was predicated on the assumption that decisive action was the essential goal of combat. At the tactical level, the command and control process of the German army became a key element to German tactical success. If victory is taken as a measure of quality, the quality of the German tactical command and control during World War II must rank with the very best.

German tactical prowess has been evident since the time of Frederick the Great. "During the latter half of the nineteenth century and the first half of the twentieth, one factor consistently influenced European affairs: Prussian-German military excellence."[2] The Wehrmacht, the name for the German army during the Second World War, enhanced this reputation. "Its campaigns in France (1940), Russia (1941), and North Africa (1941 and 1942) are still regarded as masterpieces of the military art and have indeed become almost legendary. Its operations in Norway (1940) and Crete (1941) are examples of smaller-scale triumphs achieved through hair-raising boldness."[3]

What is more extraordinary is the fact that the German army achieved these victories "in the teeth of considerable numerical odds, and, as often as not, inadequate logistic preparations."[4] Fighting virtually the entire world on multiple fronts, "aided" by unreliable allies, cease-lessly hammered day and night from the air, blockaded by sea, and forced to fight under the irrational leadership of one "all-knowing" Führer, the German Army continued to fight right up to the final Battle of Berlin in May, 1945. Although Germany lost the war, the Wehrmacht did not run. "It did not disintegrate. It did not frag its officers. In-stead it doggedly fought on. . . . It fought on for years after the last hope for victory had gone. . . . Yet for all of this, its units, even when down to 20 percent of their original size, continued to exist and to resist—an unrivaled achievement for any army."[5]

The Wehrmacht's command and control process was the product of three essential German concepts: the institution of the German General Staff, the philosophy of "forward command," and the concept of "mission tactics" or *Auftragstaktik*. It was the high standard of the command and control process which enabled the Wehrmacht to wage success-ful maneuver warfare. "It was the principle of control by directives (*Auftragstaktik*), giving commanders of all levels 'long distance tick-ets' which, together with the thorough and uniform standard of Gen-eral Staff training, exploited creativity and responsible independence to the utmost."[6]

## WEHRMACHT COMMAND AND CONTROL PROCESS

A thorough understanding of the Wehrmacht's command and con-trol process is not possible without an understanding of how the Ger-mans expected their process to work. The German army's view of the command and control process is outlined in the official 1933 manual *Truppenführung* (Command of Troops). This two-volume regulation is signed by two successive commanders in chief. These regulations explain the German concept of war and elaborate techniques to con-duct the command and control process.

The *Truppenführung* stresses decisive action. Decisive action is achieved by the decentralized action of subordinate commanders who are guided by their commander's intent. The *Truppenführung* clearly establishes the commander's role in issuing orders in time to act faster than the enemy. It emphasizes clarity over technique. The following quotations are taken directly from the *Truppenführung* (bold letter-ing is the author's emphasis):

36. The mission and situation form the basis of the action. The mission designates the objective to be attained. The leader must never forget his mission. A mission which indicates several tasks easily diverts from the main objective.

37. The decision arises from the mission and the situation. Should the mission no longer suffice as the fundamental of conduct or is changed by events, the decision must take these considerations into account. He who changes his mission or does not execute the one given must report his actions at once and assumes all responsibility for the consequences. He must always keep in mind the whole situation. . . . **However, in the vicissitudes of war an inflexible maintenance of the original decision may lead to great mistakes.** Timely recognition of the conditions and the time which call for a new decision is an attribute of the art of leadership.

The commander must permit freedom of action to his subordinates insofar as this does not endanger the whole scheme. . . .

68. The more pressing the situation, the shorter the order. **Where circumstances permit, oral orders are given in accordance with the terrain, not the map.** On the front lines and with the lower commanders this is particularly so.

73. An order should contain everything a subordinate must know to carry out his assignment independently, and only that. Accordingly, an order must be brief and clear, definite and complete, tailored to the understanding of the recipient and, under certain circumstances, to his nature. The person issuing it should never neglect to put himself in the shoes of the recipient.

75. **Orders may bind only insofar as they correspond to the situation and its conditions.**

76. Above all, orders are to avoid going into detail when changes in the situation cannot be excluded by the time they are carried out. . . .

77. **Insofar as the conditions permit, it is often best for the commander to clarify his intentions to his subordinates by word of mouth and discussion.**[7]

Operating under a mission-oriented command system that embraced mission tactics as the guiding principle of tactical success, the Wehrmacht's command and control process was verbal, streamlined, and flexible. The goal was to designate the mission and leave the details in the hands of able, subordinate leaders. With this philosophy, the Wehrmacht was consistently able to get inside the enemy's decision cycle and act faster than its opponents. This point is clearly established in a quote from Maj. General J. F. C. Fuller where he describes the Wehrmacht's 1940 campaign in France in his book, *A Military History of the Western World*:

> The speed with which the enemy exploited his penetration of the French front, his willingness to accept risks to further his aim, and his exploitation of every success to the uttermost limits emphasized, even more fully than in the campaigns of the past, the advantage which accrues to the commander who knows how best to use time and to make time his servant and not his master.[8]

## THE WEHRMACHT OPERATIONS ORDER

A typical German operations order, as shown in *Manual for Command and Combat Employment of Smaller Units* (pages 23–26), consisted of:

1. Enemy Situation
2. Friendly Situation and Friendly Intentions
3. General Plan—Organization and combat mission of each subordinate unit or weapon. Attachments and/or detachments are discussed in detail.
4. Detailed Plan—A clear explanation of the extent that the unit is to participate in the execution of the higher commander's intent. Specific details to such matters as reconnaissance, missions, supply and evacuation, communications, and the command post.

Every German commander was expected to conduct an estimate of the situation. The estimate of the situation consisted of (1) estimate of the enemy, (2) estimate of friendly forces, and (3) an evaluation of the terrain. The estimate of the situation was followed by the decision. The transformation of the decision into a tactical action was accomplished by means of the order. The order contained all the factors that changed the existing situation into the situation necessary to carry out the decision.[9]

The operations order "must contain all knowledge that is necessary for its execution. It must not contain anything unnecessary or anything apt to decrease its clarity."[10] The typical Wehrmacht operations order consisted of the following components: (1) The enemy situation, (2) the friendly situation, (3) friendly intentions of the next higher unit, (4) the organization and the combat mission of each subordinate unit or weapon (in order of infantry, armor, supporting armor, reserves, antitank defense, artillery, engineers, signal communication, and supply troops), (5) supply (ammunition, fuel, equipment, arms, rations, clothing, equipment, and the evacuation of sick and wounded), and (6) the location of the command post.[11]

The amount of detail of the operations order and the exact format was left to the discretion of the commander issuing the order. The difference in detail was a matter of time and confidence. Time was saved by emphasizing the intent of the orders rather than specifying how things were planned to occur. "Orders must convince the troops even without explanations. For them to do this, prior discussions with subordinates or discussions before execution of the order are indispensable."[12]

Commanders were expected to personally brief their subordinates and ensure that the intent was clearly communicated. Subordinates were expected to explain their instructions to their commanders to ensure understanding. A "brief back" technique was employed to give the subordinate leader every opportunity to "clear up any doubts he may have had and, having acquired an idea of the general situation, he will be able to act according to the intentions of the commanding officer if the situation should change."[13]

The operations order, at division level and below, was almost always issued verbally, by the commander, preferably overlooking the ground on which the battle would be fought. Maximum use was made of warning orders to give the troops plenty of time to prepare for combat and to initiate movement. Parallel planning techniques, where each subordinate echelon of command began planning as soon as the warning order was received, was normal procedure. Often, a written order was only prepared after the operation was conducted in order to have a record for the unit's official history.

The level of detail required in the combat order was determined by the level of proficiency of the leaders and troops. Well-trained units with experienced commanders needed few instructions. They were expected to think and accomplish the mission. "The order tells its recipient to what extent he and the troops under him are to participate in the execution of the intentions of the higher headquarters."[14] For these types of units, an identification of their mission and the higher commander's intent was all that was needed. For poorly trained units with mediocre leadership, more detail was required.[15]

The result was an orders process that achieved a remarkably short decision cycle. In Russia during World War II, German division commanders were able to receive orders at 2200 and issue their own orders to the regiments by 2400. *In effect, the Germans operated on a two-hour, division-echelon, decision cycle.* "Division, corps, and army staffs were small and contained few decision makers. The decision process was usually very fast and not characterized by exhaustive details and analyses by the staff and specialists. This was accompanied, however, by very competent and detailed ongoing staff work and superb staff planning and execution once decisions had been made."[16]

The following quote, from an interview taken in 1979 with Maj. Gen. F. W. von Mellenthin, highlights the employment of mission tactics at its best. Mellenthin's statement gives the proponents of detailed order tactics, proponents who visualize the control of combat forces by more efficient information processing systems, some important food for thought:

**Bill Rennagel**: General, in mobile operations in maintaining a fast tempo . . . what are the coordination mechanisms that the staff and commander have to resolve to keep the *Schwerpunkt* going in the direction and to the objectives that you want? Can you sort of just generalize about those kinds of control mechanisms?

**von Mellenthin**: You know, in a tank division there are no written orders. There are only verbal orders and the commander of the division can have assistant officers with radio connection to him at the place of the various regiments which inform him about movement. This keeps him informed, by radio.

**Pierre Sprey**: What would be your impression of the effect on operations and the effect on the speed of your divisions and the mobility of your divisions if you had to transmit all your orders by teletype—perhaps via a computer?

**von Mellenthin**: Forget about it.[17]

The Wehrmacht orders process, as derived from *Manual for Command and Combat Employment of Smaller Units*, is shown below:

1.  Receive / Deduce the Mission
2.  Estimate the Situation
    a. Estimate of the Enemy
    b. Estimate of Friendly Forces
    c. Terrain
3.  The Decision
4.  Prepare and Issue the Order
5.  Forward Command (supervision)

## TACTICAL EXAMPLE

A useful way to bring this subject to life is to illustrate how the Germans conducted their command and control process by relating a typical small unit action. Our example is explained in the Department of the Army pamphlet, *Small Unit Actions during the German Campaign in Russia*. This pamphlet was written under the supervision of Gen. Franz Halder, Chief of the German Army General Staff from 1938 to 1942. As a direct source narrative, it shows those actions that the Germans felt were valuable lessons learned in fighting with the Russians.

The example for our study involves the German 3d Panzer Division, operating against the Russians in 1944. The German 3d Panzer Division, recently moved in by train, was operating against the Russians near the southern Polish town of Kielce during the 13th and 14th of August 1944. "The division's mission was to stop the advance of Russian forces that had broken through the German lines during the collapse of Army Group Center and to assist the withdrawing German formations in building up a new defense line near the upper Vistula."[18]

To speed up the deployment of his division, the division commander formed an armored task force to secure his route of advance. The force was led by the commander of the 2d Tank Battalion, consisting of two companies of Panther tanks, one panzer grenadier company in SdKfz (*Sonderkraftfahrzeug*) 251 halftracks, and one battery of 105mm self-propelled howitzers. The task force was to launch a surprise attack on Village Z and seize the bridges south and east of the village in order to allow the main body of the division to advance along the Kielce-Opatow road toward the Vistula River.

Air reconnaissance information was obtained at 1800 on 15 August that showed Village Z to be lightly defended. No major troop concentrations were found in the area. The only German unit in the area was the 188th Infantry Regiment. At 2000 on 15 August the task force commander received his orders. Sunrise would occur at 0445. Sunset would occur at 1930.

The task force commander immediately began to study a plan of attack on Village Z. Since his units had not yet been alerted of the mission, he would be unable to move out before 2300. The maximum speed his forces could safely drive at night, without the aid of headlights, over dusty roads, was six miles per hour. The approach march to Village Z would take, therefore, approximately five hours. Taking into account refueling and deployment time, the commander came to the conclusion that he could not attack before dawn. Since he would lose the advantage of surprise, the task force commander decided to send forward an advance guard, a tank company reinforced with one panzer grenadier platoon, ahead of the main body of the task force.

At 2020 the task force commander assembled his orders group and issued his orders. *He did not write them out; he issued verbal orders.* He ordered the advance guard to seize Village Z and the two bridges across River B. He ordered a reconnaissance unit to direct the advance guard as far as Village X. Two gasoline trucks were to accompany the advance guard and refuel the small force two miles west of Village Z. The main body of the task force would follow the advance guard at 2300. The task force commander directed that the advance guard commander accompany him to the command post of the German 188th Infantry Regiment in contact in the area, at 2100. The advance guard commander, a Lieutenant Zobel, immediately started planning for his new mission.

Zobel returned to his unit, assembled his platoon leaders, first sergeant, and maintenance support chief, and briefed them. He indicated the march route, which they copied on their maps, and ordered the ranking platoon leader to command the column as far as Village X while he accompanied the task force commander to the 188th Infantry Regiment. Zobel arranged for hot coffee to be served to his troops at 2130.

The reconnaissance detachment was to move out at 2130 and post guides along the road to Village X. Start time was set for 2200. Zobel then met the task force commander at 2130 and accompanied him to the command post of the 188th Infantry Regiment. There, they were given detailed information concerning the enemy. This information confirmed the original plan of attack. The task force commander ordered Zobel to carry out the attack as planned.

At 0145, Zobel met the advance guard at the outskirts of Village X. He reformed the march column with tanks leading. At 0230 Zobel linked up with the most forward reconnaissance detachment. The guides gave Zobel an intelligence update and reported that they had observed no Russian movement during the night. At 0345 Zobel halted in the woods and refueled his vehicles.

While the refueling was going on, Zobel gave his platoon leaders and tank commanders a final briefing. Zobel began his attack at 0430. Visibility was approximately 1000 yards. As they were driving down the road to Village Z, Zobel's lead tanks were taken under fire by Soviet antitank gunners, skillfully waiting in ambush. Three German tanks were disabled.

Zobel, realizing that surprise was lost, ordered his elements to withdraw. He abandoned his original plan of attack, radioed in his failure and awaited the arrival of the main force.

At 0515 Zobel's units were joined by the task force. Zobel reported in person to the task force commander, who immediately drew up a new plan of attack. The plan called for Zobel's company to conduct a feint along the same route of his earlier attack while the task force commander maneuvered the rest of his force to the south and raced a few platoons across to seize the bridges. Once the bridges were secured, the village would be cleared by follow-on forces of the task force. The attack was to start at 0600.

Under the concentrated fire of the task force artillery, tanks of the lead company brushed through light enemy resistance in the south. The lead tank platoons drove through the village, overran several Russian infantry platoons, knocked out two Soviet tanks, and captured the east bridge. All units reported that they had accomplished their missions, and the task force commander organized the defense of the village and awaited the arrival of the main body of the 3d Panzer Division.[19]

This example shows the value the Germans placed on mental agility and quick tactical planning. They saved time by employing a simple and streamlined command and control process. Time was understood to be the critical element of war. The term "sufficient planning time" was unknown in the Wehrmacht. Leaders were educated not to expect "sufficient" time to think through each mission, because in combat there was no way of knowing what the situation would allow.

> To come to rely on some imaginary increment of time as necessary to execute a mission properly would subtly inject a degree of doubt, if that time did not materialize, into the minds of the leaders before the operation ever commenced. That could create dangerous reservations among the leaders and led before battle was joined. The men and unit must simply improvise and conduct the operation to the best of their capabilities under the prevailing conditions.[20]

The Wehrmacht did not require a ten-page operations order at the task force level. In fact, the task force commander gave his orders verbally, and after analyzing his mission for only twenty minutes. This gave his subunit commanders time to prepare and brief their own men. The task force commander gained a time advantage over his enemy by implementing a quick decision cycle.

The key to the plan was surprise. The task force commander, basing his decision on the available aerial reconnaissance information, set the task force in motion early. He developed the intelligence picture continuously throughout his command and control process. Both the task force commander and the advance guard commander used the technique of an intelligence update to determine if the situation had changed prior to the attack. If the intelligence update revealed that the situation had changed, both commanders could have changed the plan accordingly. Had the Germans moved less swiftly, the Russians would surely have detected their move and reacted accordingly.

Most importantly, the tactical thinking was extremely flexible. When Zobel's quick race to the bridges failed, he did not attempt to make the original plan fit the changed circumstances. Reading the situation correctly, he awaited the main body of the task force and reported to his commander. The task force commander then readdressed the situation, acted decisively, and accomplished the mission with minimal casualties. It is interesting to note that the official critique of this action stated that the unit had jeopardized surprise by conducting a refueling operation too close to the enemy and that the task force commander should have gone forward to lead the advance guard in person. Other than that, the "attack by the fully assembled task force was properly planned and executed with the expected quick success."[21]

## SUMMARY

The Wehrmacht's command and control process was an important combat multiplier. The German army exhibited a consistently short decision cycle and gained a decided time advantage over their opponents. The Wehrmacht command and control process was simple, verbal, and mission-oriented. The process was geared to decisive action. It emphasized the integration of intelligence information and based planning flexibility on the intelligence product.

The Wehrmacht system decentralized command responsibility to well-trained officers, who were expected to act decisively. The heart of the Wehrmacht command and control process was the concept of *Auftragstaktik*—mission tactics. The use of mission orders became a habit of thought in the Wehrmacht. The intentions of the two next higher headquarters were routinely provided to all units. The commander provided the who, what, where, and why in very succinct and implicitly understood terms. The details of accomplishing the mission were left to the subordinate.

This system was possible because, in the Wehrmacht, it was normal for superiors to trust their subordinates to do their duty without supervision. Quality junior leaders, trusted to take decisive action, led by trained commanders who commanded from the front, turned the Wehrmacht into a remarkable tactical fighting machine. The Wehrmacht's command and control process was a victory of intent.

# Notes

1. Martin van Creveld, *Fighting Power: German and U.S. Army Performance, 1939-1945* (Westport, Conn.: Greenwood Press, 1982), pp. 29, 32.

2. Col. Trevor N. Dupuy, *A Genius for War: The German Army and General Staff 1807–1945* (Fairfax, Va.: Hero Books, 1977), p. 7.

3. Creveld, p. 4.

4. Ibid., p. 4.

5. Ibid., p. 5.

6. Bryan Perrett, *Knights of the Black Cross* (New York: St. Martin's Press, 1986), p. xiii.

7. Center for Army Tactics, *Truppenführung (1933)* (Ft. Leavenworth, Kans.: U.S. Army Command and General Staff College, 1989; 1989 transcript of 1936 translation of *Truppenführung* [1933]), pp. 5–13.

8. Maj. Gen. J. F. C. Fuller, *A Military History of the Western World,* vol. 3, *From the Seven Days Battle, 1862 to the Battle of Leyte Gulf, 1944* (New York: Minerva Press, 1967), pp. 409, 410.

9. Field Marshal Albert Kesselring, *Manual for Command and Combat Employment of Smaller Units (Based on German Experience in World War II),* (originally prepared by the Chief Historian, Headquarters, European Command, United States Army, 1952), p. 18.

10. Ibid., p. 13.

11. Ibid., pp. 18–29.

12. Ibid., p. 12.

13. Ibid., pp. 13, 14.

14. Ibid., p. 26.

15. Ibid., p. 26. Page 26 of *Manual* highlights this point:
"If the one who is to carry out the order is a factor in a plan strictly organized as to time, place and procedure, the order must itself be strictly organized and must contain all necessary details. This form of order is also necessary if the subordinates are insufficiently trained. If, however, the commander believes his subordinates are capable of completing a mission themselves, because they have the necessary training, experience and fighting qualities, he will content himself with stating the purpose and objective of his order. Further details of the execution can be limited to the elements absolutely necessary for coordinating activities of adjacent, supporting or supported

troops with respect to time and place. This last mentioned form of giving orders, the assignment of a mission, with latitude being given as to the execution, will induce all commanders and combatants to think. It will increase their self-confidence and their sense of responsibility and, in case of a sudden change in the situation, it will insure that the spearheads act according to the intentions of the commander. On the other hand, forces accustomed to waiting for an order, or who need an order for each action, will simply freeze to the point of inaction unless they receive such an order."

16. Richard F. Timmons, "Lessons From the Past for NATO," *The Parameters of War, Military History Journal of the U.S. Army War College*, vol. xiv, no. 3 (Washington, D.C.: Pergamon–Brassey's International Defense Publishers, 1987), p. 272.

17. Battelle Columbus Laboratories, interview with Maj. Gen. F. W. von Mellenthin, *Armored Warfare in World War II, Conference Featuring F.W. von Mellenthin, German Army, May 10, 1979* (Columbus, Ohio: Battelle Columbus Laboratories, 1979), p. 47.

18. U.S. Army Pamphlet, *Small Unit Actions during the German Campaign in Russia No. 20-269* (Washington, D.C.: U.S. Government Printing Office, July 1953), p. 118.

19. Ibid., pp. 118–125.

20. Timmons, p. 277.

21. Ibid., p. 125.

# Maneuver Warfare and the Art of Deception

## Arthur T. Hadley

"Truth," said Winston Churchill, a constant if not always successful practitioner of maneuver warfare, "must be protected in wartime by a bodyguard of lies."[1] Or to use a more American idiom: "Find them, fix them, fight them, finish them," should be expanded to read, "Find them, fool them, fix them, fight them, finish them." Fooling the enemy is an essential ingredient in fixing him in a position that will benefit your attack, as to physical location, and also mental beliefs and emotional stress.[2]

How do we do this in the age of satellite surveillance, electronic intelligence, target drones, and stealth aircraft? A question much more easily asked than answered. Operation Fortitude was the creation in early 1943 of a mythic Army Group in southeast Britain threatening the Pas de Calais area.[3] Today it would be close to impossible to create such an artifice under satellite surveillance. Yet this deception so played in the minds of German commanders that they refused to accept two vital pieces of evidence that the June invasion of France was underway and would take place in the Normandy area. These were the "Verlain" message, which alerted the French Resistance to an imminent invasion, and the interception by German signals intelligence of ground-to-air radios being tested in the ports of southern Britain closest to Normandy.

About the results of Fortitude, this vast invasion of the enemy mind, one can do no better than quote Max Hastings: "A climate of uncertainty had been masterfully created, which would decisively influence German behavior until deep into July."[4] Expert British deception had changed the old saw from "seeing is believing," to "believing is seeing."

Closer in time, would the brilliant "Hail Mary" left hook used by CENTCOM against the Iraqi army in Operation Desert Storm have

360

worked so successfully if the Soviet Union had been providing their former client state with satellite intelligence?[5] This hidden left hook was well supported by several classic strategies of deception. The holding of the Marine task force offshore in a position that threatened Kuwait's sea flank contributed much to the Iraqi mind-set that made the land battle a success. This feint gained strength from the use of SEALs in a diversionary roll to simulate the landing of a large Marine combat force. Swimming ashore at night and implanting noise makers and flares on the beaches, as well as staging a few brief attacks, these small forces pinned down at least one and probably two Iraqi divisions.

In addition to the threat from the Marines, CENTCOM employed other masterfully deceptive maneuvers. The media were given ample access to the Marines and the forces in the southeast, but only limited access to the vital forces in the west. At the same time TV crews were permitted to photograph long columns of vehicles moving north, when in fact the main movement at that time was west. As in Fortitude, a bogus radio net was activated to indicate a massive troop buildup just south of Kuwait. As the ground campaign began, both a task force of the 1st Marine Division and parts of the 1st Cavalry Division made feints in the east in the Wadi al Batin area. All this reinforced Iraqi beliefs that they would face a head-on attack up through Kuwait, augmented by a Marine landing from the sea.[6]

Let us note that there were a number of deceptive actions both sides could have taken but did not. On the other side of the hill, it would have been greatly to the Iraqi advantage to sow a large number of cheap, fake mines in the Persian Gulf along with their active mines to further restrict the maneuvers of the allied navies. Nor was there any Iraqi effort to get inside the minds of the coalition's Muslim forces (including American Muslims) and their commanders, to raise questions about whether they should be fighting their Muslim brethren. Once the air attack started, the Iraqis were unable to use radio, but during the buildup they had a prolonged opportunity for the use of strategic radio and even balloons bearing leaflets.

On our side, there were also missed opportunities. Interviews with captured Iraqi officers revealed a mind-set that they were safe from flank attack through the desert because only Arabs can fight in the desert; Americans would get lost and die. This idea was already in their minds and could have been reinforced, for example, by fake distress calls from supposedly terrified lost cavalrymen picturing themselves out of fuel and dying of thirst.

While American TV programs and newspaper pictures showed a commendable use of loudspeakers to weaken the morale of the Iraqi force, these loudspeakers were all mounted on soft-skinned vehicles. This works in low-intensity conflicts such as Vietnam or Panama, but in any high- or even medium-intensity conflict, particularly one involving rapid tank or armored infantry advances, such vehicles cannot keep up. And this is precisely the time they are most effective.

Without detracting in any way from the American armed forces' splendid performance in the Gulf War, anyone who has followed recent American military actions, maneuvers, and war games is still entitled to ask: How hard is the American military working on deception plans and other forms of psychological warfare? Two things cause concern here. One is the military neglect of deception in recent American history. The Americans remained skeptical of the worth of Fortitude until well after D-Day. While I am always suspicious of the old soldiers' disease of "looking backwards," the "psyop" effort in Vietnam seemed to me at least in 1979/80, to be less sophisticated than that of World War II. The same could be said with certainty of Korea.

Then there is the failure of psychological warfare (the supposed home of thoughts about and plans for deception) to find a consistent Army home. The overall planning and direction of psyops has bounced around the Army Staff since the close of World War II; sometimes it has been a special staff section, sometimes lumped with Civil Affairs, sometimes beneath the G-2, other times placed beneath the G-3. In the field the active psychological warfare units have had equal difficulty finding a service home. It is significant to note that 73 years after World War I disclosed the need, the military has yet to develop and field a shell that can fire leaflets accurately without damaging them.

I do not mean to be unduly harsh on the U.S. military; other countries have also dropped the ball. It was Stalin's own illusions that prevented him from being prepared for the German attack in June of 1941. The German military showed scant appreciation for deception. Nazi plans and troop movements for the great battle of Kursk in the summer of 1943 were so open that the Russians successfully met the attack with thorough preparations of their own. It was operational secrecy rather than deception that led to the initial German successes in the Battle of the Bulge, though American delusions about German strength also played a part.

The use of the battlefield feint in warfare—particularly in maneuver warfare—can probably be traced to the first caveman pretending to wobble on his feet and drop his guard to lure his opponent into the killing range of his club. One battle truth that successful commanders at all levels learn fast is: "That little distracting attack on your right flank may actually be the enemy's main effort." The intent of this essay is not to deal at great length with such operational art maneuver deceptions. FM 100-5 is eloquent on this matter. In the Gulf War such deployments were handled rather well. At other times the eloquence of the manual has not been translated to the reality on the ground. The intent of this essay is to focus on units, staffs, and operations that have for either their primary mission or a prominent secondary mission the planning for and practice of deception—the art of fooling the enemy. From where I stand—and I admit to being an outsider—it seems that deception is a rather neglected part of strategic planning, operational art, tactical maneuver, and training.[7]

To develop plans and units whose sole or principal secondary function is deception will be extremely difficult in the open society of America. Successful deception requires a high degree of secrecy. But still it should be possible. Both Delta Force and portions of the Green Berets in America and the Special Air Service and Special Boat Service in Britain have successfully maintained a high degree of security. Another American cultural factor that works against the development and augmentation of units and plans for deception in the U.S. military is the remains of an attitude, fortunately growing less prevalent, that warfare is akin to a game. This game should be played by certain sporting rules in which it is unfair to steal the enemy's playbook, throw sand in his face, spit tobacco juice in his eyes, or use the hidden ball trick. Such a belief is, of course, man-killing nonsense.

The successful "pure" deception operation need not be as complex as Fortitude or the capture and subsequent turning of the Nazi agents slipped into Britain during World War II in the Double Cross (XX) System.[8] Information relayed back to the Germans from these supposedly in-place agents was used successfully to deceive the Germans in a variety of ways. Two of the most important were false information on convoy routings and bogus order of battle information used to support the overall deceptive purposes of Fortitude.

Effective deception actions need not be far-flung, expensive, and highly complex. A classic entry into the enemy mind, again accomplished by the British in the Second World War, involved nothing more complex than a soccer ball filled with helium and coated with a thick layer of luminous paint, one single-engine fighter, and an exceptionally brave and able pilot. The purpose of the operation was to distract the attention of as many German scientists as possible for a long period of time by making them scurry off on a wild goose chase rather than concentrate on serious war work.

The prepared ball was loaded into the fighter aircraft of an intrepid and skillful wing commander who had volunteered to drop it on the runway intersection of one of Germany's largest airports. Streaking in beneath the then-primitive radar screens, he launched the ball successfully. The soccer ball drifted slowly toward the runways, attracting intersecting lines of tracers; the fire slowly petered out as it dawned on gunners and their commanders that perhaps they were meant to hit this slowly descending target. Perhaps it was some new kind of explosive. By the time it touched the runway every German in the vicinity was cowering deep in shelters. The ball then took off from the runway, rising slowly and majestically into the air. Brave heads were raised. A few commenced to shoot, only to be told to stop because of the possible extreme danger.

When some half an hour later the ball finally came to rest, senior scientists all over Germany had been awakened and told to drop whatever they were doing and prepare to go to work on a most important discovery. A special train was laid on to transport the ball to a secret and remote science laboratory where this supposed wonder weapon, which had miraculously misfired, could be thoroughly tested. At the same time an elite bomb disposal unit was alerted to move the ball from the airfield to the train. Some two weeks later after exhaustive and cautious research the scientists rendered their report. The weapon was a helium-filled soccer ball. They were laughed out of court and told to continue investigating. Surely no one could be so stupid as to believe that the British would risk an aircraft and pilot to drop a gas-filled football on an airdrome. The scientists, neglecting their other work, labored on.[9]

Other British attacks on the mind of their enemy involved less deception and more direct power. Believing, correctly as it turned out, Hitler to be slightly unhinged, they developed various strategies to drive him further round the bend. One method, carried on with some loss of aircraft, was to celebrate Hitler's birthday by bombing the Munich beer hall where Hitler's first putsch had originated and which was recognized as the birthplace of the Nazi Party. One can imagine the command clout necessary to divert planes of Air Marshal Arthur "Bomber" Harris from what he considered the all-important mission of destroying German industry.

Was such a course followed with Saddam Hussein? Do we have plans to work on the mental processes of other leaders who may cause us trouble? One hopes they are better conceived than the efforts to cause Fidel Castro's beard to fall off. Surely at some moment we could have used Manuel Noriega's belief in voodoo to our immediate advantage.

In focusing on deception as an important part of maneuver warfare in the satellite/electronic age, we are neither claiming the discovery of some entirely new concept for this century nor trying to reinvent the wheel. The planning and use of deception is as old as warfare itself. The problem is to bring plans and practice up to date. And equally important to foster an atmosphere in which, faced by a military problem, the question immediately springs to mind: "How can deception help?"

In any brief historical overview the Trojan horse is the image that is remembered—a mighty piece of victorious deception if there ever was one. Here a specific unit, a horse built large enough to house fighting men, was combined with a tactical deception plan: the seeming departure of the Greek fleet. These both cleverly played into a custom of the time, that the defeated force left behind some gift or sacrifice to appease the gods. All these—beliefs, traditions, actions, and construction—worked together to breach walls that had withstood a lengthy and violent siege, with much dying on both sides.

Yet this brings up a problem that lies at the very heart of the American reaction to deception: the phrase: "a Trojan horse" has not come down to us as an example of a brilliant maneuver, but of deceit. For deception to take its proper place in maneuver warfare, commanders at all levels must not view this most successful ruse in such a light. Instead, visualize the horse standing on the plain before Troy's Scamander gate, jewels for its eyes, garlands round its neck, a bridle set with precious stones, and a note hanging from one ear that said: "To our brave, victorious Trojan foes." And from the horse's feet protrude the well-greased wheels that almost seem to move this gift of victory inside the walls of Troy under its own power. This is deception at its highest. Every commander should constantly ask himself or herself: "What Trojan horse can I employ today to gain such a great victory so cheaply?"

The invasion of England in 1066 followed the carefully laid deception plans of William of Normandy. Using a combination of deceit and diplomacy, he brought off, along with Julius Caesar and Eisenhower, one of history's only three successful cross-Channel attacks. William had persuaded (freely, the French claim; duped, the English claim) Earl Harold of Wessex, England, to swear on most sacred relics, that he, Harold, would bestow his claim to the throne of England on William. When Harold took that throne of England for himself, William contested the claim and sent an emissary to the Pope. This emissary's brief was prepared by Bishop Lanfranc, who later became Archbishop of Canterbury. Lanfranc was himself an Italian and a highly respected logician. He was also a skilled politician, who never let a possible truth stand in the way of military victory. Lanfranc's arguments managed to persuade the Pope that the English church had backslid into heresy. The Pope, moved by these arguments, and for certain considerations paid, ruled that the oaths were indeed valid, the English church heretical, and that the throne belonged to William. He gave William a holy ring and a papal banner to carry into battle. These convinced many of those fighting for Harold that they fought against God and risked damnation.[10]

The battle of Hastings was close enough as it was. Indeed, had unfavorable winds not held William in port for several days, Harold and his thanes would have fought the Normans before the Vikings instead of right afterward. The whole course of history might then have been changed, with England becoming an outpost of the Scandinavian empire rather than a Norman province. With the battle that close, the fact that many of Harold's warriors believed they were risking the eternal burning of their immortal souls in the fires of hell cannot help but have affected the battle.

The part deception plays in warfare is also enshrined in literature. The following is from William Shakespeare's *Macbeth*. Some argue that Shakespeare's knowledge of military affairs was so correct and extensive that he must have spent time in the army. In act five, scene four, Malcolm, Macduff, and their forces are encamped in Birnam Wood before Macbeth's castle of Dunsinane.

Malcolm: "Let every soldier hew him down a bough/And bear't before him. Thereby shall we shadow/The numbers of our host and make discovery/Err in report of us."

So it was that another part of the prophecy of the weird sisters was fulfilled: "Macbeth shall never vanquish'd be until/Great Birnam Wood to high Dunsinane Hill/Shall come against him."

Enough of the past. What of the present? One certainty about successful maneuver warfare is that it requires the closest of coordination between all arms and services. This begins with plans and doctrine, these must be followed by training. As Williamson Murray has brilliantly argued, it was the very absence of such doctrine and training in the use of combined arms that led to the fragmented and often ineffective performance of the British army against the Germans in World War II. Tanks, infantry, artillery, and close air support never came together to the extent that they did in the German army and eventually in the American. Also in the American army deception—invading the minds of the enemy—finally came into integrated use at the battalion level.

Such close coordination was achieved during the final phases of World War II with the 2d Armored Division during the thrust towards the Rhine and from the Rhine to the Elbe. At this time it was not unusual for a battalion's tanks to pause for a moment before the attack on an enemy position. As the tanks menacingly traversed their guns back and forth at the target, the tank-mounted loudspeaker would make a surrender broadcast, the artillery would fire a few rounds of surrender leaflets, and the P-74 would loose a leaflet bomb over the target.

The enemy soldier, with the broadcast ringing in his ears, the leaflets fluttering down on his head from air and artillery, and the menacing tanks pointing their weapons at him, would feel far more vulnerable than he really was. The shock action of tanks, artillery, and air power had been augmented by psychological shock to induce a mind-set in the enemy that resistance was hopeless. Such tactical deception will work only where there is not only total cooperation at all levels, but also belief on the part of those involved that such use of deception is an integral part of easing the way to victory. Such intimate cooperation of the various arms and services in deception must be practiced in peacetime. It will never be achieved, or only achieved after much pain, by an organization hastily patched together during, or on the eve of, battle.

However, in World War II, such coordination of deception, maneuver, and shock action was the exception rather than the rule. A great many divisions forbade loudspeaker broadcasts or leaflet firing in their division area, believing that they unnecessarily threatened the lives of their troops by drawing enemy fire. This was undoubtedly true; deception is not some form of armchair strategy that wins wars without casualties. I used to get around this prohibition on deception by ordering the collection "for intelligence purposes" of all the German leaflets fired at our troops. Since these were wildly pornographic, they were in much demand by higher headquarters and staffs. I would negotiate the turning over of a certain number of pornographic leaflets to a division headquarters in return for permission to make a certain number of loudspeaker broadcasts and leaflet firings—hardly the model of battlefield cooperation taught in the service schools. Cooperative Air Force (Army Air Corps) units that dropped accurate leaflet bombs got a supply of filthy picture leaflets too.

As we go to "lean and mean" fighting forces, which, God willing, will not mean cheap and inadequate, the necessity for deception becomes even more important. With force numbers so reduced we will need to use all aspects of warfare and all the strengths of our national educational and industrial base to achieve the victory that in the past we would have gained by strength of numbers and materiel. Many potential adversaries are authoritarian dictatorships of one sort or another which rely for their military power on numbers of trained, but not necessarily flexible, forces. They would seem to be obvious targets for deception. But again, if they are clients of one of the great powers, they will have access to a great deal of sophisticated information and analysis. This information must either be countered or, better yet, turned to our own purposes.

What steps do we need to take to make certain that deception becomes an essential part of U.S. doctrine? Starting at the National Command Authority (NCA) level, there has to be an agreed-upon war aim.

How many people do we want to kill to achieve our objective? What are the acceptable limits to our own and allied casualties? Some deceptions may kill more enemy in an effort to save the lives of our own soldiers. Do we want to do this to enemy soldiers? To enemy civilians? Again, a World War II example: The White House, the Office of War Information, and the Justice Department wanted to establish on record that after the war was won they were going to try members of the SS for war crimes. A directive therefore went out that before any battle with SS troops we were to tell them that even if they surrendered, they stood a good chance of being tried as war criminals. This was a directive obviously not written by anyone with a son in the tanks or infantry.

That did not seem to us in the field to be a very good way to save American lives by inducing SS surrenders. So, starting with Brest, those on the ground developed the rubric that said to the SS troops facing us: "Every man in uniform is a soldier and will be treated as a soldier." When Washington finally learned about what we were doing, they wanted to court-martial those that had used that formula to induce surrenders. Fortunately, the combat arms prevailed over the political theorists. But this is the type of national policy that should be the subject of decision at the highest levels, with impassioned argument from all departments, especially Defense and those within the military, rather than handed down by some department or bureau far from the dying end in compliance with its own agenda.

For example: One of the more horrendous deception choices Britain faced during World War II grew out of the false information sent back by the turned agents of the Double Cross System. The agents' handlers inside Germany desperately wanted to know where the buzz bombs (also called flying bombs) that the Reich had launched against London were actually landing. But any deceptive information provided by those controlling the turned agents would cause the bombs to land on some Englishman. No one in the armed services was willing to choose where the bombs meant for central London would actually hit. The decision fell to Churchill himself. So, at his direction, the suburbs to the East of London became an aiming point and were put in harm's way. Deception does not mean the absence of pain in warfare.

Below the NCA, a deception plan needs to be a part of all the myriad war plans the Pentagon has on its shelves to face the scores of contingencies likely and unlikely in the real world. Nor is it merely enough to have such plans. In the immortal words of that legendary maneuverist Gen. James Hollingsworth: "Any damn fool can write a plan; it's executing it f - - - s you up." Deception needs to be rehearsed in war-games and maneuvers also.

The problem of creating special units that concentrate on deception and that vital part of deception, propaganda, is complicated by the present debate over what portion of the military forces should be in the reserves, and how the reserves and their units are to be managed and commanded. To be effective, both deception and propaganda require a profound knowledge of the enemy culture (particularly military culture) and, above all, the enemy language. The late C. D. Jackson, chief of print media at SHAEF during World War II and later publisher of *Life Magazine*, used to remark that if he had a choice of a first-rate man who didn't speak the target country's language and a third-rate man who spoke the target country's language fluently, he would pick the third-rate man. Fortunately, in World War II the language was no problem. There were a number of refugees from both France and Germany; the "grand tour" still existed and many young men of even moderate wealth had traveled in Europe; and both French and German were required in the better secondary schools and for many undergraduate degrees.

However, all three of our last extensive military deployments—Korea, Vietnam, and Saudi Arabia—have placed us in parts of the world where there is an American shortage of native language skills and cultural knowledge. During the Korean War I was shown an American leaflet whose drawing was meant to depict a Chinese Communist soldier stabbing the Korean nation in the back. Unfortunately what this leaflet's picture conveyed to the Koreans was that an American private was stabbing an elderly Korean opium smoker in the back to get at his stash.

As the Cold War began to heat up in the early fifties, Congress passed the Lodge Act. Under its provisions, foreigners with critical language and cultural skills who volunteered to serve for a time in the American armed forces were granted U.S. citizenship on their discharge. One can see the present need for such an act to bring in a trained pool of individuals who speak some of the more exotic Near Eastern, Far Eastern, Balkan, and Baltic languages, which may suddenly be important. The cultural studies can be accomplished on contract to various universities or through graduate study for serving selected officers.

A practical place to pool men and women with such skills is in the reserves. Either in specially created reserve units or in the Individual Ready Reserve, as we do with certain medical specialties. But designing a program to locate such people, recruit them, and then devise programs to be sure they stay interested and current will be a challenge. And then there is a question of what their parent unit will look like. How will it stay abreast of the problems of deception and propaganda in a multi-threat world? It is an unfortunate fact of life that such special units tend to draw more than their fair share of "big-time operators" and nutty enthusiasts. The peacetime creation and nourishment of units dedicated to the arts of deception will be difficult, extremely difficult.

The bombing by the RAF on Hitler's birthday of the beer hall in which the Nazi movement started illustrates the importance of detailed order of battle studies about the leaders, particularly military leaders, of our putative and presumed enemies. This also illustrates another important fact. Those who order such work and the study of such ideas must have the command clout to put theoretical results into hard action for the benefit of the fighting troops in harm's way.

Again, much of the more esoteric parts of such action is either interagency work, or academic work that can be farmed out to various semiautonomous agencies, such as the Air Force's Rand Corporation, or done by selective reservists on short tours of duty. But at bottom there must be a commitment to entering the enemy's mind for purposes of deception. This must be done in peacetime, and not just for the results in battle. Of like importance is to persuade able officers of all services that assignment to such deception units or staffs, where the focus is about plans for and research on deception and propaganda, as well as weapons systems specifically designed for such purposes, is no longer the career dead end it has been for some in the past.

To be successful in the age of satellites, deception must permeate all levels of the military—from the lead platoon to the Supreme Allied Headquarters. Combat soldiers and airmen love to fight. They tend—*tend*, I say—to regard sneaking around, pretending to be the main effort with noise and smoke and fake radio signals, as not quite the "right stuff." Also, scouts and reconnaissance pilots love to gain that vital information and transmit it back. They too tend—again I stress *tend*—to regard deception as a bit outside their purview. Clearly the place to start to rectify this is in the training base. As Gen. Bruce Clark is often quoted as saying: "As you train, so will you fight." If the OPFOR, or the U.S. forces, get lured into a killing zone now and then by deception, a lesson will have been well and thoroughly learned.

Fooling the satellites appears to be a major problem. Any major power is capable of placing several satellites in surveillance orbit over that portion of the globe it wishes to watch closely. If such a power is an enemy of ours, or has a client state that is temporarily our enemy, how will deceptions occur? "Take the high ground" is an ancient axiom. The satellite is the new high ground. What do we do to neutralize its eyes? Must we kill it? Is that the only answer? Or better yet, is there a way to have its eyes behold not the truth, but what we ourselves wish our enemies to perceive as the truth? I trust that experts and advocates of maneuver warfare are exploring such problems. They seem to me vital, albeit both difficult and expensive.

Perhaps it is wise to end with a note of caution. The enemy too tries to get inside our minds. "Americans can't fight at night," is a typical example; it caused us problems from World War II, through Korea, and on into Vietnam. We came to believe it ourselves; and soon the enemy owned the night. We had been outmaneuvered again. At the National Training Center I have watched OPFOR elements reconnoiter freely at night while "American" forces were buttoned up tight. I have seen OPFOR electronic warfare experts easily enter "American" radio nets to direct "friendly fire" on the attacking "American" forces, and so cause them to loose faith in their own artillery.

The highly complex and individualistic nature of our society should make us superb at maneuver warfare. Thinking fast on your feet is a trait we prize. But we must recognize that we also can be led to see what we believe and not what is actual fact. "Believing is seeing" works for us as well as our enemies. Like bullets, deception can travel both ways.

# Notes

1. Cave Brown, *Bodyguard of Lies* (New York, Harper and Row, 1975).

2. The reader should be warned that the author, then a 1st Lieutenant, and OSS agent Alexis Sommaripa, subsequently killed behind the lines in action, created the first tank-mounted loudspeakers for the American Army.

3. The British Public Record Office WO 205/33 contains the details of Fortitude's creation.

4. Max Hastings, *Overlord* (New York: Simon and Schuster, 1984).

5. Several intelligence officials have suggested to me that perhaps the Soviet military, not wishing to have the Iraqis and their Soviet military equipment embarrassed by an overwhelming defeat, did furnish such information; however, the Iraqi C3 was too destroyed to act upon it. To which I can only reply: They couldn't even send such information out by motorcycle?

6. In addition to my own interviews, I wish to acknowledge the excellent work done by William J. Taylor, Jr., and James Blackwell in "The Ground War in the Gulf," *Survival*, May/June 1991, p. 230ff.

7. The best tactical use of deception I have seen, and it was excellent though limited, was by the OPFOR at Fort Irwin in 1989.

8. Sir John C. Masterman, *The XX Double Cross System* (New London: Yale University Press, 1972).

9. As far as I know this "ploy" has never been publicly reported. It was a favorite of the late Robert A. Lovett, Secretary of War for Air during World War II, and later Deputy Secretary and Secretary of Defense during the Korean War. He used the trick as an example of how much could be accomplished with a minimum of effort and a maximum of imagination.

10. David Howarth, *1066: The Year of the Norman Conquest* (New York: The Viking Press, 1977), gives an excellent account of William's and Lanfranc's machinations. For those visiting the World War II D-Day battlefields in Normandy, the town of Bayeux is but a scant half hour away, just before Caen. In the town museum the whole depiction of the 1066 deception and invasion is laid out in the 11th Century Bayeux Tapestry, some thirty yards long, woven right after the event; and one of the most extraordinary historical documents of all time. Students of military history as well as art lovers should not miss it.

# Operation *Weseruebung*:
# A Case Study in the Operational Art

## Richard D. Hooker, Jr., & Christopher Coglianese

Military history finds few examples of nations and armies that consistently excel in maneuver operations based on speed, focus, decentralized execution, high levels of initiative, and strong small-unit leadership. The German Army in the Second World War was such an organization. The Werhrmacht earns high marks from historians for its mastery of the operational level of war in particular, but one of its shining moments as a military force—the invasion of Scandinavia in April 1940—remains almost a historical footnote. This campaign, the first ever joint operation involving significant land, sea, and air forces operating under unified command, remains an outstanding example of maneuver warfare at the operational level of war.

Due to its close proximity to the more strategically significant Plan *Gelb* attack on the Low Countries, the invasion, code-named Operation *Weseruebung*, has received scant attention from most military historians. Despite this lack of attention, *Weseruebung* is worthy of close study by today's practitioners of the operational art. The campaign is replete with examples of successfully implemented tenets of a maneuver-based doctrine. It also demonstrates the importance of a firm link between the operational art and strategy, and between the various arms and services that typically cooperate in joint campaigns.

In this operation the German forces employed a joint force of Army, Navy, and Luftwaffe air and parachute units in a centrally planned assault, along multiple avenues of approach and against numerous key objectives. The decentralized execution by these different forces occurred simultaneously, with minimal need for the excessive command and control structures that are the hallmark of modern armies. Furthermore, the objectives seized accurately identified and exploited the Allied centers of gravity. Pitting strength against weakness, the Germans brought about

Danish capitulation in a single day and the complete domination of Norway in less than two months, despite the introduction of large British and French forces.

The stunning German success in rapidly seizing Denmark and Norway resulted from a few basic factors. First, the Germans possessed good intelligence leading to an accurate appreciation of enemy strengths and weaknesses, enabling them to focus their efforts on critical enemy vulnerabilities. Second, the Germans, for the most part, applied their strengths, including airpower, surprise, and a well-led, professional military force, against Allied weaknesses, which included timid commanders, an ineffective mobilization system, and an easily paralyzed command and control network. Third, the bold use of German warships to carry troops right up to their objectives in the teeth of the Royal Navy contributed significantly to the operational success of the campaign. Fourth, Norwegian regular forces were outnumbered, ill-equipped, poorly organized, poorly led, and generally neglected. Also, simultaneous, multiple threats throughout the country at key points paralyzed the Norwegian decision-making structure, thus allowing early successes against unsuspecting defenders.

Finally, the German invasion of France in May 1940 forced the Allies (the British, French, and a smattering of Poles) to pull all their troops out of Norway in an effort to stave off disaster on the Western Front. This final element, essentially based on good fortune, saved the beleaguered German forces at Narvik and permitted the Germans to complete their conquest of Norway.

## STRATEGIC AND OPERATIONAL PLANNING

The German High Command turned its gaze toward Scandinavia soon after the successful invasion of Poland. While preferring to keep Scandinavia neutral, German planners feared that Britain and France might violate Norwegian neutrality in order to position forces for an attack on Germany's northern flank.[1] Hitler repeatedly argued to OKH (*Oberkommando des Heeres*, or Army High Command) that if he did not act first, the British would establish themselves in the neutral ports. German naval commanders touted Norway's suitability as a staging area for surface, air, and submarine operations to gain control over the Norwegian Sea and to support eventual operations against Great

Britain, which in turn would facilitate naval access to the North Atlantic.[2] An important consideration was continued access to Swedish iron ore, which supplied the German war industry and which traveled overland from Kiruna to Narvik and thence by sea along the Norwegian coastal leads to German ports in the Baltic.

German strategic objectives can thus be summarized as the need to secure raw materials, protection of the German northern flank for subsequent operations in the west, and the desire to free German naval forces for operations in the open sea. Adolf Hitler, who had exercised supreme military command since February 1938, was also influenced by the tentative steps taken by the French and British to reinforce Finland in the Winter War (which he interpreted as proof of their malicious intentions in Scandinavia) and later by the *Altmark* incident of 14 February, when British sailors boarded a German ship in Norwegian territorial waters to free 300 British POWs.

On 14 December 1939, Hitler ordered OKW (*Oberkommando der Wehrmacht*, or Armed Forces High Command) to conduct preliminary planning for the invasion of Norway. This effort, called Studie Nord, included reports submitted by the staffs of all three branches of the armed forces. Naturally, given the Navy's keen interest in the matter, the Kriegsmarine report was the most exhaustive. The dominance of naval planning derives in part from Army and Luftwaffe involvement in preparation for the upcoming invasion of France and the Low Countries, Plan *Gelb*.

The Kriegsmarine Staff worked out an expanded version of Studie Nord between 14 and 19 January 1940. In this additional work, the Kriegsmarine reached two important conclusions. First, surprise would be absolutely essential to the success of the operation. If surprise could be achieved, it was believed that Norwegian resistance would be negligible and the only significant threat would be those vessels of the Royal Navy on patrol off the coast of Norway, thought originally to be one or two cruisers. The second conclusion called for the use of fast warships of the German fleet as troop transports for part of the assault force. This use of the surface fleet would overcome the range limitations of air transports and allow for the simultaneous occupation of numerous points on the Norwegian coast, including Narvik.[3]

These two conclusions well substantiate the type of thinking that permeated the German operations community. German planning exhibited the "bias for action" already evident in the Polish invasion,

emphasizing speed, shock, and deception. The study called for landings along the entire Norwegian coast from Oslo to Tromsø. On 20
January 1940, the report was submitted to Hitler, and the next day he
ordered the formation of a special staff within the OKW dedicated to
the task of formulating the operational plans for *Weseruebung.*[4] Hitler
apparently had at least two reasons for bypassing the Luftwaffe, who
would play the dominant role in the actual operation, and taking personal control of *Weseruebung.* First, Hitler probably felt that the operation was too complex and ambitious for his most junior and untested service to plan and control. Second, Hitler vented his rage at
the Luftwaffe over an incident earlier in January 1940 in which a Luftwaffe
major carrying plans for *Gelb* was forced down in Belgium, thus allowing the plans for *Gelb* to fall into Allied hands.[5]

On 5 February a joint planning staff was assembled at OKW to prepare
detailed plans for the invasion. Significantly, the operations staffs of
the services were excluded from the planning process. The principal
planner was Capt. Theodor Krancke, commanding officer of the cruiser
*Admiral Scheer*, assisted by a small number of officers from the Army
and Luftwaffe.

Studie Nord had initially called for only one division of army troops.[6]
The Krancke Plan established a requirement for a corps of army troops
consisting of one airborne division, one mountain division, a motorized rifle brigade, and six reinforced infantry regiments. Small parachute units were to seize selected airfields so that follow-on forces
could be delivered by air. Krancke identified six operational objectives, the simultaneous capture of which would cripple the country
militarily and politically and achieve the strategic goals set by Hitler.[7]
These were:

1. Oslo, the capital
2. The populated southern coastal areas
3. Bergen, a major southern port and likely British landing site in
the event of counterattack
4. Trondheim, a major rail terminus and the key to control of central Norway
5. Narvik, the chief city in northern Norway and the crucial rail link
to the Swedish ore fields
6. Tromsø and Finnmark (the northernmost areas of Norway)

The loss of the ports and airfields in these areas was expected, not only to crush Norwegian resistance at the outset, but also to forestall intervention by the Western powers until it was too late. Seeking security in boldness and enterprise, the Germans intended a large-scale coup de main to dislocate their true opponents, the British and French, by preempting their intervention in Norway through the simultaneous attack and occupation of all the important points in the country.

To do this, the Krancke Plan called for movement of German troops both by air and by sea. Only a sudden descent on the Norwegian coastline and rapid buildup of forces by airlift and sealift (supported primarily by tactical aviation) offered hope of success without interference by the Royal Navy. Both the large-scale use of warships as assault troop transports and the strategic movement of large troop formations by air were innovations in modern warfare.

The German intent was to induce the Danish and the Norwegians to surrender quickly without a fight. To help ensure this, Hitler ordered that the escape of the King of Denmark and the King of Norway be prevented at all costs.[8] The Germans felt that capturing the two monarchs would shatter resistance at the outset and ensure a bloodless occupation.

After the *Altmark* incident, Hitler appointed Gen. Nikolaus von Falkenhorst to prepare the forces for the coup de main to seize the Norwegian ports.[9] General der Infanterie von Falkenhorst was a mountain warfare expert who had acquired some experience in Nordic operations during the German operations in the Baltic in 1918.[10] Falkenhorst quickly concluded that it would be desirable to occupy Denmark as a land bridge to Norway.[11] Although the size of the landing force was ultimately raised to six divisions, daring and surprise were to be relied on rather than overpowering force. If resistance was encountered, landings were to be forced, the beachheads secured, and the nearby mobilization centers of the Norwegian army occupied.[12] The ability of the Norwegian army to mobilize was their Achilles' heel—a critical vulnerability and obvious target for German military action.

The final plan assigned 3d Mountain Division and five untested infantry divisions—69th, 163d, 181st, 196th, and 214th—to the conquest of Norway under command of XXI Group. Three divisions made up the initial assault echelon while the remainder were scheduled to reinforce thereafter (a seventh, 2d Mountain Division, was added later).[13] The

Luftwaffe provided three companies of parachute troops for airfield seizure. The initial landing detachments were small, with the bulk of the invasion force scheduled to arrive by air and transport ship in subsequent echelons during the first week. In the south, the 170th and 198th Infantry Divisions, supported by the 11th Motorized Brigade, formed XXXI Corps for the assault on Denmark. X Air Corps, a very large formation of some 1,000 aircraft of all types, was tasked to support *Weseruebung*, its principal tasks being to keep the Royal Navy at bay and to supply German forces by air.[14]

## LIGHTNING STRIKES

Hitler's initial desires to place all *Weseruebung* forces under a single army commander were not carried out. Despite his status as supreme warlord, Hitler was unable or unwilling to overrule the strong objections from the Navy and Air Force, who rebelled at the notion of committing large forces under the command of a land force officer. Although the operation remained under Hitler's personal command (exercised through the OKW operations staff), in the event Falkenhorst was only designated senior commander, exercising no direct command authority over air and naval forces. In the official after-action report, German commanders reported that the harmonious cooperation achieved by the engaged forces was a compliment to the personalities and professionalism of the commanders involved, but not a result of the command arrangements, which they recognized as unsatisfactory.[15]

Mindful of signs that the Allies were preparing to occupy Scandinavia first (British planning, code-named *Wilfred*, was far advanced and the British did, in fact, lay mines in Norwegian waters on the 8th), Hitler ordered *Weseruebung* kicked off early on the morning of 9 April with landings at Oslo, Bergen, Kristiansand, Trondheim, and Narvik. Supply ships camouflaged as civilian commercial craft actually preceded the assault ships and lay in wait in Norwegian harbors. Despite some intelligence indicators, British surface units were not deployed to detect the large-scale German movements. The British fleet, with troops embarked to conduct landings of their own in Norway, did sortie on the 7th of April from Scapa Flow, but the fleet did not intercept the fast-moving German ships or interrupt their landing operations. In a tragic blunder, the Royal Navy marched off its soldiers and steamed away in search of German battlecruisers reported in the area, leaving Falkenhorst to carry out the landings unopposed.

The magnitude and speed of the German landings completely paralyzed civilian and military leaders in both Denmark and Norway, as well as the Allies. Denmark was quickly overrun on the first day, allowing German close support aircraft to stage from Danish airfields in Jutland. Norwegian coastal defenders put up a sharp fight in the Oslo fjord, sinking the cruiser *Bluecher* (which sank with the staff of 163d Infantry Division aboard) and delaying the conquest of the capital by half a day. (Oslo fell that afternoon to a few companies of airlanded troops flown into Fornebu airfield.) Except at Narvik, the remaining landings met only minimal resistance. After clashing with German land-based aviation and small destroyer units on the 9th, the Royal Navy drew off, permitting the remainder of the German assault echelons to land unimpeded. Except for a successful escape by the Norwegian royal family, the day was one of breathtaking success for German arms.

The ineptness of the Norwegian army was a significant factor in the planning and actual success of the campaign.[16] General Laake, the Norwegian Army commander-in-chief, was selected for his position less for his military prowess than for his willingness to accept deep cuts in the military budget.[17] On the day of the invasion he was reluctant for many hours to grasp what was happening. When he had finally accepted that his nation was under attack, he returned to his headquarters to find it deserted. Included among the departed was the general's aide, who had all of the general's uniforms with him. Lacking even a personal vehicle, Laake tried to catch up with his headquarters using public transportation—a microcosm of the debacle that afflicted the Norwegian army that day.[18]

The mobilization centers were under constant assault. Most weapons depots and mobilization lists were in the hands of the Germans almost immediately. However, hundreds of young men came streaming out of the cities and towns to join the forces of General Ruge, appointed commander-in-chief after the invasion. His highly improvised fighting force was untrained and included makeshift battalions and companies with little equipment. The troops were not able to maneuver and were deemed useless for offensive operations. Furthermore, most had never trained with artillery, planes, or tanks. Some units would eventually get organized and fight effectively, but aside from brief clashes here and there, Norwegian opposition at the outset was sporadic and ineffectual.[19] In agony, Norway could only hope that the Allies arrived soon.[20]

## THE ALLIES RESPOND

Fear of German airpower and the rapidity with which the Germans manned Norwegian air and coastal defenses kept the Allies from striking back in the south. However, in central and northern Norway, farther removed from German airbases, an Allied riposte seemed more feasible. In a race against time, Allied planners strove to mount a relief expedition before German forces could organize for defense, even as German units raced northward along the valleys and coastal roads to link up with isolated detachments and complete the occupation of Norway.

The first effective blow by the Allies came on the morning of 13 April, and it was a disaster for German naval fortunes. Following a failed air attack from the British carrier *Furious* against Trondheim the previous day, a British destroyer group commanded by Adm. Sir Charles Forbes encountered German surface units screening the landing forces off Narvik. Supported by the battleship *Warspite*, British destroyers advanced into the fjords and engaged the German warships sheltering there. Unable to reach the open sea, the German ships fought until their fuel and ammunition were exhausted, after which they were beached by their commanders or sunk by British gunfire. These losses, combined with those of the previous days, deprived the German navy of half its destroyer force and dealt its surface fleet a blow from which it never recovered.

In marked contrast to their earlier indecision, the Allies now moved to break the German hold on central and north Norway. On 14 April a party of Royal Marines landed at Namsos (127 miles north of Trondheim), followed days later by the British 146th Infantry Brigade and French 5th Demi-Brigade of Chasseurs-Alpins (mountain troops). On 18 April the British landed the 148th Infantry Brigade at Andalsnes. Five days later 15th Brigade disembarked at Gudbrandsdal to cooperate in the drive to retake Trondheim. Thus, by 23 April four brigades of Allied troops with naval support were positioned north and south of Trondheim, assisted by some 6,000 Norwegian troops.

Against these numerically superior forces, the German commander in Trondheim, Gen. Kurt Woytasch, could initially deploy only seven infantry battalions. Nevertheless, he responded vigorously by pushing out strong parties to the north and south to deny the Allies use of the limited road net. Calling for reinforcements and air support, Woytasch counterpunched aggressively at Steinkjer to the north, stopping the cautiously advancing Allied units in their tracks. Assisted by German forces pushing up from the south, which drew off the British threat to his rear, Woytasch easily dealt with the halfhearted thrusts of the French and British.

Although their losses were light, the combination of a pugnacious opponent and devastating air attacks on their bases at Andalsnes and Namsos convinced the Allied commanders that their situation was hopeless. On 3 May the last Allied troops sailed away from Namsos just ahead of advancing German troops, precipitating the surrender of 2,000 Norwegian troops in the area. Outnumbered by more than six to one, the supremely confident Group Trondheim force and their able commander had inflicted an embarrassing defeat, further eroding the Allies' confidence. Southern and central Norway now lay firmly in Hitler's grip.

## EPIC AT NARVIK

German airpower had played a key role in the battles around Trondheim, but range and weather limitations greatly restricted the ability of the Luftwaffe to support German forces at Narvik, far to the north. Even as the first troops went ashore at Andalsnes, British cruisers and destroyers were massing off Narvik and the first detachments of British troops arrived to join the fleet.

The German situation in Narvik was tenuous from the beginning. Loss of sea control prevented German reinforcements from reaching the area. The 3d Mountain Division, under Gen. Eduard Dietl (minus its 138th Mountain Infantry Regiment attacking Trondheim to the south) found itself cut off from the rest of the country. Days after his successful seizure of Narvik, Dietl was only able to muster 2,000 of his mountain infantrymen along with 2,600 disembarked sailors. Fully 1,200 miles from Germany and cut off from the weak German garrisons in Trondheim to the south, Dietl and his mountain troopers waited grimly for the counterblow to fall.

The British Imperial General Staff believed that an Allied success at Narvik would go far to restore their flagging fortunes. Aside from denying the German war machine the Swedish iron ore it needed desperately, a convincing defeat of the isolated German forces in north Norway would boost Allied confidence and prick the German aura of invincibility. Yet the reasoning of the General Staff was fundamentally misplaced. By dissipating precious air and naval forces in two separate efforts (the attempts to retake first Trondheim and then Narvik), they ensured the failure of both, while a resounding success by stronger forces at Trondheim would have established Allied forces ashore in possession of a good port, rendering the small German contingent in Narvik irrelevant.[21]

Allied ground operations in the north began in earnest on 24 April, as four Norwegian battalions attacked Dietl's outposts at Gratangen, supported by a French brigade that landed four days later. In early May a second French brigade and a Polish brigade arrived; with the addition of British forces the Allies built their strength up to 24,500 troops. British naval forces were further strengthened with a battleship and aircraft carrier.

Dietl's problems were mounting quickly. The Allies were building up their forces far faster than the Germans (on the 18th, Hitler ordered that no new forces be committed to Narvik). German troops in Narvik were exposed to continuous shelling from destroyers lying offshore. Freezing temperatures, fog, and snow hampered mobility and sapped the morale of even the tough mountain soldiers. The supply situation was critical. The naval companies were untrained in land warfare and armed completely with captured Norwegian weapons. Food and ammunition stocks were dangerously low.

Despite these vulnerabilities Dietl resisted stubbornly, aided by a curious lack of energy and aggressiveness by the British commanders, Admiral of the Fleet the Earl of Cork and Orrery, and Gen. P. J. Mackesy. Lacking the troops, artillery and air support needed to conduct major engagements, the Germans fought delaying actions to maintain their precarious foothold in Narvik as well as control of the rail line leading eastward to Sweden. Norwegian forces pushing down from the north made slow but steady progress. Although the 2d Mountain Division was pushing hard from Trondheim to relieve Dietl (at one point marching 90 miles in four days through terrain judged "impassable" by British intelligence officers[22]), distance, poor weather, and lack of roads made reinforcement overland from Trondheim problematic.

On May 13th, under attack from both north and south and suffering from constant sea bombardment and continuous threat of landing, Dietl informed OKW through XXI Group that the situation at Narvik was critical. Dietl reported that his troops were too exhausted to even retreat southward toward the advancing relief columns. His plan was to give up the city if the Allies persisted in their offensive and hold a bridgehead on the railroad, but this hinged on speedy reinforcements, something the Germans had not planned for. Otherwise, there was no alternative but to cross into Sweden and be interned. Group XXI requested permission for Dietl to do so should it become necessary due to enemy action. Hoping for some miracle, 3d Mountain Division (actually a weak regiment by this time) prepared for the end.

Dietl got his miracle. Under pressure from XXI Group and OKW, Hitler approved limited reinforcements (Plan *Gelb* was already under way and diversion of large formations to Norway faced serious opposition from commanders in France). On the 14th of May, a token force of 66 paratroopers arrived. Over the next three weeks, a parachute battalion and two companies of mountain infantry (hastily trained in parachute operations) were dropped into Narvik.

These forces enabled Dietl to hold on long enough for the full weight of the German invasion of the Low Countries to make itself felt on the Allies. Although finally compelled to give up Narvik to vastly superior forces on 28 May, the remnants of 3d Mountain Division continued to fight astride the Kiruna rail line. On 8 June 1940, the Allies secretly evacuated the Narvik area. The next day, the Norwegian Command signed an armistice and ended the fighting, giving Germany total control of Norway.[23] The reputation of the Wehrmacht as an undefeated fighting force remained intact. In honor of the heroic stand at Narvik, all participants were awarded a sleeve device commemorating their service at Narvik during the battle.

## THE AFTERMATH

The true strategic significance of Germany's conquest of Norway and Denmark remains in dispute. Possession of the entrance to the Baltic and effective control of the Scandinavian peninsula secured Germany against attack from the north until the end of the war. German air and submarine units gained bases for attacks against Britain and later the Allied resupply convoys being run into Murmansk. Sweden was cowed into remaining on the sidelines for the rest of the war. Germany was also enabled to support Finland in its second war against the Soviet Union (1941–1944), which tied up large Russian forces at minimal cost to the Germans.

These gains must be weighed against the loss of German surface shipping, the requirement to maintain large forces in Scandinavia, and the relative ineffectiveness of air and naval operations subsequently launched against the British Isles from Norway. On balance, and given the fact that American intervention and defeat in Russia lay in the uncertain future, it is difficult to be too critical of German strategists. Britain would have undoubtedly occupied Norway, and possibly Denmark, had the Germans not done so, with obvious implications for the subsequent invasion of France and the Low Countries.

As an example of mastery of the operational art of war, however, *Weseruebung* has few peers. Throughout the campaign, German planners and commanders ensured that tactical concerns were subordinated to strategic and operational requirements. The early tactical engagements, widely separated in space and, in some cases, in time, were considered in light of the operational plan and were not allowed to take on lives of their own; the decision not to sacrifice the campaign or disrupt *Gelb* to save a desperate situation in Narvik is only the most obvious example.

In the planning and execution of the campaign, Krancke and Falkenhorst showed an impressive ability to distinguish between risk and foolhardiness. Where the British dismissed the chances of landing large German formations in the teeth of the Royal Navy,[24] Wehrmacht planners correctly surmised that speed, surprise, and airpower combined to give *Weseruebung* a good chance of success. The campaign has occasionally been interpreted as a desperate gamble, but the Germans undoubtedly considered it a bold venture with better-than-even odds of victory. They had good reason to feel confident.

Although few of the units employed in the campaign had served in Poland, German commanders were sure of the tactical superiority of their leaders, soldiers, and doctrine. They demonstrated this superiority in virtually every engagement with Allied troops. Where French, British, Polish, and Norwegian units were handled with hesitation, indecision, and timidity, German units showed dash, aggressiveness, and tenacity under extremely adverse conditions. Particularly at Trondheim and Narvik, the Germans were faced with numerous obstacles: bad weather, naval inferiority, unfavorable force ratios, poor roads, and failing resupply. Their triumph was as much a victory over the hardships of northern warfare as it was a decisive strategic setback for the Allies.

A key lesson is that resolute leadership can keep the hope of victory alive when everything else indicates otherwise. Outnumbered and outgunned, the Germans continuously held on due to superior strength of will. Certainly, luck had a part in the outcome, but had Falkenhorst or Dietl taken counsel of their fears, the outcome of the Norwegian campaign might have been much different. Well-trained and well-led troops, able to improvise when necessary, effective use of the German sailors in service support roles, and smartly falling back and shortening their line when absolutely necessary gave the Germans a marked advantage. Lesser commanders unable to fight when cut off, who had limited reinforcements, whose logistics were always straining, who feared taking risks when necessary, and whose lines of communication were never secured would have easily capitulated.

Dietl in particular, a strong product of the German military education system, took all these disadvantages in stride. Even if the Allies had not pulled out, significant seaborne, overland, and airborne reinforcements were on the verge of being committed to the German defense of north Norway following the collapse of the West if only the German commanders could induce their troops to hold on.[25] Here, superior attitude and will to win, fundamentals of success in any endeavor, helped overcome a potentially disastrous situation.

In what sense is *Weseruebung* illustrative of maneuver warfare at the operational level? First and most importantly, the Nordic campaign reveals a characteristic preoccupation with achieving a rapid decision. Like *Gelb*, its more famous sibling, *Weseruebung* shunned a systematic advance through the enemy's territory in favor of a series of lightning strikes designed to knock the enemy out of the fight at the start. This obsession with decisive battle, which obviates the need for protracted and costly campaigning, is perhaps the most defining feature of maneuver warfare.

In comparing the operational plan and the methods of command and control of the contending sides, it is clear they operated very differently. The German decision/action cycle, which operated on the basis of brief mission orders, was crisper and faster. Where the British passion for detailed planning and ponderous execution revealed itself at every opportunity, the Germans emphasized mobility, speed, and tempo—in Forrest's phrase, they consistently got there "first with the most." The German system granted maximum independence to subordinate commanders, requiring only that they remain faithful to the operational goals of the campaign. Where the Allies advanced cautiously and methodically, the Germans fought more fluidly, focusing more on the enemy and less on retention of specific terrain features.

One striking difference that stands out was the strong preference for methodical battle shown by the Allies and its absence on the part of the Wehrmacht. It is almost impossible to imagine Britain tossing isolated detachments along 1,200 miles of coastline, hoping to link up with them later in the face of a much stronger navy, bad flying weather, and large amphibious counterattacks. The German plan relied on the sudden disruption of Norwegian mobilization and the simultaneous seizure of all likely landing sites for Allied reinforcements, with little regard for secure flanks or a continuous front.

In so doing, the Wehrmacht directed its strengths—speed, shock, tempo, airpower, and superior tactical prowess—against the weaknesses of a less resolute adversary and crushed its will to fight. Falkenhorst and XXI Group did not win a campaign of attrition. Although casualties for both sides were roughly equivalent (with German naval and air losses being significantly higher),[26] German morale remained high throughout the campaign while the Allies from the beginning showed little heart for the fight.

In retrospect, *Weseruebung* was a minor operation compared to later actions throughout the war. Despite Hitler's expectation that the British would not abandon their strategic aim of cutting off the German ore imports,[27] German forces in Norway (except for minor commando raids) were never attacked throughout the war. As an isolated operation, *Weseruebung* was a resounding success for the Wehrmacht. The conquest was achieved without any material subtraction from the forces on the western front, or interference with the preparations for Plan *Gelb*. Moreover, the operation was the first carried out under a unified command system.[28]

These features make the conquest of Norway and Denmark an interesting and worthwhile study for the student of the operational art. Many of the lessons of *Weseruebung* are still valid today, when complex joint operations mounted over great distances have become almost the norm. Though technology changes rapidly, campaigns and battles between comparable adversaries ultimately remain a clash of wills. In this sense, Operation *Weseruebung* still has much to teach.

# Notes

1. B. H. Liddell Hart, *History of the Second World War* (New York: G. P. Putnam's Sons, 1970), p. 52.

2. B. H. Liddell Hart, *The German Generals Talk* (New York: Quill, 1979), p. 37.

3. Matthew Cooper, *The German Army* (Chelsea, Mich.: Scarborough, 1991), p. 191.

4. Francois Kersaudy, *Norway 1940* (New York: Saint Martin's Press, 1991), p. 43.

5. Earl F. Ziemke, "The German Decision to Invade Norway and Denmark" in *Command Decisions* (Washington, D.C.: U.S. Army Center for Military History, 1960), p. 58 (hereafter cited as *Command Decisions*).

6. Earl F. Ziemke, *The German Theater of Northern Operations* (Washington, D.C.: U.S. Army, 1959), p. 13 (hereafter cited as Ziemke).

7. Ibid., p. 15.

8. Kersaudy, p. 49.

9. Liddell Hart, *German Generals Talk*, p. 37.

10. Ziemke, p. 16.

11. John Keegan, *The Second World War* (New York: Viking, 1990), pp. 50, 51.

12. *Command Decisions*, pp. 62–64.

13. Christopher Buckley, *Norway: The Commandos Dieppe* (London: Her Majesty's Stationery Office, 1951), p. 10.

14. In all, the Luftwaffe moved 29,280 troops and 2,376 tons of supplies in the first weeks of the invasion, an impressive feat given the bad flying weather and limited size of transport aircraft in that period. Ziemke, 56.

15. Ziemke, p. 32.

16. Kersaudy, p. 68.

17. Ibid.

18. Ibid., pp. 68 and 72.

19. Bernard Ash, *Norway 1940* (London: Cassell, 1964), p. 44.

20. Ibid., p. 109.

21. Ash, p. 98.

22. Ziemke, p. 97.

23. Ibid., pp. 102–104.

24. J. L. Moulton, *The Norwegian Campaign of 1940* (London: Eyre and Spottiswood, 1967), p. 60.

25. Ziemke, p. 104.

26. The Germans lost 1,317 dead and 2,374 lost at sea. 127 German combat aircraft were shot down, and the British succeeded in sinking 1 heavy cruiser, 2 light cruisers, 10 destroyers and 6 submarines. The British lost 1,896 troops in the fighting and approximately 2,500 sailors, as well as 1 aircraft carrier, 1 cruiser, 7 destroyers and 4 submarines. The French and Poles together suffered 530 dead and the Norwegians 1,335. A total of 87 allied planes were shot down. Ziemke, p. 109.

27. Cooper, pp. 258, 267, and 492.

28. *Command Decisions*, p. 68.

# Operation 25:
# The Wehrmacht's Conquest of Yugoslavia

## John F. Antal

The eternal uncertainty is over, the tornado is going to burst upon Yugoslavia with breathtaking suddenness.[1]

Adolf Hitler

War came to Yugoslavia in April 1941. That spring the Wehrmacht launched a combined-arms blitzkrieg through the difficult mountain terrain of Croatia, Bosnia-Hercegovina, Serbia, Montenegro, Kosovo and Macedonia—the polyglot of ethnic and tribal nations that had come to be known as Yugoslavia. The German invasion of Yugoslavia in the early years of the Second World War fanned the flames of hatred and division that are burning furiously today on the battlefields of Bosnia-Hercegovina. The Balkans has always been a fertile cauldron for international crisis, but this bloody heritage is partially the result of the tumultuous events that occurred in Yugoslavia in the spring of 1941. Understanding how the young Republic of Yugoslavia was crushed by German military might is an illuminating study of the origins of today's terrible problems.

On the 27th of March, 1941, Adolf Hitler ordered his army and air force to crush Yugoslavia as the first step in his plans to secure the Balkans and complete the conquest of Greece. The code name for the German attack was Operation 25. Hitler, enraged at Yugoslavia's defiance to his ultimatums, termed the attack "Operation Punishment." Hitler's goal was to destroy Yugoslavia in a surprise attack. "No diplomatic inquiries will be made nor ultimatums presented. . . . Politically it is especially important that the blow against Yugoslavia is carried out with unmerciful harshness and that military destruction is done in a lightning-like undertaking."[2]

The battle-tried and tested Wehrmacht, led by the Panzerwaffe (tank corps), rolled into Yugoslavia on 6 April 1941. In a series of staggered timed assaults the Germans and their Italian, Romanian, Bulgarian, and Hungarian allies brought Yugoslavia to her knees and then raced on to conquer Greece. The German army disintegrated the Yugoslav army in a combined-arms campaign that was characterized by rapid tank and mechanized movement, skillful execution of coordinated air-ground operations, and superior tactical and operational planning. On 17 April, after only twelve days of fighting, Yugoslavia surrendered. The casualties figures of the Wehrmacht totaled 151 killed and 407 wounded for the entire campaign.

## THE STRATEGIC IMPORTANCE OF THE BALKANS

Why did Hitler's vaunted Wehrmacht invade Yugoslavia? The answer to this question lies in Germany's need for secure resources and secure flanks. The Balkans was a critical supply source for Germany's war machine. Half of the animal livestock and grain to supply Germany in World War II would come from the Balkans. "Greece, with Yugoslavia, was the source of 45 percent of the bauxite (aluminum ore) used by German industry, while Yugoslavia supplied 90 percent of its tin, 40 percent of its lead and 10 percent of its copper."[3] The oil fields in Bulgaria and Romania would supply over half of the oil to fuel the tanks of the Wehrmacht and the airplanes of the Luftwaffe.

More importantly, Hitler had ordered that the German Army seek a decision against the communist arch-enemy of Nazi Germany, the Soviet Union. Hitler's massive invasion of Russia, code name Operation Barbarossa, could not be launched if the Yugoslavs, Greeks, and British were able to threaten the German southern flank. Barbarossa was designed to knock out the Soviet nemesis and was to be the largest land campaign ever executed by the German army. Before the invasion of Russia could be executed, Hitler needed to secure the Balkans.

Initially, Hitler preferred a political, rather than military, solution to the Balkan problem. He had hoped that his powers of persuasion, backed up by the victorious might of the German army and air force, would intimidate the small Balkan countries into joining the Axis. In this endeavor, Hitler was fairly successful. Romania, Bulgaria, and Hungary bowed to this pressure. Yugoslavia, whose Serbian majority were proud of their fight against the Germans in the First World War, remained reluctant.

Then, to complicate matters, the Italian dictator, Benito Mussolini, launched an attack on Greece. Italian forces attacked through Albania and ran into a stone wall of determined Greek resistance. Mussolini attacked without Hitler's consent and did not coordinate his attack with the German High Command. The result was a near disaster. The Greeks, allied with Great Britain, were soon on the offensive and the Italians were reeling back in retreat. Hitler, furious over this uncoordinated move by his ally, became convinced that Greece's entry into the war would bring the Romanian oil field under British bombing range. In addition, Hitler realized that the Duce's creaky empire might fall if things were left to themselves.

On 4 November 1940 Hitler had decided to intervene in the Balkans and conquer Greece from Romania and Bulgaria. He had not instructed the General Staff to plan the conquest of Yugoslavia, for he believed that he could threaten the Yugoslavs into submission or at least force their neutrality. With this in mind, the Führer pressed the Yugoslavs to join the Axis to allow German armies to move through Yugoslavia for an attack on Greece. The Yugoslav government council, realizing that any reluctance on their part would result in war with Germany, submitted to Hitler's will. On 18 March 1941, Prince Regent Paul, the constitutional leader of Yugoslavia, signed his country over to the Axis. On 25 March 1941 Yugoslavia officially joined the Tripartite Pact. Germany's invasion routes to Greece and his continued source of Balkan supplies seemed assured.

Hitler's diplomatic success, however, was short-lived. The ink was not yet dry on the Tripartite Pact when Gen. Richard D. Simovic, a Serbian who commanded the Yugoslav Air Force, successfully executed a coup d'etat against the Yugoslav government led by Prince Paul. The coup occurred on 26-27 March 1941. Seventeen-year-old King Peter was placed on the throne by Simovic, and the treaty with Nazi Germany was declared null and void. Inspired by the bold act, the majority of Yugoslavs responded with spontaneous jubilation. Schools and businesses closed, patriotic songs were sung, and anti-German demonstrations occurred in almost every city. The Serbian majority of Yugoslavia rejoiced, shouting the words "Better war than pact. Better war than pact!"[4] The "pactasi," Yugoslavians who advocated the pact with the Axis, went into hiding. A general state of euphoria swept Yugoslavia as the nation prepared to defy Nazi Germany.

Hitler was informed of the Yugoslav change of sides on 27 March. The change of events in Yugoslavia had a negative and drastic impact on the preparation for the planned Barbarossa operation. Dealing with the Yugoslavs would waste valuable time and would place additional stress on the Wehrmacht's Panzerwaffe. Enraged by the defiance of the Yugoslavs and the disruption of his plans, Hitler vowed revenge. The Führer ordered the destruction of "Yugoslavia militarily and as a nation." He ordered the German air force to "destroy Belgrade in attacks by waves."[5] He told his generals: "It is my intention to force my way into Yugoslavia . . . and to annihilate the Yugoslav Army."[6] General Jodl, the Chief of Operations Staff at the German High Command, was ordered to prepare the plans that very night.

## THE YUGOSLAV DEFENSE PLAN

Opposing the Wehrmacht was an army of one million Yugoslavs. On paper it was a force capable of defending the homeland. Although the Yugoslav army's equipment was old, no one made light of its soldiers' courage or will to fight. The Serbians had earned a fierce reputation for resistance against invaders as guerrilla fighters during the First World War. This tradition was reinforced by the rugged terrain of Yugoslavia. The Balkans was considered "poor tank country" by most military planners. Many military experts in the West expected that any German attack of Yugoslavia would be a slow and costly affair. It was widely accepted that the German blitzkrieg would meet its match along the treacherous winding roads, the steep mountain passes, the wide rivers, and the poorly bridged defiles of Yugoslavia. The Yugoslavs believed this too. In consultation with the Allies, the Yugoslav High Command let it be known that they expected to hold out against the Germans for several weeks, if not months, and wait for the British and the Greeks to come to their rescue.

But wars are not fought on paper. General Simovic, the leader of the Serbian-sponsored coup d'etat, had a monumental task to perform. In spite of the recent tensions, Yugoslavia was not prepared for war. The army, a million men strong, was organized into twenty-eight infantry and three cavalry divisions. Much of its equipment was out of date and of Czechoslovakian manufacture. Since Czechoslovakia had been absorbed by the Axis, the Yugoslavis could no longer get the spare parts it needed to keep its military machine running. The Yugoslav army had just two battalions of antiquated tanks—a grand total of less than one hundred. Few of these tanks were a worthy match for German panzers. "The whole army belonged, indeed, to the era of the Balkan wars of 1911-1912 rather than to the modern world—its movements depended on the mobilization of 900,000 horses, oxen and mules—and, moreover, it was not mobilized."[7]

The Yugoslav army began full mobilization on 29 March. The borders were sealed and units deployed to the countryside. After the initial euphoria of the coup subsided, the new government attempted to devise a serious plan for the defense of the nation against a German attack. General Simovic had several options. One was to concentrate his forces in the difficult mountain regions of Yugoslavia and wage a long guerrilla war against the enemy. Another was to concentrate his forces along the border with Greece, in order to fight in concert with the nearest Allied force. The third option was to try to defend the cities and the vital regions, in order to hold the loosely knit state of Yugoslavia together as long as possible and hope for Allied intervention.

Due to political considerations, Simovic chose the third option. The High Command felt compelled to garrison Slovenia and Croatia in order to maintain a fictitious internal cohesion. The army was ordered to defend the borders, protect every inch of Yugoslav territory, and fight the enemy wherever he appeared. Trying to defend everywhere, the Yugoslav army dispersed itself across the country. Surrounded on all sides by enemies, Yugoslavia hardly stood a chance of defending the entire country by employing this defensive strategy. Anyone who had studied the 1939–1940 campaigns in Poland, Norway, and France should have been able to understand that this strategy of defense was wrought with error. "But no country has perhaps ever as irrationally dispersed its forces as the Yugoslavs did in April 1941, seeking to defend with ancient rifles and mule-borne mountain artillery one of the longest land frontiers in Europe against Panzer divisions and 2000 modern aircraft."[8]

The leaders of Yugoslavia's armed forces expected the same tempo of war that many of them had experienced in World War I. "But there was no strategic plan."[9] Warfare had changed since the slower-paced days of 1918. No one expected the Germans to attack quickly, with massed armor, over the rough mountain tracks and poor narrow roads of Yugoslavia. "The mistakes of years cannot be remedied in hours. When the general excitement had subsided, everyone in Belgrade realized that disaster and death approached them and that there was little they could do to avert their fate."[10] The Yugoslav army's capability to fight, untrained for modern war and ill-disposed to meet the German blitz-krieg, was considerably overestimated.

In addition, age-old ethnic problems plagued the Yugoslav army and nation. General Simovic, a Serbian, did not have time to heal the eth-nic wounds that were inherent in the make-up of the Yugoslav state. The coup d'etat was largely a Serbian-run affair. Attempts by the new government to guarantee solidarity with the Croats had been answered with lukewarm assurances. Many Croatians openly sided with Ger-many, considering themselves ethnic Germans rather than Slavic Serbs. Croatians complained that they were suffering under Serbian domi-nation and were considered by Serbs to be second-class citizens in their own country. Scores of Croatians openly welcomed the idea of Ger-man intervention. In spite of these problems, Simovic ordered his forces to move to defensive positions to meet the foe. "At this moment all the might of Germany within reach was descending like an avalanche upon them."[11] Blind to reality, almost everyone in the Yugoslav High Command believed that the Allies would come. Simovic and his gen-erals thought there would be plenty of time to prepare for the Axis attack.

## THE WEHRMACHT ATTACK PLAN

Time, however, was a precious commodity that the Yugoslavs did not have. The Wehrmacht planners believed that any campaign in the Balkans would have to be executed in a manner similar to the cam-paigns in Poland, Norway, and France. "The strategically important features would have to be seized in blitzkrieg fashion."[12] The German General Staff, working under tremendous pressure, developed an outline plan for the combined Yugoslav and Greek campaign within twenty-four hours of the revolt in Yugoslavia. The plan emphasized the principles of the blitzkrieg:

The principles of the blitzkrieg were surprise, speed and concen-tration. All three were interdependent. Speed was only made possible by surprise and concentration. Surprise itself was achieved principally by concentration and speed. Concentration could only reap decisive results if in conjunction with speed and surprise it tore open the enemy's front, penetrated deeply behind it, paralyzed opposition, and led to a battle of annihilation. Suddenness, violence, blitzkrieg schnell—these were the very nuclei of blitzkrieg. But there was something more. Once this violent all-destroying thrust had got going, it must never stop until the battle is won. If it halted it would be found, checked and attacked. To maintain momentum, night and day, was everything. The forces engaged must penetrate ever deeper, ever broader, and so bring about the absolute disruption of enemy positions, reserves, headquarters and supplies. The key to it was a never-ending flow of mixed panzer groups constantly supported and supplied by fire power and transport aircraft of the Luftwaffe. Thus the two indispensable agents of blitzkrieg were still Panzer and Stuka.[13]

General Franz Halder had directed OKH's (Oberkommando des Heeres or Army High Command) planning staff to prepare plans in October 1940 for a future invasion of Greece. The forces for this operation, code-name Operation Marita, would be used for the invasion of Yugoslavia. Additional forces were quickly moved by rail and road from their positions in France, Germany, Czechoslovakia, and the Russian border. Bad weather and icy roads made the concentration of forces difficult and incomplete. Few of the German units had assembled all of their equipment and formations prior to D-Day.

The plan called for staggered timing of the attacks, launched from Germany, Bulgaria, Romania, Hungary, and Italy. The Second Army, stationed in Austria, would drive southward, destroy the Yugoslav armies in Croatia, and advance between the Sava and Drava rivers, directly on Belgrade. The Twelfth Army, positioned to attack Greece through Bulgaria, would move into southern Yugoslavia, attack along the axis Nis-Kragujevac-Belgrade, take Belgrade, and secure the Danube River before continuing the attack into Greece. The intention was "to keep the enemy in a state of uncertain ferment with every fresh penetration, and in the way the country was quickly carved into sections by converging attacks on the main cities executed by different formations."[14]

A three-pronged drive on the Yugoslav capital by Panzer Corps was planned. The mobile divisions of each army would coordinate their attack with other attack forces as they closed in on Belgrade and deny the Yugoslavs the ability to make an orderly withdrawal into the mountains. These attacks would converge on Belgrade at the same time, putting the Yugoslavs in a vise that would make withdrawal impossible, and force them to surrender. Liddell Hart, the great military theorist who inspired the blitzkrieg, explained this concept in a letter to General Guderian, the father of the German tank corps, after the Second World War.

> The secret of the blitzkrieg lay partly in the tactical combination of tanks and aircraft, partly in the unexpectedness of the stroke in direction and time, but above all in the "follow through"—the way that a breakthrough (the tactical penetration of the front) was exploited by a deep strategic penetration carried out by an armored force racing ahead of the main army, and operating independently.[15]

The First Panzer Group of the Twelfth Army would attack from assembly areas in Sofia, Bulgaria, crossing the Yugoslav border near Pirot, and advance in a northwesterly direction along the axis Pirot-Nis-Kragujevac-Belgrade. The XLI Panzer Corps, operating as an independent force, would lead the drive across the southeastern part of Yugoslavia, jumping off from Timisoara, Romania, along the axis Vrsac-Pancevo-Belgrade. The XLVI Panzer Corps of the Second Army would attack from Hungary along the axis Barcs-Osijeke-Mitrovica-Belgrade.

Secondary attacks were planned to be conducted by infantry and mountain troops before and during the main drive on Belgrade. These attacks would support the main effort and would be conducted across the Austrian-Yugoslav frontier where the terrain was unsuitable for motorized units. Along almost every line of attack the German armor would have to negotiate formidable mountain roads before reaching their objectives. If the Serbians established a well-organized defense of these mountain areas, the German attacks would be at considerable risk.

To minimize these risks the Germans sought to disrupt the Yugoslav defense plan early by destroying Serbian command and control. The Luftwaffe played a vital role in the operation by focusing its combat power on the destruction of the Yugoslav air force and the neutralization of Yugoslav command-and-control structures and facilities. The plan called for an intense bombardment of the center of Belgrade, where important government and military centers were located.

The campaign plan also involved the integrated employment of five different armies in the Axis coalition—German, Romanian, Hungarian, Bulgarian, and Italian forces. Italian forces would attack from Italy toward Zagreb, capital city of the Croats. The Hungarians were directed to send their Third Army to seize the trans-Danubian province of Vojvodina, where Hungary claimed rights. Coordination of the coalition's forces was orchestrated through the German High Command. Coalition forces were issued explicit instructions and were seldom asked to do more than execute orders. In every case the Germans did not expect too much from their allies.

## THE BATTLE FOR YUGOSLAVIA

The story of the Wehrmacht's campaign was sadly different from the brave expectations of the Yugoslavs. The Luftwaffe spearheaded the invasion with the saturation bombing of Belgrade in the early hours of 6 April 1941. One hundred and fifty dive-bombers, and hundreds of fighter escorts from Lt. Gen. Wolfram von Richtofen's VIII Air Corps, devastated the capital with almost one and a half hours of non-stop aerial bombardment. The German aircraft operated from airfields in Romania and Bulgaria and attacked in three distinct waves. The first wave destroyed the Yugoslav air force and flak defenses. "Against the loss of two German fighters, twenty Yugoslav planes were shot down and forty-four were destroyed on the ground."[16] With the city virtually defenseless, the second and third waves obliterated the principal military and government facilities. When the attack was over, 17,000 Yugoslavians lay dead in the smoldering ruins of Belgrade. Before 9:00 A.M. on the first day of the war, the Yugoslav government, along with the military nerve center for the Yugoslav armed forces, ceased to exist. Successful in this mission, the VIII Air Corps transferred the weight of its deadly effort to the additional Yugoslav airfields, troop concentrations, and, most importantly, to close air support of the attacking German ground forces.

Initial attacks were conducted on 6 April in the XLVI Panzer Corps area (Second Army) to seize intact critical bridges along the line of advance. On 8 April, after two days of preparation by the Luftwaffe, the main attack kicked off. The weather was miserable, with cold winds and intermittent snowstorms. In spite of the bad weather, and tough resistance from the Yugoslav Fifth Army, the 11th Panzer Division, spearheading the First Panzer Group, broke through the Yugoslav lines on the first day. With dive-bombers clearing the route of advance, the panzers of the First Panzer Group quickly reached Nis. From Nis northwestward the terrain opened up and the German tank columns rumbled steadily up Morava Valley all the way to Belgrade. The Yugoslav Fifth Army attempted to regroup and block the Germans southwest of Kragujevac, but this attempt was quickly defeated. The Yugoslavs lost over 5,000 prisoners for their effort.

The XLI Panzer Corps likewise got off to a quick start. Spearheaded by the "Gross Deutschland" Division and followed by the 2d SS Motorized Infantry Division, the XLI Panzer Corps raced to Belgrade, encountering only light and scattered resistance. On 11 April, its lead elements entered Pancevo. "So feeble was the resistance that the invaders suffered only 151 fatal casualties in the course of the campaign; the XLI Panzer Corps lost a single soldier dead, though it was in the forefront of the advance to Belgrade."[17] The Yugoslavs seemed to have placed the "same sort of misguided reliance on their native mountains as a defense against armor as had the Poles and the French on 'tank-proof' forests."[18]

The campaign soon became a series of operations against river lines and mountainous terrain. "In both instances, independent combined arms teams with the mission of seizing key bridges and hills proved effective and successful."[19] Using this technique, the three advancing German Panzer spearheads were not slowed by the poor roads, the weather, or the Yugoslav army. The pressure caused by this relentless drive of German panzer columns deep into Yugoslav territory began to crack the fragile unity of the Yugoslav army. The psychological dislocation of the Yugoslav defenses was the result. This was particularly evident in the Croatian areas of the country.

The XLVI Panzer Corps was given the duty of attacking into Croatia. Opposing them was the Yugoslav Fourth Army, which had a high percentage of Croatian soldiers. "All but one of the army's divisions was under Serb command, and most of these divisional generals surrendered to the panic which rapidity of the Wehrmacht's onslaught induced."[20] Croatian soldiers mutinied, refusing to fight the Germans. Some individual Croatian soldiers threw down their weapons and surrendered. Other units turned themselves over, en masse, to the Germans. By 10 April the "disintegration of the Yugoslav forces had reached an advanced stage."[21]

The plight of the Yugoslav army was now desperate. With fast-moving panzer formations cutting deep into Yugoslav territory, a synchronized defense became impossible. Bewildered, isolated pockets of resistance were quickly mopped up by the Germans. General Simovic, unable to coordinate his defense against an enemy with superior agility, appealed for his troops to attack the Germans wherever they were. The appeal was beyond the capability of the commanders in the field. All three Panzer spearheads, unstoppable, arrived at the outskirts of the capital at almost the same time. Finally, on 13 April, at 11:52 A.M., the 8th Panzer Division drove into Belgrade, occupied the center of the city, and raised the swastika flag. The city, its population battered and dazed, offered no opposition. Belgrade surrendered unconditionally.

With the fall of Belgrade the Wehrmacht moved swiftly to deny the stunned Yugoslav forces the ability to withdraw to the mountains in the interior of Serbia. With a quick thrust into the interior of Yugoslavia, General Weichs, the German Second Army commander, pursued the Yugoslavs withdrawing in the vicinity of Sarajevo. The German forces converged on Sarajevo, as they had on Belgrade, and destroyed the final semblance of Yugoslav resistance. "By 14 April the fighting between the Serb and Croat factions had gained momentum and had spread throughout Dalmatia."[22] On 15 April the trap at Sarajevo closed and the Yugoslav Second Army, the last remaining Yugoslav fighting force in the field, surrendered. The Yugoslavs asked for an armistice, which was signed on 17 April 1941. The fact that 345,000 Yugoslav soldiers agreed to surrender unconditionally, "while the total German casualties amounted to a mere 558, undoubtedly confirms the suggestion that a sledgehammer had been used to crack a nut, yet this cannot disguise the sheer professionalism with which the panzer divisions carried out the mission."[23] The Wehrmacht's Yugoslav campaign was over. The highly trained combined-arms force of panzers, stuka, infantry, and artillery then switched their attention to Greece.

## CONCLUSION

When diplomatic intimidation failed, and the Yugoslav coup d'etat occurred, Hitler immediately ordered a plan be drawn up for the military conquest of Yugoslavia. The German High Command had little time to prepare plans for the subjugation of the country. There was no German contingency plan to conquer Yugoslavia. The Wehrmacht was positioning for the attack of Russia and was not ready to launch a major operation in Yugoslavia. In spite of this, the efficient German General Staff quickly improvised a campaign plan to conquer Yugoslavia and developed the sequel, which involved the conquest of Greece and the removal of British power from the Balkans. The Germans developed this plan within twenty-four hours of Hitler's order to "destroy Yugoslavia as a nation."

The German campaign plan was based upon an attack along the lines of least resistance, penetrating the enemy's linear and dispersed defenses, and rapidly moving into the depths of the enemy's country to capture critical political and military command centers. The attack first emphasized the destruction of the Yugoslav command-and-control system. It then depended upon the rapid penetration and exploitation of the Yugoslav defenses by three powerful panzer wedges. Once these centers were captured, the Yugoslav will to resist was broken and the enemy was mopped up at will.

The Yugoslav campaign is a study of successful maneuver warfare conducted by a first-rate military force against a second-rate opponent. Notwithstanding, there are important lessons to be learned from the Wehrmacht's Yugoslav campaign. Throughout the campaign the Wehrmacht specifically targeted and attacked the Yugoslav command-and-control structure. The Germans fought a battle of maneuver, focused on the disruption of the enemy force. This, coupled with the fast tempo of the armored advance, maintained the initiative for the Germans. The lead panzer columns, working closely with the Luftwaffe's dive-bombers, were able to overcome the weather, the terrain, and the enemy.

In twelve days of fighting the Wehrmacht conquered a one-million-man army at the loss of only 151 dead: no small task. By maintaining a relentless pressure on the obsolete Yugoslav army, the Germans never let the Yugoslavs "catch their breath." Once the Yugoslavs were knocked off balance, the Germans drove home the thrust in the form of their fast-moving tank columns. Speedy combined-arms execution, aimed at the correct operational objective, brought about the strategic paralysis of the Yugoslav High Command and destroyed the Yugoslav army's will to resist.

In addition, the Germans did everything they could to pit Serbian and Croatian forces against each other. With very little effort, the Germans were able to drive an ethnic wedge into the heart of the Yugoslav defense effort. The defections and mutinies of Croatian soldiers in the Yugoslav army spread confusion and indecision, further weakening Yugoslav command and control. Toward the end of the campaign Serbian and Croatian forces were in open combat with each other. The Wehrmacht then turned on the demoralized and largely paralyzed enemy army and forced it into an uneven battle of maneuver that the Yugoslavs were ill prepared to fight. The result was a lightning victory, accomplished through force and speed, which brought about the political and military collapse of the Yugoslav state.

Lastly, the campaign in Yugoslavia was the Wehrmacht's first taste of coalition warfare. Coalition forces composed of Bulgarian, Romanian, Hungarian, and Italian forces attacked Yugoslavia from all sides. The military effect of coalition units was not impressive, but they added an important political element to the German campaign plan. Each coalition partner was promised a share of the spoils after the successful completion of the campaign. The Wehrmacht, in every case, however, had to be the "driving spirit and carry the brunt of the fighting during operations. The participating allied and satellite forces achieved success only when they were under German command."[24] Later on, in the long years of occupation, the Germans would require more and more manpower from their Axis partners to hold Yugoslavia from the actions of the Chetniks and Tito's partisans. The hatred between Serb, Croat, German, Romanian, Bulgarian, and Italian, because of the bloody partisan warfare that erupted from 1941 until 1945, is the current legacy of the Balkans.

The German military philosopher, Hans Delbrück, said in his famous work *Krieg und Politik* that "every people is the child of its history, its past, and can no more break away from it than a man can separate himself from his youth." This truth is evident today in the former nation of Yugoslavia. The current crisis in Bosnia-Hercegovina, Croatia, Kosovo,

and Serbia is the result of this history and, in particular, the tumultuous events of the German invasion and occupation during the Second
World War. In order to understand how military operations should be
conducted in this area of the world, it is important to review past military
performances. Operation 25 is a case in point.

# Notes

1. John Keegan, *The Second World War* (New York: Viking Penguin Publishing, 1990), p. 154.

2. Winston S. Churchill, *The Second World War, The Grand Alliance* (Boston: Houghton Mifflin Company, 1949), p. 163.

3. Keegan, p. 146.

4. Milija M. Lasic-Vasojevic, *Enemies on All Sides: The Fall of Yugoslavia* (New York: North American International Publishers, 1976), p. 5.

5. William L. Shirer, *The Rise and Fall of the Third Reich: A History of Nazi Germany* (New York: Simon and Schuster, 1960), p. 824.

6. Ibid., p. 825.

7. Keegan, p. 154.

8. Ibid., p. 155.

9. Churchill, p. 173.

10. Ibid.

11. Ibid.

12. A. C. Smith, *The German Campaigns in the Balkans* (*Spring 1941*) (Washington, D.C.: Center of Military History, U.S. Government Printing Office, 1953), p. 4.

13. John Strawson, *The Battle for the Ardennes* (New York: Charles Scribner's Sons, 1972), pp. 10-11.

14. Bryan Perrett, *Knights of the Black Cross: Hitler's Panzerwaffe and Its Leaders* (New York: St. Martin's Press, 1986), p. 77.

15. Liddell Hart Papers, Letter from Liddell Hart to Guderian, dated 7 October 1948.

16. Smith, p. 49.

17. Keegan, p. 156.

18. Perrett, p. 76.

19. Smith, p. 66.

20. Ibid., p. 156.

21. Ibid., p. 53.

22. Ibid., p. 63.

23. Perrett, p. 77.

24. Ibid., p. 65.

# Biographies of Contributing Authors

**The Editor**

**Richard D. Hooker, Jr.,** is a student at the U.S. Army Command and General Staff College. An infantryman, Major Hooker was previously assigned to the National Security Council as a White House Fellow and taught politics at West Point in the Department of Social Sciences. He has served three tours with airborne units and participated in contingency operations in Grenada and Somalia. Major Hooker holds master's and doctoral degrees from the University of Virginia in international relations.

**The Authors**

**John F. Antal** is an Army major currently assigned to the 1st Infantry Division (Mechanized). An armor officer, Major Antal commanded tank units in the 1st Cavalry and 2d Infantry Divisions and served as executive officer with the Opposing Forces tank battalion at the National Training Center. He holds a master's degree in military science from the U.S. Army Command and General Staff College and writes widely for military publications. His book *Armor Attacks* was published in 1992.

**Daniel Bolger** is an Army major assigned to the 101st Airborne Division (Air Assault). He previously served with the 24th and 2d Infantry divisions and taught history at West Point. An infantryman and prominent military writer, Major Bolger holds a doctorate in history from the University of Chicago and has authored several books, including *Americans at War 1975–1986: An Era of Violent Peace.*

**Bruce B. G. Clarke** is Director of National Security Studies at the Army War College. An armor officer, Colonel Clarke served in Vietnam at the siege of Khe Sanh and later commanded a squadron in the 11th Armored Cavalry Squadron and a tank brigade in the 1st Infantry Division (Mechanized). He attended graduate school at UCLA and later served with the Department of Social Sciences at West Point and with the Arms Control and Disarmament Agency.

**Christopher Coglianese** is an infantry officer now serving with the 24th Infantry Division (Mechanized) at Ft. Stewart, Georgia. Lieutenant Coglianese graduated from the U.S. Military Academy in 1992, where he majored in Military Studies.

**Robert A. Doughty** is Professor and Head of the History Department at West Point. An armor officer, Colonel Doughty commanded tank units in the 4th Armored Division, and later served as an advisor to Vietnamese armored cavalry units and as executive officer to the Supreme Allied Commander Europe. He holds a doctorate in history from the University of Kansas and is the author of several major works, including *The Evolution of U.S. Army Tactical Doctrine 1946-1976* and *The Breaking Point: Sedan 1940 and the Fall of France.*

**David A. Grossman** is a student at the British Staff College and taught at West Point as an Assistant Professor in the Department of Behavioral Sciences and Leadership. Major Grossman served in the 9th Infantry Division and later commanded a rifle company in the 7th Infantry Division (Light). A former noncommissioned officer, Major Grossman attended graduate school at the University of Texas. His book *On Killing: The Price and Process of Killing* is forthcoming.

**Bruce I. Gudmundsson** is a historian and former instructor at the U.S. Marine Corps School of Advanced Warfighting. A reserve Marine officer, he is the author of *Stormtroop Tactics: Innovation in the German Army 1914–1918* and *On Artillery*. He is presently the editor of *Tactical Notebook.*

**Arthur T. Hadley** is a prominent military journalist and writer. As a young officer in the Second World War, Mr. Hadley pioneered psychological warfare techniques in Northwest Europe, earning two Silver Stars and the Purple Heart. A Yale University graduate and former *New York Times* Washington Bureau chief, Mr. Hadley has authored nine books, including *Straw Giant* and *Crisis Now* (with James Gavin).

**Robert R. Leonhard** is a student at the School of Advanced Military Studies at the Army Command and Staff College. Major Leonhard commanded a mechanized infantry company in Germany and served with the 3d Armored Division in the Gulf War. He holds degrees in history and international relations and is the author of *Art of Maneuver*. His work has appeared previously in *Infantry* and *Army* magazines.

**William S. Lind** is Director of the Center for Cultural Conservatism at the Free Congress Foundation in Washington, D.C. A former legislative aide to Senator Robert Taft, Jr., and Senator Gary Hart, Mr. Lind writes frequently for military journals and is co-author (with Senator Hart) of *America Can Win* and *Maneuver Warfare Handbook* (with M. D. Wyly). He is a graduate of Dartmouth College and received a graduate degree in history from Princeton University in 1971.

**James McDonough** is Director of the School of Advanced Military Studies at the Army Command and General Staff College. Colonel McDonough served in Vietnam with the 173d Airborne Brigade and later commanded an infantry battalion at Fort Hood, Texas. He attended graduate school at MIT and later taught with the Department of Social Sciences at West Point. Colonel McDonough is the principal author of the Army's revised FM 100-5, *Operations* manual. He also authored *Platoon Leader*, a widely read account of small unit leadership in Vietnam, and *Limits of Glory*, a novel about the Battle of Waterloo.

**Michael J. Meese** is a student at the Army's Command and General Staff College. He served in field artillery units in the United States, commanded a cannon artillery battery in Europe, and later taught in the Department of Social Sciences at West Point. Major Meese has master's and doctoral degrees in public administration from Princeton University.

**Harold E. Raugh, Jr.,** is an Army major currently serving with the 7th Infantry Division (Light). Major Raugh has a doctorate in history from UCLA and previously served with the Berlin Brigade, the Department of History at West Point, and the United Nations Truce Supervisory Organization in Cairo. He writes widely for military journals and recently published his first book, *Wavell in the Middle East, 1939–1941: A Study in Generalship.*

**Franz Uhle-Wettler** is a retired lieutenant general in the Army of the Federal Republic of Germany. A tanker and General Staff officer, General Uhle-Wettler served in the German army in the Second World War as a conscript and later earned a doctorate in history before returning to military service as a commissioned officer in the Bundeswehr. During his long career he commanded at all levels from company to division, ending his military career as Commandant of the NATO Defense College.

**Ricky L. Waddell** is an engineer officer now serving as a Council on Foreign Relations Fellow in New York City. Major Waddell served in the 9th Infantry Division (Motorized) and with Joint Task Force Bravo in Honduras, and later commanded an engineer company at Ft. Leonard Wood, Missouri. A Rhodes Scholar and former international relations instructor at West Point, Major Waddell has master's and doctoral degrees in foreign affairs from Columbia University and graduate degrees from Webster University and Oxford University.

**Michael D. Wyly** is a retired colonel in the U.S. Marine Corps and former Vice President of the Marine Corps University. An author and lecturer, Colonel Wyly earned a graduate degree in history from George Washington University and served two combat tours in Vietnam as a commander of Marine infantry units. He is co-author of *Maneuver Warfare Handbook* and contributes regularly to the *Marine Corps Gazette* and other military journals.